…Gardening the sister art to building, was at the lowest ebb in Rome. Brown had no guide to follow in the whole extent of Classick ground, left thus entirely to himself, with great sagacity and elegance of taste, He calls in Nature to his assistance, and in company with Her makes new Creations in every place He comes to; Hills arise and undulating plains; where a dead flat appear'd before; the black morass, the [space] and Bulrush vanish and are succeeded by a noble River, such are the marks of real genius, unfettered and untaught, …

Extract from John Stuart, 3rd Earl of Bute, *Travel Journal and Essay on Travel Writing, c.*1770, Cambridge University Library, MSS.Ad.8826. My grateful thanks to Nora Shane

MOVING HEAVEN & EARTH

CAPABILITY BROWN'S GIFT OF LANDSCAPE

STEFFIE SHIELDS

This book is dedicated to my husband Michael,
our daughter Gabrielle and her husband Peter Gaunt,
and our granddaughter Emily

EIGHTEENTH-CENTURY CURRENCY

According to www.measuringworth.com
In 1750 the value of a £100 0s 0d Commodity compares to 2014:
the real price of that commodity is £14,050.00;
labour value of that commodity is £178,100.00;
income value of that commodity is £278,200.00.

In 1750 the value of £100 0s 0d of Income or Wealth compares to 2014:
the historic standard of living value of that income or wealth is £14,050.00;
economic status value of that income or wealth is £278,200.00;
economic power value of that income or wealth is £1,638,000.00.

In 1750 the value of a £100 0s 0d Project compares to 2014:
the historic opportunity cost of that project is £13,920.00;
labour cost of that project is £178,100.00;
economic cost of that project is £1,638,000.00.

Between 1750 and 2013, prices rose by around 145 times. References to money in the script will be followed by an equivalent amount based on these statistics; for example, a very good bottle of claret that cost 6 shillings in 1750 would cost in the region of £42 today.[1]

Pound sterling (silver)	= 20 shillings	= 240 pennies	= 480 ha'pennies	= 960 farthings
Shilling (silver)		= 12 pennies	= 24 ha'pennies	= 48 farthings
Groat (silver)		= 4 pennies	= 8 ha'pennies	= 16 farthings
Penny (copper)			= 2 ha'pennies	= 4 farthings
Ha'penny copper)				= 2 farthings
Farthing (brass)				
Guinea (gold) (after 1707)				= 21 shillings
Crown (silver)				= 5 shillings

EIGHTEENTH-CENTURY MEASUREMENT

Length was measured as follows:

Inch	2.54 centimetres
Foot	30.48 centimetres
Mile	1.6 kilometres
Span	22.86 centimetres
Cubit	0.46 metres
Hand	10.16 centimetres

Furlong (220 yards)	201.16 metres
Palm	7.5 centimetres
Rod (16.5 feet)	5.03 metres
Chain (22 yards)	20.12 metres
League (approx. 3 miles)	4.8 kilometres

(page 1) **August 1981, Broadlands, Hampshire** A scene along the River Test that misled me into thinking it was natural countryside. I later learned that 'Capability' Brown had designed the setting. The exotic swamp cypress (left) and grove of native white willows (right) are typical of his planting.

(pages 2 and 3) **October 1989, The Pastures, Alnwick, Northumberland** A seemingly natural view from Alnwick Castle's Pic-Nic Tower. Brown altered the course of the River Aln and transformed unkempt, craggy moorland into grazing grounds. Alnwick townsfolk have always been free to walk here; many believe it has always been like this.

NOTE: in captions, NT is National Trust; EH is English Heritage; HE is Historic England.

A star or arrow, superimposed on certain plans, highlights particular design features.

All images by the author unless credited otherwise, including images of National Trust properties with permission.

CONTENTS

PREFACE

*People will not look forward to posterity
who never look backward to their ancestors.*
EDMUND BURKE

Everyone has landscapes lodged in their memories, many from childhood.

I remember my first real urge to take a photograph. I was eight years old, visiting the Dutch tulip fields of Keukenhof. Such glorious settings have the power to evoke deep emotions or, simply, take the breath away. Whatever the view, we all see things differently from each other. We see with memory.

My father once told me he found it difficult to appreciate landscape. Such was his training as a gunner in WWII that any time he surveyed a beautiful scene, sadly, his eyes saw only possible gun emplacements. His compensation was that he delighted in writing verse, and would read to me from this memory bank, or snippets of his favourite poets, especially Robert Frost. Some lines have never left me.

*Two roads diverged in a wood, and I –
I took the one less travelled by,
And that has made all the difference.*[2]

My 'different' journey began in Hampshire, at Broadlands. I ignored the classical charm of the house as a sweeping lawn led me down to the edge of the meandering River Test. A pair of swans piloted their cygnets under leaning white willows. A spreading copper beech attracted attention at the river bend, great trees punctuated the water meadow, and upstream a stand of Scots pines dominated the river bank. All seemed serene, reassuring. Nothing disturbed the eye or the peace.

I fell under the spell of the place, and later discovered that this pastoral setting had been to a great extent man-made – by the celebrated 'Capability' Brown.

Five years passed. I had given up teaching to bring up a family, and taken up garden photography, a passion kindled by two years of living in California sunshine and later properly stoked by the trail-blazing photography of Andrew Lawson.

My husband, an officer in the Royal Air Force, was posted to a radar station on the east coast of Northumberland, and we moved there with our young daughter. In October 1987, as I dashed to catch my train to Newcastle, the great hurricane devastated vast tracts of land in the south of the country, and uprooted millions of trees, a loss that greatly affected me – it was almost as bad as losing one's friends.[3]

I discovered that Brown was born and raised in Northumberland, before spending his working life improving all four corners of England. My daughter spotted a paperback edition of Dorothy Stroud's seminal biography *Capability Brown*, which became my trail guide (still much used). This prompted me to drive to his first landscape, Kirkharle, a quiet hamlet some twenty miles north-west of Newcastle-upon-Tyne.

Brown's family home is long gone, as is his older brother John's house near the pond. A plain stone cairn bears the legend 'Capability Brown of Kirkharle 1716–1783'.

Curiosity about my local Brown landscape led me to Alnwick Castle's Estate Office. The archivist, Dr Colin Shrimpton, responded to my enquiries for old engravings or early photographs: 'There's a Canaletto painting, about 1750, but that was *before* Brown. There are plenty of illustrations and photographs of *castle* renovations. No, I do not think we have any of the *landscape*.' His answer shocked me.

Colin led me up to the ramparts of the 'Pic-Nic Tower'. The first Duke and Duchess of Northumberland liked to entertain their guests there, watching progress as Brown improved the environs of the castle. Where once fast-running waters divided craggy, almost barren, moorland, the horizons are clothed with trees. The River Aln, now mirror-smooth, falls tamely over a series of shallow lip cascades, winding to the North Sea through undulating meadows dotted with trees and sheep walks.

Of course, the passage of time, other designers' works and tree disease had already altered the Brownian feel of many parks. The hurricane was closely followed by two more great storms, in 1989 and 1991, bringing his signature planting even closer to annihilation. Wondering how many other great parkland vistas had gone unrecorded, I resolved to visit as many of Brown's works as possible. I had no idea how far I would travel – and the journey is ongoing.

My excursions, enabled by the peripatetic lifestyle of an RAF family, opened my eyes to this exceptional man, his methods and values. As I learned landscape photography from the ground up, I captured some key surviving features, a faithful distillation, I trust, of an extraordinary legacy. Time has confirmed Brown as a man of vision.

Landscape eases solitude, blows away cares, makes one feel happy to be alive. Landscape is where we choose to celebrate commitment, or remember a loved one.

I hope this celebratory book will open eyes and encourage the reader to explore Brown's generous landscapes. Don't be anxious about having to make challenging aesthetic or critical judgements. Simply pause occasionally, ponder the view and, above all – enjoy looking at the landscape!

July 1989, Kirkharle, Northumberland A peaceful small estate and hamlet, the birthplace of Lancelot 'Capability' Brown.

LAUNCELOT BROWN Esq:
of Fenstanton, Hunts.
"Capability Brown"
B.1716.   D.1783.

INTRODUCTION

Aformal portrait of Brown at the pinnacle of his career was undertaken by Sir Nathaniel Holland-Dance (1735–1811), a founder member of the Royal Academy. The fact that, at the same time, the artist was also working on portraits of Brown's employers, King George III and Queen Charlotte, tells us their royal gardener had significant status.[4] According to this portrayal, his eyes protruding, and the angle of neck and shoulder, Brown may have suffered goitre-related health problems, a possible cause for his over-active life.

One other portrait is more informal. Richard Cosway (1742–1821) shows Brown just as alert and resolute, but wigless, more relaxed, as his associates and workforce would have known him – a kind face, manly yet gentle, good looks, the same thick eyebrows and high forehead. His fine, curly, receding hair, fair to light brown, shows vestiges of grey. Sculptor Jon Edgar has recently compared the facial details in the two paintings. He suggests that the one by Cosway, just as several other known copies, could have been copied from the original Dance portrait. Certainly, both artists took pains to capture Brown's animated confidence, and, because of his reputation, his direct, famously unfailing, 'comprehensive and elegant eye'[5] with a perceptible twinkle.

'Capability' was a word frequently uttered by Lancelot Brown, it seems. Horace Walpole (1717–1797), Earl of Orford, attributed the nickname to the man himself, in first assessing possible improvements to any given country estate. The name proved strategic in promoting potential for all kinds of improvement. Walpole found the word amusing when gossiping about people and gardens. Besides being accurate, the nickname effectively distinguished the improver from *other* Mr Browns.[6]

Walpole, a wealthy Member of Parliament, a self-confessed 'quiet republican', moved in the same circles as Brown. He too was a frequent traveller with a connoisseur's passion for improvement, but revelled in making copious, occasionally malicious observations concerning distinguished contemporaries and their properties. Somehow Pope's emotive grotto garden beside the River Thames drew Walpole to Twickenham, where he built a fanciful, castellated home overlooking the river at neighbouring Strawberry Hill, with interiors of 'gothic gloom'. Outside, in complete contrast, he desired his garden to be light, romantic and, above all, *riant* (smiling).

This lively, perceptive commentator was among the first to offer public praise for the improver's designs at Warwick Castle. Brown's reputation spread. He was 'capability' personified, later moving churches, let alone mountains. The two men were soon acquainted and came to value each other's taste and judgement. Walpole went on to publish his *Essay on Modern Gardening*, hailing the increasing beauty of England thanks to progressive improvers such as Brown and his collaborators:

Enough has been done to establish such a school of landscape, as cannot be found on the rest of the globe. If we have the seeds of a Claude *or a* Gaspar *amongst us, he must come forth. If wood, water, groves, valleys, glades, can inspire or poet or painter, this is the country, this is the age to produce them.*[7]

Soon, everyone in society circles seemed to be chattering about 'capabilities' of estates worth visiting around the country:

We went to pay a visit to Mrs Annesley, Bletchingdon House, Oxon. In this part of our county there are more fine houses near each other than in any, I believe, in England. We were reckoning nineteen within a morning's airing worth seeing. I must say something of that we were at, as Mr Brown would style it, 'A place of vast capabilities' stands high, the ground lays well, and the views round it far preferable to most in that county.[8]

Nowadays, an array of settings of magnificent scale contributes to the historic and cultural fabric and beauty of this country: Alnwick, Blenheim, Burghley, Chatsworth; Harrow and Wimbledon; from Petworth, Broadlands and Sherborne in the south to Trentham and Temple Newsam in the north; Prior Park, Newton and Ugbrooke in the south-west to Kimberley and Heveningham in the east; from Cardiff Castle and Dinefwr in the west to Warwick Castle and Croome in the Midlands; and many more.

A few private estates are little-known, but the majority of Brown's surviving landscapes are open to the public, valuable cultural and sporting amenities, wildlife havens and breathing spaces. To appreciate how Brown left his mark, the reader needs to picture the landscapes he encountered at the beginning of his career.

A brief summary charts the evolution of English landscape up to his day. Early nomadic settlers surrounded their homes with deep ditches, fishponds and moats for security and sanitation. Their livestock grazed surrounding common land, as men excavated roads and built large barrows to bury their dead. Native trees defined field and property boundaries, with oak the dominant species in wood pasture. Farmers cut back trees (pollards) above grazing height for building material and divided agricultural terrain with ridge and furrow. Trees were valuable assets. Managing woodland for fuel and income by coppicing, cutting down to the stump, proved a sensible way to

revive healthy woodland, letting in light so that trees flourished and seedlings grew at no cost.

A conscious drive for development, over and above survival, differentiates mankind from the animal kingdom. By Tudor times, imported trees were shading delightful, herb-scented potagers and enclosed private physic gardens, reminiscent of the cloistered garths of early religious houses. Prosperous landowners planted avenues to their manor houses, which were often adjacent to a wood, and established long rides to link their lands.

Successive kings and queens introduced European design to royal gardens, setting a trend for mathematically precise, manicured grounds with strong axes, eye-pleasing vistas and reflective linear canals in place of irregular fishponds, and building pavilions or 'standings' at high vantage points for watching deer-coursing. Earthworks were no longer defensive in origin. Mounts and raised terrace walks, a convenient solution for quantities of excavated earth and canal spoil, offered charming views of the gardens and surrounding countryside. English gardeners laboured to measure and lay out levelled grounds and long walks, orderly orchards and kitchen gardens, to emulate the spectacle of much-visited palace gardens in France and Holland. They pleached lime trees, clipped box, holly and yew hedges, and created intricate, cutwork, patterned 'floors' or 'parterres', in season dotted with colourful flowers, visible from the upper windows of the great houses.

Land slowly devolved from royal control. Ownership of deer parks, once the prerogative of the monarch, became more widely permissible, though devastating civil wars left estates abused by soldiers badly neglected. Coke-fired blast furnaces for glass-manufacturing and smelting of lead, tin and iron consumed vast timber resources, which were also needed for housing and for shipbuilding, critical to defence and overseas trade. Besides providing

LEFT **May 2010, Boughton House, Northamptonshire** A recently restored canal, 'Dead Man's Reach', in formal early eighteenth-century gardens inspired by Versailles.

ABOVE **September 2004, Castle Howard, Yorkshire** The pine cone finial is a symbol of eternity.

industry with resin, turpentine and tar, wood was necessary for mining.

The diarist John Evelyn (1620–1705), a founder of the Royal Society, voiced concerns, following the Civil War, about the supply of quality timber for building and the iron industry. His milestone publication *Sylva – A Discourse of Forest Trees* (1664, reprinted three times by 1706) advocated planting avenues, 'cabinets of fruit' and walnut trees with 'codlin' (apple) hedges and copses with 'tufted' trees (raised stems).

Early eighteenth-century 'bird's eye' engravings show great houses approached by elm or lime avenues, the trees often planted a rod apart, and walled gardens surrounded by extensive radial rides for galloping through new, densely packed plantations and clearings 'enamelled' with wild flowers. Horizons changed. Landowners had obviously heeded Evelyn's forward-thinking advice, despite profits not being as immediate as from agriculture. Much-travelled, moneyed aristocrats developed country retreats along refined, classical lines, variants of Dutch, French and Italian/ Roman styles. Their elm walks had intricate wrought-iron gates and carved stone arches to define thresholds to a series of sheltered garden 'rooms' furnished with shade houses, arbours and exotic wall-trained fruit trees.

Extensive hedged walks and forest rides became symbols of status, as much as canals, fountains and plunge baths, allegorical stone statuary, heraldic beasts, urns and balustrades, and banquet houses where sweetmeats were served. Generals retiring from Flemish battlefields asserted dominion over their local terrain by investing in groves of clean-stemmed trees. They created crossed walks and vistas to monumental urns and obelisks 'for eternity', and prospect towers to entertain spectators of hunting and racing.

Nurseries and seedsmen multiplied in response to the demand from progressive landowners, intent on surrounding country retreats with parks and requiring quantities of trees and 'quick' hedges (such as hawthorn) for arable, waste and common lands claimed by parliamentary acts of enclosure.[9] Slightly better wages in industry, road-building and river navigation schemes inevitably attracted manual workers, leaving high-profile gardeners who faced critical shortages in manpower to advocate simplified, more relaxed designs requiring less maintenance.

The invention of the seed drill by a farmer, Jethro Tull (1674–1741), and the four-field crop rotation promoted by Charles, 2nd Viscount Townshend (1674–1738), contributed more to changing country views than essays in *The Spectator* by Joseph Addison (1672–1719), heralding, over and above agricultural or sporting prowess, 'the pleasure of the imagination'.

One influential designer, Batty Langley (1696–1751), loathed 'abominable mathematical regularity', the elaborate business of cutting and trimming, and motivated owners to turn a whole estate into a 'non-stiff' garden by getting their gardeners to 'humour' nature.[10] By the time the legendary supervisor of Chelsea Physic Garden, Philip Miller FRS (1691–1771), was enthusing about diverse groves of fir trees, yew bowers and wildernesses of flowering fruit trees, the planting of trees had become, without doubt, the most popular pursuit for gentlemen.

The poet Alexander Pope (1688–1744) loved the way forest scenery intensified feelings. His writings found favour with Lord Burlington (1694–1753), a prominent amateur architect who pressed his *protégé* William Kent (1685–1748) to create captivating garden settings for Chiswick. This Italian-trained artist's flair for summerhouses, temples and rustic buildings, with rich Rococo flourishes in interior furnishings, found equal expression in clients' gardens. A burgeoning mining industry fuelled a craze for geology, providing fossils, sparkling minerals and shells to decorate garden seats by springs of water. Kent conjured such natural and lyrical views that Pope consulted him regarding his Thames-side

LEFT **2007, Hartwell, Buckinghamshire** The goddess Juno.

BELOW **September 2011, Rousham, Oxfordshire** The best surviving example of William Kent's garden designs, with a serpentine rill.

villa garden at Twickenham. Visitors entered Pope's garden through a grotto in the undercroft inspired by underworld myths, where the mind could play with elements of fancy or fantasy.

If twenty-first-century mechanical landscaping equipment is now hugely more versatile, efficient and sophisticated, the ethos of improvement and ongoing management in the face of climatic challenges remains relevant. The eighteenth century offered arguably the greatest and most dramatic changes in garden style. Even when incorporating older trees from earlier designs, Brown masterminded polished, fresh and modern settings that proved a revelation.

A sea-change in the look of English gardens accompanied a surge in agriculture, forestry and water-engineering. This brought more than physical change as centuries of straight, rigid lines and enclosing walls gave way to continuous curves.

Georgians shared their expanded boundaries and new adventures, like prisoners emerging from strait-jackets, celebrating liberation and visual sensation. Men and, more unusually, women actively engaged with 'safe' exploration of the wider natural world. Brown, quicker and bolder than most other improvers, grasped this unexpected freedom from formality to exploit seemingly endless capabilities wherever he was employed.

Each generation since has made their value judgements, their own choices as regards taste and style, as fashion dictates and fluctuates. There have been many myths, misapprehensions and misconceptions about Brown. Perhaps this book will convey the sheer variety and surviving drama of his stage sets, and will counterbalance negative jibes vilifying him as the 'vandal destroyer' who demolished exquisite, formally organised gardens surrounding the country's great houses.

OPPOSITE **April 1994, Beechwood Park, Hertfordshire** Middle-distance planting – Brown's signature cedar of Lebanon, Scots pine and oak are, sadly, all past their prime. A round grove beyond, one of a receding series of plantations, alleviates the flatness of the land.

RIGHT **August 2008, Madingley Hall, Cambridgeshire** Brown surely considered the view to the lake from this window of the first-floor reception room.

I challenge historian Christopher Hussey's curious assessment in the Introduction to Dorothy Stroud's pioneering biography: 'Brown was not a painter. I do not think he was particularly sensitive to visual impressions.'[11]

With painting and fine arts high on society's agenda, the land Brown loved was his canvas, nature's resources his materials. Largely as a result of his endeavours and legacy, 'natural' parkland is one of the few English arts to achieve worldwide recognition. It is no coincidence, and no exaggeration, that his work later inspired the country's greatest landscape artist, J.M.W. Turner (1775–1851).

More immediate than paintings and engravings of the period, I trust my photographs will engage and inform. Centuries later, they reveal altered, aged and weathered landscapes. Many Brown trees have been lost, or cropped, as was often his intention. Some sites have been restored sympathetically in Brownian fashion. Others contain formal terracing once more. Whatever the case, many maintain an enduring link with Brown through his greatest gift: 'sense of place'.

Let us examine 'Capability' Brown's world before his last footprints disappear: his many journeys, the money and energy he expended, the professional associations and friendships he forged, his ground-breaking trials and setbacks. He never published his designs, let alone his ideas. Ascertaining exactly what he accomplished is not easy. He studied, and learned to exploit, the same colours and textures as landscape architects today, the same earth and grass and plant material, the same timber, stone and brick, gravel, sand, glass and iron, and, best of all universal elements other than the air we breathe, life-enhancing water. After perusing these pages, the reader might be prompted, I hope, to 'walk the ground' with sufficient confidence to compare and weigh up some authentic, surviving examples of this remarkable man's achievements.

I share these windows in time, and while factoring in climatic conditions I discuss Brown's pioneering engineering methods for creating expansive water features. Along with his words, where possible, my images in shades of seasonal light, which Brown and his associates would also have seen, focus on specific sites, pinpoint his planting, and reveal his architectural innovation. I hope they will serve to answer those age-old questions: how – and why – did he do it?

CHAPTER ONE

NORTHUMBERLAND

No one lives in **Northumberland** without being touched by its wild terrain. High hills unfold beneath vast skies. Ever-changing light accentuates infinite sweeps of craggy, wind-whipped moorland, punctuated by dense stands of Scots pine protecting lonely farmsteads.

Rugged slopes of coarse tufted grass are dotted with thousands of sheep. Warmed in season by gorse, heather and bracken, the hills are silent in winter, their contours softened by pillows of snow. Space and solitude reign.

This ancient territory, north of the River Humber, colonised by Romans, converted by fervent monks and Holy Island saints, was once claimed as a kingdom by invading Norsemen. Eastward, in place of Viking invaders, castles and abandoned ruins command endless, empty stretches of coastal dune.

Inland, the raids of the Border reivers long since history, granite peel towers and fortified farmhouses, or 'bastles', continue to stand guard over small farming communities.

This is Border Country, the 'back pocket of England',[12] home to Northumbrian pipes, fireside stories and gentle humour, a land of singular charm and majesty, the birthplace of Lancelot 'Capability' Brown.

OPPOSITE **April 1990, near Alnwick, Northumberland** A wintry view, with snow still lingering and the distant Cheviot Hills silhouetted by the setting sun.

ABOVE **February 1988, Holy Island, Northumberland** Lindisfarne Castle warmed by late-afternoon sun.

Little of Brown's early life is recorded. As far as is known, his parents, Ursula and William Browne, were tenant farmers.[13] They moved down from Elsdon, a rough and lawless reivers' community above Redesdale, to peaceful grazing land some ten miles further south-east. **Kirk Harle**,[14] their small village (now a hamlet called Kirkharle), on the ancestral estate of the Loraine family, nestled in the secluded valley of the River Wansbeck. Here, in 1716, the second youngest of their six children was born one (unrecorded) summer's day.

On 30 August 1716 (probably soon after the birth) the baby boy was christened Lancelot in St Wilfrid's, a fourteenth-century church, little more than a chapel.

Four years later, his father William died. At about this time, Sir William Loraine, 2nd Baronet (1658–1744), a barrister and one-time MP for Northumberland, inherited the estate. It seems likely that he developed a close, supportive relationship with the bereaved Brown family, since he later became the children's patron and first employer.

This Brown's schooldays were spent in Cambo village some three miles north-east of his home. He followed his older brothers John and George to the plain, stone-built schoolhouse, where the Master, Thomas Gastle, was much respected. All three Brown boys achieved professional status, but Lancelot, by all accounts, was particularly quick to learn, eager for any opportunity for self-improvement.

On the daily three-mile trek to and from school he crossed the Wansbeck, pausing to watch comings and goings at the largest country house in the neighbourhood. A wealthy Whig, Sir Walter Blackett, had inherited the Wallington estate and immediately began building. Lancelot witnessed great changes, especially when grandiose new stables were commissioned and his brother, George, was taken on as builder and mason. George assisted the architect

LEFT **July 1989, Kirkharle, Northumberland** Later in his life, Brown suggested adding the bell-cote to the fourteenth-century St Wilfrid's Church.

BELOW **February 2000, Kirkharle, Northumberland** Traces of eighteenth-century parkland planting surround Kirkharle Hall, with the Cheviot Hills in the distance. The road (left) leads to St Wilfrid's Church. My camera lens has flattened the view, but I was pleased to see new tree-planting since my last visit.

LEFT **July 1989, Cambo, Northumberland (NT)** The Old Schoolhouse now bears a stone memorial plaque dedicated to its most famous pupil, Lancelot Brown.

BELOW **April 1990, Wallington Hall, Northumberland (NT)** Brown went to school in Cambo village above Wallington Hall in the picturesque Wansbeck Valley. Later, in the 1760s, he gave advice to improve Wallington's grounds. A few traces of his planting remain, for instance on the hill behind the house.

OPPOSITE RIGHT **February 2000, Kirkharle, Northumberland** Despite the peaceful rural setting, the Loraine Memorial is a disturbing reminder of man's barbarity.

Daniel Garrett (d.1753), who had worked for Richard Boyle, 3rd Earl of Burlington (1694–1753), well known for his Palladian taste. Brown was intrigued, and certainly stimulated, as Gateshead nurseryman William Joyce improved the grounds with widespread plantations.

Closer to home, Loraine at Kirk Harle set about planting: '24,000 forest trees, 480,000 quicks, 580 fruit trees, divided his grounds, built new farmhouses, drained morasses, cleared land of ponderous stones for the village'.[15]

The local community admired him for his learning, and especially for the garden fountains and fishponds he installed, 'the first regular ones known in that country'.[16]

In 1728, Loraine decided to replace an old monument on the hill near his house. As a twelve-year-old, Brown may have watched, or even helped to position the restored stone. The inscription reads:

This new Stone was set up in place of an old one by Sr Will. Loraine Bart. in 1728 In Memory of Robert Loraine, who was barbarously murdered in this place by the Scots in 1483 for the good service to his Country against their thefts and Robbery as he was returning home from the Church.

On leaving school, Lancelot followed his eldest brother John into employment on the Loraine estate. He received basic training in the cultivation of fruit trees, the art of hedging and the practicalities of trenching, creating drainage for tree plantations that improved the views from the manor house. This is where he was well grounded in both levelling and fieldwork, learning to assess and survey the land.

Every Brown landscape repays exploration and offers surprise – rounded hill and hollow, cascading burn and sinuous pool, hanging wood and hidden grotto, a grown-up 'hide and seek'. Wherever he worked he recreated, perhaps subconsciously, the open, undulating countryside of his boyhood, dominated by the ever-present hills, Cheviot and Hedgehope.

Weather was a challenging factor in farming, gardening and lake-making initiatives, especially in the dry years of the early 1730s. He learned how to dam and redirect streams safely, how to tap springs, to lay pipes, build conduits to channel water, and then restore any disturbed terrain.

Managers of coalmines were operating horse-driven pumps that by the late 1730s were also assisting tunnelling and pile-driving in bridge-making. Considering there was a local open mine nearby at Wallington, Brown must have been fascinated and enthused by experiments using the hydraulic power of Savary or Newcomen steam engines[17] to pump out water from shafts.

Men with his expertise were often shared among neighbouring landowners to direct the labour force. Brown worked for Mr Shafto at Benwell Tower as well as assisting in the creation of a lake at Bavington, the construction of a grotto and cascade at Hartburn, and conceivably the enlargement of fish ponds at Wallington and possibly Capheaton.

His brother John had been promoted to steward (and would later marry Loraine's daughter), and Brown was equally determined to advance, despite being afflicted with asthma. Outdoor work then was advised for sufferers.

Prospects in the area were limited for someone with Brown's experience, and Loraine, by then in his eighties, was beyond contemplating any more large-scale projects. Aged twenty-three, a typical Borders man with a strong sense of identity, Brown made the bold decision to leave home, perhaps with his first patron's letter of introduction tucked reassuringly inside his coat.

B

C

ABOVE **March 2005, Kirkharle, Northumberland** Brown's first landscape, where he received a good grounding in land management: drainage, levelling and planting. A few remnant trees survive from his later professional improvement plan (c.1766): a singleton on the rise (A), a beech clump (B) and an enclosing tree belt on the distant horizon (C).

LEFT **July 2015, Kirkharle Hall, Northumberland** Returning recently, I was delighted to see the landscape restoration inspired by Brown's improvement plan (c.1766) for the Loraine family, with the lake Brown envisaged at its heart reflecting the ever-changing Northumberland skies.

CHAPTER TWO

MR BROWN ENGINEER

Picture the landscapes young Brown encountered, on perhaps his first long expedition away from home, en route to **Lincolnshire**, a politically powerful, sheep-farming county producing much of the nation's food. Did he board a coastal vessel in Newcastle, destination Boston? Perhaps he endured an uncomfortable coach ride. Maybe he rode alone, negotiating a growing network of improved turnpike roads,[18] or avoided tolls by heading cross-country over rough terrain, along old Roman roads, muddy drovers' ways and rutted pack-horse tracks. Was he wary, stopping to ask strangers for directions, or to recommend inns for board, lodging and welcome company?

Woods and windmills, church steeples and towers interrupted the horizon, the monotony intermittently relieved by a glimpse of a medieval stone castle, with here an abbey ruin, there an isolated manor house, surrounded by walls and orchards, with labourers toiling in the fields, to remind him of home.

OPPOSITE **May 2014, Grimsthorpe Castle, Lincolnshire** A courtyard gateway frames a view to the lake in the Vaudey valley below.

ABOVE **August 1998, near Sleaford, Lincolnshire** Flat, fertile fenland landscape created by seventeenth- and eighteenth-century landowners with extensive, deep drainage ditches to further grazing and agricultural opportunities.

25

The world that Brown surveyed appeared more optimistic. Memories of civil and continental wars were fading, views were changing radically as a result of politics and travel. Except for London, a few industrial towns in the north-west and the mining areas in the north-east, England was still largely rural. Family networks of sophisticated, landowning aristocracy[19] and educated gentry continued to dictate a hierarchical society. If fewer than half the population were literate, however, the hard lives of workers were beginning to feel more secure and more progressive.

Better communications by road and sea were enabling an expansion of commerce and banking, making additional finance available for building, collecting fine art and leisure pursuits. Gentlemen journeyed abroad on an educational Grand Tour almost as much as nobility. On their return, enthused by new sights and trading opportunities, the prosperous chose to imitate continental fashions, refining their homes with souvenir furniture, statuary and paintings, and making ostentatious new gardens in the 'grand manner'.

An ethos of self-improvement was beginning to filter through to even the most rural community. Pioneering land reclamation schemes for grazing, following techniques introduced in the previous century by the Dutch, were transforming Lincolnshire's marshy fens. Engineers and 'fen artisans' raised huge flood banks with clay core walls, built bridges for access, sluices to hold the water back, and large, wind-powered wheels with paddles, known as 'Dutch' engines, to pump water out into rivers.[20]

A wealthy lawyer and former High Sheriff, Joseph Banks II (1696–1741), grandfather of the renowned botanist explorer Sir Joseph Banks, had invested greatly in developing his rural estate at Revesby, some seventeen miles inland from Boston, the capital of the fens and England's second largest port after London. Like his father, a contemporary of Brown's first patron Loraine, Banks was an influential MP, Fellow of the Royal Society and, of considerable consequence locally, was agent to the Duke of Ancaster at **Grimsthorpe Castle** in the south of the county.

In 1738 an Act of Parliament, calling for more engineers, committed the Court of Sewers to raising finance for deepening and straightening navigable rivers for shipping and for further fen drainage, in direct competition with the 'Adventurers', another group of landowners.[21] This Act had played a major role in Brown's decision to leave Northumberland. Joseph Banks, as Clerk of Sewers, was well placed to find employment for an already experienced young man, with engineering part and parcel of his chosen career in land improvement.[22] His neighbouring landowners, Lewis Dymoke and Bennet Langton, told Banks that 'Mr Brown' made a good impression, and was worth consulting on matters of enclosure and improvement.[23]

Banks may also have introduced Brown to his future wife. Bridget Wayet was born in 1719 to a 'very respectable county family', William Wayet and his wife Margaret Kelsall, and christened in Boston.[24] During the summer months, the Wayet family rented a house near the River Bain at Tumby, a small hamlet on Banks's estate, a perfect place for courtship. Years later, Brown's youngest son Thomas would recall the lifelong friendship his father had enjoyed with the Banks family.[25]

A London seedsman, who trained under Brompton nurserymen George London (c.1640–1713) and Henry Wise (1653–1738) to become a designer to the aristocracy, Stephen Switzer (?1682–1745) deserves a special place in the story of the landscape garden. His work, especially his continental-style axial gardens at Grimsthorpe Castle, and his writing, particularly authoritative research into the properties of water, later made quite an impact on young Brown.

In 1715, following George I's accession, Robert Bertie, 4th Earl of Lindsey, was created Duke of Ancaster and hereditary Lord Great Chamberlain of England. A city merchant and a founder of the Bank of England, the new duke invited the versatile playwright and architect Sir John Vanbrugh (1664–1726) to make fitting alterations to the county's premier seat.

Grimsthorpe Castle, Vanbrugh's last work, was arguably his best in terms of scale and proportion,

RIGHT **August 2006, Grimsthorpe Castle, Lincolnshire** The ducal crest on the castle parapet, also seen (far right) on wrought-iron gates in the *clairvoie* screen, bears a ducal crown, battering rams, the wild man of Grimsthorpe and the monk, with Ancaster's motto: 'Loyalty Me Oblige'.

BELOW The fine north front, Sir John Vanbrugh's last work. The splendid 'gate guardian' oak veteran (left) may date from Brown's later advice (1770s).

appropriate to its high, narrow ridge location. He brought in Switzer to enhance the castle setting – the two had collaborated to great effect at Castle Howard and Blenheim. Along the main approach from the north, Switzer designed The Oaks, a fashionable 'wilderness', in reality carefully structured, with exploratory paths snaking among new plantations. To the south he created wide-ranging garden walks along the ridge, while his 'arrowhead' bastion garden reflected Vanbrugh's theatrical emphasis on the great military traditions of the Bertie family: a star-shaped fortress design, consisting of a series of low stone walls and ditches enclosing groves of mixed trees and garden walks, with arresting views over parkland and pasture. Similar to the continental-inspired baroque gardens Switzer had laid out for the royal gardener Charles Bridgeman (d.1738) at Blenheim, such ideas essentially stemmed from north European defences.

This country commission afforded Switzer the time, peace and motivation to write, seeking to advocate commonsense ideas such as a circuit riding, or *enfilade*, to survey the whole extent of the park, where eye-catching clumps of trees, left to grow naturally, were placed on every prominent rise.[26]

Switzer's treatise, *The Nobleman, Gentleman, and Gardener's Recreation* (1715, later published as *Ichnographia Rustica*, 1718), was dedicated to the Duke of Ancaster. It succeeded in raising the profile of his profession by combining the history of gardening with much literary quotation set alongside judicious, practical advice, thoughtfully printed in small books for owners and foremen to consult in the field. Over and above the power of panoramic rural prospects, as at Grimsthorpe, he emphasised their economic significance, which naturally appealed to landowners:

> *Utile dulci....* By mixing the useful and profitable parts of Gard'ning with the Pleasurable in the Interior Parts of my Designs, ... are thereby vastly enlarged and both Profit and Pleasure may be said to be agreeably mix'd together ... if the Beauties of Nature were not corrupted by Art, Gardens would be much more valuable. ... It cashiers those interlacings of Boxwork, and such-like trifling Ornaments, and substitutes the plain but nobler Embellishments of Grass, Gravel and the like, in which we so excel other Countries.

Switzer went on to publish *The Practical Fruit-Gardener – Being the Newest and Best Method of Raising, Planting, and Pruning, All Sorts of Fruit-Trees* (1724), and an even more significant work, *An Introduction to a General System of Hydrostaticks & Hydraulicks, Philosophical & Practical* (1729, two volumes), addressing how water was stored and used in the countryside.

Writing from Spye Park, Wiltshire, Switzer made a point of seeking advice from Dr William Stukeley (1687–1765), specifically on how to exploit falls and levels for mills and pumps. The antiquarian draughtsman of earthworks, ruins and gardens had become a friend and confidant. He was also a map-maker, having surveyed both Lincolnshire and Cambridgeshire fens. In one letter Switzer boasted about his cascade at Spye: 'equal to any in the French Gardens, the Falls of the Water being over Steps and rough Work of different Kinds and different Heights, of about 30 or 40 Foot Fall'.[27]

Switzer may have intended to take similar advantage of the natural springs and fishponds that once served an old Cistercian foundation, St Mary's Abbey, in the Vaudey valley below Grimsthorpe Castle. (The name Vaudey comes from 'Valle Dei' or Valley of God.) Convenient, healthy ponds and efficient watercourses were as essential for plants and produce as for gentlemen's houses and attendant offices, stables, laundries, dairies and brew-houses. However, owing to the South Sea débâcle and Ancaster's consequently depleted coffers, only Vanbrugh's magnificent Romano-Palladian north front was realised. Remodelling the entire castle, let alone any sizeable experimental hydraulic works, was now totally out of the question.[28]

A decade later the situation changed. On 15 October 1739, the 2nd Duke of Ancaster's son and heir (also named Peregrine Bertie) married Lady Nicol, a rich widow. Joseph Banks II, the duke's agent, acted as trustee for a generous £70,000 marriage settlement (the equivalent today of about £10 million). This union provided enough finance for major improvements to the castle park, including Switzer-inspired waterworks. Moves to enlarge fishponds and canals or dam small rivers and streams to create 'natural' irregular lakes were rarely driven solely by aesthetics or persuasively lyrical commentators. Banks, as Clerk of Sewers, paid by Ancaster to hold tribunals and to organise Court of Sewers dinners at Grimsthorpe, knew just the man for the job. Mr Brown, newly arrived in the county, had sufficient know-how and drive to act as overseer.

It seems possible that the duke lent the young improver his dedicated copies of Switzer's books to study. Brown initiated an experimental hydraulic scheme to exploit the 'Ladie Spring', situated high above the Vaudey valley, which had served the Cistercian monks. He took up residence at nearby Witham Manor for the duration of the project, his rent paid by his new patron.

OPPOSITE LEFT Dr William Stukeley, *A View from Grime's Walk in Grimsthorpe garden* (1736). All images here Courtesy © Lincolnshire Archives, with the permission of Grimsthorpe & Drummond Castle Trust

OPPOSITE RIGHT Dr William Stukeley, *The Duchess Bastion in Grimsthorpe Gardens* (1736)

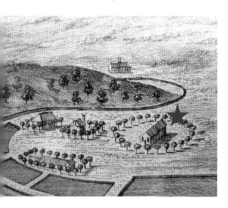

ABOVE Kip/Knyff, *Grimsthorp in the County of Lincoln, the Seat of the Rt. Hon. Robert Earl of Lindsey* (bird's-eye engraving, 1707). Detail: The River West Glen (Jockey Lodge indicated by star).

RIGHT Tycho Wing, *Survey of Grimsthorpe Park* (c.1745). The same area, now Mill Dam Pond, an irregular, naturalised lake. An island (arrow) is on view from Switzer's bastion garden (bottom arrow).

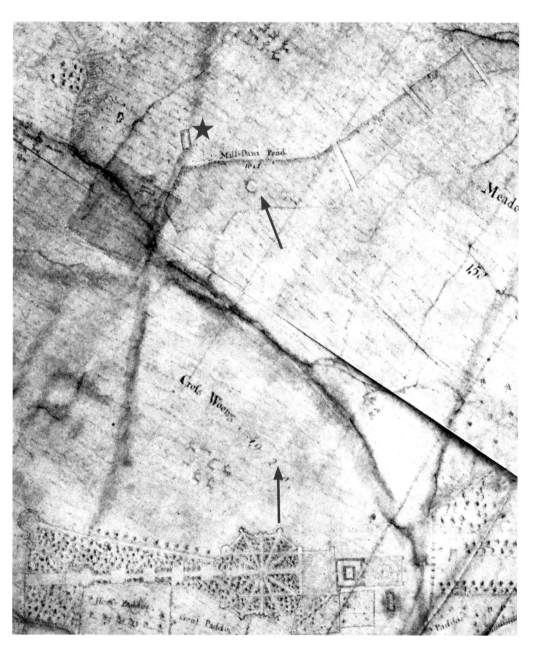

Bitterly cold winters in 1741 and 1742 saw work in the park involving plumbers, blacksmiths, ironmongers and carpenters. The plan was to pump fresh spring water from a deep well, and channel it several hundred yards by gravity to store in a cistern on the edge of Bishophall Wood. The idea was eventually to attempt to pump the water from the cistern up to another tank by the castle, over a mile and a half away. In preparation for this, Brown moved orchards from the proximity of the castle to an appropriate east-sloping site further south (later made into an extensive walled garden).

The duke paid Brown for 'paviour' work: earth-moving, conduit building, ramming clay, levelling and laying stone. Men carted clay to reinforce both the dam banks and the edge of the southernmost fishpond and probably reused stone from the old ruins of the abbey and Bishop's Hall or from barns along the water's edge that he dismantled. In this way they realised a ten-acre, irregular basin, 'Mill Dam Pond' below Mill Hill, the solution to an area of the River West Glen susceptible to flooding. With an eye for detail, he created an island to hide the unnatural-looking straight dam, thus protecting the principal prospect of the park from Switzer's bastion garden.

Brown then began rebuilding and reinforcing the causeway dam that carried the Four Mile Riding from Bytham to the castle. This sham 'Red Bridge' (possibly named for underlying red brick foundations) had water filtering through a sluice under the central arch. Later, its thirteen arches were faced with stone.[29]

In summer 1744, long after Brown had left the area, the 3rd duke looked to a local engineer, John Grundy Jr (1719–1783), to complete the project that Brown had initiated to pump spring water to the castle. Grundy also built a new dam to support an even greater body of water encompassing all the fishponds. His survey book includes a pen and wash drawing of the Red Bridge across the lake, and another

LEFT John Grundy, *A perspective View of the Engine House and Bishophall Wood,* Survey Book (1753) (see opposite). The hexagonal engine house was once central to the park view.

BELOW **May 2006, Grimsthorpe Park, Lincolnshire** A foreshortened view from the castle gardens to the lake, initially naturalised by Brown.

depicting an elegant hexagonal stone engine-house and a nearby cistern-house.[30] To judge from the dearth of trees in the vicinity, and considering another Grundy illustration of his great dam and the lake in an equally barren landscape, some historians doubt that Brown was ever involved. He did work at Grimsthorpe, but at this early stage in his career water engineering, rather than planting, had taken precedence. In fact, years later, the scale of changes Brown had made, especially initiating the large-scale hydraulic project, prompted the 3rd duke to add his signature to a petition, with other eminent patrons, recommending Brown for the position of Master Gardener to King George III. However, long before that, his endeavours in the Vaudey valley led directly to a promotion to one of the most prestigious gardens in the land.

ABOVE **May 2006, Grimsthorpe Castle, Lincolnshire** King John's tower (right) dates from the twelfth century. The rest of the south front, in marked contrast to Vanbrugh's north front, is sixteenth-century. Four stone torches signify 'Enlightenment'.

BELOW John Grundy, *A Perspective View of the Red Bridge from the Keeper's Lodge*, Survey Book (1753). This and top left opposite Courtesy © Lincolnshire Archives, with permission of the Grimsthorpe & Drummond Castle Trust.

A Perspective View of the RED BRIDGE taken from the KEEPERS LODGE

CHAPTER THREE

THE FINEST GARDEN

Winter 1739–40, one of the severest on record, saw the River Thames frozen over for more than six weeks, from Christmas Day to the middle of February. At **Stowe**, Buckinghamshire, Richard Temple, 1st Viscount Cobham (1675–1749), was one of many landowners encountering serious problems from the weather. Brown was recommended to him and travelled some eighty miles across country.

Arriving at Stowe, he immediately addressed the drainage issues, including the water supply to the mansion. The faint sketch of watercourses, apparently in the background of Charles Bridgeman's earlier survey (1719),[31] may well be by Brown, pencilling in his proposal for the excavation of a 'New River', involving an underground conduit leading from natural springs in Conduit Field.

Here was no 'kitchen garden hand', a myth later invented, and then perpetuated, by his critics. From his first day on site, hired in a temporary capacity, his pay, plus board, was more than that of ordinary surveyors, equivalent to a good head gardener's income, £25 a year (£3,625 today). He was an accomplished journeyman overseer, able to measure, estimate and value work. Moreover, at least four key associates from Grimsthorpe, including a plumber and a carpenter, accompanied him to Stowe, men he could rely on for hydraulic work. The following winter was just as harsh. Brown was again called across country to mend a broken dam in the gardens, 'the Head of the River in ye wood'.[32]

OPPOSITE **September 1997, Stowe, Buckinghamshire (NT)** The colonnade of the Temple of Concord and Victory frames a veteran Scots pine, a remnant of Brown's planting in the Grecian Valley.

ABOVE **September 1997, Stowe, Buckinghamshire (NT)** The sham Shell Bridge, designed by William Kent.

33

LEFT **April 1991, Stowe, Buckinghamshire (NT)** One of two Oxford Lodge gate piers by William Kent (later moved to its present location) frames one of two Boycott pavilions by James Gibbs, Brown's first home on marrying Bridget (1744).

RIGHT **October 1999, Stowe, Buckinghamshire (NT)** William Kent's Temple of Ancient Virtue dominates the Elysian Fields.

In March 1741 Joseph Banks II died of 'atrophy'. Brown continued to oversee works at Grimsthorpe until the harvest was in. That November, having journeyed to Stowe to continue his scheme there, he heard some distressing stories. The previous summer, Cobham's steward had committed suicide. What was perhaps just as upsetting, his successor, Potts, with whom Brown had conveniently boarded, had absconded after stealing money from his patron.

On the first day of the New Year, the Great Lord Chamberlain, the Duke of Ancaster, also died. This news was swiftly relayed to Cobham as a Privy Councillor, who, with Brown on site, wasted no time. Having been let down twice, he desperately needed a trustworthy supervisor for his ambitious building programme. He had witnessed Brown's aptitude and focused energy at first hand, noting the way he, at not yet twenty-five years of age, handled his men. As one of Marlborough's generals, Cobham recognised innate leadership and decided to offer the young improver a permanent position as his steward and head gardener, a classic case of 'the right man, in the right place, at the right time'. Not having to test or compromise his loyalty, with both his patrons now gone Brown was free to seize this prestigious career opportunity.

Matching the ambition of his new patron, Brown welcomed the unprecedented chance to shoulder responsibility for both the ornamental and the productive aspects of the most famous garden in England. He set to work straight away and, because he kept accounts conscientiously, any suspicions were soon dispersed.

Imagine the impressive scale and layout of canals and fountains, parterres, temples and triumphal arches now in the care of Brown and his workforce. Bridgeman had surrounded the ornamental gardens with a deep, dry ditch and retaining wall, an occasional bastion jutting out where the long walks met, overlooking the park. His obelisk, in the centre of the Octagon pond below the house, was meant to have a gravity-fed jet of water but it never functioned satisfactorily and was later moved. Stimulating views called to mind ancient legends, Roman monuments and more recent battles. A series of straight walks, with trees left unclipped, intended – some say – as a more romantic interpretation of life's journey along earthly paths, through love and war towards heaven's gate, focused the attention westward towards the hub of Bridgeman's asymmetrically skewed design in response to the topography. The Rotunda was Vanbrugh's shrine for the curvaceous Medici Venus or her Greek equivalent Aphrodite, Goddess of Love, the most popular statue of the day.

William Kent had been invited by Cobham to develop the 'Elysian Fields', the heaven of the Ancient World, in place of a public road.[33] His choice naturalistic planting, largely Scots pine and clipped laurel 'lawn', was beginning to look established, setting off the winding, artificial 'River Styx', to mirror more architectural conceits, the Temples of Modern and Ancient Virtue and, on the opposite bank, positioned to catch afternoon and early evening light, his unique, curved exedra Temple of British Worthies, with the Roman god Mercury, guide to souls in the underworld, in the central niche. Brown, just as every visitor, could pause to contemplate this great seat, and doubtless, from time to time, reflect on the legacy of sixteen remarkable individuals in the story of England, among them King Alfred, Queen Elizabeth I, King William III, Sir Francis Drake, William Shakespeare, Inigo Jones and Sir Isaac Newton. Lastly, unusually, was the Catholic poet Alexander Pope, still living.[34]

ABOVE J.C. Nattes, *View of the Round Tower in the park, Stowe* (1805), also called the 'Saxon Tower'. Courtesy © Buckinghamshire County Museum, Aylesbury. Originally an engine house, now known as 'Keeper's Lodge'.

RIGHT July 2001, Stowe, Buckinghamshire (NT) Keeper's Lodge, the site of an early steam pump.

Brown's forty-man team included, besides gardeners, four masons under contract, with stone supplied from three different quarries, working on new stables and no fewer than seven new garden buildings, such as the Queen's Temple; they were also to finish the Palladian Bridge. Opportunities to learn were manifold and Brown took full advantage. Embarking upon a more scholarly approach to construction and architecture, he copied out a fifteen-page glossary of architectural terms so as to be able to communicate with artisans. The urge to create and innovate was strong. Soon he began to draw his own designs, and went on to undertake interior improvements to Cobham's private apartments, including building a new staircase and altering the chapel. Brown was an uncompromising taskmaster, ordering unsatisfactory walls to be taken down and rebuilt, and steps relaid. He also assiduously kept his employer informed about every move with transparent honesty: 'An acct shall come on Tuesdays post all the work people have been employ'd & likewise the plan of the Long Room. I should have sent it this post but could not get it finished.'[35]

The early 1740s were unusually dry, in particular June to September 1741 and 1743, evidently one of the worst dry spells of the century. Works in the gardens reflect the need for water. A round, rustic stone 'eye-catcher' surrounded by oaks and Scots pines on Stowe's highest hill, the Keeper's Lodge has an unnaturally wide chimney and, at ground level, unusual circular openings in the stonework (now walled up). It was originally designed to house an engine. For five months, from Lady Day through to Michaelmas 1741, the blacksmith Thomas Bennet collaborated with ironmongers, a cooper and a 'collar worker' to dig a new well and install a steam engine pump (also known as a 'fire' engine). When required, water could be pumped across from springs in Conduit Field, stored in cisterns and gravity-fed to irrigate vegetables, flowers and fruit trees in a new 'kitching' (kitchen) garden that Brown, in November 1742, conveniently tucked below the hill, putting six men to thatch its cob (not brick) walls. The following three months' accounts detail great activity:

> *Brown and his boys laying turf ... sweeping leaves and weeding gravle, ... repairing and helping the Elpalliards' (espaliers), pruning, ... staking and 'nailing' new planted trees. ... Washing the trees to prevt the Deer barking them, ... weeding and Rooling (laying out) the Garding..., trees Weeding, harrowing gravle, Rolling laying turff Filling up Holes in Nelsons Seat whear the trees had been taken out.*[36]

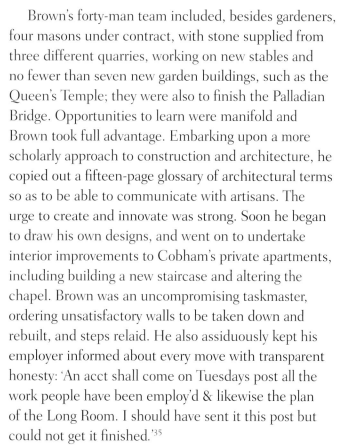

June 2001, Stowe, Buckinghamshire (NT) Bridgeman's straight ha-ha (right arrow) between Vanbrugh's Lake Pavilions (c. 1722) and Brown's sunk fence dividing the pasture (left arrow) are barely evident.

As the Palladian Bridge neared completion, Cobham also paid 'Brown and his boys' handsomely for conduit building and moving an immense volume of earth. Nearer the house, they levelled the terrain away from the building to ease drainage. They filled in garden pools, dismantled fountains, and, probably to prevent a repeat of problems caused by acute frost, lowered existing pipes in order to drain kitchen and office waste-water into Eleven-Acre Lake.

Over time, Brown's simplification transformed labour-intensive and water-dependent gardens to open up a manageable, watered landscape of scale. Was this because of aesthetics or pragmatism? Almost certainly a combination of both, as his men tore up hedges and parterres, and replaced them with a broad, smooth, more drought-resistant turf sward, seeded with Dutch clover. The lawn calmed the scene and successfully set off the architectural splendour of the house, sloping gently down to a freshly gravelled Abele Walk (Poplar Walk) leading towards the reflective waters of the Octagon.

On several occasions during the drought, Cobham's nephew Richard Grenville called Brown across to Wotton for advice, and probably to clear out silt from the great pond called 'The Warrells' while water levels were low. Each time he paid him a guinea (today

£152).[37] Again, ideas sketched on an old survey are probably Brown's. In December 1742, labourers began transforming an existing fishpond and low-lying parts of Cleere Field below Wotton Launde (Lawn) into a 'Great Pond' (see p.74). In an attempt to recycle water back at Stowe, where once a large water-wheel existed close by the Temple of Venus, Brown cannily hid a horse engine underneath the rear of the building.

The more changes made and solutions to problems found, the more open space Brown created, the more his confidence and aesthetic finesse grew. In 1742, Samuel Richardson (1689–1761) noted: 'Some grand walks are now making by the Side of a fine Lawn from which we see numerous herds of Deer.'[38]

In adapting the third edition of his travel book, *A Tour thro' the Whole Island of Great Britain* (1724), Daniel Defoe devoted seventeen of a total thirty-two pages to the gardens of Stowe, at a time when Brown was engaged in improvements. Taking in the vistas from the Belvedere, he detected one snag: 'Here we had likewise a view of the South Front of the House up an Avenue of stately Trees; but great Objections have been made to the Narrowness of it.'[39]

In 1744, Stowe became the first garden to open to the public, with an illustrated guidebook produced by Benton Seeley (1716–1795), a writing-master at Buckingham:

… to give a plain Account
of the GARDENS of the Lord COBHAM at STOWE:
As they are esteemed, by Persons of the most exact Taste,
to be the finest in this Kingdom,
and perhaps in Europe.[40]

All this undoubtedly brought Brown wider acclaim, but there were other matters on his mind. That November, Joseph Banks's daughter Elizabeth eloped from her home in Revesby to marry a neighbour, James Hawley MD, at Gray's Inn in London. We can only speculate whether this gave Bridget, tired of waiting for her sweetheart's return to Lincolnshire, the courage

to set off for Stowe two weeks later. Whatever the case, on 22 November 1744, shortly after her arrival, Bridget Wayet and Lancelot Brown exchanged vows by special licence in St Mary's Church, in the gardens.

The young couple then settled down to married life in the unusual West Boycott Pavilion, 'a very good habitable house',[41] on the main approach to Stowe. Here their first four children were born: Bridget (1746), Lancelot (1748), William (1750, who lived only one month) and John (1751).

For the gardens, ½ lb of 'Scotch Fir' seed headed one order (1744/5) from a specialist London nurseryman, James Scott.[42] The seeds for the new kitchen garden included Persian melons, Turkey cucumber, Italian broccoli, Dutch turnips and Strasbourg onions. What seems surprising, since Brown is mostly associated nowadays with acres of grassland and parkland trees, is that he planted bulbs, including four dozen 'largest roots of Double Ye sweet-smelling Junquil roots', an old variety of double narcissus, now known as *Telemonius plenus* 'Van Sion'.

BELOW **April 1991, St Mary's Church, Stowe** (thirteenth century)

BELOW LEFT **March 2007, Lincolnshire** Jonquil *Telemonius plenus* 'Van Sion'.

RIGHT **September 1997, West Boycott Pavilion, Stowe** (NT)

ABOVE A nineteenth-century engraving shows a 'timber-bob', similar to the tree-planting device invented by Brown.

LEFT **September 1997, Stowe, Buckinghamshire (NT)** The Gothic Temple of Liberty and, still bright after restoration, the memorial to William Pitt, Lord Chatham.

Though he is often accused of banning flowers behind kitchen garden walls, his accounts record men 'digging the flower boarders in the laines' and sowing twenty-three different annuals. Picture laurels sited for shelter, with periwinkles as ground cover, and blue and pink larkspur, wallflowers, hollyhocks and carnations planted along the meandering walks leading to the newly tiled, thatched grotto, a suitably quixotic setting for the family to entertain distinguished guests by evening torchlight.

Ingeniously thinking up new solutions to problems, Brown invented a device, effectively a pole on wheels, to assist the manoeuvring of mature trees. First pollarding larger branches, before strapping the tree trunk to the pole, his men levered out the tree using horsepower, the axle of the wheels acting as a pivot, gradually teasing out roots with as much rootball as possible. They wheeled the heavy tree on the contraption to a new location, where they built up the soil around its roots, ensuring that the trunk was

supported with guy-ropes until it had settled. Little by little over the years, the atmosphere of the gardens softened. In thrifty fashion, 'thinnings' on the west supplemented vistas towards the east, where the latest and most prominent features could be appreciated in the best possible light. Brown's seemingly more natural planting was far from random. Making use of a 110-yard measuring chain costing £3 5s 0d (today about £460), he took great pains positioning trees, considered each individual setting just as Kent had done and refined every view from every angle.

Although Catholics were still mostly shunned by society, Cobham chose to commission a highly regarded Catholic architect, James Gibbs (1682–1754), perhaps persuaded by his *Book of Architecture, of use to Gentlemen concerned in Building* (1739). Brown was able to observe the architect's close collaboration with craftsmen as they raised his unusual, triangular building in rusty-orange Northamptonshire ironstone.[43] When it was

finally finished in 1748, Cobham dedicated the Gothic Temple, in celebration of traditional British architecture, 'To the Liberty of our Ancestors'. In complete contrast to Kent's secluded Elysian Fields, in its open meadow setting on the brow of Hawkwell Field, this temple towering above the great gardens could be seen from almost every corner, and offered, more than any other building, dramatic and extensive views of the countryside. Brown chose select trees, cedar of Lebanon, holm oak and beech, to set it off, allowing space for them to grow well. Without question Stowe's most memorable, most affecting prospect left a powerful impression on the Northumbrian.

Despite increasing frailty, Cobham determined on another new venture, a 'Grecian diagonal': a neo-classical temple aligned on the rising sun, 'one of the noblest objects that ever adorned a garden'.[44] On close inspection, a certain naivety of design, together with typically convenient features, indicates that Brown was the driving force.[45] The idea was for the temple to be reflected in 'new waters'. Labourers dug out a massive volume of earth, 23,500 cubic yards, to create a basin with steep slopes, surrounded by a laurel terrace, and found the best clay at Brick Kiln Farm to make the walls of the dams. Following the latest trend

September 1997, Stowe, Buckinghamshire (NT) The Temple of Concord and Victory dominates the Grecian Valley, where the hollowed-out levels of Brown's failed lake are still discernible.

Brown intended filling an 'Oval Pond', on two levels, by pumping spring water through his 'Barn River'[46] conduit, controlled by sluices with iron gates. However, when 1746 proved a very hot summer, he had to confess that drought was once again causing problems:

> My lord,
> As to finishing the Head of the Oval I had never formed any other idea on it than what your Lordship gave me which was to Forme the Laurell Plantation with a sweep under it and Concave to the Ovall that the Slope of the Heads your Lordship thought might some time or other have statues put on it, but gave me no absolute Orders to finish it and indeed I think it would be better not finishing this season, I thinking that a sumer's talks and Tryels about it may make it a very fine thing. The Springs fill the Oval much about a barleycorns head a Day. I can only add that my hope is still biger than my fear that your Lordship will see it full.[47]

Experiments continued but, with water in short supply, and early pumps notoriously inefficient, the scheme was eventually abandoned. Failure, a rare experience for Brown, was sobering. There was little time to mope for a man who could make lakes. His water-engineering skills, as also his building know-how, were increasingly in demand. Cobham showed great benevolence, especially during 1747, when the house was let while he remained in London, in permitting Brown to advise other local landowners.[48] That May, a nephew of Cobham, Captain Thomas Grenville, was killed during a naval engagement against the French. Cobham chose the north side of the half-empty basin in the Grecian Valley to set a fitting memorial column inscribed 'The Muse forbids Heroic Worth to die'.[49]

Brown began tackling another major project, building an octagonal prospect tower, with enough confidence to alter the original design by Gibbs. Sadly, before the end of 1748, Cobham too passed away. Lady Anne commissioned a statue of her husband, dressed as a noble Roman emperor, to surmount Brown's tower, overlooking his precious gardens and offering views over five counties.[50] A memorial shield bears Alexander Pope's inscription: 'As we cannot live long, let us leave something behind us, to show that we have lived'.

Though there was plenty of work in the immediate locality, well-connected clients with disposable income were more accessible in London. Brown made plans to leave, dutifully remaining long enough to oversee the underpinning of the garden front of the house, and finishing both the Grecian Temple interior and the Conduit House. The summers from 1746 to 1749 had been exceptionally hot and 1749 was also very dry. His first design in virgin territory had proved a catastrophe through lack of water – an experience that probably proved the making of the man. One of his final tasks was to sign a receipt for 45 lb of Dutch clover seed, white-flowering *Trifolium repens*, enough to clothe approximately seven acres of bare earth. This helped to create a 'Grecian Valley' in place of his failed lake, perfect for grazing sheep.[51]

In 1751, Brown moved Bridget and the family to London. They rented a house (now gone) on Hammersmith Mall overlooking the River Thames, where Queen Catherine, widow of Charles II, had planted tall elms to shade the promenade, 'the finest specimens of the kind in the west of London'.[52] Lord Burlington's Palladian villa at Chiswick, an archetype of fashion, was less than a mile away. Brown was spoilt for choice of nurseries, besides having established a reliable working relationship with James Scott nearby at Turnham Green. Hammersmith was a hamlet of Fulham, a flourishing market garden suburb. Together with neighbouring parishes and several prominent nurseries, the area was known as the 'great garden' of London.

By this time most major roads out of London had become expensive turnpikes by Acts of Parliament. Those serving Cambridge cost 6d (today £3.50) for a gig, a light two-wheeled one-horse carriage, and 3d (£1.75) for a saddle horse. Over the next twenty years, the booming economic climate enabled prosperous towns to organise the formation of hundreds more turnpike trusts, particularly in the west and north-west. All the same, travel, if steadily more convenient, was still slow, uncomfortable and unreliable. In 1754 a coach journey from London to Manchester took four and a half days.

Stowe had afforded Brown a period of stability, nurturing his young family while consolidating and refining his *modus operandi* and eye for planting. A range of aristocratic commissions had broadened his horizons and so he returned to journeying with optimism. Independent, well-placed and positive, he could offer clients the best possible comprehensive advice. He prudently kept in contact with several dependable craftsmen and overseers he had come to know in the Midlands who would prove invaluable in the establishment of a complex practice dedicated to building, water engineering and land improvement. The Thames, London's main artery for transport, was always awash with barges and ferrying watermen, yet it was also seen as 'one continuous garden', a perpetual source of inspiration. Word spread through society's salons concerning Mr Brown's 'capability', leading to several important commissions both up- and down-river.

CHAPTER FOUR

CLIENTS, SURVEYS & PROPOSALS

Over the next fourteen years, six more brothers and sisters arrived for Bridget, Lancelot and John. Sadly, only two survived: Margaret, christened 2 November 1758 at St Paul's Church, Hammersmith, and Thomas, 21 July 1761. One particularly exciting challenge proved a distracting consolation. The Earl of Coventry invited Brown not only to tame the boggy environs of **Croome** in Worcestershire, but also, his first integrated commission, to design a new house, with a view of the Malvern Hills.

As work on his house progressed at Croome, Coventry numbered among several clients who became closely attached to the genial, outgoing Northumbrian, who was, by all accounts, as uncomplicated and as easy-going as the levels he crafted. Brown was a man who enjoyed playful puns, according to Lord Harcourt. For those contemplating the sweeping scale and wide range of his landscapes, the question 'How on earth did he do it?' is as apposite as answers are manifold. His many attributes – force of character, intelligence, integrity, diligence, empathy, loyalty, charm, sense of humour – plus a generous dose of self-belief are neatly summed up in one word: charisma.

OPPOSITE June 2009, Croome, Worcestershire (NT) The view from the garden door of the house to the distant 'Owl Seat' overlooking the 'river' landscape. Two sphinxes keep guard either side of the house steps, inspired by Burlington's designs.

ABOVE May 2010, Packington, Warwickshire A sentinel beech (now a stump) once shaded Brown's coursed sandstone spring head, taking the eye off his great dam beyond. Did a later dam restoration demolish his grotto?

Many stimulated landowners parted with enormous sums of money for 'place-making', apparently with consummate ease. Occasionally there were long delays before work 'to correct and mend' could begin, for expensive Acts of Parliament to divert roads or footpaths, or to change the common field system by enclosure. A magnetic, persuasive personality, with acute spatial intellect, this superlative salesman was able to communicate ideas for audacious schemes with convincing authority, to client, king, artisan or labourer, and to demand tolerance to bring them, eventually, to fruition.

His good-humoured, constructive visits offered such a potent mix of novel ingenuity and practical experience that his reputation spread rapidly, often leading to further commissions nearby. Freethinking opposition patriots numbered among Brown's earliest patrons. Later, inheriting sons valued his counsel just as their fathers had. Some clients looked on him as a trusted go-between. Whether house-hunting for Lady Bute or negotiating the sale of the Earl of Exeter's London townhouse, he enjoyed many a bottle of wine with society's leaders, wisely choosing to stay on the periphery of politics with no apparent bias towards Whig or Tory, Protestant or Catholic.

His confident expertise and honest professionalism facilitated his freedom of movement in the highest social circles. Where the polite manners of the day required deference towards high-ranking clients, Brown was direct, without pretension, as easy as the levels he designed. If he sometimes waited ages to be paid, he never seemed to charge interest. Yet he was not averse to pointing out arrears or non-payment of fees. The Earl of Northampton received a curt letter admonishing a broken promise: 'The wine did not come.'[53]

It was still rare to emerge from a farming background to dinners 'at all the tables of the House of Lords', not to mention entertaining conversations with discerning wives. The ladies, appreciating that he addressed their quality of life, often prompted a commission in the first place. Barbara Mostyn[54] admired great changes as she grew up at Kiddington, Oxfordshire, where, in a typical response to the problem of lack of prospect, Brown had widened and dammed the River Glyme to contrive a sinuous body of water that would mirror enfolding hills: 'I will make it so agreeable that no one will want to look beyond it.'[55]

After her marriage, Lady Mostyn approached him about alterations to her new home in Wales, Talacre (Flintshire). Likewise, the newly married Countess of Northumberland made notes about her visit to Stowe gardens, before Brown was summoned to Syon, their Thames-side property on the outskirts of London. Lady Chatham, Lady Ossory and Mrs Elizabeth Montagu numbered among other distinguished clients who became long-standing friends. While he irritated young Lady Shelburne by spending the evening after dinner issuing orders to his men,[56] Lady Bruce took a keen interest in plans and staffing, and found Brown's northern wit irresistible. Lady Digby hurried back to Sherborne Castle from Weymouth so as not to miss seeing Mr Brown who, according to her brother-in-law, Captain Digby, was 'very agreeable'.[57]

Horace Walpole, more than anyone, spread the word about the designer's talent and integrity in copious correspondence. He could not resist sharing gossip about Brown, especially when it concerned the Duke of Marlborough:

> Mr Brown's flippancy diverted me. It is what was called wit two thousand years ago... The first peer that experiences it, laughs to conceal his being angry at the freedom – the next flatters him for fear of being treated as familiarly, and ten more bear it because it is so like Brown.[58]

With Brown fast becoming a celebrity, the famous Shakespearean actor/manager David Garrick (1717–1779) adapted his first play, *Lethe or Aesop in the Shades*, to satirise the current gardening craze. He delighted in playing an ageing peer, 'Lord Chalkstone', waiting to cross the River Styx into the Elysian Fields. They were laid out without taste, he complained, and should have been given a serpentine sweep: 'the whole wants variety, extent, contrast, inequality'.[59]

Brown had been remodelling Garrick's Thames-side garden at **Hampton**, building a tunnel under the high road, and embellishing a setting for an Ionic temple in tribute to William Shakespeare.[60] Had he regaled the actor with humorous stories about his former employer, Cobham, alias 'Lord Chalkstone', obsessed with his garden buildings? Whatever the case, Garrick knew it was safe to tease. They had become good friends. Both men were patriotic in the extreme, energetic, innovative and relaxed. He also later admitted to an acquaintance not only his respect for Brown's genius, but that he 'simply doted' on the man.

Zoffany's radically informal conversation piece (*above*) reveals how society figures were relaxing and unwinding in their gardens. Colonel George Bodens, with cane, recommended plants for the garden.[61] Who is the gentleman taking tea, standing between Mr and Mrs Garrick? All in brown, too well-dressed to be the butler, both the angle of the man's head and his wig

ABOVE Johann Zoffany (1733–1810), *Mr and Mrs Garrick Taking Tea at Hampton* © Courtesy Garrick Club. Is Mr Brown standing behind?

BELOW Peter de Wint (1784–1849), *David Garrick's Villa Garden by the Thames at Hampton.* Brown's grotto tunnel is just discernible (right).

suggest that Zoffany copied Dance's original portrait of Brown. Surely this has to be Brown in attendance here, the colour of his clothing the artist's visual pun.

June 1998, Chilham Castle, Kent A holm oak on the lawn, framed by the wings of the old manor house, with Brown's curvaceous ha-ha beyond.

Brown's restraint in laying out the small garden is apparent here. The smooth lawn, right to the uncluttered river-bank, gives an illusion of space. A seat around a mature tree makes a feature opposite the temple. As visitors arrive through Brown's tunnel, young weeping willows and evergreens guard his grotto, including, typically, three Scots pines planted diagonally across from Walpole's cypress, all framing an Arcadian view of the Thames.

Consider one other instance to understand the effect Brown had on people. Thomas Heron's letters to his brother Richard, serving abroad in Ireland, mostly plead for more money to run their family estates, administered from **Chilham** Castle in Kent. They are brief, often depressed, altogether tedious. The minute the celebrated Brown arrives, the length and, above all, tone change radically as Heron, stimulated, uplifted and quite obviously impressed, reports every recommendation, word for word:

Mr Brown left me yesterday. He staid two days. The weather was so extremely bad we could scarcely take our views. He proposes to lay down that part of the garden before the House, except the upper terraces which he considers as a set-off to it. The nursery to be the kitchen garden, and have a small addition at the bottom from the Paddock; this situation for the garden is from necessity; there being no other in any degree convenient.

The stables he, at first, thought might keep their ground but afterwards condemned them and pointed out two situations for them.... He says no building should appear with the Castle and he thinks the valey on that side very fine, and that the view of it from the Park should not be intercepted.

The farmyard and wood-yard he would place below the stables. He says there is little to do in the Park; it is so well wooded that it only wants a little opening. The River he would enlarge and lay the earth on the low parts of the meadows, and drain them; that the expense will be more than repaid by the improvement of the ground. He admires the situation and beauty of the grounds. He attends to Economy. [62]

As it happened, Chilham's terraces presented Brown with something of a dilemma. The garden had been laid out over a hundred years previously by the royal gardener John Tradescant (d.1637). Brown's initial instinct had been to demolish the terraces, level a sloping lawn and excavate the requisite ha-ha. His solution was an unusual compromise, maybe out of respect for his predecessor: 'The wall of the Upper Terras to be taken down and the ground from the house sloped to the wall of the next Terras to correspond with the slope before the house, the next Terras to remain entire.'[63]

By the mid-1770s Brown's fame had spread, with newspapers regularly talking of his exploits. There is no doubt that the designer was compulsively driven, prepared to travel hundreds of miles in every direction, with little regard for inconvenience or the strain on his health, apart from the odd grumble in letters to his wife whom he affectionately called 'Biddy': 'I am tolerable well after a most shocking passage over the Humber'.[64]

When invited by the Duke of Leinster to Dublin, Brown turned down an extraordinarily generous inducement for his advice: £1,000 (today £145,000).[65] He must have had his reasons, over and above his loathing for a sea crossing, but famously gave as his reason, with a wit regarded as conceited by those who fail to grasp his humour, that he had not yet finished England!

Dedicating his life to advance his gospel of improvement, Brown was never short of commissions from senior officers in government, admiralty and law. Writing one Christmas Eve, the Earl of Hardwicke expected him to complete a specific plan of operations, detailing estate improvements for the next three years, including 'our Minute of proceeding at Wimple' (Wimpole, Cambridgeshire), and all by the New Year.[66] Such pressing demands were typical.

Travel arrangements were complicated. A servant would ride on in advance to order fresh horses at various coaching inns. Brown took care to keep foremen and, naturally, family, informed of his whereabouts, 'to Lord Donegall's by Tuesday post to Lord Craven's by Thursday post'.[67]

Clients were always eager for work to begin, and just as anxious, if not more, for it to finish. He was often elusive despite reassurance to the contrary: 'P.S. a line directed for me to Hampton Court will always find me'.[68]

Most were prepared to suffer setbacks, content to await the designer's reappearance, simply because he eventually achieved spectacular results. His contractors also had to exercise patience. When the master plasterer Thomas Stocking of Bristol expressed exasperation at not receiving drawings for elaborate mouldings for the Picture Gallery at Corsham, Brown's excuse could not be questioned: 'The Queen not coming has made an exceeding great trouble in my Business.'[69] In the end, he found it expedient to submit a design for a ceiling that another client, William Constable, had already rejected.

Letters were swiftly penned, usually brief and to the point and littered with phrases such as 'on my western expedition', almost as if he were a world explorer with a mission. Brown hated wasting time. A missive to Lord Methuen confessed: 'I cough Night & Day. I mean to take a little Journey by way of changing the Air and when I return you may depend of seeing me.'[70]

Whether stress exacerbated his asthma, or his health provided a convenient excuse for delays, it seems remarkable how many contracts and underwritten payments were completed by agreed dates, despite bouts of illness disrupting his overloaded schedule. Of course, there was added frustration if clients were away from home when he called:

> *I am obliged to go to Blenheim [Oxfordshire] on Wednesday or Thursday. I must go round by Lord Coventry's [Croome, Worcestershire] & Sr Wm Codrington's [Dodington, Gloucestershire] which will take me at least eight or ten Days. I wish your Lordship could stay a few Days longer in the Country or be a few days longer before you go. I have been calculating my time entirely for your Lordship & it will be an extreme mortification to*

me not to meet your Lordship. I beg your Lordship will contrive as much about this matter as possible because I have been contriving to make every body meet me at their respective Places which puts out of my power to alter my rout. I fully intended to have waited on your Lordship tomorrow. Your Lordship will oblige me with an answer.[71]

Middle-aged yet indefatigable, he was simultaneously masterminding major projects at Blenheim, Burghley, Claremont, Fisherwick, Luton, Sandbeck, Thorndon, Tottenham Park and Wimpole. A pattern of travel evolved, with journeys to southern properties in spring, to northern ones in autumn. A letter to his younger daughter, Peggy, describes making a seventy-mile journey from London to Broadlands (Hampshire) in ten hours, this time by coach: 'We came all the way as hard as four horses could lay feet to the ground.'[72]

The Game Book at Sherborne Castle in Dorset shows Brown still riding at sixty years of age and records one of many early morning starts: 'Thursday 18th January 1776 Mr Brown set out between seven and eight o'clock in the morning to go on horseback by Wincaunton to London.'

A postscript in a missive to his friend Elizabeth Montagu, dated October 1782, proves that, despite his age and ill-health, he was still covering considerable mileage. 'I have travelled fifty miles today & have twenty-five more to go before I attempt to sleep.'[73]

The only surviving account book refers to various proposals, surveys and plans dating from the second half of Brown's career.[74] These financial records confirm his growing prosperity and firm grip on finance. They are not comprehensive, with only sparse detail regarding the architectural side of the business, nor do they chart every mission. There must have been occasional payments in cash. A single journey, for instance, is noted to Burton Constable (Yorkshire), September 1774, where estate minutes detail a regular pattern of visits, almost annually in late summer or early autumn over more than ten years. At times he seemed happy to advise friends and

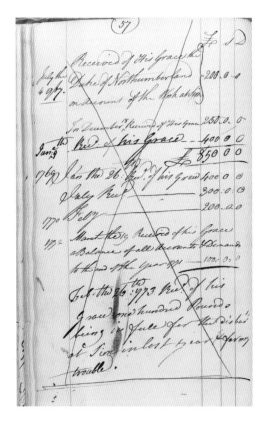

LEFT Brown Account Book © Mr M. Morrice/RHS Lindley Library. Page 57 relates to payments from the Duke of Northumberland, over a period of five years, totalling £1,850 (today £268,250) for work at Syon House, Middlesex.

RIGHT **May 1997, Aske, North Yorkshire** The veteran beech in the foreground draws the focus to a loose grouping, three oaks, in the middle distance. These lead the eye to a 'tree of liberty', a sycamore visible from the house windows. This singleton contrasts with three single-species groves (left) on the horizon, counterbalanced by a clump of mixed trees beyond. I believe this view is a surviving example of Brown's planting advice.

acquaintances in exchange for occasional bed and board on the way to other commissions. Months, even years of toil, in which many noteworthy landscapes were significantly altered, were credited as simply 'out of doors work'.[75]

Accurate maps were fundamental to Brown's livelihood, each survey a springboard for his problem-solving imagination. He set such store by his survey equipment and tools that they featured in his will. His equipment in a mahogany box, carried everywhere with him on a pack-horse, included ranging rods, measuring chains (probably 'Gunter',[76] with 100 links, 66 feet in length), a surveying compass, a plane table for plotting in the field, and a simple theodolite, measuring both horizontal and vertical angles between two points either by sights or a telescope.[77] A surveyor's wheel, a 'way wiser', recorded each revolution of the wheel to measure distance.

The French writer François de la Rochefoucauld, travelling extensively in rural England with his brother, joked that 'Le Brun' could create a design after riding around a park for only an hour and needed just half a day to mark out the ground with theodolite and notebook. He would have ridden to the highest point on any given estate to take in existing layout and views. Such was the speed and precision of his visual comprehension that some clients received only two visits, one to assess the estate (rarely lasting more than three days), the second to explain (and sell) his 'grand plan' in detail and a suggested process of improvement. A keen spatial awareness, together with what is now called photographic memory, helped him observe and log water sources and boggy areas, existing boundaries, contours and features, natural or man-made.

Often pressed for time, the pragmatic businessman was not averse to using others' surveys or designs as a basis for his own modifications. A royal gardener's plan for Kirtlington (Oxfordshire) is endorsed: 'Greening's plan totally changed by Brown'.[78]

As he rushed off to his next appointment, trained assistants would remain behind to take detailed measurements, in order to draw up a complete survey on which he would base his plan. William Donn and Thomas White are among highly regarded surveyors who worked for Brown before going on to establish their own improvement practices. Another experienced surveyor, Cornelius Dickinson, charged 18s (today £130) a day at Sherborne.

Sometimes Brown would call in local county surveyors. In September 1769, George Jackson, surveyor and mapmaker, was paid one guinea a day (£152) to attend Brown for two days at **Aske** (North Yorkshire). That December, Jackson presented his account for a finely drawn survey:

To Surveying and Planing on a larger scale and in a very particular manner for Mr Brown the Improvers use all that part of the Aske Estate lying East of the Road leading from Richmond to Kirby Hills and describing exactly on this Plan is all the Hills, Hollows, Levels, Walks, Waters, Woods Trees and Buildings, with a book of References thereunto answered … £47.5.0 [£652.10].[79]

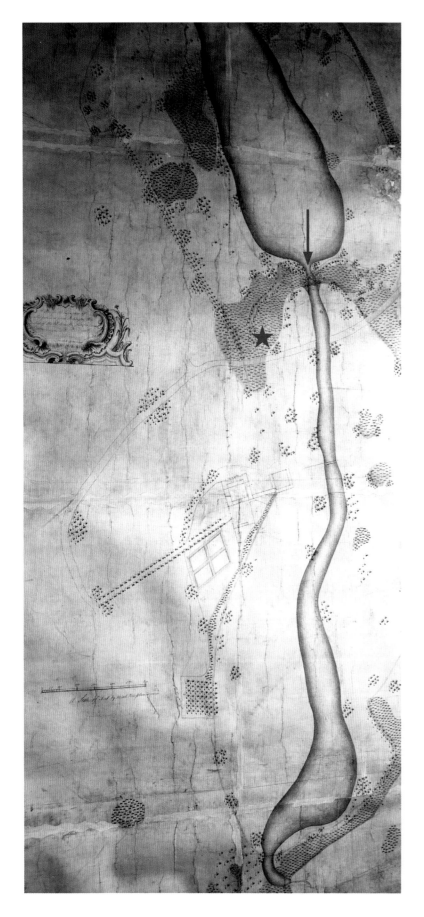

LEFT Brown's Packington Plan (1751) © The Earl of Aylesford. The uniform trees and shrubs, as on Brown's Petworth, Syon and Aynho plans, were probably stamped by the draughtsman with a carved woodblock. Note the strength of line for the lake-edge. The star indicates the spring-head (see p.43), the arrow 'The Situation for a Cascade' (below), a grotto cascade similar to one still extant at Stowe.

MIDDLE **October 1999, Stowe, Buckinghamshire (NT)** Brown and Sanderson Miller may have collaborated (c.1751) on alterations to the cascade, distracting from the level-change between the Octagon and Eleven-Acre Lakes. This was probably originally designed by William Kent.

BOTTOM Detail No. 18 from Brown's Packington Plan (1751) © The Earl of Aylesford. 'The Desinge [sic] for my Lady's Lodge'. Later, smaller architectural plans, framed with a single or double outline, were mostly signed or initialled LB.

May 2010, Packington Park, Warwickshire Old alders edge the lower lake, Brown's 'new river'.

Neither date, nor fee for his advice, feature in Brown's account book, only the following: 'A journey to Aske Hall & plan for a Bridge & the Head of the water where the new road was to go over Paid.'[80] The mapmaker charged the client, Sir Lawrence Dundas, for the paper for the plan, for the reference book and for a tin case and carriage to Northallerton. Brown, presumably on his way back from Northumberland, or one of his men, would pick it up. Note the phrase 'planing on a larger scale and in a very particular manner'. Jackson had been impressed by Brown.

Years earlier, following several hot, dry summers, 1751 had been exceedingly wet and offered opportunities for expansion of water features. To promote the scheme for Packington (Warwickshire), Brown had sketched out his initial ideas and suggestions on another's survey, including, perhaps to give an idea of scale, amusing details, a three-mast ship and a man fishing in a boat. He envisaged extending the existing 'Great Pond' and bringing his 'new river' waters through the landscape so that they would then be pleasingly on view from the house windows.

Later, he presented a grand plan, 6 ft long by 2 ft 4 ins wide, eight folio pages gummed together, and here, as was often the case, on a scale of 1 in. to 100 ft. The drawing bears little resemblance to his later, more informal plans. A formal cartouche and accomplished

pen and wash vignettes in indian ink ornament both top and bottom of the proposal: a classical Palladian pavilion, 'My Lady's Lodge', a three-arch stone bridge, and a Palladian entrance gate and screen. An elaborate grotto cascade is reminiscent of the Stowe cascade that Brown had recently altered.[81] The likelihood is that he sketched out the most important lines in pencil, given their strength: water's edge, winding paths and main approach road, before investing in employing a professional draughtsman,[82] in the hope that this important commission would advance his practice. He then numbered twenty-three features in coloured ink, penned the corresponding references on the legend (including a spelling mistake for 'design') and signed the cartouche. The water is clearly the main focus and selling point for his proposal.

Brown listed a total of twenty-three elements, including the approach, 'a Great Road which in my opinion would be much better turned', and winding gravel paths a standard 8 ft wide. Inappropriate aspects, fences, avenues or buildings, shown by dotted lines, were to be replaced with Scots fir clumps, flowering shrubs and flowers, a pillar and two seats. In the event Lord Guernsey commissioned the 'new river', the 'turned' road and some planting. It seems that the

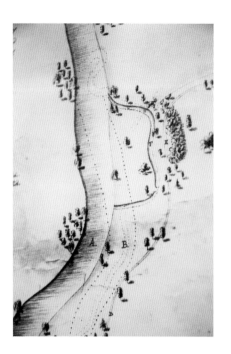
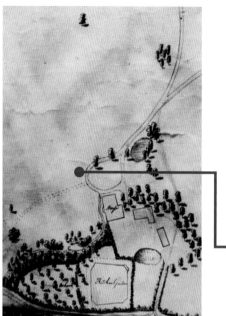

built features amounted to just the small spring head, a neat two-arch stone bridge where his approach road crossed the 'narrow river', and probably the wooden bridge later replaced with ornamental cast iron.

Where the water was his main focus, this consummate professional, at this point thirty-five, had aspirations for grandiose buildings and bridges in his portfolio. The earliest surviving Brown proposal for an entire landscape garden, the Packington plan (1751), is highly significant evidence of a confident, all-encompassing, cohesive and surprisingly mature design and shows that Brown's sophisticated 'natural' style had already become fully fledged.

Later, all-inclusive plans for improvement, in pen and ink, and sometimes wash, on four, six or even more folio sheets of drawing paper pasted together, developed more consistent definition. I suggest that most of these more fluent, three-dimensional, easy-to-read plans, such as that for Youngsbury, a modest country seat in Hertfordshire, were likely to have been quickly and confidently drawn by Brown himself. They compare well with his proposal for Hills in Sussex, the title of which is annotated 'By LB, 1768'.[83] Shading indicates inclinations or hollowing out of roads, reinforced dams and embankments, and stretches of water. Ribbon-like drives wind through boundary planting and, skirting sinuous lakes, curve

towards the mansion, the heart of the design. North is not indicated, but might just be ascertained.

Some surviving rough drawings, differentiating little between practical and aesthetic improvement, confirm a diverse range of work, probably guidelines for foremen: serpentine plantations, shrubberies, flowerbeds and seats, Gothic stables, doorways, and a 'swan-neck' bend in a river. Other proposals, with limited land, were intended to give an illusion of much greater space. Ponder, for example, Brown's modest yet holistic plan in pen and ink, 28 x 29 ins, commissioned by George Fiesci Heneage MP for his small estate, Hainton, the oldest family seat in Lincolnshire.

The straightforward plan is immediately comprehensible. The owner could quickly grasp his suggestions for improvement. The house was the hub, the views considered from every window. Both the necessary kitchen garden and the garden are linked in his thinking. Though somewhat old-fashioned in maintaining space for a bowling green (perhaps the whim of the client), this plan is nevertheless exceptional. Two distinct straight lines of dots coming from the house, labelled 'View to Mr Brackenbury's House' and 'View to the Village of Sottby', direct openings in the shelter belt. Such important vistas to the wider world of the charming Lincolnshire Wolds were not to be obscured. They would add an impression of greater extent to a modest-sized park. Then again, two clearings in the tree belt would offer both an attractive opening for an approach drive and an appealing, tree-framed glimpse of the house across water for passers-by on the road, the essence of the picturesque.

These instructional dotted sight lines, making the most of 'borrowed' views, provide unequivocal proof of Brown's advanced intellectual capacity and new methodology. This particular technique is now common practice in landscape architecture. In the event, his suggested small, oval lake was never created in this flat site, perhaps because of a lack of water. One proposal led to another, as was often the case, with Brown landing a more lucrative £5,000 contract (today £654,200), agreed with Heneage's father-in-law, Lord Petre, at Thorndon in Essex. Meanwhile, between 1764 and 1766 a reliable Pontefract seedsman/nurseryman, William Perfect, recommended by Brown, completed his reasonably modest projects at Hainton, including planting shrubs along 'Lady's Walk', the route to the kitchen garden.

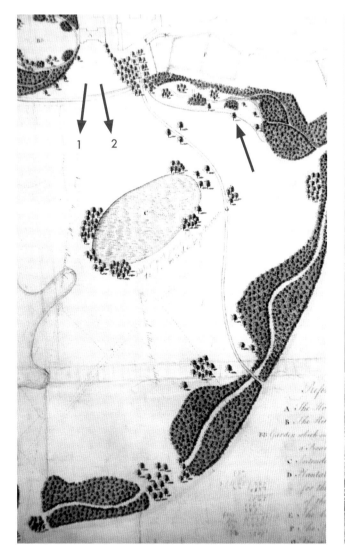

Brown Plan (1763) for Hainton, Lincolnshire
Courtesy © Christopher Heneage
RIGHT Detail in pen, ink and wash on four joined folio pages, with the house (top) and walled garden nearby. (The amoebic lake, left, is a proposal added in 1780 by designer William Emes.) Brown's serpentine lines define an approach drive through the park, a shrubbery walk along the ha-ha and the edge of the enclosing tree belt. Note two straight sight-lines directing openings in the boundary shelter-belt labelled: (1) 'View to Mr Brackenbury's House' and (2) 'View to the Village of Sottby'.

FAR RIGHT **February 1996, Hainton, Lincolnshire** Brown's now veteran beech tree (right arrow on plan) breaks the line of the snaking ha-ha.

CHAPTER FIVE

CONTRACTS & ASSOCIATES

From the early days of his professional practice, over a period of more than a dozen years, Brown negotiated several contracts with the Earl of Egremont to improve **Petworth,** an estate in Sussex owned by the Northumbrian Percy family. In October 1751 he visited Petworth, accompanied by two men to help measure the park. The following June he presented several plans, including a 'Grand Plan', initialled LB, for which in August 1754 he was paid £62 10s 6d (today £8,600). The delay apparently caused no difficulty, because in May 1753 he had already landed a valuable, twelve-article contract for £1,175 (£170,400) for a year's work, with an advance payment of £300 (£43,800).

The reduction of the level of the coach road in front of the house took precedence. He went on to demolish the 'Cypress Walkes', Italianate rampart terraces along the nearby hill, before completing a parterre in front of the greenhouse. He renovated the Horse Pond by the old stables, built kitchen garden walls, hidden by a graded slope, and planted trees, promising to replace any that died. Lastly, he saw that all new-made ground was sown with grass and clover. Before the year was out, in April 1754, he had signed a second £1,000 (£136,500) contract:

1st The making a Ha Ha from ye End of ye intended Iron Fence in front of Green house to ye London Road to be Eight Feet deep & wide on the Bottom ten Feet, & to finish ye Slopes and sow or turf it.

OPPOSITE **May 1992, Petworth Park, Sussex (NT)** The ha-ha divides the pleasure grounds from the deer park.

ABOVE **May 2011, Petworth Park, Sussex (NT)** Brown completely altered the setting: the park lawn was brought up to the house, allowing deer to graze in front of the windows.

2ᵈ To build a wall along ye said Ha Ha from an End to ye other, coping it with a sloped Turf leaving two Doorways, for a Communication with the Park.

3ᵈ To clear away all the Rubbish of Stones and Brambles betwixt above mentioned Ha Ha & ye Wood so as to give ye Walk form'd by it a proper & Corresponding level with ye Park & ye Trees in ye Garden.

4 To begin at ye Passages ye lead from ye House to ye Office & give ye Chapel Court a proper Level to keep ye Buildings dry and to lay ye same with Turf. The paved & pitch'd Part to be at my Lord's Expense…[84]

And so on for fourteen articles, in short:

to build a wall between the Poultry Court and the house;

to remove the basin in front of the greenhouse;

to turf over walks and make a proper place for orange trees;

to pull down terraced walls;

to prepare the ground and plant flowering shrubs and trees in the pleasure ground;

to make a walk up the hill beside the wood (now known as Lawn Hill).

The following year brought another contract, for £814 (£114,000): to demolish yet more walls, to drain and level the ground, and to create a grass road, in place of the London Road in the valley, snaking instead along the brow of the hills to take in park views, especially across the 'Pond', which he planned on enlarging. He established three tree clumps, oversaw further planting, removed kennels, a pigeon-house and other elements cluttering the scene, built an ice-house on the approach and made improvements to the stables, besides commencing an ambitious and costly fourteen-mile perimeter wall around the park.

Agreements became noticeably more legally structured, coinciding with regular, large payments from Brown's Drummond's Bank account to the attorney John Edison, who was to become a close friend. Contracts detailed each article of work and costings for journeys, survey and plan, with underwritten times of payment with 'the good and lawful money of great Brittain'. Signed by both client and designer, they were later endorsed with dated receipts paid to Brown, usually by a draft on Drummond's including the final payment, to be made when work was completed satisfactorily. Further contracts (including laying out Egremont's London garden for his new house in Piccadilly, now known as

Cambridge House)[85] brought great long-term benefit to the Petworth estate. Some ideas, particularly ambitious planting on the original grand plan, were never fully implemented. Nevertheless, the mixture of gardens and fields disappeared, replaced mostly by manageable and enduring parkland and pleasure grounds, works that underpinned Brown's London-based practice financially.

Once Brown's reputation was secure, some clients were easy-going regarding contracts. Lord Palmerston, having commissioned the alteration of Broadlands, his home in Hampshire, intended going abroad, and confirmed: 'only settled the plans with Brown, and have left everything in the execution of them to him'.

Early on in his career, Brown's neat, legible copperplate script displays a perfectionist's precision. Surviving correspondence reveals an astute business sense, wise ideas and decent sentiments expressed in good, if economic, style, couched in the respectful manner of the period. Perhaps his signature, bolder than his normal script, is symptomatic of an ego and a desire for personal standing. Progressively more confident as his achievements grew, even though often written in haste, it revealed an artistic nature with a touch of flamboyance. Besides, a bold flourish underlined with loops and curls was difficult to forge

and, for one with a common surname, declared his individuality. A professional analysis of Brown's handwriting reports:

> *He was obviously a determined and focused individual, but also generous to others. The close spacing between the words indicates a need to be near people and know their thoughts and business, and where the words actually connect one to another means a person of high moral standards, and someone who wants to create order with a tendency to categorise, although it has to be said, not always appropriately.*[86]

Later, perhaps with a more pressing need to achieve, rather than be perfect, his handwriting loosened, particularly when dashing off an affectionate letter to his wife, Bridget. (She also wrote letters on his behalf to save him time.) His letter seal, an engraved intaglio ring, appears to be a classical head, perhaps a copy of Michelangelo's *David*.

His word was his bond. Clients took comfort in the knowledge that Brown led a professional team and was scrupulously honest. On the odd occasion when accounts were queried, Brown was understandably defensive: 'if anything is wrong it shall be put to rights but this acct is taken from Blair's Accts which is all the guide I had'.[87]

After dining with his neighbour at Ingestre (Staffordshire), the Earl of Breadalbane penned a letter to his daughter, Marchioness de Grey, reporting the number of men employed there.

I was vastly surprised at seeing this transformation, which has made a greater difference than I ever saw in any place, and has made it from being bad and disagreeable, beautifull and grand. Lord Chetwynd, who breaks fast, presses the work on that he may enjoy it; he has 70 men at constant work for a year, and an overseer sent by Mr Brown, another year will compleat all.[88]

As countrywide commitments multiplied, Brown openly confessed to inevitable mistakes, for instance to the Duke of Marlborough:

I hope Mr Read has altered the level of the ground at the Oak tree which her Grace wished to have altered. I have lost the dimensions I took of the space under the New Stairs which her Grace wished to have a seat in; which prevents me from sending a sketch for that purpose.[89]

There were few disputes. A Yorkshire landowner, Edwin Lascelles, expressed dissatisfaction with slovenly, badly finished work at Harewood. Brown swiftly promised to return to make amends. In providing work for 'navvies', unskilled 'tramps' and the unemployed, an adequate brew-house was one of his first stipulations, making sure there was copious, invigorating beer to dull their aches and alleviate boredom. If hiring proved difficult, he cajoled idle soldiers to help with 'muck-moving', putting the North Staffordshire Regiment stationed at Richmond to good use on the king's land.

Brown monitored the progress of those from the labour force whom he promoted. He trained them assiduously in the adjustment and integration of 'natural and easy' levels, freed from distracting clipped hedging and intricate patterns needing constant attention in the summer when clients were mostly in residence. He ensured regular, if sometimes intermittent, payment to foremen who in turn paid the labour gangs.[90] Fiercely protective when any were wronged, he noted a rare and angry confrontation in his account book when a Suffolk landowner refused to pay his dues: 'W Brown could not get the money for the Extra work. I tore the Acct before Mr Dickens face & said his say upon that Business to him.'[91]

The Brown in question was probably Brown's cousin, which may explain his angry embarrassment. William Brown was a mine overseer who worked mainly in the north of England: at Hartley Colliery he developed a fire engine and collaborated with the mill and canal engineer James Brindley (see p.101). Fortunately, most relationships, whether with landowner or labourer, were excellent. In many cases, Brown brought in skilled independent local contractors to complete the work. Success largely lay in his choice of experienced, trustworthy men who were sufficiently competent to direct estate workers and hired hands in 'land business' until he returned for a half-yearly or annual consultation. Men on site who impressed, such as Adam Mickle at Badminton (Gloucestershire), he remembered and recruited later. Soon he built up a network of reliable, hard-working foremen and clerks of work, contractors and associates, some of whom were prepared to travel. From their point of view, it was surely stimulating to work for a reliable and honourable director who remained open to new developments. Proven managers were sometimes expected to superintend work at several estates concurrently. He inspired tremendous loyalty.

Lord Craven pressed him for a plan for his Warwickshire seat, Combe Abbey (today Coombe Abbey):

I desire you will exert yr utmost abilities to improve the place & shall leave everything else to you.

I hope you will not leave Combe till you have made a plan & Estimate, & that you will get the man you mentioned to me, & begin directly.[92]

There were some foremen Brown could always trust to begin implementing his design; for instance, he informed Paul Methuen at Corsham in Wiltshire: 'I have desired Sanderson my foreman at Longleat to come over and give a few Directions he will want the Plan.'[93]

An enduring working relationship with Peter Blair spanned twenty-four years. Blair, his overseer at Petworth, moved to Luton, where he was joined by William Ireland. Ireland implemented contracts at Wallington, Burghley, Stapleford and Trentham, but also, on occasion, worked independently, as did other associates of good standing.

Just as a talented sports captain cajoles his team, or a general his officers, Brown delegated daily concerns regarding the groundwork and encouraged his men to aim high, to be of good service. Meanwhile agents and stewards soon saw the wisdom of writing down his lucid, verbal instructions, to be carried out 'to the letter'.

> *I have given the necessary direction for our work there & ordered it to be expedited with all possible care. If anything is wanted at the Temple [Temple Newsam, Yorkshire], my man that is at Lord Scarborough's shall come over bout the gravel or anything that your Lordship may want to have done.*[94]

Good men, as always, were hard to come by. At Brocklesby, Lincolnshire, Brown was unhappy with work executed in his absence and elected to redo some of it himself.[95] The head gardener, William Dicker, was given his marching orders. A year later, the Burghley gardener, Stephen Dicker, whether related or not, was similarly despatched.[96] Recommendations for sober, dependable head gardeners, their wages, and even whether they were to dine in the Servants' Hall, became part and parcel of the improver's life.

In January 1765 Brown sent a note to Lord Bruce at **Tottenham** (Wiltshire): 'The bearer Mr Winkles is the Person I recommended to your Lordship who is now disengaged and ready to obey. Any Commands your Lordship has to honor him with; I hope he will give intier satisfaction.'[97]

In early March he wrote again from London: 'I shall however come there as soon as I can. I will then make Winkles Master of the work & remove the man that is there & in all matters relative to the Plan I will do the best I can.'[98]

One autumn visit, three years later, prompted forty-one detailed memoranda on a wide range of issues concerning drainage, buildings, sunk fences, tree and hedge planting: 'those mark'd with a finger to be done this year [24 in total] and as many others as can be'.[99]

Winkles had his work cut out. Andrew Riddell, the head gardener, looked on Brown as more than an employer and wrote to him about his wedding plans: 'I think it my Duty as my Best Friend to acquaint you of my Intention of Leving Lord Bruce's service in a month or six weeks.'[100]

At times Brown's commanding and positive dedication engendered somewhat fearful respect. Mr Bill, the Tottenham agent, reported: 'If the high Bank & Trees had been taken down, great would have been the fall indeed, Brown would have excommunicated us all.'[101]

Inevitably, the stress of managing a large practice took its toll. He defended his accounting, having paid the surveyor 'by the book', 6d (today £3.50) per acre:

> *I am now in Staffordshire where I was honoured with your Lordship's Letter I believe ten days ago or more, but I have been much out of order, that I have not been able to write nor do anything else…. as to my Journeys and Plans I have no fixed rule about it nor is it possible to do it if but to charge less or more, according to the size & trouble. All I can say upon it is that I should be very sorry to diminish my Friends, and very sorry to increase my business, for I have so much to do that it neither answers for profit nor pleasure, for when I am galloping in one part of the world my men are making blunders and neglects which [make] it very unples't.*[102]

In an era of unconstrained manpower, improvements involved much road-building, including turnpikes, large-scale mining and tunnelling, better river navigation and canal-building, let alone lake-making and ground modelling.

Levelling an even gradient of slope was no easy task. Plans and contracts involved many thousands of tons of earth, measured and paid for by the yard, dug up, shovelled into barrows and removed. Earth-moving on such a huge scale was exhaustingly intensive and unrelenting. Labourers, paid for 'Dig Work' between 2d and 5d (£1 and £2.50) per cubic yard of soil removed, had only muscle-power and unsophisticated tools at their disposal, usually made locally by estate blacksmiths: picks, spades, rakes, iron turf-lifters, rollers and wheelbarrows.

Quantities of fresh beer, besides encouraging and keeping them healthy, helped to instil a sense of community. Gangs of men worked in rhythm as they dug low, loaded each shovel and swung high to empty the soil into barrows and horse-drawn carts. These all needed constant repair from such unremitting use. Ensuring he was not liable for broken barrows, Brown was wise to negotiate for clients to provide carts with horse and harness, and their own wheelbarrows – for instance twenty-three at Sherborne, forty for Longleat.

Winter working after the harvest was the norm, when it was easier to break up ground that had been frozen. The land was scarred at first but, during upheaval, clients could retreat to London or Bath or journey abroad. For those patrons who lacked visual imagination, Brown soon persuaded them that all would eventually not only be restored, but greatly enhanced. Exploiting every opportunity to turn infertile or boggy areas into profitable, friable land, he was undeterred by the effort and time it would take or the

cost involved. He knew precisely where an immense quantity of lake spoil could be safely transported and disguised as small rounded hills or 'swells'.

Over and above straightforward movements of earth, he employed 'cut and fill' mining techniques to build underground ice-houses and subterranean passages, cleverly concealed under naturalistic land forms so as to have minimal impact on the wider landscape. He built up islands in the middle of lakes, filled in unsightly quarry-pits, smoothed and 'humoured' graduated slopes as a sculptor moulds clay, creating hollows and rises where previously none existed.

Lord Anson spent £6,000 (today £816,400) on remodelling Moor Park, Hertfordshire, under the direction of the surveyor and nurseryman Nathaniel Richmond as foreman. Once again, Walpole was hard to please and remained unimpressed:

We went to see More Park, but I was not much struck with it, after all the miracles I had heard Brown had performed there. He has undulated the horizon by so many molehills that it is full as unnatural as if it was drawn with a rule and compasses.[103]

The writer may have been correct in his assumption. In mastering the art of earth redistribution, Brown was scientific and precise in his methods, using an underlying geometry to achieve harmony and balance. He maintained a healthy respect for nature, and trusted the process of regeneration. Scars need time to heal.

The Belhus agent reported to Lord Dacre that Mr Brown had 'slaved at setting out the road and the rest of the shrubbery all day and drew plans all Evening and was in the best humour'.

A well-built approach was part and parcel of Brown's success, with 'twinings and windings … to diversify the views' as Switzer recommended, giving both comfort and economic benefit.[104] His men engineered 'barrel' roads to a high standard, raised for drainage using hard-core (often from demolished buildings and garden walls) covered with layers of gravel estimated by the cart-load.[105] Clients such as

OPPOSITE **May 1991, Petworth Park, Sussex (NT)** Over and above simple aesthetics, the smooth shores of Brown's lakes were intended to encourage landings of wildfowl such as Canada geese.

Henry Fox were responsible for obtaining gravel, which sometimes lay under tons of earth that needed shifting:

I am hard at work digging gravel & have made a Bargain for 800 Load of Ballast which will move above 2000 Load of Earth. If you could come here Saturday to put in a few stakes it would be a great guidance to me, & save much future Trouble.[106]

The contract for the main road from the Pound at Petworth to Upperton (almost two miles) cost £1,163 (today £158,300) and included building arches to keep it dry, making a footway, altering levels, making side fences and planting quick hedges, and building two hundred rod of wall (1,100 yards) 10 ft high. It is interesting to note that in 1760, at Chatsworth, Derbyshire, Brown brought in the gentleman builder Henry Holland Sr from Fulham in London to construct a major new road through the park. Holland became a lifelong family friend as well as a reliable collaborator.

Brown brought his easy line of approach to a fine art, selecting pleasant contours, often with two drives converging at the house for smooth arrival and departure. The politician and writer Thomas Whateley (1726–1772) commented in admiration: 'The ground [the approach to Caversham Park, Berkshire] … is cast into an infinite number of elegant shapes, in every gradation from the most gentle slope, to a very precipitate fall.'[107]

As soon as the water, roads and plantations were in place, Brown himself worked at marking out the direction of paths amid pleasure grounds and shrubberies dotted with specimen trees. He would choose the best, most effective and eye-pleasing line, appreciating that a winding path allowed easy negotiation of changing gradients as well as a variety of viewpoints. He had the prudence and common sense to inform absent clients of progress – for instance, he told Viscount Irwin, concerning his southern estate, Hills in Sussex: 'I intend setting out the gravel walk from the Dairy Place to the river & to make the necessary plantations.'[108]

April 1992, Petworth Park, Sussex (NT) A newly laid path of sand invites easy exploration along the circuit walk around Brown's lake.

Materials varied according to availability: sandstone, gravel, or charcoal cinders ('clinker' from steam engines). The essayist Revd Joseph Spence (1699–1768) reasoned that a gravelled path in town gardens should be the same width as either the front door or the windows. At Madingley (Cambridgeshire), Brown gave similar thought to the most appropriate dimension for his short circuit walk (still extant and well used). He stipulated a width of 7½ or 8 ft, with a quantity of rubble underneath as drainage to keep the gravel dry. Later, 8 ft was deemed the best measurement for Gray's Inn Walks in London. His 1762 contract for Bowood, Wiltshire, promised: 'Carrying a sand walk … in the best direction for Shade, Prospect etc.'[109]

At Wynnstay, Denbighshire, Brown responded to the scale of the surrounding Welsh hills: 'There are nineteen men employed in the Park who are making a gravel walk of 1,738 yards.'[110]

Occasionally, Brown or the client opted for 'green walks'. At Audley End in Essex, there were eventually seven miles of grass walks.[111] An outstanding and enlightening archive of memoranda recording Brown's

directions survives at **Burton Constable** in Yorkshire. In September 1772, James Clarke started as 'Director of the Ground Work Planting etc' on £50 (£6,000) a year, notably six shillings (£35) a week more than the head gardener. Later, advising on his replacement, Brown recommended Joseph Nutt, who had been working there for several years, rather than the head gardener, Hugh Mitchell. The latter, though a good plantsman, 'knows nothing about how to lay out grounds – he has never been used to it'.[112]

Brown went so far as to recommend removing parts of a hill to allow more light into the park. He directed supply wagons bringing coals and lime to use the old road, the back drive, which allowed his new road, the front drive, to be used for riders or a coach and horses: 'make a good Road from the Gate above mentioned to Burton – An easy Barrel 35 or 40 feet broad, & gravel'd about 12 or 15 Feet wide'.[113]

On his next visit, he amended the width to 20 ft and suggested an additional 'swarth' or green road, again 'with an easy barrel', to circumnavigate the estate. A quiet excursion, rather than being noisily tossed about in carriages on stony roads, added much to visitors' enjoyment of the estate. In addition to narrow paths encircling the lawn and leading on through the pleasure ground, Brown divided the rather featureless, flat terrain here with a 6-ft wide gravel walk across to the lake from the gate in the sunk fence. A narrow ribbon meandering between plantations led the eye to his distant bridge over the water. On the return, the trail offered a gratifying view of the house. Redundant avenues or rides also made for longer and wider walks.

'Gravel walk 20 ft wide & crowned with Gravel from the Deerhouse Close gate … to Yaud wood gate – directly in the middle of the Avenue as staked out'.[114] This instruction is just one from a list of twenty-seven refinements following ten years' consultation. Still gainfully engaged, Brown had not yet exhausted the 'capabilities' for improvement. We will return several times to those detailed archives and memoranda surviving at Burton Constable, Petworth and Tottenham in order to evaluate, and appreciate, his water engineering and planting.

CHAPTER SIX

GROUNDWORK

Picking up the baton of landscape improvement after Brown's death in 1783, the designer Humphry Repton (1752–1818) observed such a plethora of walled trenches separating gardens from parks in Brown's works that he wrongly believed his predecessor responsible for the introduction of the ha-ha. Interestingly, he thought it his greatest gift.[115]

In fact, before the turn of the eighteenth century, a French gardener, Guillaume Beaumont, working at Levens Hall in Cumberland, had brought the ha-ha to England.[116] Such a concealed boundary between gardens and parkland kept marauding rabbits and deer at bay and prevented stock from trampling flowerbeds and lawns, while allowing uninterrupted views to the wider countryside. No wonder others adopted the idea.

Brown's early ha-has, with supporting stone or brick walls at least 5 ft deep, contrived a pronounced, semicircular apron or 'terras' (terrace) of lawn sloping away from the house to ensure its surroundings remained dry. Later, further developing drainage and planting potential, his longer ha-has stretched out hundreds of yards into the park. For new houses, as at Luton Hoo (Bedfordshire), Brown built the ha-ha before work on the house started. At Trentham (Staffordshire), as his contract specified, labourers dug out a 6-ft-deep fosse (ditch), 22 ft wide, with a 12-ft slope, according to Brown's line of stakes, before seeding the ground with grass and Dutch clover. A protective coping, hidden under turf, helped to prolong the life of his ha-has and prevent deterioration of his pleasing line.[117]

OPPOSITE **October 1996, Prior Park, Bath, Avon (NT)** The Palladian Bridge (1755) was built by Richard Jones for Ralph Allen. Note the masterful handling of three different levels of water.

ABOVE **March 2007, Burghley Park, Cambridgeshire** A recent restoration of Brown's snaking ha-ha.

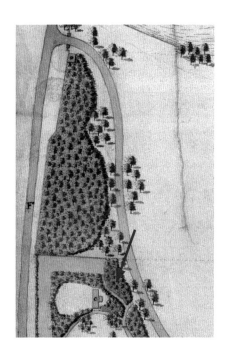

Clever use of gravity and precision levels channelled water down to Brown's lake, together with waste water in underground conduits from stables, brew-houses, dairies and laundries. In the middle of the park, long 'sunk fences' proved effective for drainage and separation of grazing stock, creating seemingly uninterrupted space (see p.187). Cleft oak supported banks of soil, possibly reusing the paling that Brown had advised dismantling, which had divided the meadows.

A term derived from the Dutch 'landskip', the word 'landscape' essentially means 'land craftsmanship'. Making the landscape had become a specialised art, a skilled job, more highly valued than gardening – an art in which Brown excelled. Did the world's first three-dimensional land artist also influence the English language by his men's endeavours? Brown and his teams 'moved mountains' and made 'mountains out of molehills' to deliver fresh perspectives of 'fine taste'.

Any study of Brown's works should begin from the ground up. Where did he move all the earth? At every site where he worked, quantities of earth were shifted to create undulating, sensuous form in changing light, particularly in winter. Fine examples of his subtle skill at moulding the terrain are seen in the Denwick Hills, rising and dipping east of Alnwick Castle (Northumberland), in the celebrated Golden Valley at

Ashridge (Buckinghamshire), or the shallow Warren Dell in variable terrain at Luton Park (Bedfordshire). Today, all are mistakenly believed to be natural, rolling countryside, so that sceptics doubt he ever did much at all!

At **Madingley** in Cambridgeshire Brown agreed 'to take down such Trees as shall be thought proper to come down in order to make the Laun on this [north] Front large enough'.[118] On the east side, beginning at the front door and finishing at the public road a few hundred yards away, he intended giving 'the whole lawn a natural and easy level'. Here his man-made, natural-looking bank, a reverse ha-ha raised beyond the lake, succeeds in obscuring the main road passing through the grounds. In endorsing the contract, despite the confusing use of a double negative, the final outcome was that the client, Sir John Hynde-Cotton, was more than happy with Brown's work. 'Never executed nor any other but all way done upon honor on both sides or never repented by either.'[119]

Curving lines on Brown's plan (1763) for **Audley End** in Essex also indicate a 'reverse ha-ha'. Brown engineered an extensive, sloping embankment, doubtless made by the redistribution of spoil from widening and controlling the flow of the River Cam to create a mirror lake (see also pp.228–29). This reverse ha-ha, the bank shored up by a wall of bricks salvaged

OPPOSITE RIGHT **June 2014, Audley End, Essex** Brown's land craftsmanship married the old walling, as shown on the plan (opposite left), with the setting by creating both a hillock in otherwise flat terrain and a secluded area for a private flower garden.

Brown plan for Audley End (1763) © Reproduced by permission of Historic England:

OPPOSITE LEFT Detail of the substantial high brick walls that Brown had to blend into the setting.

RIGHT Detail with curving lines to indicate an intention to screen the main road with a reverse ha-ha.

ABOVE AND BELOW **June 2014, Audley End, Essex** Brown's reverse ha-ha, detailed on the plan (middle right), once effectively hid the main road. (The road has since been raised, so traffic is now visible.) His skilful levelling of the lawn ensured that the ha-ha's brick wall is not seen from the house. Cricket is still played in this memorable lawn amphitheatre.

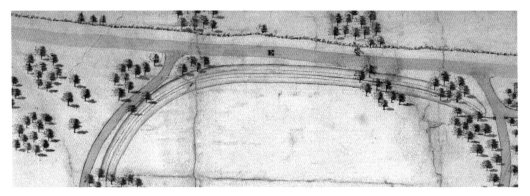

June 2012, Ampthill, Bedfordshire A knoll, part of Brown's earthwork, juts out from the greensand ridge to act as a viewing platform. The landscape historian John Phibbs has shown how Brown devised 'natural' terraces blending into the greensand ridge topography as 'carriage-stops' arranged to enliven drives around the park. Visitors were encouraged to dismount so as to admire each of the improved views to the house and the surrounding landscape.

from the part-demolition of the Jacobean house, courtyard and garden walls, helped to implement Article 4 of his agreement with Sir John Griffin Griffin, which promised 'giving the Whole a Natural easy and corresponding Level with the House, the Water and the Roads'.[120] 250 years later, all remains in harmony. The eye, oblivious to earlier buildings swept away by Brown, is led unhindered across a seamless lawn, river, and pasture towards Robert Adam's Temple of Victory on the hill beyond.

While details of the early days of Brown's independent practice are scarce, with a small number of surviving estimates, contracts, letters, and some accounts, his Drummond's Bank account throws light on his later career, his clients and his surprisingly numerous collaborators. Competition with a growing number of professional 'gentlemen improvers' caused Brown to improve the presentation of his proposals utilising the skills of his chief surveyor. In 1775, John Spyers, also a competent watercolourist, contributed to the creation of a fine leather-bound folio of architectural plans, and Brown's ideas for the grounds, for a banker's retreat at Cadland (Hampshire). Spyers also took pains over a Survey Book (1777) for Fenstanton, his employer's own estate.[121] A similar set of proposals for Beaudesert in Staffordshire is mentioned in a memoir, though neither book nor plan has survived.[122] What is more, Spyers sold two

beautiful folio albums of his watercolours, recording Hampton Court gardens when Brown was in charge, for 1,000 roubles to Empress Catherine the Great of Russia, so as to inform and inspire English 'taste' for her own gardens.[123]

Despite a long, active career, and the large number of sites at which Brown gave advice, comparatively few plans exist. True, his ideas may be found added in pencil to a number of old surveys, and perhaps some plans still go unrecognised as Brown's hand. A few small presentation drawings, approximately A4 in size, show bridges, various garden buildings, a temple on a mount or an ice-house, or a 'Sketch of Mr Brown's directions' with measurements and materials for a 'stuccade' or deer fence.

Following substantial alterations to boundaries, layout and park use, it was essential for landowners to have an accurate record for tax and legacy purposes. Thomas Richardson of York moved to London to complete new surveys of Wimbledon Park, Blenheim and Richmond, perhaps on Brown's recommendation.

If, at first, projects involved problem-solving and up-to-date advice in practicalities and land management, the designer's thoughts always turned to aesthetics. Brown excelled at 'middle distance' schemes but did not confine his ideas. He succeeded in presenting an entirely new look, stimulating and delighting his clients with fresh ways of appreciating and utilising their lands, often to the far horizon. 'I must say he bit off the slip of the garden ground well'.[124]

TOP **September 2003, Sherborne Castle, Dorset** Drought accentuates 'Dry Grounds Walk', one of the main views from the house windows. Subtle man-made mounds lead the eye effortlessly, even subconsciously, on an easy progress towards the entirely natural eminence beyond: Jerusalem Hill (see p.189).

ABOVE **March 2010, Clumber Park, Nottinghamshire (NT)** An old wooden wheelbarrow, much like those Brown's workforce would have used.

LEFT **August 2012, Madingley, Cambridgeshire** Another example of a reverse ha-ha. Brown chose the right level so that the eye would not be disturbed by traffic on the road (since raised). His magnificent oak tree has flourished in open space beyond the lake, a choice location in the view from the house.

CHAPTER SEVEN

LAKE-MAKING

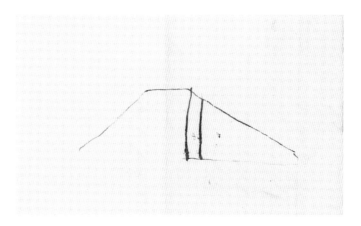

One wonders if the eighteenth century's unprecedented 'out of doors' work spawned, or at least reinforced, our legendary English obsession with the weather. When torrential or incessant rains, or melting snow and ice, caused swollen rivers and flooded grounds, the resulting drainage measures often necessitated certain alterations to the geometry of gardens – much to the wrath of later critics. Equally, in dry summers, as water levels diminished, the clay lining of man-made reservoirs would crack, causing tiresome leaks.

Regrettably, surviving accounts and plans from this decade lack meaningful detail about managing water. When the Earl of Denbigh commissioned work at **Newnham Paddox** (Warwickshire), for instance, his 'Building Book' recording mentions only briefly what was a considerable project:

Apil 28th 1746 Begun the alteration of ye great Canal, & carrying it onto ye head of ye pond in the Park by a plan & the Direction of Mr Brown, Gardiner to Lord Cobham, with other work done in consequence of this.[125]

Cleaning out the park pond, levelling the end, 'laying it with hanging slopes' before linking it to the ornamental canal in the gardens, resulted in a river-like stretch of water appearing to meander down a valley towards the house. The effect must have caused quite a stir – though fashion had not dictated changes in the first instance. In the midst of a drought, improvements to the water supply had been essential.

OPPOSITE **April 1999, Newnham Paddox, Warwickshire** Brown's upper lake, 'the pond in the park', with remnant groves of trees placed asymmetrically.

ABOVE Dam sketch on the back of undated Petworth estimate © West Sussex RO, PHA.

Nature then redressed the balance. Ten consecutive summers, 1751–1760, were extremely wet, as luck would have it, creating opportunities just as Brown was building up his independent practice from his Hammersmith base. On the road, mostly in the Midlands, Brown was a problem-solver, often called in a crisis to address saturated land and incidents of serious flooding.

In 1755, the provincial press reported two earthquakes in quick succession. The first, early on 31 July, was centred on Newark in Nottinghamshire, with damage to villages as far as the east coast and north to the Humber.[126] The next day, a second sizeable quake shook Stamford in Lincolnshire, with tremors reaching as far as Nottingham, Leicester and Rushden in Northamptonshire. At Boston, aldermen addressed the damage: 'Resolved that the Mayor be desired to write to Mr Brown an Engineer at Hammersmith to come over and view several buildings belonging to this Corporation and to pay him five guineas [today £730] for his journey.'[127]

The mayor in this case, Bridget Brown's brother John Wayet, an apothecary, was confident that his brother-in-law's advice on repairs and rebuilding would be well worth the corporation's paying his travel expenses from London.[128] Typically, Brown found a use for considerable amounts of stone and brick rubble resulting from the earthquake as, shortly after, the town began to raise funds for a ten-mile turnpike from Boston to Donnington.[129] Far from being a mere gardener, Brown's professional reputation as an engineer was well established in Lincolnshire.

Many clients paid Brown in cash because he was responsible for the hire and wages of a travelling workforce. Specialist water-men, 'drowners', 'grippers' (making open drainage ditches called 'grips'), 'paviours', plumbers, 'poolmakers', 'pudlemen' or 'pudlers', crossed county borders for piecework or 'catch-work'. Since the sixteenth century, agricultural improvers had learnt to manage water by the organised flooding of water meadows. Rather than flooding the ground with standing water, they maintained a constant flow over the meadows. Usually organised early in the year, this 'floating' irrigation fertilised fields, reduced the effects of frost and started grass growth early, besides gaining a further hay crop later in the year. Where water was over-plentiful, the improvers would systematically dig ditches around new plantations and trench boggy areas to drain and divide the land, as in Brown's 'sunk fences', in order to reclaim it for farming.

Much of Brown's engineering has already been destroyed, though archaeological surveys during recent restorations have been enlightening. **Croome** (Worcestershire) was undoubtedly his 'watershed', his first major commission for both house and landscape. After filling in parts of the inadequate and poorly situated original lake, Brown's men built a system of subterranean channels to drain Lord Coventry's 'morass' and fill up his snaking 'river'. One typical drain, a mile and a half long, has been found to have a drop of only six inches, 'a feat of incredible engineering'[130] by Brown's expert levellers.

As designer, improver and would-be architect, Brown thought through modern, costly but enduring refinements, ensuring that contaminated waste water from kitchens, laundries and stables could be flushed down drains and directed through substantial, brick-walled 'barrel' culverts (large enough to allow for men to clean them out) hidden under 'lawns', and designed to disgorge discreetly below a weir to facilitate pollution dispersal downstream.

Brown's first task was to ride out across any given client's domain, aiming for the high ground, to take in the surrounding topography. Then, turning his attention to water sources, rivers and springs, he would note any significant points of convergence or advantageous natural depressions in the land that would require less work to hollow out a new water feature. The typical engineer, Brown advised 'there wants a good plan' in order to expand fish ponds and stews, perhaps dating from medieval times, to connect existing trout streams, canals and catchments, or adapt a decoy or mill leat.[131]

Sometimes Brown's foremen would make boreholes, lined with bricks, to tap underground aquifers; by exploiting gravity and the contours of hillsides, they would then feed fresh water down through a series of elmwood pipes in lengthy drainage ditches loosely lined and covered with stone.

Elm does not rot under water. It proved tougher if cropped from the open hedgerow rather than woods, bored to make hollow pipes, smeared with linseed oil putty and joined with iron bands. Elm logs fitted into a frame served as both a temporary coffer dam and a removable relief drain for rivers or streams. When the main dam was finished, and the time came to fill the reservoir, the logs were plugged with clay to maintain the water level.

The work involved close collaboration between skilled plumbers, carpenters, masons and blacksmiths, who constructed weirs and increasingly sophisticated permanent sluices hidden underground. Known variably as 'penstocks' or 'trunks', with iron grilles used to filter out debris, these sluices were made of elm with iron hatches or 'gates' controlled by winding gear and revetted with ashlar or brick masonry to counteract water erosion.

Walpole kept a critical watch on estate improvements, writing to George Montagu about Ragley (Warwickshire): 'Browne has improved both the ground and the water, though not quite to perfection.'[132] Later, he found it amusing to satirise such works in terms of the fashion for tea-drinking: 'the home-brewed rivers that Mr Brown makes with a spade and a watering-pot'.[133]

'To float a valley' required considerably more ingenuity, nerve and resilience than Walpole could ever imagine. Casual observers never appreciated how much effort, manpower and time were needed to achieve the required effect. It was doubtless exhilarating for bystanders to watch the first trickles of water being diverted, but with large dams holding back millions of gallons, the massive power of water demanded great care and respect. Unfortunately, at **Sherborne Castle**, two men drowned 'making a piece of water'.[134] Lord Digby spent 18s (£125 today) on their burial and gave their widows each five guineas (£730).

September 2003, Sherborne Castle, Dorset Tall cedars of Lebanon, said to have been planted by Sir Walter Raleigh (c.1554–1618), frame the old castle ruin, reflected in Brown's 50-acre lake, made by demolishing seventeenth-century garden terraces and damming the River Yeo.

'Puddling' clay, a method similar to kneading bread introduced by Dutch engineers, had long been employed to line extensive embankments in canal building, to stabilise river navigations, in fen drainage, and to prevent seepage in mines. A number of such schemes had been created prior to Brown's time, especially in the 1720s. John Vanbrugh had envisaged an inland 'sea' at Blenheim and planned a 50-acre lake at Welbeck Abbey, but neither materialised.

Brown expected clients to source clay from 'borrow pits' for both dam and lake-bottom, and stone for the water's edge. The use of on-site materials reduced outlay considerably. A ready supply of fuller's earth, a type of clay, found on the River Yeo terrace at Sherborne, for instance, precluded the necessity for 'puddling' the lining.

Some lake-makers used oven-dried marl, a chalky, clayey and crumbling limestone soil, crushed to powder, before spreading it thinly, wetting and hammering it with wooden mallets in order to form an impermeable lining. Gentleman improvers such as William Emes, Francis Richardson and Richard Woods trained estate workers and field labourers in lake-making procedures, described in Switzer's significant publication which advised a 'pond must be 8 inches thick clayed' to hold water.[135] Brown's designs were arguably the most experimental and ambitious in developing the potential of water. His endeavours to pump clear, soft, good spring water to the environs of the house were a blessing, a welcome bonus for washing and brewing, besides insurance against fire. Schemes were not prompted, in the first instance, to produce the perfect 'Claudian' landscape, although, it must be said, his dams and waterworks were hidden just as carefully as Wren had disguised the engineering in building St Paul's Cathedral.

Wherever it proved impossible to provide an enchanting sheet of water in full view of the house, Brown would propose building a new approach road to skirt round a more distant lake, to add to visitors' enjoyment on arrival and departure. Invariably, the principal picturesque view involved looking across the lake to the house. Clients required considerable capital to cover labour costs, and great tolerance. The harmony of their estates was disrupted for several years, but they appreciated that, over and above a complete new look, serious investment in draining land brought huge benefits for farming and arboriculture. An expanse of healthy, flowing water increased the oxygen supply and so produced better fish stocks, while attracting greater numbers of wildfowl for both sport and table.

Occasionally, as happened at **Southill** in Bedfordshire, a flooded water-meadow made enough of a feature by catching the light and reflecting a summerhouse temple beyond.[136] More often than not, numbers of labourers had to clear rank-smelling, overgrown pond vegetation and scrub before they could begin to dig out soil by hand, pick and shovel to the required depth of the lake – often surprisingly shallow. They then had to wheel away heavy loads of earth and spoil for redistribution by wheelbarrow or horse and dung cart. Workmen built up the sides of the lake and constructed a durable 'head', the dam, with equally sturdy spillways or sluices, with which outflow and water levels could be regulated by opening or closing gates.

In 1748, the year William Kent died, the Duke of Grafton had approached Lord Cobham's protégé to oversee the completion of Kent's **Wakefield Lodge**, his 'hunting box' in Northamptonshire. The house, a short ride from Stowe, overlooked a triangular 'great pond' surrounded by coppice woods, 'lawnes' and water-meadows.[137] Offered a further fee for 'making the water', Brown went on to construct an immense, broad-based earth dam, some 700 ft in length, 25 to 30 ft wide at the top and 80 ft wide at the bottom, that succeeded in raising the water 25 ft to create a much larger, slug-shaped lake.

Several rain-sodden summers later, Brown completed a second reservoir at Newnham Paddox. Likewise, at Wakefield, more than fifty men excavated a second river-lake, and built necessary drains and flood-gates (sluices).[138] In August and September the grass was specially mown, making a pleasant, raised walk for the family and their visitors. Carpenters made seats to place on the dam so that the visitors could enjoy new views cut by estate workers through the woods towards nearby villages, Potterspury and Castlethorpe.

The next May, carpenters mended old fish 'trunks' and made new ones, so that in June there was somewhere to store the fish gathered up as the old lake slowly drained into the new reservoir. By September, they were able to repair the sluice gates. They then planted hawthorn 'quick hedges' and trees on the contoured dam slope to screen the artificiality of the change in level between upper and lower waters.

This systematic approach has all Brown's hallmarks, among them the attention to visual detail, particularly the walk, to deflect the eye from the dam's unnatural structure. If proof were needed, his name appears, between December 1750 and 1755, alongside nine payments for either £50 or £100, 'upon Acct. of the water at Wakefeild' amounting to £707 10s 0d (about £102,000).[139] Later, Grafton tasked Brown with widening the river and finishing Kent's landscaping at his family seat, Euston, on the Norfolk/Suffolk border.

Landowners began to appreciate Brown's tactics. A second lake could solve overflow problems in wet seasons. This led to the drainage of further agricultural tracts, while enabling essential maintenance. If there was seepage when testing the second dam for water tightness, the original dam could be used to hold back the main body of water safely, while temporary coffer dams of stop logs diverted surplus water, to allow repairs to the lining of the lake, or bridges, dams and sluices.

Brown counselled regular intervention to assist upkeep, ensuring the conservation of fish stock and waterfowl by using one reservoir while the other was drained and silt cleared out. A dam usually consisted of two mortared stone walls infilled with a strong clay core, supported by banks of excavated soil. Labourers spread tons of clay in thick layers mixed with lime and flints on the bottom of the lake, ramming exhaustively

March 1998, Wakefield Lodge, Northamptonshire A cannon beside a stone-edged sluice on Brown's great dam and walk recalls the mock sea-battles once popular in the eighteenth century.

to exclude air pockets and flatten the surface. At Ashburnham (Sussex) 'pudlers' walked farm oxen up and down, again and again, to help the process of sealing the clay. Brown went on to extend the existing lake to create 'Broad Water' by raising the level and, eventually, purposefully submerging the main road.

Water was seldom allowed to find its own level. Of course, to make space for a lake, trees often had either to be felled and the timber sold off, or moved, for instance in the case of an elm avenue at Blenheim. Brown led his men energetically, personally staking out the ground to indicate the right plane and chosen contour and showing how to avoid unevenness or irregularity along the periphery of the lake. Everything was to appear as easy and natural as humanly possible, with no straight lines, tangled brambles or eyesores to spoil the view.

Possibly the earliest surviving pictorial evidence regarding Brown's lake engineering is found on the reverse of an undated estimate for work at **Petworth** in Sussex, where the Earl of Egremont asked him to transform a boggy corner of the deer park by building underground conduits to feed into a 'Lower Pond' in the view on the approach to the house. The hastily drawn, rough sketch (see p.71), apparently a cross-section of a dam, shows two vertical walls, slightly offset from the middle. Perhaps Brown used the drawing to argue the merit of an extension to the 'Horse Pond' in the upper park, a second lake, this time in the view from the house. He was able to convince Egremont of his 'double sure' method of dam reinforcement and so secured the contract:

> *Article 1st To enlarging the Pond according to the Stakes for y'. Purpose & digging out all such parts as are not deep enough (making the shallow Places three foot and a half) & making the necessary Clay walls & levelling the Bottom of it, and pitching the Sides which are 2460 feet round to prevent the Cattle from Damaging it, as likewise to turf the edges of the water & to lay in the Plug. £580.0.0 [today £84,210] to levelling the same & sowing with Dutch Clover & Grass seeds. £120.0.0 [today £17,800]... etc.*[140]

Maintaining a pleasing, serpentine edge was crucial to the look. The lake-makers laid stone 'pitching' below the intended waterline and also went to the trouble of edging the shore with stone paving, hidden under a coping of turf, so that the verge would not be broken down by livestock and the pleasing line ruined. Straw placed to protect the verge in frosty weather also helped to protect against duckweed.

Finally, the moment arrived to open sluices. Filling up an entire, man-made reservoir was dependent on weather and the strength of the source – this was not something that happened overnight, and occasional leaks could cause delays. Sometimes it took months for sediment to settle, and often a further two years before stinking and unsightly algae dispersed.

ABOVE **May 1992, Petworth, Sussex (NT)** The grass coping has worn away to reveal the stone holding the pleasing line of the lake edge.

OPPOSITE **May 1992, Petworth, Sussex (NT)** The foreground sycamore was planted to distract the eye from the artificial dam. An island haven for wild birds, doubtless created with spoil, also screens this end of the lake, so the water appears never-ending.

Two months later, Brown was forced to write to Egremont to allay his concerns about the expense because the work was still unfinished:

> *...there is a vast deal of earth that must be moved or else your Lordship will have nothing but weeds and dirty water. As to money expended on it, I am not very certain of at present because I have not recd my Accts from the Man but yr Lordship shall have a faithfull Acct or at least such a One as I have paid.*[141]

During the course of the next winter Brown's foreman, Peter Blair, installed a system of field drains, following the folds of Arbour and Snow Hill, one and a half miles of underground brick conduits, so as to gravity-feed water from springs to fill up Brown's sinuous artificial river. Reading between the lines

of the next contract, all did not go quite according to plan once again, this time concerning the sluice: 'To make a proper Plug and trough to draw down the Water, as likewise a Grate for the discharge of the waste Water. My Lord to find the timber.'[142]

Egremont, for his part, provided five horses and all necessary carts and wheelbarrows, in addition to trees for obscuring the dam and for ornamenting the edge of the shallow lake. There were setbacks in sourcing enough stone for pitching the sides and lining the edges of the new lake. Finally, Christmas 1757 found Brown arranging the finishing touches, sowing all broken ground with grass seed and Dutch clover.

It was not long before he turned his energies to another project at Petworth: widening the River Rother between Coultershaw Bridge and the mill, 'making the tumbling Bay at the end of it'.[143] A river meander and weir, and beyond them the high downs at Duncton, crowned with Brown's clumps, would enhance the way to Chichester.

Lake-making progressed simultaneously in several other locations, including nearby Shillingley,[144] with

gradual, deliberate trials and occasional improvisation, sometimes linking with water supply improvements to the house and walled gardens (to be discussed later). It has been said that he coined the phrase 'I shall go to bed and sleep on it.' Certainly, when crises arose, a good night's rest would have replenished his reserves of patience, pragmatism and resolution.

In Lincolnshire, 'home of decoys', Brown witnessed how fen men set willow traps for eels, 'fen men's gold', and, especially in winter months, exploited abundant bird-life using a technique introduced the previous century by Dutch engineers.[145] Men beat through marshland ponds and dykes to drive wild duck, funnelling them with reed screens into a narrowing passage of water or 'pipe' where they were netted and caught by hand. Just as with the rabbit warren, working a decoy pond produced meat on a commercial scale. Mallard, widgeon and teal were taken alive to London and sold in large numbers, on average about 5,000 a year per decoy. Duck were protected by landowners. Poachers were treated harshly, often with transportation.

BELOW Sketch of Skellingthorpe Decoy, Lincolnshire, an EH Grade II registered landscape. An outer, moat-like ditch encircles an early eighteenth-century decoy west of Lincoln, enclosed by trees, with a range of artificial earth banks around a central, irregular 'landing pond'. From here, several tapering, clearly defined channels or 'pipes' curve away, each about 200 feet long. A raised boundary walk allowed convenient access to net wildfowl.

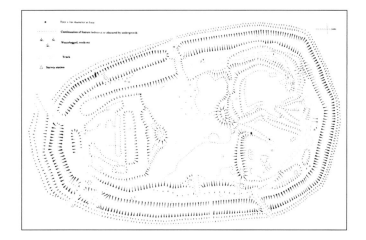

By mid-century, the management of sheltered decoys had changed. Rather than large numbers of men having to be employed to drive wildfowl into nets, one man alone, in necessary quiet, could now operate a single netted pipe. Decoys started to appear elsewhere. At Stowe, mainly in December and January, men shot wildfowl. Wooden decoy birds were deployed near the Chinese House on the island near the Grotto. So there was more purpose to the sublime 'River Alder' and the Worthies' 'River Styx' than watering Elysium: 'In the pond are the figures of two Chinese birds about the size of a duck, which move with the wind as if alive.'[146]

On two occasions, Brown charged fifteen guineas (today £2,200) for advice at Boarstall, Buckinghamshire, where a decoy still exists. It is near Wotton, where he worked for the Grenville family. Meanwhile, at Packington (see pp.51–52), Brown addressed the extension of an existing decoy, the 'Great Pool', to 30 acres, including four islands at the Decoy Wood end.[147] New islands, carefully positioned (often shored up by timber), helped to hide the artificial termination of a lake, so the stretch of water would seem more river-like and limitless. A good solution for depositing excavated spoil and silt, islands made excellent bird sanctuaries for nesting. Many of Brown's islands continue to host long-established heronries.

The embanked circuit walk around many of Brown's water features bears a marked resemblance

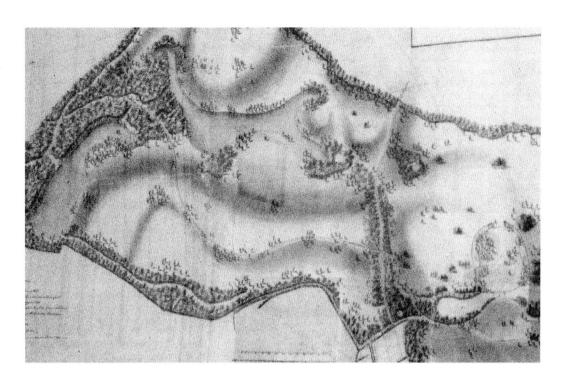

to a decoy's raised, grassy track encompassing landing pool and pipes.[148] It seems that Brown deliberately subsumed decoy ideas into his plans, typically on a more impressive scale.[149] Moreover, his insistence on uncluttered banks was not solely for calming simplicity and eye-pleasing effect. Open areas of lawn near water encouraged large numbers of wildfowl landings, enticed by the sight and call of tame ducks. At Chillington (Staffordshire) a canal running off Brown's lake allowed fuel and weighty articles to be transported to the house, and probably doubled as a decoy for netting wildfowl.[150] The architect James Paine (1717–1789) was effusive in his praise:

> *one of the finest pieces of water, with an inclosure that this Kingdom produces; the verges of which are bounded by fine plantations, intermixed with groves of venerable stately oaks … at another neck of this beautiful water is erected another bridge, concealing the other extreme of the water, built by Lancelot Brown Esq., who designed and conducted the execution of the improvements of this justly admired park.*[151]

A proposal for the larger lake at **Highclere** in Berkshire shows narrowing water channels which would assist the control of flow and make useful duck 'gathering ponds'. In this case, negotiations failed and no contract resulted. Henry Herbert chose to employ his own estate workers to undertake improvements. Despite failing to win the commission, Brown's clear plan and ideas influenced subsequent grandiose landscaping improvements, as they do to this day.[152] Several similar grand plans, including those for **Wimbledon** and Blenheim, evolved into a pioneering 'tricorn' design for an organic-shaped, curving lake with pronounced convex sides directly opposite concave banks on the other shore. Young George Spencer wrote to his mother Georgiana, Countess Spencer, about developments 'in the pure air' at Wimbledon (formerly Surrey): 'There is a pretty boat put in the pond and a thing made for the swans in an island of the pond.'[153]

Everywhere Brown worked he advised strategic maintenance, including regularly lowering the waters for silt clearance. This also gave an opportunity for easy fishing, as Lady Georgiana observed: '1781 Nov 15 The Great Water is almost let off [drained] and we had a most extraordinary draught of fishes there. We caught 63 brace of carp, most of them very large, and a brace of very fine pike at one haul.'[154]

CHAPTER EIGHT

RIVERS REAL & ILLUSORY

Sir Richard Grenville called Brown back to **Wotton**, Buckinghamshire, during the wet 1750s. Water was much more abundant than the first time he had worked there. He was able, with great subtlety, to make two channels to extend the basin, known as the Warrells, below the house to fourteen acres, making it seem as if it were the convergence of two streams.

These stretches of water appear to join another river (in reality, a five-acre embanked canal, much like a fen dyke) that, thanks to its higher level, flowed seamlessly into Brown's 'Great Pond' beyond. He enclosed the new, narrow, finger-like canal between the lakes by planting, and this too doubtless acted as a decoy. 'China Island' hid the end of the second channel, and made an excellent spot for the Chinese summerhouse that was specially brought across from Stowe.

By enlarging and raising the level of 'Neptune's Bridge', an existing rubblestone five-arch 'sham bridge', Brown succeeded in disguising the termination of his new canal. A sluice and spillway under the middle arch of the bridge controlled the water coming in from Wotton Brook down Brill Hill. The figure of Neptune was replaced by a shell, and the feature renamed 'Shell Bridge'. Neptune proved useful elsewhere, conveniently helping to take the eye off Brown's massive artificial dam on the 'Great Pond' as if surveying the waters of an inland sea.

OPPOSITE **October 2009, Wotton, Buckinghamshire** In the foreground Brown's embanked canal is on a higher level than the Warrells, the lake beyond, though this is not apparent.

ABOVE **October 2009, Wotton, Buckinghamshire** The five-arch Shell Bridge (two storeys high) acts as an eye-catching termination of Brown's canal, giving a romantic illusion of a river. This intimate, secluded reach contrasts with the open expanses of the Warrells (opposite) and the great lake (p.83).

Bringing across his 'safe pair of hands' from Croome, Brown introduced his foreman, the young improver Benjamin Read (1734–1794), possibly the son of the paviour 'Mr Read' with whom Brown had collaborated at both Grimsthorpe and Stowe. The younger Read spent two years overseeing the building of the necessary network of sunk fences and field drains. Two large culverts also served as boathouses on the Warrells, hidden under mounds. These made ideal raised platforms for seats from which visitors could take in the tranquil view.

The Grenville family and their advisers, William Pitt and Sanderson Miller, engaged Brown to adapt some of the views inherited from the earlier schemes of Brompton nurserymen London and Wise. In 1758, in the midst of concerns over the Seven Years War against France and Spain, Pitt found solace in writing to his wife Hester (*née* Grenville), thinking of her in a much more serene place, 'amidst the sweet amenity of fragrant Lawns quiet Woods and gentle Waters. My Angel will not be surprised that to crown all sweetest Mussel Hill must ever hold a distinguished Place in my Landskip of Verdant delightful Wotton'.[155]

The vast 'Great Pond' came to serve as a training ground for young naval cadets, with mock sea-battles, war games known as 'naumachia'.[156] Later, as Brown intended, the potential of the considerable fall of water leaving the lake was harnessed to power a saw-mill.[157]

Such a quantity and variety of water radically changed the face of Wotton. A subtle, complex juxtaposition of sightlines evolved, each framed or controlled by taking down and moving trees, or introducing new planting, to create a 'natural' landscape, ironically with painstaking, geometric precision. The water featured in every equation: it determined views with reflected eye-catchers, plantations, lawns and shrubberies, and made destinations for romantic walks. Informal countryside pursuits multiplied as the Grenville family and their coterie responded to an altered and more accessible and usable topography: drawing and painting, shooting or netting wildfowl, and boating for pleasure. More significantly, rentals of fields let out within the park rose as a direct consequence of the improved grazing land.

Thomas Whately admired the 'succession of perpetual variety' that he found at Wotton, where

ABOVE **October 2009, Wotton, Buckinghamshire** Brown's embanked canal leads seamlessly into his great lake, where Grotto Island diverts attention from his extensive dam. Sanderson Miller's Octagon Temple (newly restored) is counterbalanced by a rotunda, in the distance (right).

OPPOSITE LEFT **September 2006, Wotton, Buckinghamshire** The top storey of the Shell Bridge.

OPPOSITE RIGHT **August 2009, Wotton, Buckinghamshire** The spillway under the Shell Bridge, with remnants of the sluice gate.

visitors, attracted into relaxing exploration of the grounds, walked or rode in a bumpy two-wheeled horse-drawn 'chaise' for a three-mile circuit around the lakes. They could also enjoy a peaceful sojourn, gliding along in a boat, and admire the novelty of mirrored views of the house and surrounding plantations.[158]

In 1786, Thomas Jefferson (1743–1826), the future third American President, carried a second edition of Thomas Whately's book *Observations on Modern Gardening* (1770) as a guide on his tour of English gardens. He was determined to visit Wotton after reading descriptions such as this:

> *All seem to communicate with one another....*
> *A profusion of water pours in from all sides round*
> *upon the view.... However interrupted, however varied,*
> *they still appear to be parts of one whole, which has*
> *all the intricacy of number, and the greatness of unity;*
> *the variety of a stream and the quantity of a lake; the*
> *solemnity of a wood, and the animation of water.*[159]

Jefferson reckoned Stowe's waters, on four levels, covered no more than twenty acres (estimating the central basin as seven, the lake below ten acres) whereas, much to his admiration, Wotton's lakes totalled seventy-two acres (the Great Pond fifty). However, he found the grounds at Wotton neglected, kept only by two garden hands, but was impressed that the great lake supplied 2,000 brace of carp a year.[160]

In contrast to the rural quiet at Wotton, the River Thames, the capital's major artery, was always awash with the hubbub of constant river traffic, 'Thames wherries', clinker-built boats ferrying travellers and cargo to and from London. The Earl of Northumberland commissioned Brown to create an undisturbed ribbon of water over what were once the capital's best gravel pits at **Syon**, on the Thames near Isleworth (Middlesex). His sheltered serpentine river was perhaps meant to recall Northumbrian tributaries, such as the River Coquet, as it meandered through well-stocked pleasure grounds. A circuit walk passed the easy slope of 'Flora's Lawn' where a tall Doric column bearing a statue of Flora, Goddess of Flowers, dominated his man-made rise, created from the excavation of the lake.

A second stretch of water in the park, later crossed by a bridge on the main approach, added to the charming 'pretend' river effect. Meanwhile, the house overlooked a sparsely planted tidal water-meadow that flooded as the Thames rose, twice a day, sometimes giving the illusion of a lake beyond the pronounced curve of Brown's long ha-ha. Interesting pencil marks on Brown's undated plan indicate his Church Walk shrubberies, together with extensions and plantations, ideas that were later realised in the outer park. In this instance, the new river was the first priority, and its success caused Brown to hone other designs in similar fashion.

Faint but assured markings added to John Haynes's survey (1755) of **Burghley** must, likewise, be attributable to Brown, tracing a suggested stretch

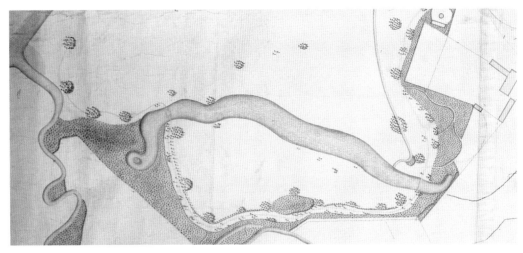

of water snaking past William Cecil's Elizabethan house and cutting through formal gardens. He went on to join together rectangular reflection pools and fishponds and a nine-acre 'Great Pond' into one long, gently winding artificial river, at the same time eradicating terraces and steps under excavated soil. The discovery of a seam of waterproof blue clay proved invaluable in constructing a necessarily massive dam, because water kept disappearing down a natural geological fault in the limestone. There were real difficulties in estimating the correct length and height of dam to control the required water level: 'twice or thrice, when the workmen thought it [water] well secured, did it elude their pains, surmount the dam, and carrying all before it, subject them to new toil'.[161]

OPPOSITE **September 1990, The Duke's River, Syon, Middlesex** Native white willow (middle) and imported swamp cypress (left) and weeping willows (right) set off Brown's lake, which resembles a natural meandering tributary to the River Thames.

TOP Detail from Brown's undated, unfinished and unsigned Grand Plan for Syon. The draughtsmanship bears a close relationship with his Packington plan (1751, signed – see p.50) and also a later plan for Aynho, unsigned.

ABOVE **March 1991, Kew Gardens, London** A late afternoon view from Kew to Syon House, topped by the Percy Lion, across the River Thames, water meadow and lawn.

LEFT **March 2007, Burghley, Cambridgeshire** A gravel path traversing the middle of Brown's huge dam distracts from the massive earthwork, with the dam bank continuing (left) behind the laurel bushes.

BELOW **April 1994, Burghley, Cambridgeshire** Brown's 'pretend river', the lake naturally divides the pleasure gardens from the park, with his model farm in the distance.

OPPOSITE **May 2005, Wrest Park, Bedfordshire (EH)** Brown agreed to leave this principal view from the house well alone. He brought a new stretch of artificial river behind one of the country's best garden buildings, the Pavilion, a banqueting house by Thomas Archer (1711), and framed it with cedars and plane trees.

A vertical well in the centre of the dam provided access to the drainage tunnel, which was plugged by an oak door and a conical wooden stopper. A second, fail-safe plug had to be retrieved from a boat.[162] A charming cascade near the cliff, along the geological fault line, disguised the outfall of water from the lake flowing into the existing 'Swallow Rill', using 'pudding-stones', aggregates of rounded flint pebbles bound with a natural silica and sand cement.

In 1775 a local contractor, Edward Thorpe and Co., earned £61 (today £8,540) and needed twenty-four wheelbarrows to dig out the mud for an eleven-acre stretch of water to extend the illusory river.[163] Where spring water supplied the lake, another innovation, Brown designed a series of stone lip cascades to act as narrow silt traps at regular intervals down the hill to prevent the silt reaching the lake. These were easier to clean out than draining the entire lake. We will return to Burghley later, to see how Brown set about changing the entire approach to the house so as to cross an elegant, three-arch 'Lion Bridge' (see p.200).

Burghley was one of the destinations that Jemima, Marchioness Grey, had on her list as she embarked on a garden tour around the country, also taking in Holkham, Stowe and Warwick Castle. In 1758, she finally decided to invite Brown to her own property, **Wrest Park** in Bedfordshire. Perhaps atrocious weather had helped to make her mind up. She commissioned him to drain all the saturated parts of the gardens and surrounding low-lying land, but on no account was he to alter the compelling and

memorable canal view centred on the Pavilion, Thomas Archer's baroque banqueting house that had been commissioned by her late father, the Duke of Kent.

Brown went on to make significant changes nonetheless, carting in ironstone from Clophill Quarry, a mile or so away, for a dam to raise the level and expand an oval lake in the park, 'Old Water'. Recently uncovered in restoration work, this double, infilled wall has an unusual concave curve on the downstream side, with adjacent spillway, and walled, sinuous banks on the upstream side. He then linked this artificial river to existing stretches, widening and naturalising straight canals lower down, and adjusting changes of levels with adjoining streams by discreet shallow-lipped cascades.

Having brought the waters behind the Archer pavilion, Brown put in a discreet weir and sluice to control the outfall round the corner in a wider 'Broad Water' on the east. He designed a Chinese bridge of oak[164] (see examples, pp.198, 199) to lead the eye towards Cain Hill, the principal attraction of the local landscape. All this effort added greatly to the sense of place that is Wrest, giving the charming illusion of a river holding the formal wilderness gardens, almost as if an island, in a unifying, watery embrace. The main benefit lay in his solving flooding and drainage problems, a fact recognised by Walpole, who, in his inimitable style, found the grounds out of date: 'execrable, too, but is something mended by Brown'.

The expert improver continued to give advice, sometimes appearing suddenly and unannounced in the gardens, much to the dismay of Amabel, Jemima's daughter. In 1765 her guests 'embarked under the shade of the acacias' on a colourful Chinese boat, a gilded swan carved on the prow, a tiger on the stern, a floating pleasure pavilion launched with due ceremony and streamers. On the west was a thatched rustic building, half Hermitage, half Roman bathhouse with plunge pool, possibly an ice-house conversion, because Brown's extended waters were now too near to allow for adequate drainage from the melting ice. This once overlooked an odd Doric pillar on the opposing bank near the tail end of 'Old Water'.[165]

*These gardens originally laid out
by Henry Duke of Kent
were altered by
Philip Earl of Hardwicke
and Jemima,
Marchioness Grey,
with the professional assistance of
Lancelot Brown Esq.
in the years 1758, 1759, 1760*

This rather odd-looking tribute to Brown in his lifetime marks how Wrest came to be a unique palimpsest of garden design. Hinting at a marriage of styles, the smooth, traditionally dressed and 'natural' rusticated stone may have been the Marchioness's idea for a visual pun. Just as interesting, this also marks one of the earliest uses of the word 'professional'.

BELOW LEFT **Wrest Park, Bedfordshire (EH)** The Doric Column commissioned by Marchioness de Grey, once on view from the bath-house, now terminates one of the Wilderness Walks.

BELOW RIGHT **Wrest Park, Bedfordshire (EH)** Brown's signature Scots pine acts as an eye-catcher near the dam at the head of 'Old Park Water', designed to look like a river, still muddied after a recent restoration. It takes a couple of years for silt to settle and for the water to fill up enough to hide stone lake edging. Brown and his men were faced with similar problems.

CHAPTER NINE

CASCADES

Horace Walpole's first encounter with Brown's handiwork, in 1751 at **Warwick Castle**, had evoked an emotional response, the loquacious commentator for once almost lost for words: 'The castle is enchanting; the view pleased me more than I can express the river Avon tumbles down a cascade at the foot of it.'

Later, Lord Ilchester, visiting his sister Charlotte at Sherborne in 1756, reported to Lord Digby:

The masons have finished and seemingly very well. In digging to lay the foundation of the cascade they are got into rock, and as there is a nicety in that work, and that rock is a bad sort of soil, I advised Mr Barnet to send for Mr Brown to give his advice.[166]

Thrilling to the eye, the splashing sounds of a foaming force were agreeable to the ear. A weir with a cascade, a straightforward solution to changing levels when lake-making, more importantly aerated the water and deposited silt. Brown had come to be recognised for expertise in building stable dams with central weirs to control the rate of flow and run-off in fast rivers such as the Avon or the Yeo. Where time was critical and a serious problem needed to be addressed, he would quickly draw suggested improvements on an owner's existing map. If commissioned he would go on to provide a more polished, measured, comprehensive proposal.[167]

OPPOSITE **August 1991, Warwick Castle, Warwickshire** Brown calmed the River Avon with a sturdy weir to offer charming reflections of the somewhat austere castle on its sandstone bluff, softened by his planting.

ABOVE Paul Sandby (1725–1809), *Caesar's Tower and Part of Warwick Castle* Private Collection, © Alamy

Whether Brown was consulted at **Enville**, Staffordshire, has long been a subject for conjecture, with no mention in surviving accounts, letters or journals. Yet one survey (*c.*1750) has telling marks in a different hand indicating snaking plantations, with crosses for the removal of hedges, and compares closely with Brown's *modus operandi* elsewhere, as will be seen. More interestingly, the author of a second, related but unsigned plan of a similar period, recently discovered, has never been identified.

The Earl of Stamford is known to have consulted a neighbouring landowner, the rural poet William Shenstone (1714–1763), and the local architect Sanderson Miller about landscaping high hills and the 'Sheep Walks' above his house. The cascades at Enville have mostly been associated with Shenstone, and enjoyed from his Gothic chapel high in the woods, once with striking views down to the Chinese Temple in the middle of Temple Pool. So the unsigned plan has been suggested as being by him. Ornate, grotto-like waterfalls ornamented with river-gods were proving popular but were expensive and not easy to build. It is more likely, given the dire weather, with prolonged rains heavy enough to cause flooding from hillside springs, or even a collapsed dam, that Miller probably recommended the experienced engineer with whom he occasionally collaborated, since Brown was working no more than twenty miles away at both Hewell Grange and Croome in Worcestershire.

A comparison of the content and style of one of Brown's first professional proposals for Packington with the Enville plan is instructive: the first was drawn up by a draughtsman, the latter, I believe, by Brown, one of those occasions where there was no time to hire a professional. Both plans display the ideas of an improver whose principal focus is to make changes to the water, each drawn to the same scale, 1 in. to 100 ft; both demonstrate a bold use of a deeply shadowed, serpentine line for the water's edge, a line also seen in winding walks, tree belts and shrubberies. Despite disparities, because of different hands and, of course, different terrains, both plans have several features in

common: an apron ha-ha, a pillar or column, a grotto and a cascade as a key highlight. Also, significantly, each displays the characteristic accuracy, clarity and holistic simplicity of a perfectionist and includes a strongly defined Brownian 'serpent head' termination at one end of the water.

Another more likely scenario is that Brown came across from Hewell in Worcestershire to solve problems of flooding and eventually to restore order. The two top pools were enlarged, dams reinforced and controlling sluices inserted to make more of a reliable feature of the spring and cascades. Acres of space were opened up by cutting down the central axis of hedging and breaking up the line of trees beyond the 'Terras in front of the House', bounded by an apron-shaped ha-ha.[168] A snaking belt of trees, 'The New Serpentine Plantation', broken by small groves, hugged the horizon above the water. Faint words, 'Visto august', are inscribed where the stream cascades down the hill.

Completely transforming the original square, brick-lined Temple Pool into a curvaceous, amoeba-like lake had proved out of the question. Stamford had probably rejected the plan to alter and extend the lake because the challenging topography in the steep valley would have required the costly movement of great volumes of earth to shore up a new dam. The level of the basin was raised, although never enlarged to the full extent suggested, and its edges softened. At this time, the earl was drawing large amounts of cash to pay for landscaping a reservoir.[169] I suggest Brown's answer to excessive rainfall was to engineer the extra 'Jordan's Pool' positioned directly below Sanderson Miller's castle-like Gothic entrance ('New Gateway' on the plan) into a vision of the 'Promised Land'. This would explain why, in 1758, Stamford numbered among several landed petitioners recommending Brown's appointment as royal gardener.

In 1769 the Chinese Temple on the island was finally removed, so as not to block an emotive vista from the house to the feature on the hill above the water. Empress Catherine of Russia's Wedgwood 'Frog

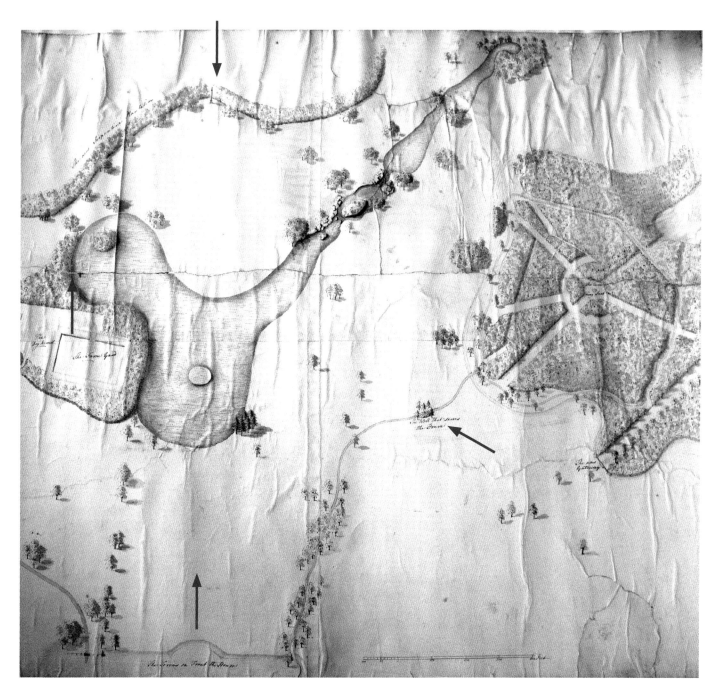

Unsigned pen and wash proposal for Enville, Staffordshire, c.1753–54.
© Mrs Diana Williams. I believe this to be a Brown plan, probably
in his own hand. It compares favourably with his other designs,
considering serpentine lines, coloured sand walks, tree forms and
groupings with shadows. Notice the emphasis on water, shading for
reinforced banks, and the 'Well that serves the House' (right arrow). A
new island with trees would screen the proposed dam (left arrow), and
the existing island would be cleared to open the view from the house
(bottom arrow) to the pillar on the hill (top arrow).

Service' (c. 1774) illustrated this charming, maturing scene, the serpentine belt of trees framing (instead of Brown's pillar) a classical memorial urn. Most of the ideas of the mystery plan had indeed been implemented by this stage. A barrel-shaped, vaulted brick grotto at the bottom of Round Hill replaced 'the Well that serves the House',[170] with the spring feeding in to refresh Temple Pool. When George Harry, 5th Earl of Stamford, inherited Enville, he may have preferred others to think that he, and his father before him, rather than Brown, had been the driving force behind improvements. He built a decorative boathouse at one corner of the lake, with an elegant, octagonal upper room, offering an intimate, relaxing view of the water. Given a signal, a workman would open the sluice gates of holding pools up on the hillside, unleashing a roaring torrent that suddenly appeared, rushing down the hill, much to visitors' amazement.[171]

The steep terrain at Enville made Brown's envisioned 'Visto august' – grand view – more dramatic than the new cascade he later masterminded, behind the Palladian Bridge at Stowe, where one 1760s planting bill mentions him. At this time, the

ABOVE AND BELOW May 2010, Enville, Staffordshire The substantially built upper dam is discernible. Arrows mark the progress of the waterfalls when sluices on the hill were opened.

RIGHT Detail from Enville plan (c. 1753–54) © Mrs Diana Williams. Rocky cascades down the hillside (arrows).

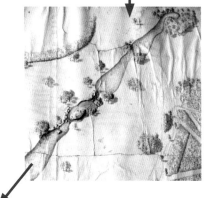

groundsmen excavated a series of holding pools to collect water on the newly acquired Lamport hillside above the 'Upper River' and built a rocky waterfall to conceal the lake termination. Brown was one of the few men capable of envisaging the practicalities of landscaping on that scale and in that manner. It must have been his suggestion to remove carved stone panels on the back of the Palladian Bridge to open up a 'new view' of the cascade, especially as the decorative panels were then added to the Grecian temple he had helped to build.[172]

Cascades are rarely mentioned in surviving contracts. The 1759 agreement for **Longleat** (Wiltshire) to create an illusory river is an exception: 'To lay the two canals next the serpentine river into one. To alter the sharp turns on the serpentine river, and to make the cascades.'[173]

Brown devised an attractive, rock-strewn cascade to hide his unnatural causeway dam carrying the approach drive, since the marked change of level between the lakes was in full view of the house. Here, and doubtless elsewhere, he left specific instructions to open sluices and raise the water level

every spring, sufficient to flush out the house drains – perhaps learned wisdom from Lincolnshire fen men: the waste water would then flood and effectively fertilise the water-meadows while, at the same time, allowing reeds to purify the water. Could this have been the first example of ecological reed-bed filtration and managed wetlands in a designed landscape, a system now commonly promoted?[174] Water-meadows were incorporated in many of Brown's plans, among

ABOVE July 1992, Longleat, Wiltshire Brown recommended that the sluices be opened every spring to raise the water level of the lake and to flush out the house drain (arrow).

RIGHT July 1992, Longleat, Wiltshire A natural-looking cascade hides a major dam taking the main approach road to the house. Discreet ironwork supports the rocks in place.

ABOVE AND RIGHT **March 2009, Chatsworth, Derbyshire** The great weir (rebuilt by Joseph Paxton, 1840). Brown widened and dammed the River Derwent to create a contrasting mirror-like surface reflecting the house and surrounding park landscape. A sluice below the lower weir allowed water to flow into a leat to power Paine's Mill, a once useful eye-catcher, in the view from Chatsworth gardens, which is now a romantic ruin.

them those for Broadlands, Charlecote, Syon, Trentham and Youngsbury.

Reaching Chatsworth, Derbyshire, in 1760, Walpole did not care for the famous Baroque waterfall that had been created at the end of the seventeenth century by Grillet, a pupil of the celebrated French royal gardener Le Nôtre: 'that absurdity of a cascade tumbling down marble steps, which reduces them to no use at all'.

The Grand Cascade remained, but many other 'foolish' waterworks had been removed. Eight years later, Walpole returned to find Chatsworth much improved. Brown's new road through the park made a striking, oblique approach to the house, running across James Paine's magnificent stone bridge. Walpole commented that the Duke of Devonshire was busy 'making vast plantations, widening and raising the River, and carrying the park on to the side of it, and levelling a great deal of ground to shew the River under the direction of Brown'.[175]

Brown had succeeded in widening the fast-flowing River Derwent, reducing the steep banks by grading the slopes and calming its turbulent flow by raising the level with two curvilinear weirs. Such was the scale of earth-moving to improve prospects from the house that all trace of medieval ridge and furrow disappeared from the area of the lower weir. Both the 'Quebec Cascade', commemorating the Battle of Quebec (1759), and Paine's Mill (1760), a corn mill in prime position on the opposite bank terminating the view from the gardens and an island down-river, were almost certainly part of Brown's works, extending the garden walks to take advantage of the new dramatic river views. His team had the know-how to harness the force of the water, reusing parts of an earlier mill downstream, demolished when the river was widened. A sluice controlled a narrow leat, or head race, running partly underground before supplying sufficient power to operate the mill's giant waterwheel, then being discharged back into the river along the tail race through another stone culvert.

The Earl of Ashburnham sought nothing but peace on his Sussex estate, **Ashburnham Place**, and took exception to the sound of rushing water. Following his 1767 proposal Brown addressed the problem of the level-change between the existing lake and his proposed vast reservoir by creating an accommodating watercourse, an interconnecting 'carrier' stream running underground. He cannily, and quietly, hid the outfall from the upper lake, 'Front Water', on an island opposite the house. Further west his extension to 'Broad Water' was topped up by a freshwater spring seeping equally quietly from a ferny cave which made a destination on the circuit walk around the lake and a tranquil spot for a secluded Lady's Grotto.

In 1763 the Earl of Bute resigned as prime minister, and was looking to procure a country estate for his retirement. Brown remembered **Luton Hoo**, a Bedfordshire estate, where he had previously made improvements for Francis Herne.[176] He facilitated the sale. This involved the extra purchase of a number of surrounding farms and the re-routing of

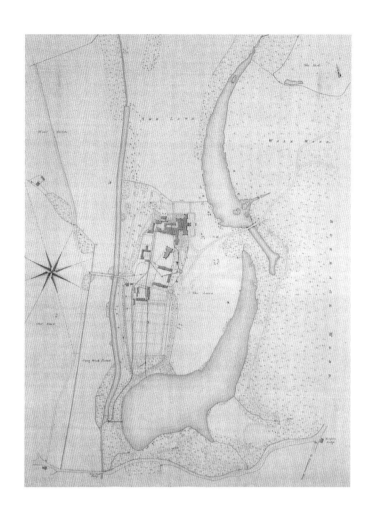

ABOVE Ashburnham Survey ASH 4357 (1832). Most of Brown's proposals were implemented.

RIGHT June 1997, Ashburnham, Sussex Brown's sluice is hidden on the island.

BELOW LEFT September 2005, Ashburnham, Sussex Brown's secluded 'Lady's Grotto'.

ABOVE **May 2007, Luton Park, Bedfordshire** Willows give Brown's upper lake a distinctive character, a largely unspoiled view (though with Luton Airport close by, not as peaceful as it once was).

RIGHT **Luton Park, Bedfordshire** Middle Weir on the River Lea. Brown's brick sham bridge (rebuilt 1783 after flood damage) hides the dam and the 12-foot change in level. Note the paint remnants underneath the arch, possibly his experiment to hide brickwork and reflect light on to the cascade (see also pp.201–202).

the Luton to Wheathampstead road by offering to make new roads and footpaths, to enlarge the park eventually to 1,500 acres. Brown also advised where to source suitable stone for Robert Adam to remodel the house.

Over a period of fourteen years, improvements amounting to £10,000 (today £1,361,000) included plantations, a large kitchen garden, an ice-house, a lodge, and possibly a boathouse.[177] Apart from Blenheim, Luton Hoo was Brown's biggest commission. The water engineering proved equally demanding. Peter Blair, Brown's right-hand man at Petworth, supervised the works, damming the inconsequential River Lea to create two serpentine lakes, fourteen and fifty acres respectively. He built an engine-house to pump water up to the house (which had seven water closets). A 'Design for planting a river meander', an unsigned guideline typical of Brown's pronounced curvaceous line, survives, confidently sketched in pen, ink and wash. This suggested a double bend edged with trees to screen a brick, single-arch sham bridge. A large island, a haven for wild birds, diverted attention from the changing levels between the two lakes, making two narrow channels like decoy pipes.[178]

A memorable approach road from the town ran almost parallel to the grand 'new river', with a variety of gentle rises and falls above water-meadows to offer visitors in carriages charming glimpses of the pastoral valley. An oak on the first man-made hillock signalled a good stopping-place to survey the pleasing ox-bow bend, framed by willows, and the river extending as far as the eye could see. Thanks to the leading agricultural writer Arthur Young (1741–1820) we can imagine the scene:[179]

If the Earl of Bute's park at Luton Hoo were not an inducement, there certainly could be none to visit that town. Notwithstanding the wretched roads I was forced to crawl through, yet the beauties of the hill & dale, wood & water in that park made ample amends. We entered through the Lodge from the town of Luton & drove along the banks of the river which was naturally a trifling stream, but is now forming, & is made further on, the finest water I have anywhere seen; the plantations on top of the hills to the right as we entered are very beautiful, on the left, the winding hollow which is prettily diversified with scattered trees, is nobly traced for continuing the water & is a spot wonderfully capable. Where the lake

is finished which is just before you come to the island, the view is very fine, the stream bends in a noble manner, is seen a long way without wanting irregularity; & from its breadth has a magnificent appearance. The island is large, has many full-grown trees upon it, with young plantations, & adds much to the beauty of the scene. … There are many fine beeches as you advance up to the house, from the dark shade of which the water is seen at a distance very advantageously … turning a little to the right the bridge fronts you; it is of wood, & though unornamented, is right and has a good effect. A little further is the cascade, which is yet but a capability; when a little improved & catched from a proper point of view, it will add to the variety of the scene … view of the ornamental pillar which is seen among the trees in a picturesque manner.

Where Brown's waters disappeared round a bend, falling over a 30-ft-high cascade, a discreet underground spillway and sluice allowed flood control. However, the lie of the land was such that, in the views from the house and gardens, the water appeared as only a narrow ribbon. Bute promptly commissioned ship's carpenters to build a sailing ship, an arresting model of a man-of-war, from estate timber to trick the eye as to the scale of his inland sea.

Meanwhile, in 1773, in north-east Yorkshire, landowner Sir William St Quentin reported on progress in the modernisation of **Scampston**.

> *I have recd the Favour of your letter, with the Plan enclosed for the Cascade, which I like very much.… I have made the sunk fence on both side of the Gate-way, which has a most charming Effect. I have also fill'd the angle of the water at the West End, & have also made an Island where the water was too broad & have widened ye North of the bridge according to your Plan which answers prodigious well, for which I return many thanks.[180]*

Here Brown recommended large pieces of ancient limestone tufa to create a waterfall, disguising the dam and level change between the upper and lower lake, just as at Longleat.[181] In addition to his substantial fee, he received a Scampston ham as a token of gratitude.

CHAPTER TEN

PROBLEMS & PUMPS

Experimentation and trials with pumps continued in tandem with lake-making. In autumn 1754, over and above regular contract payments for estate improvements at **Shortgrove** (Essex), which included widening the River Cam, Brown had received £286 12s 7d (£40,141) 'on acct. of the Building'. This was almost certainly the engine-house or pump-house, for which John Broadbent provided both a plan (p.102) 'to raise water out of a well 160 feet perpendicular' (1755) and a detailed estimate for a horse engine, which he was prepared to keep in good repair for twenty-one years.[182]

Large payments into Brown's Drummond's Bank account (sometimes £1,000 (£130,800) every six months) suggest that probably he later had a hand in building the artesian well at Wimbledon (1763), where a similar horse pump was installed to raise water to a reservoir at the top of the house.[183] The domed Well House, the only Spencer building to survive in Wimbledon, bears a striking resemblance to Brown's summerhouse at Redgrave in Suffolk.

In 1759, in the midst of improving Ashridge (Buckinghamshire) for the Duke of Bridgewater, Brown was called north by the duke's brother-in-law, Earl Gower, to address problems doubtless exacerbated by pollution from the potteries at Stoke carried by the River Trent past his house at **Trentham** (Staffordshire). A 1758 survey of the River Trent to the River Mersey, undertaken by James Brindley (1716–1772), the self-made engineer for 'Arle Gower', one of his first patrons, may have been useful.

OPPOSITE **July 2011, Trentham, Staffordshire** Brown's great lake was engineered by damming the River Trent.

ABOVE **March 2008, Trentham, Staffordshire** Brown's watercourse through cleansing water meadows.

101

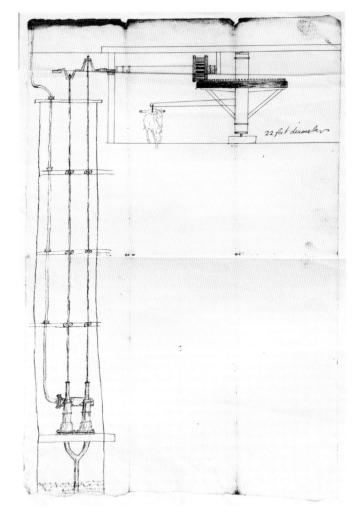

Horse Engine Plan for Shortgrove, Essex (plus inserted horse sketch)
© West Sussex RO, PHA

In wrestling with his most challenging assignment to date, Brown came up with an audacious plan (1759) to create a mile-long, eighty-acre sheet of water, four feet deep.[184] He indicated the original course of the Trent with pricked lines. Gore and Brown agreed a six-article contract, worth £2,270 (today £309,000), requiring eight horses to assist the groundwork.

Brown would change the river's direction, cleansing the water by flooding a wide, flat water-meadow, parts of which he would fill in with 'Mould to a proper level above the Water that it may become firm and Sound Land'.[185]

A narrowing, controlling serpentine channel, as elegant as a swan's neck, had water falling away downstream over a weir. By 1773 a visitor admired the transformation: 'Mr Brown has contrived to swell the narrow stream of the Trent into a River almost as broad as the Thames & to conduct it through a delightful Valley with a noble wood on one side & very beautiful meadows on the other.'[186]

A business-like footnote covered the probability that manual workers might be attracted to road and canal building in this more industrial area, work that was better paid: 'Should we be drove to the Necessity of giving a shilling [today £7.00] a day to the Labourers the advanced Expense of it is understood that the Earl should bear one Half of it and Brown the other.'

The project took longer than expected. Gower spent a further £245 (£33,500) before signing off the contract in August 1762. A month later, generously bearing the cost of remedial leakage repairs, he asked Brown to design an approach road to take in views of the splendid new waters. Once again, things were not plain sailing: 'July 3rd Memo that his Lordship agreed to give me a bond for £300 [today £43,000] the Balance due to me on all accts for repairs of the water etc at Trentham. Dec Rec'd.'[187]

Most visitors were bowled over, though had he been aware of Viscount Torrington's observation, Brown would have been disappointed: 'My old friend L. Brown is to be traced at every turn: he certainly was a grand planner and leveller of ground here is very fine, but above the house.'[188]

Experts were few for engineering on such a scale, a novel and demanding science. Brindley was called in to Trentham fairly often. His installation of a pump coincided with Brown's improvements there. Then, according to his notebook diary, early in 1762, Brindley had a new collaborator: 'to mesure the Duks pools I and Smeaton'.[189]

John Smeaton FRS (1724–1792) was another highly regarded engineer, and a specialist in large atmospheric engines, with whom Brown collaborated. In 1761 Smeaton, John Grundy Jr and Langley Edwards published a joint report on the River Witham Navigation for Boston Corporation, where Commissioner John Wayet, Brown's brother-in-law, was involved. So it seems credible that Smeaton may have travelled cross-country to take surveys from Sale Moor to Stockport on Brown's recommendation to his clients Gower and Bridgewater. Both were scheming a ten-mile 'river road', the first commercial canal linking the Rivers Trent and Mersey, to transport coal from the Duke's Worsley collieries to the spinning mills of Manchester.

In 1769, at **Temple Newsam**, Yorkshire, Brown tasked Smeaton, living close by, with the supervision of hanging his grand Sphinx Gates. A local blacksmith's estimate gave the dimensions: '12 June 1768 an estimate made by Robert Johnson of the iron railings & gates for Lord Irwin according to Mr Brown's design being 17 ft wide & 8 ft high supposed to weigh 27 cwt more or less at 35/- per cwt = £47 5s 0d [£6,850].'[190]

The following year Smeaton designed and built an engine to pump water to the house, almost certainly part of Brown's holistic plans for the estate.[191] Further south in Wiltshire, the Tottenham agent had also been glad of Brown's professional advice involving pumps:

> *Mr Brown says the best method would be to dig broad Deep ditches or trenches, across the Hillside to catch the water & from thence to lay it in pipes – says he has done this with great success at Mr Mot – [sic]. But he would by all means advise the water to be brought from Crofton in Iron Pipes (abt 2 inch bore) as the only method that can be at all*

effectual. He thinks the old engine is constructed upon proper principles by forcing the water, and that many parts of it may be useful again.[192]

Recycling useful parts was not always effective in the long run. On his return after a three-year interval, his first directive involved a new engine: 'To Erect the Horse Engine and lay the Pipes from the New Well and Thatch the Woodhouse'.[193]

In 1769 James Watt (1736–1819) patented his condenser. His engine soon became the accepted model. Keeping abreast with scientific advances in the field, a Palladian 'water house' at Redgrave, Suffolk, faced in brick and rusticated stone and probably housing a similar pump, terminated Brown's fifty-acre lake. He was still involved at Croome in 1778 when they built an engine-house for a new steam engine to pump water to the tree nursery in addition to augmenting the supply to his 'pretend river'.

Following a severe winter in 1762, Brown, almost certainly recommended as a problem-solver, was faced with flooding a stone's throw from Shortgrove, at Audley End, as earlier discussed (see pp.66, 67). His solution suggested to the landowner, Sir John

June 2014, Audley End, Essex (EH) Brown's cedar of Lebanon (arrow) frames the house. Clouds of box hedging (star) hide the offices.

OPPOSITE **September 1991, Audley End, Essex** Compare today's river bend, two concave curves either side, with Brown's proposal (right) showing concave curves opposite convex curves. He recognised that land curving away, when viewed from the house (arrow, at a distance), would make the scale of the prospect seem even grander.

RIGHT Brown's plan for Audley End (1763) © Historic England. Brown ensured that the house was the pivotal focus in an amphitheatre of restful, open space. Note his intent to 'borrow' countryside prospects beyond Griffin's land across the main road to Cambridge. Griffin later bought land here for his temple and menagerie.

← VIEW FROM HOUSE

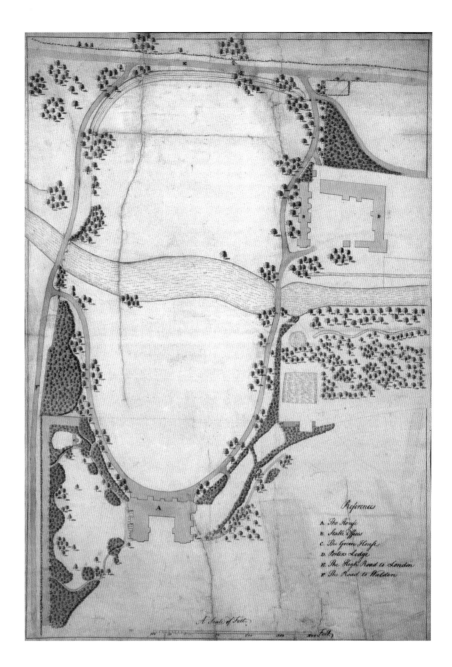

Griffin Griffin, was to make a cut across the meadow to turn the floods away from the village and into the River Cam. It did not take long before a plan was drawn up and an agreement signed to widen the swollen river to make a lake, 100 ft wide and 4 ft deep, giving an illusion of much greater distance, perspective and size of land-holding. Brown promised to distribute the excavated soil to improve and drain the low parts of the fields, to remove the straight central approach and all constraining avenues, buildings, walled gardens and a bowling green, and to tuck kitchen gardens and orchards out of sight behind the stables, to give the owner a natural landscape in contemporary style.[194]

Griffin Griffin was keen to have pumps driven by a water-wheel installed in 1763 to pump water from the river Cam to tanks in the roof of the house, from where it was piped around the house, a rare luxury at that time. Brown's workman-like sham bridge, built mostly in red brick and shaded by plane trees, carried his sweeping carriage drive from the house to the smart red-brick stables.

An elegant three-arch stone bridge (1728–92) designed by Robert Adam, a talented young Scottish architect, terminated the other, open end of the lake. All in all, it must have been a splendid sight when red-sailed boats drifted lazily past unhindered banks and acres of lawn. However, the client, far from satisfied

and less than honourable, withheld some £60 (today £7,800) of the contract. Brown angrily reminded Griffin Griffin of the outstanding debt, vowing that he would not 'labour more to convince Sir John as he knows there is none so blind as him that will not see'.

Pressured by weather events, let alone the complexity of finding the right level for his waters, a plan (1763) to create two lakes at **Bowood** (Wiltshire) overran the agreed date by two years.[195] In the course of damming two streams, the Washway and the Whetam, with a 30-ft-high dam 150 yards long, Brown ended up submerging the main Bath Road, and, even more controversial, he had to demolish the hamlet of Mannings Hill. In his poem *The Deserted*

Village, Oliver Goldsmith (1730–74), though a friend of Lord Shelburne, famously questioned the morality of destroying a community 'to make space for his lake', though Shelburne's new bride, Sophia Carteret, made no mention of this dilemma in her journal.[196]

June 16th [1766 Bowood]
As soon as breakfast was over we took a walk and were vastly pleased with the effect of the water which flows into a magnificent river, and only wants now to rise to its proper height, which it comes nearer to every day.

However, she did refer to employment and poverty issues, after commenting that Brown's plantations were 'young but very promising'.

March 17th 1768 [Bowood]
It being Good Friday we had prayers in the morning, after which I attempted taking a little walk, but was driven back by the cold. The work they are now upon is levelling the lawn before the house, to the edge of the water, for which the weather has been very unfavourable. My Lord is very much satisfied with Farmer Manfield, by whose care the park is got into fine order, and the flock of sheep increasing very fast; these circumstances and the number of workpeople employed there, make Bowood have no appearance of the scarcity so alarmingly conspicuous in most parts of this country, and so severely felt by the poor.

A century later, Charles Eliot, an American landscape architect, oblivious to such troubles of conscience and poverty, could only enthuse about the serpentine 'river' extending one and a half miles:

…very, very good … and the dam of the lake is well treated. There is a pretty region of wooded mounds, where no doubt earth from the lake excavation was dumped…. Yesterday I saw splendid Bowood, which Mr Henry Winthrop Sargent [influential American writer and horticulturalist] pronounced the second best in all England.

CHAPTER ELEVEN

ROYAL GARDENER AT HAMPTON COURT

The Earl of Coventry was more than happy to petition the Prime Minister, the Duke of Newcastle, to arrange an official position for Brown at Kensington Palace. His comfortable, stylish country house at Croome was nearing completion, amid magnificent embellishments to the setting. There was little doubt that his architect and improver was a rising star. Two dukes, ten peers and a single commoner were just as delighted to add their signatures in support of the petition (1758). Lord Brooke also approached the Paymaster, the Earl of Guildford: 'as he has been many years employed by me and as I have ever been thoroughly satisfied with his skill & undertaking in all he undertakes & as also with his just and truly honest Dealings with me in all respects'.

No notice was taken. Four years later, politics and court life had moved on. In his role as the new Tory prime minister, the Earl of Bute found he was personally responsible for realising the new young King George III's instructions for an improvement scheme for the gardens at Kensington as the Queen's Palace was being renovated. Bute called in Brown.

> *I return Brown's plan of Kensington, I am clear He ought to alter the Old part of the Garden, & that the part I objected to the other night should be more broke; by riding through the thickets I have seen many pretty forest plants which I fancy will do extrem'ly well for the plantations here; I wish my D.ˢ friend would enquire about it.*

OPPOSITE AND ABOVE **June 2008, Wilderness House, Hampton Court** The holm oak (above right) and the Scots pine (opposite, where once there were three) just outside its intimate walled garden, may date from Brown's day.

When one of the original petitioners, Cobham's nephew George Grenville, succeeded as prime minister, a royal announcement finally proclaimed: 'Lancelot Brown appointed chief Gardiner at **Hampton Court** during Pleasure on the 16th July 1764.'

Brown moved his family upriver to Wilderness House, a late-seventeenth-century three-storey red brick house in the grounds of Hampton Court Palace, conveniently next to the royal kitchen gardens. The following December he began the first page of a brand new account book, registering what was to become one of his most lucrative commissions, involving the development of the Prime Minister's estates, Luton Park, Bedfordshire, and Highcliffe on the Hampshire coast. After his retirement from politics, Bute remained the king's adviser and administrator of Kew Gardens, and continued to find the designer indispensable.

The Royal Court had not been held at the palace for thirty years, so Brown made few changes to the Privy Gardens and park, and kept wild turkeys in the Palace Wilderness. Providing fresh produce for the royal household was the priority. He had failed to become involved in improving the eight-acre

kitchen gardens at Windsor Castle. A suggestion for including them in his warrant had been made in a letter to Grenville even before he was appointed royal gardener, but ignored.[197] So now he planned instead a new kitchen garden at **Richmond**, George III's favourite palace, as well as upgrading the park for grazing. The king prized his flock of merino sheep, the first to be introduced from Spain.

Although he championed the arts and the foundation of the Royal Academy, this king is more widely remembered for his nickname, 'Farmer George', and for his parsimony. Sometimes Brown paid for plants out of his own pocket. All the same, he enjoyed a unique relationship with the monarch, more intimate than, a century earlier, his famous French counterpart, André Le Nôtre, was ever allowed with Louis XIV. Brown gave advice with such resolute authority that, from time to time, bizarrely the king was obliged to give way. Perhaps, through a shared passion for agriculture, the Hanoverian had won over the Borders man. The more Brown learned about the country's affairs, the more he became concerned, but not afraid to express deeply held sentiments over and above personal ambition: 'I love my King and my country.'

OPPOSITE LEFT **March 1991, Kew Gardens, London** A red oak, *Quercus rubra*, and cedars of Lebanon.

OPPOSITE RIGHT **June 2007, Kew Gardens, London** A veteran London plane tree shades this lowered walk.

ABOVE **May 2007, The Manor House, Fenstanton, Cambridgeshire (formerly Huntingdonshire)**

RIGHT **June 2013, The Manor House, Fenstanton, Cambridgeshire (formerly Huntingdonshire)** An old apple tree in the garden.

Full-time support was essential to help deal with royal requests at short notice, such as the provision of fruit for a banquet for a deputation from Oxford University. Needing someone to supervise his drawing office at Hampton Court, Brown engaged Samuel Lapidge (1740–1806) to oversee the gardens in his absence, and to accompany him for the occasional survey close to home. Draughtsman/surveyor John Spyers (d.1798), a nephew of the Twickenham nurseryman Joshua Spyers, became his right-hand man out of town. Promotion soon followed, and as 'Surveyor to His Majesty's Gardens and Waters at Hampton Court' and 'Gardiner' at St James's Palace, Brown was paid an additional £40 (£5,067) for 'looking after the Garden adjoining the Treasury'. Royal duties included providing plans for both Buckingham House and St James's Park.

Far from being restricted by Brown's twice-weekly royal attendances (on Tuesdays and Saturdays), his practice flourished, as clients clamoured for advice from the Royal Gardener and Surveyor. Of all his many improvements for the king at Richmond, only fragments remain. In order to create a diversion he dug out an area of the Thames alluvial flood plain. Now a part of Kew Gardens, his intimate 'Hollow Walk' winds through a bluebell dell, largely unnoticed among the wealth of other botanical attractions.

Meanwhile the Earl of Northampton was so heavily in debt that he could not afford to pay his bills for the considerable improvements at Castle Ashby in Northamptonshire. Brown was now financially secure enough to take advantage of an opportunity for investment. He negotiated the purchase of a small estate belonging to the earl, **Fenstanton Manor**

in Huntingdonshire, on the old Roman road from Cambridge to Huntingdon, including the villages of Conington and Elsworth, with rights to certain navigation tolls on the River Ouse.

Some fourteen years after leaving Stowe on £25 per annum, Brown was able to pay off the entire £13,000 (today £1,500,000) in two instalments over just six months. Northampton, seemingly more than content, endorsed his copy of the transfer deed: 'I take the Manor of Fen Standon to belong to Lawrence [sic] Brown Taste Esq., who gave the Lord Northampton Taste in exchange for it.'

If Brown ever lived in the timbered manor house, it was only briefly. A local Huntingdon nurseryman, James Wood, supplied a variety of fruit trees for 'Mrs Brown's garden'. A further 160 elms, at 6d each, were probably destined to shelter the brick and tiled manor farmhouse half a mile away. In 1770, Brown purchased land in Hardwick, Cambridgeshire, now

known as Victoria Farm, and as a prosperous, landed gentleman, with backing from the Earl of Sandwich, was appointed Sheriff of Huntingdon.

Upon leasing the manor house to a yeoman, in 1773 Brown took out an indemnity for £1,800 (today £204,300) with Sun Insurance Ltd covering both houses and, in addition, a kiln-house and dairy, both brick and tiled, and several thatched buildings: including another timber and tiled dairy, brew-house, malting office and chambers, 'quearn' (corn) house, chaff-house, cow-house, hog sties, stables, cart hovels and several barns for oat, wheat and barley. With Brown's contacts in the building trade, it was not long before this was upgraded with stone band-course dressings and pilasters and let to a yeoman farmer. Interior improvements included a wide, elegant staircase with turned and twisted balusters, and newels in the form of fluted Ionic columns.

Meanwhile at **Wardour** (Wiltshire), in 1772 the 8th Lord Arundell decided to dispense with the services of designer-cum-surveyor Richard Woods (1716–1793) who, for some eight years, had laboured to improve the estate. He had obviously heard that the Royal Gardener's fee was considerably cheaper, apparently only charging one guinea a day (today £125). Arundell was minded to commission a general plan, since, twenty years previously, his father had employed Brown. At that time the journeyman improver spent five days surveying, at £5 per day (today £725), before providing a plan for landscaping the area around the old castle for a further £25 (£3,625). Woods expressed both disappointment and disbelief: 'if the gentleman yr Lordship is pleased to mention had done business upon those terms, I know not how he could have raised a fortune of £2,500 [£362,500] per annum'.[198]

Brown took his time before finally presenting a plan (1775), a proposal for a string of three lakes. On learning the true cost of the ambitious scheme, Arundell realised his mistake and declined to engage him further. It was just as well, with the business almost too successful and under strain, and his travel schedule overloaded, not to mention the odd emergency demanding immediate action. Most other landowners deemed it worth the considerable expense of installing his experienced foreman, especially if Brown's perfectionist eye was guaranteed in return visits at agreed intervals over several years.

The royal gardener soon accrued sufficient financial collateral to set up both his future son-in-law, Henry Holland Jr (1745–1806), and his nephew, Richard Brown, in the practice. With income from his estate and rentals, he could contemplate sending his eldest son to Eton. A generous man, over and above supporting relatives, buying lottery tickets to aid various army charities, he showed interest in the diamonds inherited by his client Thomas Heron at Chilham only as a possible donation to the hospital of which he was governor. The poet Edward Lovibond bequeathed his capable and popular friend a one-third share in his Elm Lodge property at Hampton (Middlesex).

February 2007, Wimpole, Cambridgeshire (NT) Garden history students measuring a veteran beech to estimate its age.

After spending two hours in the designer's company at Wimpole, Cambridgeshire, Marchioness de Grey underlined meaningful words in a letter to her daughter-in-law, and could not contain her delight:

'Break of Break off, we tread Enchanted Ground' is almost literally true with me at present. Mr Brown has been leading me such a Fairy Circle and his magic Wand has raised such landscapes to the Eye, not Visionary for they were all there, but his Touch has brought them out with the same Effect as a Painter's Pencil upon Canvass.[199]

CHAPTER TWELVE

PAINTS AS HE PLANTS

The banker Henry Hoare II (1705–1785) was no aristocrat, but he won distinction in developing landscape gardens with dedication and flair.[200] Brown is known to have paid him a visit to Stourhead at least once, perhaps en route to other projects in the region, and in autumn 1752 opened an account with Hoare's Bank. Just six months later, something made him decide to transfer his money to Drummond's Bank, keeping his custom there for the rest of his life. Whether Brown advised Hoare, at this time making his great lake, remains an unanswered though plausible question.[201]

Naturally, with his passion for landscape, the banker kept an eye on Brown's progress. Later, hearing that his son-in-law, Baron Bruce, had commissioned improvements at Tottenham Park, he put pen to paper to register his approval:

> I am glad your Lordship has got Mr Browne [sic]. He has
> undoubtedly the best taste of anybody for improving nature by what
> I have seen of his Works. He paints as he plants; Before I doubt
> not that he will remove damps and the too great regularity of your
> Garden, far better to be turned into a park.[202]

OPPOSITE **April 2012, Roche Abbey, Yorkshire** Brown's planting included silver firs, *Abies alba*, and larches, *Larix decidua*.

ABOVE **November 2009, Corsham Court, Wiltshire** A palette of autumn beech leaves, *Fagus sylvatica*.

If, as Pope believed, 'All gardening is landscape painting', Stowe had been Brown's outdoor academy, nature's induction in universal principles of composition. Responsibility for managing this visual and intellectual feast had set in train Brown's advancement from journeyman engineer to accomplished garden designer. The ambience was grander than anything he had previously encountered. Cobham's open extravagance had implicit political and even erotic undercurrents, but Brown's initial awe of allegory in engraved stone and sculptured marble receded with familiarity as fresh, evolving 'frames' captivated his senses. Stability had allowed time to study predecessors' positioning of trees, noting foliage in early morning light or late afternoon shade, observing seasonal colour, variety in texture and density of tone. Kent's conifers lent a year-round backdrop to grotto, hermitage and temple: 'Mr Kent always used to stake out the grovettes before they were planted and to view the stakes every way, to see that no three of them stand in a line.'[203]

Like most hands-on designers, who would personally stake out principal feature trees, Brown would have followed the same method. A Grand Tour in Italy was not essential to school his eye. If he seldom ventured abroad, he witnessed a growing, European-inspired patronage of the arts.[204]

Attendance at social gatherings in decorative salons throughout the country proved stimulating, even educational, as society leaders showed off prized paintings, classical 'landskips' by Claude Lorraine, Nicolas Poussin and Salvator Rosa.[205] Some clients challenged Brown to conjure equivalent, evocative compositions outside in the grounds, framed by their country-house windows. Claude Lorraine paintings at Sherborne Castle are said to have inspired his plans for a lake between Sir Walter Raleigh's Tudor mansion house and the old castle ruins. Staying one night at Combe Abbey, Brown described the atmosphere in a letter to Bridget, telling her about the pictures on his bedroom walls, including a Charles I portrait. So observant was he, so determined to learn, it seems hardly surprising that he occasionally dabbled in watercolour, capturing the odd scene on his travels.[206]

Once he offered to collect the artist Giovanni Battista Cipriani (1727–1785)[207] for the journey from London to Bowood, eager to spend time in the company of a gifted Royal Academician. Brown also dealt in artworks. There are payments to two upcoming artists, William Marlow (1740–1813) and Thomas Gainsborough (1727–1788), in his Drummond's Bank account. Clients began to appreciate Brown's flair for interior space. At Burghley, amid exquisite tapestries and baroque murals, Brown supervised the display of paintings, pottery and sculpture that the Earl of Exeter brought back from Italy. When Exeter declined his Clérisseau paintings, he despatched them to William Constable, a Yorkshire client.[208]

Living at Chiswick, half a mile upriver from Brown's Hammersmith home, the painter and satirist William Hogarth (1697–1764) aimed at 'fixing the fluctuating Ideas of Taste' by extolling the value of the 'line of grace', the serpentine. A defining moment in the comprehension of visual pleasure came with the publication of his *The Analysis of Beauty* (1753), a

book that contributed greatly to the trend for 'natural' gardening by combining personal observations of nature with 'infinite variety' (using words borrowed from Shakespeare).[209] Brown's plans were already displaying easy, calming curves at the edge of a wood or in an oblique approach road or path snaking towards some surprise around the next corner.

Years earlier, to please Queen Caroline, Charles Bridgeman had constructed a large natural-looking lake in Hyde Park, the Serpentine, but the Rocque map of London (1746) shows a distinct lack of contoured bends. Brown became known for his serpentine line. Design conviction came with experience and careful scrutiny. He engaged onlookers by completely altering the symmetry of settings, seamlessly softening hard features, rounding squared edges, extending garden boundaries into pleasure

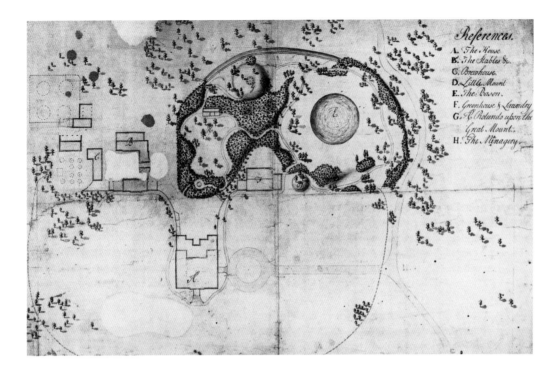

grounds, and even ensuring that open drainage ditches in plantations were not straight. He found many ways to exploit the concept on a large scale, developing pleasing meanders and 'swan's-neck' terminations to his artificial rivers. Ironically, just as greater quantities of exotic trees, plants and seeds were arriving from America, South Africa and the Far East, an expansive English style of gardening was quietly evolving in rural areas as Brown instinctively embraced the 'wavy line' that complemented the undulating topography of the English countryside.

A freer approach, rather than the regimented formality interpreted by some as a sign of autocracy, resonated in some political quarters, suiting the more mobile, free-thinking, moneyed classes for whom nature and country pursuits were all the rage. Wilder, more natural gardens symbolised liberty, as being open for observation and exploration – to chosen visitors. Besides, the wealthy could afford coal, so pollarding of trees for fuel was considered both unnecessary and unfashionable in parkland. Even if Brown broke the grand avenue from Warwick Castle mount across to Temple Hill to expose a view from Spier's Lodge back to the castle, radical felling of entire avenues was rare.

He did not cut down Burghley's lime trees, planted at the turn of the eighteenth century by London and Wise in a *patte d'oie* (goosefoot) arrangement. They were in their prime, though he curtailed and offset where they terminated. Similarly, the stately two-mile double-lined elm approach to **Wimpole** escaped his axe, as also straight woodland walks in Switzer's bastion garden at Grimsthorpe.[210] Brown's plans accommodated both the lime avenue walk at **Ampthill**, Bedfordshire, and the long rides or 'ridings' for hunting at Hallingbury, Essex. In the principal view from Hampton Court Palace, he cut only lateral park views through his predecessor's *Königslind* lime avenue, while leaving serried ranks of yew trees lining the canal to grow unclipped as nature intended, to relieve their military uniformity.

Other than one £200 payment (today £29,000), an anonymous poem (*right*) penned in 1758 is the only evidence regarding Brown's employment in converting a flooding stream into a lake at Astrop, Northamptonshire, for the lawyer and MP for Aylesbury Sir John Willes. The poem confirms the landscape improvements made and demonstrates, in transplanting the abeles (white poplars or *Populus alba*), a real

At Astrop Brown his skill display'd
In Woods & Lawns & clear Cascades
The first from fetter'd Rules set free
And made the Lawns with these agree
The murmuring Streams & chrystal Floods
Join'd to improve the Lawns & woods
The Work & Workman all commend
Nor found one fault for Taste to mend
Till Blagrave came the Place to view
Who gave each Beauty Praises due,
With piercing Eyes the whole Survey'd
Resembling much the blue-ey'd Maid
Genteel erect & tall she stood,
And seemed the Goddess of the Wood,
With perfect Shape & lively Face
Expressing Majesty & Grace.
These stiff Abeles she said displease
See there beyond those rising Trees!
A noble object I descry,
Which with a forest seems to vye.
No Artist e'er could mean she cry'd
The Glories of that Scene to hide
The wood appear'd, th'Abeles were mov'd
And Brown th'happy Change approv'd.
Anon

flexibility and willingness to listen to others' ideas, attributes with all the hallmarks of Brown.[211]

A later contract (1774) departed from the normal, practical 'down-to-earth' grammar of improvement, seeking to impress on Lord Scarborough his grasp of current aesthetic taste by a newly published epic poem, *The English Garden*.[212] Brown proposed, having spotted the artistic potential of Roche Abbey ruins, to dress a valley near **Sandbeck** (Yorkshire) 'with Poet's Feeling and with Painter's Eye'.

The workforce covered untidier parts of the old ruins with excavated soil from his lake, Laughton Dam, and levelled those areas disturbed when making the sunk fence and land drains. Finally, they sowed a mix of grass and Dutch clover to unite the scene. Brown left a few tall Gothic arches to retain an air of sanctity and mystery. They framed picturesque views like ships' masts anchored in a sea of lawn.[213] He had seen what Jane Austen later perceived: the melancholic effect of such skeletal silhouettes. Derelict abbeys recalled the ghosts of early religious communities and haunted imaginations with nostalgia and regret.[214]

Over and above beauty, land was far more essential for meat and sport, even if observation of nature, taste

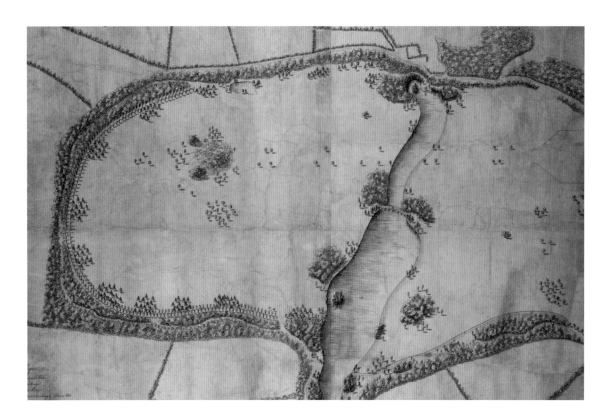

LEFT Brown Plan (c.1767) of Wimpole Estate, Cambridgeshire © NT Images. Detail for the north park. The scale of planting led to a huge order of trees. Dotted lines reveal various existing paths and hedges to be removed. What is unusual is the regimented planting and numbers of stands of conifers breaking up the perimeter (left). Brown sought to counterbalance the impressive existing two-mile-long double elm avenue south. A 'broken up' avenue leads to the intended eye-catcher, a sham castle ruin.

OPPOSITE July 2009, Wimpole, Cambridgeshire (NT) The Gothic Tower framed by a London plane in the park.

and the art of improvement were closely interwoven in landowners' ambitions and conversations. Farming had made major advances, and took priority in order to return a quick profit in the short term. Brown persuaded clients to visualise long-term benefits: well-fed horses in pastures, and herds of fattened deer, cattle and sheep grazing extended lawns and drinking at the water's edge. Most, including the Duke of Northumberland and even King George III, took a keen interest in agricultural production.

In the mid-1750s, fears of a French invasion led many landowners, especially those directly involved with the Navy who were passionate about shipbuilding for the defence of the realm and its colonies, to offer improvers moneymaking opportunities to secure future timber supplies. Brown set out his perimeter plantations, narrow, curving oak and beech belts, occasionally interspersed with Scots pine and an under-storey of yew, to enclose each park in a reassuring sylvan embrace, almost like irregular 'battalions' defending the park space from winds. A Huntingdon nurseryman, James Woods, supplied Brown's large order for Wimpole, including 3,000 large elms, 10 to 12 ft high, and 2,050 small elms,

at 6 ft.[215] Imagine, in 1769, the difficulty of delivering such quantities by horse and cart.

English elm, *Ulmus procera*, had great presence. Its hard-wearing wood was as prized for ornamental use as for its resistance to decay when wet, with many practical purposes besides, especially in furniture and shipbuilding. Brown embellished Warwick Castle Park with 1,200 elms.[216] By the end of the nineteenth century, thousands of Brown's trees had matured into 'magnificent specimens of oak and elm'.[217] Magnificent, towering elm trees were dominant in many of his parks until struck down by Dutch elm disease, a fungus spread by elm beetles in the 1970s that devastated the appearance of the English countryside and parkland. This significant element of Brown's planting is lost and now may only be imagined. Sometimes it proved impossible to 'see the wood for trees'.[218] The initial task at both Beechwood (Hertfordshire) and Caversham (Berkshire) was to grade, thin and tidy up existing overgrown woodlands and scrub to gain better growth, to let in light and to open up views. Where trees were coppiced, he advised choosing a 'leader' shoot to grow on later.

John Evelyn (1620–1706) gave oak, *Quercus robur*, pride of place in his celebrated and motivating treatise *Sylva* on trees. Switzer agreed: 'We have the more durable and serviceable Blessing of Oak, which abundantly commands them all, I mean our Ships and the Balance of Trade.'[219]

Essential for building and the Navy, oak could be turned into furniture, tools, tubs and cartwheels, and barrels for beer, cider and whisky. Rapid industrial growth, particularly in iron-smelting and glass-making, was greatly increasing demand for timber, while huge quantities of oak bark provided a vital ingredient for tanning hides in the leather industry.

Notably respecting ancient trees and pollards with character, Brown incorporated them into designs such as those at **Moccas** (Herefordshire) and Wotton (Buckinghamshire). He suggested that easy-to-grow forest trees, particularly long-lived oaks, should be thinly scattered among the plantations, even among evergreen clumps. Later works, aiming for neat plantations and flawless prospects, show a differentiation between clumps in one area of a park and numbers of single oaks in open grazing ground. Planting hundreds of new trees, young whips each

kept upright with a stake, and protected from deer by paling, was labour-intensive. Single feature trees enclosed in protective wood or iron railing were also not particularly attractive. Given time and patience, modern planting would mature to look glorious, and required less upkeep than old-style gardens, suiting those aristocrats who came to their country estate for only a few weeks or months of the year. The best bonus, timber proved a lucrative crop, worth every penny of long-term investment.

Vigilant against problems of scale, Brown ordered all small, badly grown trees overshadowed by large ones to be cut down, and ensured other selective clearances. At Ashridge, Hertfordshire, he cut through dense swathes of forest so as to leave individual, moulded copses of trees in a contrived, spacious 'Golden Valley', before directing new clumps to be planted 'so that trees do not touch each other'. Layered 'quick' hedges of prickly hawthorn made ideal stock-proof barriers around farms, and were to be conveniently 'buck-headed' so as to enable people to see over them: 'Old Thorns in the Park – Cut off the heads of half a score Thorns in a Year, & let them spring again About the month of February the proper time.'[220]

Annual tasks to maintain a degree of tidiness and to reinvigorate shrubs and small trees were assiduously promoted. As late as 1917, Brown was considered a 'famous forester'. He prompted foremen to remember to collect acorns and beech mast and actively encouraged the replenishment of the forest with oaks from the nursery, protected by furze (gorse) or thorn; he suggested spreading around ashes from brick kilns and charcoal-making 'before the Salts were washed out'. Both good stewardship and regeneration were essential to the science of silviculture.[221]

Finding the grounds at Chilham Castle well stocked, Brown considered further planting unnecessary: 'he has recommended some management of the Woods and Tillage of the Ground, which will expel the Deer, to save an unreasonable expense of fencing against them'.[222]

Laying out the gardens here, the royal gardener John Tradescant (d.1637) is reputed to have introduced European larch, *Larix decidua*. Brown went on to encourage landowners to plant great numbers of these fast-growing trees as well as pines,

because larch afforded a more secure, greater, faster profit than any other tree grown in the country. Larch also provided useful 'thinnings' that could be used at all stages of growth for shipbuilding, fencing, 'rosaries' and pergolas. Hence many are long since felled, though odd remnants lurk in corners of aged, Brownian shelter belts.

The Chelsea 'Physick' Garden, the centre of economic botany and the most important horticultural market in Europe, was witnessing a marked increase in stock. As propagation and breeding improved, approximately a hundred important nurseries and seedsmen were established in England and Wales. Plants could be bought by mail order, named and categorised by the Linnaean system, including trees imported from Holland by the thousand. The contract specification for Bowood (Wiltshire) is typical: 'Brown to find all Forrest Trees and also under Wood, His lordship to find the curious Trees and Tree Seeds, Brown to plant them.'[223]

In London Brown spread his nursery orders around, variously dealing with John Williamson, James Lee and

May 1996, Southill, **Bedfordshire** Spring-green deciduous trees and contrasting evergreen yews reflected in the shallow waters of Brown's lake.

Lewis Kennedy at the Vineyard, Hammersmith; James Scott, Turnham Green; Thomas Ash, Twickenham, and many others.[224] Occasionally he obtained sizeable trees from French nurseries.[225] He recommended William Perfect (Pontefract, Yorkshire) to clients in the north. 3,000 alders, *Alnus glutinosa*, trees that will tolerate both flood and drought, came from Rotterdam for Audley End, at a cost of £4 2s 0d (£580). Clients living in remote areas were advised to grow on their own trees.[226] Following Brown's second consultation in north Lincolnshire, Brocklesby's head gardener, William Dicker, purchased numbers of small trees: 'Mountain berryes and horse chestnuts, two bushels each; 200 "Filbert" or hazel; 6 rosemary trees'.

Nurse trees from Skitter near Beverley, 100 spruce and 42 larch, arrived by boat across the Humber via Brigg. Thanks to this patient forward planning, Brown ensured there would be sufficient resources to implement his master plan (1771). By 1776, his contract stipulated: 'Mr Pelham to find Trees and shrubs of which there are a plenty in his own Nursery'.[227]

Viscount Torrington, at **Southill**, Bedfordshire, reported to the Duke of Portland, who was employing Brown's brother John as agent:

> *Lancelot Brown came here yesterday & has given me a pretty idea of my Place which perhaps (if I am not Bankrupt first) will be better than I expected it could be made. Immediately however we are to begin a Nursery as that is the most Essentiall accessory you know and the Planting of one of the Warren Hills I think is to be our Winter Work.… the Plan he has not yet finished.*[228]

Over and above planting huge numbers of young trees, 14,000 beech and 21,000 oak trees at Tottenham, one substantial order (1766) from a Berkshire nurseryman, William Pendar, lists a surprising number of conifers, including *Thuja* (Tree of Life, *Arbor Vitae*) and *Cupressus* among mature 10- and 12-ft trees, evergreen oak, cedar, larch, bay, strawberry tree, spruce and juniper, tulip tree and oriental plane. Besides writing down questions

in advance and making sure that Brown's bed was well aired, the agent Charles Bill kept Lord Bruce abreast of Brown's work: 'Spent a considerable time in marking the Spots where he would have little choice plants such as Cedars, small Weymouth Pine, Larch, *Arbor Vitae* [Cypress, Portugal Laurels] scattered about upon the Grass near the Serpentine.'[229]

Bill noted Brown's meticulous 'Memoranda of Instructions', a litany of specific embellishments and modifications, many brief and to the point: 'Add some Spruce firs amongst the Scotch.'[230]

The creation of model vistas was fast becoming a preoccupation, though arguably field sports had an equal influence on the design equation. Game shooting, mainly for partridge, in those days a more solitary sport, was increasingly popular in the light of improving gun technology. Woodland shelter belts, where Brown provided evergreens for roosts among mixed deciduous planting, encouraged game birds to fly high. By the 1760s fox-hunting was also becoming more organised. Brown's proposals for small groves and narrow woodland thickets for cover (recorded as 'covert' plantations on later surveys) led to the conversion of hundreds of acres of nondescript bog or moorland into sporting territory. Thin strips of strategically placed woodland made little impact when first planted, so Brown took pains to add interest by laying down an attractive wavy edge to plantations.

Sir William Chambers, at this time closely involved in the design of Kew Gardens for Princess Augusta, ridiculed this rival's landscape as nothing other than a collection of 'a few American weeds'. In fact, during the 1750s Brown had pioneered mass planting of conifers in the English countryside. At Kirtlington, Oxfordshire, beyond his 'fosse' or sunk fence, he experimented by establishing a protective Scotch fir belt, together with a wide semicircle of fir clumps.

A Stowe garden guide (1769) described the Grecian valley just as Brown's first attempt at planting up virgin territory was maturing: 'a large and beautiful vale adorned with Statues of various kinds intermixed with Clumps of Trees beautifully disposed'.[231]

Not everyone was satisfied. At Warwick Castle, Lord Brooke was critical: 'I have ever undone many things he left me as I thought looking Formal in the planting way, ever making round clumps that merit nothing but being very tame indeed.'[232]

Elsewhere, numerous Scots pines planted together with wild cherry, *Prunus avium* and *Prunus avium plena*, in contrast with wind-tolerant 'forest' birches or silver birches, *Betula pendula*, acted as nursery trees to protect young hardwood plantations of beech and oak. When these were eventually cropped and sold for firewood, stands of stately oak and beech remained for generations to come. Shelter belts, as they were later known, because the trees lifted and filtered the wind, created a notion of security, either arranged along valleys to emphasise the form of the land, or on horizons to close the view, which would transfer the focus to key features within the park. Oak belts, with leaves turning nut-brown in autumn, are famously slow-growing, but stable, and in time create an impression of longevity and strength.

A resilient conifer with rusty-red bark that will grow on marginal land, acid heath and on the arid south coast, Scots pine, *Pinus sylvestris*, is the only pine native to Britain. Inexpensive and easily grown cold from seed, it proved valuable in shipbuilding, particularly as masts for ships, and as a source for resin, turpentine, tar and pitch. It was ideal for building, fencing, furniture and as firewood for ovens; its lower branches and 'fir-apple' cones gathered by local children 'appling' provided both fuel for the poor and fodder for deer and sheep. 'Forty Scotch firrs 13 foot and upwards' costing 30s (today £271) headed Brown's first order for Petworth, Sussex.

Beech, *Fagus sylvatica*, is tolerant of most soils and omnipresent in Brown landscapes.[233] At Chatsworth, Derbyshire, besides beech, Brown planted huge numbers of thorn, rowan, spruce and oak. On the high ridge east, the principal park view from the house, he organised Calton New Piece plantation in wedge-shaped sections, ensuring that, with subsequent clear felling and replanting, the tree line, with occasional stands of silvered beech trunks, would always hold fast on the horizon.

The Royal Society of Arts considered tree planting of such national importance that it offered prizes

to encourage the expansion of forestry, particularly in the barren uplands of the north. After Brown had planted 100,000 oaks and nurse conifers at Fisherwick, Staffordshire, the society awarded a silver medal to his client, the Earl of Donegal. The Earl of Upper Ossory, too, later received a gold medal, again thanks to Brown's ambitious planting programme for the charming, undulating topography at Ampthill, Bedfordshire. Clumps of mature, spiral-barked sweet chestnut intermingling with beech and Scots pine still frame breathtaking views on the high Greensand Ridge above the house.

Of course, it took considerable time and patience before, with the eventual removal of stakes and protective fencing, the desired effect was achieved. Brown went on to master the art of 'un-squaring' formality. In the 1770s 40,000 'Scotch Firs' were ordered following his advice at Grimsthorpe (Lincolnshire), a legacy of forestry practice later respected by Arthur Young.[234]

Where one or two trees were diseased, as on the rather narrow oak avenue approach to Langley (Buckinghamshire), Brown interrupted and transformed the line into groves, to open up rural vistas.[235] Expediting excavations at **Moor Park**, Hertfordshire, his task force had to invent hillocks with the lake spoil, before decking them with clusters of trees: 'I was not much struck with it, after the miracles I had heard Brown had performed there. He has undulated the horizon in so many artificial molehills that it is as full unnatural as if it was drawn with a rule and compass.'[236]

Walpole's censure suggests that the improver was digging up and repositioning mature trees with his tree machine (see p.39). Ten years' growth later, Thomas Whately had nothing but praise: 'They recede one beyond the other, and the outline waves agreeably among them. They do more than conceal the sharpness of the edge; they convert a deformity into a beauty, and greatly contribute to the embellishment of this most lovely scene.'[237]

A single clump, a company as opposed to a battalion, placed on the horizon or on top of a natural eminence, created a strong point of reference. A number of clumps contributed character, added height or emphasised upward slopes. Receding, rounded,

mixed or single-species clumps were also practical to 'take off the flatness', a contrast to linear shelter belts, and to lead the eye through the middle distance towards the horizon. The Tottenham agent confirmed Mr Brown's trademark simplification of 'ideal' country views. '[He] spoke much in commendation of shady rides as so frequently agreeable both in summer & winter, a fence both against heat & cold…. He seems very fond of leaving large clumps made upon the downs at a distance.'[238]

Radical changes to largely agricultural landscape at **Shortgrove**, Essex, are revealed when comparing two surveys (1727) and (1786).[239] The latter bears evocative names, 'Ice-house Plantation', 'Hollow Lane Plantation', '40 Acre Wood', 'Temple Plantation', 'Water Lane Plantation', which, though no plan survives, may be assumed to be mostly the product of Brown's advice, including hollowing out a road, with curving sunk fences and lawn replacing earlier axial avenues and regular gardens near the house.

Brown removed mature trees surrounding Butfield and those on two sides of another square field, leaving a shady walk along the remaining double row of trees. Two large clumps of trees, one disguising old gravel pits, served as middle-distance features, straddling a new, more convenient approach from the south. Notably, some square and in one case triangular stands of trees remained unaltered, with new, smaller, circular groves typically dotted around in focal positions. A large, rounded 'Engine Field Plantation' swallowed up a rectangular wood.

Some years later, having widened the River Cam, Brown returned to suggest further refinements, when Matthew Brettingham (1699–1769) is thought to have designed a bridge and a temple eye-catcher on the now tree-clad western boundary overlooking the river. The architect was building the palatial Egremont House[240] in London while Brown spearheaded the 'new making' of its town garden. A Kensington nurseryman, John Williamson, supplied three large standard elms, two large standard almonds and one standard horse chestnut, in modern terms an 'instant makeover'.[241]

It was out in the country that the biggest changes were seen. The Trentham contract confirms Brown's particular approach: 'Article the 4th To plant all the necessary Plantations for hiding the Village the Offices and the Edge of the Water and the Head.'[242] Dense groves of horse chestnut, sweet chestnut or holm oak screened untidy farm buildings, obtrusive kitchen garden walls or engine-houses. Meanwhile, thickets of evergreens hid outlets from main drains, and anything artificial.

On one early first visit to remote **Burton Constable**, Yorkshire, Brown provided both acorns and beech mast to start a new estate nursery. Returning every September, he rode out with landowners, agents and foremen to vantage points in the park to inspect progress. One of the first instructions advised: 'Make your clumps large and massy.'[243] Suggestions to manage and refine planting came thick and fast: lop boughs here, lift the canopy there, enlarge clumps, grub out trees to let in light, remove and transplant young trees. Exhaustive, succinct and uncompromising, instructions emphasised the importance of good drainage, bold planting and long-term planning:

> *Small Clumps are nothing, only pimples upon the Face of Nature.... Keep all the Plantations well drained with serpentine Grips [small open ditches].*[244]*... Clump on each side of the New road in the Park Pale, about 30 or 40 feet distance from each side of the New Road [to leave room for a Lodge] – Large clumps about 100 or 200 feet in diameter.*[245]*... Opening thro' the West Avenue – When the Plantation screed on the East side of the Lawn towards North wood in George Harrison's Ground is planted and grown up, then will be the proper time to make openings and not before by any means. Dare not touch till then.*[246]*... Mix the trees promiscuously in the plantations & Clumps & don't plant them in patches.*[247]

A stand of trees made a strong feature, especially where roads diverged. Large mixed plantations, some disguising an unsightly clay pit, brick pit or quarry, were intended to be closed in, solid and dark with an under-storey of hawthorn, fenced off from deer or cattle.[248] Conversely, adding variety, single-species groves with no under-planting were to be kept clear of weeds, and thistles 'paddled' down, letting the light through

so that manicured trunks threw graceful shadows. One hundred hollies, nine and ten inches high, were transplanted to create an under-storey and, as light relief, thirty-eight single and double flowering almonds. All dead or decayed trees were to be 'recruited' (cut down), and large trees shredded or 'stripped up to about 10 feet high'. In thinning out ash trees, he suggested replacing them with 'better kinds': oak, elm, beech or larch. In 1775, Grimwoods (Little Chelsea) supplied 2,000 two-year-old beech. Four years later, a further 2,000 beeches, 9 ft tall for more immediate impact, came from nearby Sigstons of Beverley. Andrew Carr of Cottingham transported 900 European larches for sandy locations in North Wood. A clump of silver fir, *Abies alba*, also featured in the design.

Castle Ashby (Northamptonshire) was one place where Brown dispensed with the existing double avenue approach. His foreman, Jonathan Midgeley, reported every achieved improvement: 'I have taken down both the elms, as I could not bring the ground very well together without; and I have shortened the spinny and taken down some of the limes and trimmed some up, so as to let your eye through, without making an avenue'.[249]

CHAPTER THIRTEEN

NOW THERE
I MAKE A COMMA

Strolling in Hampton Court gardens one mild December day, in 1782, Brown came across Hannah More (1745–1833),[250] an intelligent young playwright, and close friend of the Garrick family. She was evidently good company, for the overworked designer enjoyed her conversation for two hours. Afterwards, in a letter to her sisters in Gloucestershire, Hannah relayed how she had been both charmed and amused by 'my friend Mr Brown' who 'promised to give me taste by inoculation'. He had arrived at a witty analogy for his endeavours, injecting a literary interpretation that, as a writer moving in the same circles as Dr Johnson, she readily appreciated:

> 'Now there', said he, pointing his finger, 'I make a comma, and there,' pointing to another spot, 'where a more decided turn is proper, I make a colon; at another part, where an interruption is desirable to break the view, a parenthesis; now a full stop, and then I begin another subject.'[251]

More than a playful way with words, perhaps his spatial understanding of survey triangulation influenced the balanced subtlety of his planting. Feature trees, or clumps, are often in loose arrangements of three. Brown effectively introduced a new and entertaining activity for people to enjoy, encapsulated in this one sentence, the art of reading landscape.

OPPOSITE **May 2010, Packington, Warwickshire** Great cedars of Lebanon screen the kitchen garden walling.

ABOVE **May 1989, Denwick Hills, near Alnwick** One of the first panoramas, on the Duke of Northumberland's estate, that drew me to explore Brown's works.

Building on ideas first learned from Stowe, Brown was perhaps the first to realise that landscape, or more particularly his natural method of design, is something akin to perusing a book. The eye could be trained to read the scene. There was real underlying geometry, a harmonious system between the species chosen and their arrangement to suit location and relationship to other trees.

At some sites Brown spied, and probably appreciated, remarkable veteran trees, some named for Queen Elizabeth I, such as the surviving 'Elizabeth Oak' at Heveningham (Suffolk) and the 'Elizabeth Tree' at Wynnstay, once the largest tree in Wales.[252] His original plan for the sunk fence at Lee (Lewisham in London) was amended in order to enclose a fine spreading oak, considered unique.

Traces of Brown's distinctive 'grammar', now veteran trees, remain in well-preserved sites that, although apparently random, are notable for strength of position – good trees in good places: at the bottom of a fold between two hills, on a horizon, or at the end of a lake. Some act as guardians to architectural features. Others divide a panorama into separate sections, frame vistas or draw the eye to a notable highlight. Brown's secret was an ability to envisage the long-term, three-dimensional quality of every tree he planted. He thought in terms of foreground, middle and distant space, so a 'natural' pattern evolved. Foremen and head gardeners accompanying him to stake out tree positions and plantations soon learned Brown's guiding principle and attempted to school their imagination by observation just as he had done: 'Allow each tree Room, supposing it to be full grown.'

The Shortgrove contract refers to retention and transplantation.[253] A handsome, fully-grown tree was repositioned for immediate foreground interest, so as to break the horizontal line of the snaking ha-ha or take the eye from a young, monotonous and spindly tree belt. Brown's unique 'tree-bob' machine (see p.39) used horse traction to move mature trees of some bulk, helped tear up roots and transport both tree and almost intact root ball to another site 'to suit the prospect and the landscape'.[254] Rather than labouring to dig a big hole in the new spot, labourers firmed soil

up around the roots, a quicker, easier task. Hence the transplanted tree, initially stabilised with guy ropes, appeared to stand on top of a small mound, a useful diversion, especially in flat terrain.[255] By the 1770s, with hindsight, Brown concluded that there was no real advantage to such practice: 'Not fond of removing large Trees as they never make Trees good for anything afterwards; the lopping of the Boughs (without which they cannot be removed) spoils them.'[256]

What may seem astonishing is that Brown planted sycamores.[257] These trees, like the distinctive, palmate, large-leaved horse chestnut, *Aesculus hippocastanum* (introduced in the 1600s), could withstand wind and would grow almost anywhere

LEFT **June 2013, Lowther Castle, Cumbria** A magnificent, 'gate guardian' sycamore, *Acer pseudoplatanus*.

TOP **March 2008, Belvoir Castle, Leicestershire** The bark of *Robinia pseudoacacia* on the approach, with recognisable Gothic texture.

ABOVE *Catalpa bignonioides*, Indian bean tree, in flower.

in England's temperate climate. Look again at the conspicuous position and profile of the lone sycamore in Brown's parks, sometimes on a horizon in full view of the house (see p.49) or near an entrance lodge, its branches stretching wide as if in welcome, for some a subtle reminder of eighteenth-century politics. Where Hanoverians favoured the common small-leaved lime, *Tilia x europaea*, a sweet-smelling tree that helped to mask odours,[258] Whig sympathisers heralded the plane as a symbol of liberty.

One Petworth order included a button tree, *Platanus occidentalis* (a type of American sycamore), two Virginia maples, *Acer saccharum* (sugar maple), and two American maples, *Acer platanoides*. A hundred 6–8-ft planes, *Acer pseudoplatanus* (European sycamore maple), cost in total 50s (today £342), saplings that he knew were deer-proof, and if planted singly in open ground would mature to magnificent size and shape.[259] At Blenheim two sycamore maples marked the site of the old palace at Woodstock.

Walpole credited the introduction of foreign trees and plants to Archibald, 3rd Duke of Argyll, calling him the 'tree monger' who 'contributed essentially to the richness of colouring so peculiar to our modern landscape'.[260] For Freemasons like Walpole, the 'Sprig of Acacia', a biblical tree, the building material of the tabernacle and Holy Ark, signified initiation and innocence and symbolised the immortality of the soul. The quick-growing, relatively long-lived American native, *Robinia pseudoacacia* (false acacia), was his favourite tree. Brown too appreciated its light, feathery foliage and the fragrant racemes of drooping white pea flowers in May, and placed it often on an approach as an effective contrast for dark evergreen cedars. Brown too would have delighted in the acacia's winter silhouette, its ridged and furrowed bark, like Gothic tracery. A William Tomkins painting of Audley End (1788) depicts an immature cedar of Lebanon near

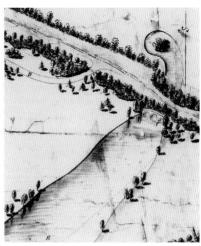

LEFT **March 1998, Wakefield Lodge, Northamptonshire** Native white willow, *Salix alba* (left); imported weeping willow, *Salix babylonica* (right).

ABOVE Thumbnail detail from Brown's plan (1768) for Hills, Sussex. The sham three-arch bridge and lake are screened from the approach. A view of the lake, framed by conifers and weeping willows in the Chinese fashion, came as a charming surprise.

the house on a small knoll, with a false acacia nearby. The cedar stood for 'Strength' and 'Think of Me'.[261] Several friends, including Garrick, some clients and a fair number of people with whom he collaborated, belonged to various Lodges. The majority, brought up as Christians, Brown included, believed they were doing God's work, but there is no record of Brown being a member of a Freemasons' lodge.

On every nursery visit the eagle-eyed Brown selected the best specimens of flowering trees for his pleasure grounds at Petworth. Alongside twenty-one 10-ft acacias from Hammersmith nurseryman John Williamson, a 13-ft specimen of *Catalpa bignonioides*, a handsome, spreading deciduous tree with large leaves and bell-shaped flowers in August, cost the huge sum of three guineas (today £431). According to Mark Laird, this was probably one of Mark Catesby's original American plants, introduced to London in 1726.

Twickenham nurseries supplied the royal gardens at Richmond and Kew. As villa gardens followed suit, imported exotics began appearing all along the Thames. Pope and, later, Garrick edged their Thames-side garden slopes with graceful weeping willows, *Salix babylonica*, from China (see p.45). Unsurprisingly, Brown ordered six to border the Upper Lake at Petworth, to give his client a fashionable touch of the orient. Plans for Wimpole (Cambridgeshire) and Hills (Sussex), among others, are dotted with silhouettes of trees with their distinctive, trailing habit on the edge of his 'pretend rivers'.

> *Lord Bruce has had the offer of some setts, Cuttings or plants of* Weeping Willows *which he thinks are Picturesque and in the taste of Forest Birch Trees, a few of which might be scattered about one or two corners of the lower Canal if Mr Brown approves of it.*

The response to the Tottenham agent, anxious not to upset Brown, was typically economical: 'No objections to the Weeping Willows'.[262]

Native white willow, *Salix alba*, with subtle, light silver foliage, and grey poplar, *Populus canescens*, a cross between white poplar and aspen, may have been more to Brown's taste, and readily obtainable.

During a long association with Croome, consignments of plants arrived from America (1750s), St Petersburg (1771) and the Far East (1770s). Arthur Young later rated Croome second only to Kew in botanical interest, noting 'tripple-thorned acacia' (or honey locust, an American introduction), *Gleditzia triacanthos* together with birch, and a handsome turkey oak, *Quercus cerris*, native to south-eastern Europe and Asia Minor. He also spotted a *Gingko biloba*, a rare Chinese maidenhair tree, first introduced in 1754 when the craze for *chinoiserie* was at its height.

Fast-growing, male fastigiate black poplar, *Populus nigra italica* or Lombardy poplar, was first introduced into England in about 1758. The full architectural effect of Brown's planting of these, 'sparingly and in a judicial manner', did not become apparent until some forty years after his death. They required plenty of water. Once established on river bank or lakeside, in groves or standing solitary in an expanse of marshy grassland, they added an Italianate feel to classical temple views. Their salient vertical dimension in expansive, often flat park panoramas made slender, upright foils for bridges, and proved a perfect counterbalance to church steeples or monumental pillars.[263] Nineteenth-century paintings, engravings, early Victorian photographs and ordnance surveys confirm the presence of Lombardy poplars in Brown's parks.[264] Blue and white Staffordshire china also depicts 'poplar pines',[265] as Walpole called them, in idealised country house scenes.

Later generations of landowners probably appreciated, as Brown had foreseen, their columnar purity of form standing out against trees with generous, spreading or rounded canopies, at Bowood, Denham, Madingley, Luton and on the Thames-side walk at Nuneham, for instance. However, Lombardy poplars are not generally long-lived. Many parks have completely lost this key component of Brown's planting. Richmond Old Deer Park hosts a few aged specimens, possible replacements for original Brown poplars, framing the significant prospect from the King's Royal Observatory towards Kew's distant pagoda.

OPPOSITE, CLOCKWISE 1. **May 2008, Castle Ashby, Northamptonshire** A *Quercus cerris*, turkey oak, by the lake. 2, 3. The maidenhair tree, *Gingko biloba*. 4, 5. **May 2013, Luton Park, Bedfordshire** A veteran pollarded copper beech, *Fagus sylvatica atropurpurea*, centre stage (arrow), is possibly one of the first imported trees supplied to Brown by the Kew gardener John Haverfield. 6. **May 1991, Luton, Bedfordshire** Lombardy poplars (post-dating Brown) draw the eye to the beech tree, the last survivor of Brown's horizon beech stand – now gone – that used to frame a view to Someries Castle ruin. 7. **May 1997, Aske, North Yorkshire** Three beeches on the corner of the house.

BELOW **March 2007, Madingley, Cambridgeshire** Lombardy poplar, *Populus nigra 'Italica'*, introduced from Northern Italy c.1758, in prime middle-distance position in the lake view from the hall.

By the 1770s, a wider palette of imported trees brought greater variety to designs. Splendid veteran examples of distinctive, handsome purple beech, *Fagus sylvatica* var. *purpurea*, a large ornamental tree, survive in key locations at High Wycombe, Basildon, Luton and Brocklesby that might suggest Brown's hand in planting. Specimen American red oaks, *Quercus rubra*, also add outstanding autumn colour, varying from red to nut-brown. One in Richmond Old Deer Park was once admired from the salon windows of the Royal Lodge (now demolished).[266] Veterans survive at Wotton (Buckinghamshire) and nearby Finmere Rectory. Swamp cypress, *Taxodium*

distichum, imported from America from the seventeenth century onward, feature beside Brown's lakes at Syon, Bowood and Broadlands, turning rich, rusty-gold in autumn.

One of the trees most associated with Brown is the cedar of Lebanon. Seeds of the aristocratic *Cedrus libani* became available only from the 1730s, and then not readily. For an immediate 'designed' effect, he often chose a cedar to make a year-round frame for the house. Nearby, in direct contrast, he staged deciduous trees with presence even when immature, beech or London planes, often in threes, as the other side of the frame, as it were. He positioned one group reasonably near the front door in line with the angles of the house, on the diagonal so as to divide and frame separate views (see Tomkins painting, p.132). The contrasting group would be planted asymmetrically at a distance. Always careful not to block out the light or obstruct the wider panorama, never planting too close to the house, he imagined his feature trees fully grown, standing the test of time and providing a foreground edge to the view from the windows.[267]

Cedars offered great aesthetic value and were portrayed by artists as guardians to many a grand country house. Brown was not afraid to position dominant, stately cedars well out into the landscape to enliven otherwise ordinary scenery, either individually to create a focal point, or severally staggered to take the eye towards a horizon. Very distinct from native trees, with 'dancing skirts' when immature, these conifers were a satisfying year-round presence. Only a month after Brown's Petworth order (March 1759) for 200 cedars, 6 ins high, a further sixteen were delivered, 2–3-ft high, each costing 5s (today £35). By 1775 a trend for 'cedar walks', as at Mount Clare (Surrey), increased demand to 3s (£21) a foot. The trees' eventual dignity, strengthened by biblical allegory and Christian sentiment, justified a client's investment.

A count of the tree rings of cedars laid waste by the October 1987 hurricane at Claremont (Surrey) proved unequivocally that they had been planted when Brown was restoring the grounds. He chose to retain

Bridgeman's showpiece grass amphitheatre overlooking the lake, and planted a few cedars either side, envisaging them fully grown as theatrical 'wings' to the stage set. Once, Brown declined a commission, a rare occurrence. Perhaps he was overstretched by other commitments. In token recompense, he presented the landowner, the Earl of Harrington, with six cedar seedlings, now swallowed up in the long, mixed avenues of today's park at Elvaston (Derbyshire).[268]

Another story handed down at **Castle Ashby**, Northamptonshire, has the Earl of Northampton's son jumping over one of the designer's young cedars, which had been specially positioned on the hill above the lake. Fortunately no damage was done. Now this veteran commands the principal prospect, the crux of Brown's design, almost beckoning as a destination on the circuit walk. Standing beneath its ample branches, visitors may take in the lake, the church and the house, indeed most of the park landscape, in one all-encompassing, approving glance.

OPPOSITE **February 1992, Langley Park, Buckinghamshire** Swamp cypress, *Taxodium distichum*, lead the eye towards the house.

BELOW **November 2001, Castle Ashby, Northamptonshire** The strategically placed cedar of Lebanon frames a memorable view.

ABOVE **2012, Grays Inn, London** The attractive bark of a hybrid veteran London plane, *Platanus* x *acerifolia*.

LEFT **November 2009, Corsham Court, Wiltshire** The champion Oriental plane, *Platanus orientalis*.

OPPOSITE **October 2009, Wotton, Buckinghamshire** Veteran holm oaks frame vistas to and from the Octagon Temple.

The north lawn at Corsham Court (Wiltshire) is completely taken up with a handsome, veteran *Platanus orientalis*, a 'shade tree', planted by Brown in 1760. Since its lower branches have been layered, this is the most spreading oriental plane in the country, a champion tree. The more upright, hybrid 'London plane', *Platanus hybrida*, is equally long-lived and more often seen in Brown's settings. Both types have large leaves, creating an immediate effect when still immature. A rounded copse of towering planes disguises the upper dam at Wimpole. They would have contrasted with all the conifers (most long since cropped) in Brown's rather military-style belt planting. On a nearby hill, a lone London plane attracts attention. Did Brown purposefully position this tree, calling the visitor into the heart of the park, where the best, most affecting views are revealed? Many a dappled plane tree, admired for its attractive trunk and bristly seed balls, continues to make a perfect

foil for Brown's dark green cedars with elephant-grey bark.[269] A majestic plane guarding Wakefield Lodge is balanced by stately cedars on the other side of the lake. Another takes the eye off the sham bridge at Madingley (Cambridgeshire), diagonally across the east lawn from where a great cedar once framed the house, a signature combination surviving at Audley End (Essex).[270]

In the summer of 1771, Captain James Cook returned from a three-year voyage on board HMS *Bark Endeavour* charting new world territories, including Australia. The organiser of the famous expedition, Sir Philip Stephens, Secretary to the Admiralty, had commissioned Brown 'to mirror' his new Mulgrave House near the Thames in Fulham, and now invited Cook to plant a commemorative London plane. One wonders if both the royal gardener and the ship's collector/botanist, Joseph Banks, witnessed the ceremonial tree-planting. The

legendary tree heralding the success of the expedition still ornaments Brown's lake.[271]

Another much favoured feature tree, *Quercus ilex* or holm oak, added year-round structure and diversity to many Brown designs. Small groves served to edge picturesque views at Ashridge (Buckinghamshire) and Mamhead (Devon). Chilham Castle, a derelict Norman keep in Kent, has lost Brown's custodian cedar. A holm oak remains, planted in 1616, so the story goes, when Sir Dudley Digges finished building his manor house. An engraving (*c*.1791) shows the tree still relatively small, either a Brownian replacement, after alteration of levels around the house, or kept in check by hard pruning. Also known as 'holly oak' for its leathery, evergreen leaves, holm oak is just as forgiving of pruning as holly, and, originating in the Mediterranean and southern Europe, will withstand a maritime climate. In the 1770s Brown planted holm oaks at Cadland (Hampshire) and at nearby Highcliffe

(Dorset) to frame delightful coastal prospects across the Solent to the Isle of Wight, while allowing other less salt-tolerant trees to become established in his protective tree belts.

Brown was as intrigued and stimulated as others with imported oak varieties, experimenting and augmenting his planting with them. A hybrid between *Quercus cerris*, the Turkey oak, and *Quercus suber*, the cork oak, originally raised by an Exeter nurseryman in 1762, *Quercus* x *hispanica Lucombeana*, the Lucombe oak, is found on several Brown sites, such as Brocklesby, Syon, and in the Thames view opposite in Richmond Old Park.[272] *Quercus frainetto*, Hungarian (also Italian) oak, with shiny dark green leaves in summer, survives from Brown's planting at Peper Harow (Surrey). In 1776 Hungarian oak mast arrived from Livorno for Knowsley (Lancashire), following Brown's consultation and General Plan, for which he charged Lord Derby £100 (about £14,500).[273]

In planting native Scots pines, *Pinus sylvestris*, in great numbers, Brown made quite a name for himself. Although born soon after the first Jacobite rising, when for some the trees hinted at both Stuart and Catholic allegiance, he deliberately chose to set out great plantations, 10,000 pine seedlings at Audley End, Essex, for instance.[274] Evergreen with a trunk maturing to attractive, variable reddish-brown to grey, these pines, sometimes arranged in stands to strengthen the inconsequential line of a mixed tree belt, or else in a single-species grove in contrast to

larger deciduous clumps, changed the whole nature of the English countryside.

Imported conifers, cypress, *Arbor vitae*, the 'Tree of Life', and the Austrian pine with a dense crown, *Pinus nigra*, also made feature trees. The Mediterranean straight-stemmed Corsican pine with grey bark, *Pinus nigra* var. *maritima*, and the maritime or cluster pine *Pinus pinaster*, also planted in great numbers, proved an effective timber crop. At Syon, Mediterranean stone pines, *Pinus pinea*, are now the largest in England. At Longleat, Wiltshire, he cultivated great numbers of *Pinus strobus*, Lord Weymouth's pine, together with the perfect foil, beech, both in the park and on high ground above the house. The commentator J.C. Loudon (1783–1843) later acknowledged the Scots pine: 'an admirable tree for planting near ruins, castles and all gothic and irregular buildings'.[275]

One Scots pine once topped the famous Warwick Castle mount as a focal point. Just as noteworthy in the centre of any park panorama, the Scots pine was to Brown's eye the slim, evergreen, invaluable marker tree, the pivot of a subtle, straightforward geometry. Armed with marker stakes, he probably directed foremen to position a reasonably tall singleton to divide the terrain and simplify arranging the remainder of the planting. One such (now veteran) pine stands centre stage (what John Phibbs calls 'point blank') in the south park at Langley, Buckinghamshire, framing the perfect vista of the house.[276]

Earlier, Alexander Pope had planted a focal clump of Scots pines on Jerusalem Hill at Sherborne Castle (Dorset). Brown added singleton Scots pines, accompanied by the occasional cedar of Lebanon to heighten sensibilities, to progress beyond the old castle walk in the direction of this iconic hill. A handful of singleton pines snaking at intervals through the Vaudey Valley at Grimsthorpe Castle (Lincolnshire) performs a similar service, leading the eye towards the castle on the ridge beyond. Scots pines created perennial strength, whether at the end of a lake, in the middle of a tree-belt, defining the

edge of a mixed clump, or occasionally planted in threes where roads converged.

Called across to **Newton House** (now Dinefwr Castle, after twelfth-century ruins), Brown was inspired by its picturesque location in Carmarthenshire, the heart of Wales, with views over the deer park and Tywi Valley, and approving of the new model farm and all that George Rice had achieved on the estate: 'I wish my journey may prove of use to the place, which if it should, it will be very flattering to me. Nature has been truly bountiful & art has done no harm.'

Such flattering charm was infectious and, like all who plant trees, Brown helped others to look to the future with more optimism. At best, Brown witnessed an uplifting, maturing beauty on estates with which he held a long association: Wotton, Burghley, Syon and Croome. If he never saw fully grown the trees he planted, he surely enjoyed the gratifying mental exercise of picturing them in his mind in full majesty, enriching the scene. In the twilight of his career, he

envisaged a dark, rounded clump of cedars on a hill at **Belvoir Castle** (Leicestershire), an idea from one of his last grand leather-bound folios of plans, some of which were implemented after his death. Cedar Hill still makes an imposing feature in views from both the neighbouring Croxton estate and the castle.[277] Whether he recalled punctuating the undulating Sussex Downs at Petworth with conspicuous groupings of cedars and pines at the dawn of his career, history does not relate.

In Brown's day, besides the political status of the Established Protestant Church, Deists were questioning the Trinity. Where he looked out from the windows of his home, Wilderness House, there was once a trio of Scots pines; one survives. Could his triple planting have been a believer's gesture?[278] A tell-tale Scots pine in a considered location assists easy reading of the landscape and recalls Brown's hand in the design – *Pinus sylvestris*, an enduring postscript or PS.

CHAPTER FOURTEEN

SHRUBBERY 'SWEETS' & FLOWER GARDENS

Legend has it that Henrietta, Lady Luxborough, an avid gardener, invented the word 'shrubbery' in a letter (1748) to the poet William Shenstone.[279] At the time, shrubs were a luxury to which the middle classes could only aspire. Where some landowners indulged in collecting maples, North American conifers and 'curious' blossom trees, these were not Brown's sole consideration. Evergreens such as native common box, *Buxus sempervirens*; the tough, reasonably long-lived common English laurel, or cherry laurel, *Prunus laurocerasus*; and the equally vigorous, dark green-leaved Portugal laurel, *Prunus lusitanica*, introduced in 1742, provided a distinctive, year-round under-storey. From the start, when he launched into independent professional practice, Brown's all-inclusive plans, such as that for Packington (1751), incorporated 'Flowering Shrubs and Flowers'. One of his many Petworth contracts proposed alterations to the grounds: 'A gravel path through the mena[gerie] etc with its borders adorned with Flowering Shrubbs'.

OPPOSITE **October 2010, Cadland, Hampshire** The miniature landscape garden setting in its prime, following a restoration after the 1987 hurricane by Gilly Drummond with advice from the landscape architect Hal Moggridge.

ABOVE **May 2014, Rycote, Oxfordshire** A pleasure ground walk to the lake, edged with roses and lilac.

The emphasis ostensibly on 'flowering' shrubs was to edge and enliven sinuous walks overlooking the park, possibly planted in modish graduated stages or theatrical tiers, as Mark Laird suggests. Brown contrived to create an under-storey and bring fragrance to the fringes of the woods. Clients and their visitors gained pleasure from diversity, 'getting shade from the large Trees & sweets from the smaller sorts of Shrubbs'.[280] Brown selected specimen flowering trees, English cherry, *Prunus avium*, or more exotic double-blossom cherries from overseas, the much-admired 'Golden Rain', *Laburnum anagyroides*, and perfumed lilacs, *Syringa vulgaris*. Evergreens, valuable in season for their bright, jewel-like berries, also provided much-needed shelter, contrast, and sometimes concealment.[281]

Attentive to management, Brown furthered the traditional art of coppicing alder and hornbeam and cutting back and thinning osier beds to encourage neatness and new growth.

> To continue thinning the Plantations in the Pleasure Grod. [Ground] Particularly that Quarter next to the Umbrella Seat where there is to be a background of Laurells planted (thick) the long Plantation, and all other Plantations and Clumps as the Wood is wanted.[282]

Brown recommended low-growing shrubs and herbaceous plants 'that 'will not prevent the prospects'. Distant views were as essential to the design as foreground colour and texture. His Burton Constable shrubbery was 'to lie open and not enclosed', though 'tented off' from sheep grazing the lawn.[283]

When he first moved to London, it seems likely that Brown haunted Hammersmith nurseries nearby to study botany and familiarise himself with newly imported exotics, with the same dedication with which he had taught himself architecture at Stowe. In 1753 comprehensive proposals at Petworth involved finishing the parterre in front of the greenhouse, an aloe garden of semi-tropical African plants to 'give a fine prospect from the Arcade at the House'.[284] Sometimes he was just too busy to concentrate on planting flowers. At Madingley, Cambridgeshire (1756), he agreed to refresh the garden by digging a trench:

> to supply us with such a Quantity of Earth as may be wanted in the Garden. NB it is not meant to finish this Fosse, only to remove so much earth as may be wanted in the Garden and to make a pattern of it, to be done after and when Sir John [Hynde Cotton] pleases.[285]

A recognised authority in raising produce, Brown was involved with every aspect of gardening. His task was sometimes restorative, involving a softening and enriching of earlier wildernesses and groves, London and Wise's 'woodwork' inspired by Versailles. A freer movement towards the picturesque was already in train, as Brown, and other designers such as Richard Woods, moved on from where Batty Langley's and William Kent's artistry had left off. At Stowe, William Marshall noted 'tufts of trees, shrubs and flowers growing promiscuously'[286] around Cobham's Monument. Brown's planting had included double jonquil bulbs and a variety of flowers, both perennial and annual, in addition to 'embroidered' or 'enamelled' scatterings of wild primroses, violets, cowslips, red and white campion and bluebells. Brown surely encouraged gardeners to utilise available, freely naturalising, springtime 'sweets', local wild flowers, but there were occasions, particularly when working for botanically educated owners, when he ordered a wider variety of flowers from nurserymen.

Old paintings and engravings are now the only clues to the variety of Brown's shrubberies, often as protective arms either side of the house, reaching out into the wider landscape to invite exploration further afield. Occasioned glimpses of a 'river-lake' shimmering in the distance charmed visitors as they negotiated agreeable, scented walks snaking towards feature clumps or seats to survey the landscape. Undulating shrubbery walks differed from earlier enclosed, formal, mazy wildernesses. Those, leading from Syon House in one direction along the 'Duke's River' towards

TOP LEFT *Laburnum anagyroides*

TOP MIDDLE *Prunus laurocerasus,* laurel blossom

TOP RIGHT Portuguese laurel, *Prunus lusitanica*

ABOVE LEFT **May 1992, Petworth, Sussex (NT)** The rotunda on a mount in the pleasure ground, set off by ornamental trees and shrubs (some later nineteenth-century introductions).

ABOVE RIGHT Yew berries, *Taxus baccata*

RIGHT *Phillyrea* seedhead

FAR RIGHT **May 2008, Castle Ashby, Northamptonshire** Lilac, *Syringa vulgaris,* in the pleasure ground by the Menagerie.

TOP LEFT Hawthorn (*Crataegus*)

TOP MIDDLE Bladdernut (*Staphylea pinnata*)

TOP RIGHT Hazel (*Corylus*, catkins)

MIDDLE RIGHT Staghorn sumach
(*Rhus typhina*)

MIDDLE LEFT Sea buckthorn
(*Hippophae rhamnoides*)

BELOW **October 2011, Syon, Middlesex**
A variety of trees with form and scale create
a backdrop for Flora's Lawn, though barely
apparent is an under-storey with fragrant
flowering shrubs and roses.

Flora's Lawn, and, in the opposite direction towards All Saints Church at Isleworth, were much-admired highlights of Brown's work for the Duke and Duchess of Northumberland. Most shrubs in his acclaimed pleasure grounds have long since disappeared, but you might still chance upon an irregular set of yews once directing sight-lines to eye-catchers or, as Lady Luxborough chose to call them, 'eye-traps'.

Yew, *Taxus baccata*, a dark marker or 'setting out' plant, proved effective in screening and protecting clearings in the woods; they were sometimes planted higher on spoil mounds to allow for better drainage.[287] Rowan or mountain ash, *Sorbus aucuparia*, in folklore a sign of welcome, featured regularly in nursery orders, a useful ornamental tree with white pompoms of blossom in spring and cheerful red berries in autumn. Brown favoured evergreen *Phillyrea*, imported from Virginia, and any hardy 'shining greens' to catch and reflect light.[288]

At Belhus (Essex) Brown expressed pleasure, having 'slaved at setting out the road and the rest of the shrubbery all day', uplifted by the promise of blossoming variety and vibrant colour. Archive evidence of his palette of hardy, reliable English stock includes shrubs imported from southern Europe:

Persian jasmine – Jasminum officinales
Italian buckthorn – Rhamnus alaternus
'Barbajovis' – Anthyllis barba-jovis
bladdernut – Staphylea pinnata
staghorn sumach – Rhus typhina
juniper – Juniperus communis
holly – Ilex
hawthorn – Crataegus[289]
guelder rose – Viburnum
Spiraea
dog rose – Rosa canina
honeysuckle – Lonicera
clematis
dogwood – Cornus
elder – Sambucus nigra
sea buckthorn – Hippophae rhamnoides
hazel – Corylus – *catkins*
Cercis

RIGHT A page in a late-eighteenth-century sketchbook by the topographical draughtsman and watercolourist J.C. Nattes (1765?–1822) shows Brown's mature shrubbery after his death, encircling the Church of St Mary Magdalene at Castle Ashby, Northamptonshire. 'Rarely is a church made so much of the private garden furnishings of a mansion' (N. Pevsner). Courtesy Northamptonshire Archive Office, reference: ZB1455

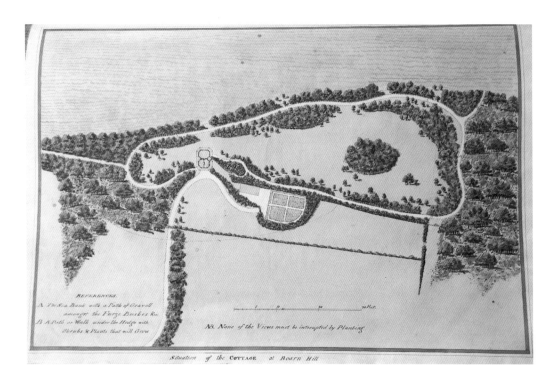

ABOVE **March 2004, Patshull Park, Staffordshire** Gorse still grows near Brown's lake.

LEFT Brown's plan (1775), 'situation of the COTTAGE at Boarn Hill'. From Spyers folio. © Cadland Trustees.

BELOW **October 2010, Cadland, Hampshire** The miniature landscape garden setting after restoration following the 1987 hurricane, with shrubberies and Scots pines beginning to mature.

Robert Drummond, a banker, and the nephew of the banker Andrew Drummond, for whom Brown had worked at Stanmore, commissioned ideas for improvements for his seat, **Cadland** in Hampshire. Competition with a growing number of professional gentlemen improvers motivated Brown to develop better methods of proposal presentation by exploiting an assistant's skills as a competent watercolourist. John Spyers produced an impressive, leather-bound folio of architectural plans and a plan for the grounds (1775) for Cadland. Later, he also took trouble over a Survey Book (1777) for Fenstanton, his employer's own estate.[290] Brown selected trees to suit Cadland's coastal location, part dry and sandy, part marshy, those that he knew could cope with salt-laden winds, mainly oak and holm oak, beech, sweet chestnut, *Castanea sativa*, and Scots pine. His plan envisaged a short, informal, coastal circuit, with holes cut through the trees to frame captivating 'peep' vistas across the Solent to the Isle of Wight.[291]

This nucleus was enclosed by wider, random, plentiful planting to filter the wind and to screen small kitchen gardens from the approach drive. The circuit comprised two walks, A and B, each on different levels, each with a distinct character, one intimately shaded and sheltered, with occasional glimpses of the sea, the other more open and sunny, before leading back to the house. Brown wove a varying tapestry of scented and textured shrub foliage and made the most of every charming seaside aspect; it was not long before a delightful, unique miniature landscape knitted together to protect walkers from the worst of the elements. Realising he had been overpaid £100 (£14,500), he was quick to reimburse the money to Drummond.

Interestingly, Brown advocated planting 'furze', now better known as common gorse or *Ulex*. Besides having bright yellow flowers with a distinctive, sweet coconut scent, it proved excellent for winter fodder, for stock-proofing, and as cover for fowl and game; it was useful to insulate water-pipes and, because of its high calorific content, made excellent fuel for bread ovens.[292] He favoured a London nurseryman,

Williamson & Co., for broom, *Cytisus scoparius*, and furze for **Brocklesby**, rather than nurseries in the Midlands region.[293]

Walpole, quick to find fault, considered Brown's shrubs out of proportion with the existing surrounding trees, which must have sometimes been the case when they were first planted. He was of course right in recognising that there would be future problems, with some short-lived flowering shrubs being 'past their beauty in less than twenty years'.

Most ladies exerted considerable influence over kitchen garden plans and plant purchases, including the newest imported roses, with some purposely requesting a private flower garden to show off the latest introductions. Lady Greenwich consulted Brown

Cadland, Hampshire In contrast to the grounds open to sunshine, the textured restored shrubbery is seen here in enclosed shade along the circuit walk, where a sprinkling of Brown's trees survives to make focal points.

regarding the Treasury Garden in Whitehall. Lady Dacre recorded seeds bought from James Gordon, in London's Fenchurch Street, and plants from Samuel Driver in Lambeth.[294] The very first article of his Audley End contract (1763) concerned 'Lady Griffin's Garden in all its parts', in a separate, secluded area not on view from the house. What might surprise the reader, the Audley plan includes an unusual detail: potted plants on paving outside the drawing-room windows.

Contrary to popular belief, evidence suggests that Brown did not banish flowers to the kitchen garden – quite the reverse. One instruction, at Tottenham, Wiltshire, paints a specifically relaxed and colourful picture: 'All the Rose Trees in the Kitchen Garden to be planted in the most conspicuous parts of the Pleasure Ground'.[295]

Here, in addition to hundreds of trees and 200 unnamed flowering shrubs, the Berkshire nurseryman William Pendar's order (1766) further underscores the floral scale and sweet-smelling variety of Brown's planting:

25 *True Phillyreas*	*6d each*
50 *Phillyreas Strip'd & plain 6d each*	*£1. 10. 0.*
10 *Sumach's large*	*3d each*
4 *Shining leav'd sumachs*	*6d each*
100 *roses 10 sorts*	*£1. 10. 0*
100 *'sweet briars'* (Rosa rubiginosa)	

Roses: 100 Moss Red Provence, Damask Provence Hundred-leav'd, Blush, Monthly, 'Double Yellow', York and Lancaster, and Velvet roses 2 sorts £2. 10 [total today £784].[296]

A close study of Mrs Delaney's unique flower collages, crafted in the mid-1770s at Luton Hoo, shows a fascinating range of plants plucked from the gardens.[297] In addition the Bute archive contains a comprehensive, lengthy plant catalogue, with times of flowering throughout the year: single and double snowdrops, mixed tulips and agapanthus among others. In 1783 the *General Evening Post* proclaimed:

'Excepting the King's Residence at Kew, a botanical garden is an appendage peculiar to this place and his Lordship with a liberal zeal for science, has given orders that it is to be open to all comers.'[298]

Brown ordered a hundred mixed tulips for Syon (another recent revelation), though whether these were grown in urns, flower beds or scattered alongside Flora's Lawn is not known.[299] A remarkable miscellany of flowers in his surviving orders, here and elsewhere, indicates the range of his horticultural experience:

germander – *Teucrium*
white hellebores – *Helleborus niger*
Veratrum album
spiderwort – *Tradescanti*
starwort or Michaelmas daisy – *Aster*
wallflowers – *Erysimum*
star of Bethlehem – *Ornithogalum*
lily of the valley – *Convallaria majalis*
blue & yellow flag iris – *Iris versicolor & Iris pseudacorus*
orange & white lilies – *Alstroemeria & Lilium candidum*
trumpet flower – *Brugmansia*

Some say Brown earned his reputation by being an autocrat. However, the proposal concerning the close environs of Lord Bute's house at Luton, Bedfordshire, with a larger scale than the norm, 1 in. to 50 ft, departs from his usual formula of uninterrupted

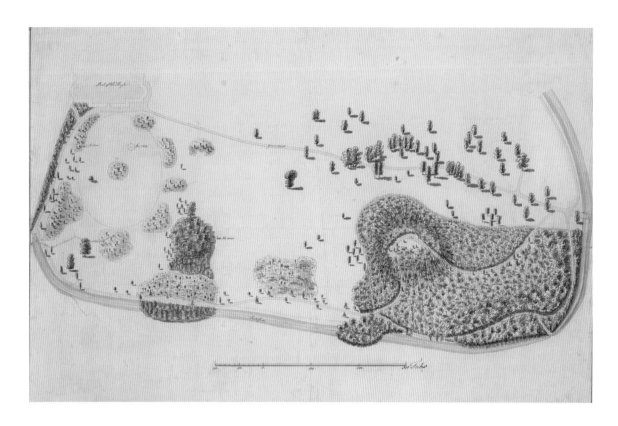

lawn near the house and, in working to satisfy the client, illustrates a flexible versatility and openness to change.[300] Both men shared a passion for science, and the apparently random appearance of this special Botanical Garden was far from the truth.

A circular bed within the lawn features seven small trees or shrubs, offset from the main axis to allow a glimpse of a Tuscan pillar eye-catcher on Column Hill beyond (since removed to Mount Stewart, Isle of Bute). Two mature trees, one surrounded by a seat, draw the eye through the design.[301] A gravel walk then circles the flower garden and leads along the ha-ha, past the Dell plantation, with planting breaking its line. The path follows shaded contours down into a surprise, a densely planted old quarry, past a secluded seat in a clearing, before looping back to the house.

At the height of his career, Brown stimulated much discussion and comment on gardening arts, which continued long after his death (this is still the case, nearly two and a half centuries later). That is not to say that he remained impervious to others' ideas. In 1768 essayist George Mason suggested that

a geometric layout was still quite acceptable for an orangery garden within a natural landscape setting.[302]

Perhaps to please Sophia Aufrère, Charles Pelham's striking young bride, Brown's grand plan (1771) for Brocklesby (Lincolnshire) proposed, on the one hand, to eliminate the original geometric bastion gardens (shown by dotted lines), while, on the other, paradoxically outlining a regular, octagonal flower garden in front of a new greenhouse. Ten petal-shaped flowerbeds, each a considerable 50 ft in length, arranged around a central oval bed and apparent ornamental urn, were to be tucked into a corner next to the menagerie, and sheltered from prevailing winds by a belt of trees.[303] Rare specimens, florists' flowers and tender 'exotics' overwintered in the greenhouse could be planted out to great decorative effect in summer. A later four-page contract with Pelham includes the pertinent article:

To finish in all its Parts the Garden Ground enclosed by the above mentioned [sunk] Fence, (Viz.) The taking down of the Trees, new Planting, Shrubs, Trees and Flowers, making Gravel Walks, and Leveling the Ground, Turfing

response. This poem, dedicated to Viscount Irwin, who had commissioned Brown to improve **Temple Newsam** in Yorkshire and Hills in Sussex, is worth appraising in its entirety as a source for appropriate plant material in effecting a pleasure-ground restoration:

> *But your great artist like the source of light*
> *Gilds every Scene with beauty and delight*
> *At Blenheim, Croome and Caversham ye trace*
> *Salvator's Wildness, Claud's enlivening grace,*
> *Cascades and lakes as fine as Risdale drew*
> *While nature's vary'd in each charming view*
> *To paint his works wou'd Poussin's powers require,*
> *Milton's sublimity & Dryden's fire.*[306]

and Sowing with Grass seeds all those Parts which are to be in Grass, marking out a place for a small flower garden and Greenhouse near the Farm-yard within the Garden Fence which may be finished whenever it is agreed with Mr & Mrs Pelham.[304]

By this time, plans for the three-acre grounds surrounding a new townhouse, Sloane Place, for his newly wed daughter Bridget and son-in-law Henry Holland, had included stylish flowerbeds near the house, as in smaller town gardens. Amenable to the London-based younger generation's fashion-conscious aspirations, Brown kept pace with contemporary style. With barely half an acre of garden on Richmond Hill, Frederick Nicolay was not deterred from asking for his advice: 'I hope it is no offence to wish for a Miniature Picture from a Raphael.'[305]

Those with a flair for words and poetry were readily receptive to a change of style and greater variety of planting. In the 1760s Brown's shelter belts were still in their infancy, so it must have been the combination of colourful pleasure grounds reflected in his stretches of water that elicited the following anonymous

Meanwhile, returning to Wotton, Brown suggested changes to the flower garden near the house. This was not always the case. John Phibbs has drawn attention to flower gardens designed by Brown at some distance from the house.[307] It was natural to experiment and enjoy a creative intermingling of native shrubs with exciting, colourful imports and to pander to clients' enthusiasm for unusual new plants. Brown also incorporated a circular flower garden into his plan for Lowther Castle, Cumbria, and, beyond, a serpentine walk among further flower beds and shrubs: 'The most dramatic evidence of Brown's capabilities in the art of the pleasure ground'.[308]

For a generation for whom enlightenment was all, the ephemeral business of planting safe and shaded circuits had become an affecting form of art, designed, and then constantly revised, to entice the landowner, his family and congenial visitors on private walks and rides, amid fragrant, blossoming and berried shrubs, trees and flowers that 'in fair confusion rise'.[309]

> *The great end of all those arts is to make an impression on the imagination and the feeling. The imitation of nature frequently does this…. The true test of all arts is not whether the production is a true copy of nature, but whether it answers the end of art, which is to produce a pleasing effect on the mind.*[310]

CHAPTER FIFTEEN

COMFORTS & CONVENIENCE

The 1760s were better times. Almost everyone seemed to be engaged in building as the country emerged from recession. Upper and professional classes experienced unprecedented economic and political growth and clamoured for grander houses with classical profiles. Inigo Jones (1573–1652) had introduced in the Queen's House at Greenwich a new architecture inspired by the Italian Palladio (1508–1580), whose original countryside villas, with clean lines, gratifying scale and beautiful proportion, were harmonious reinterpretations of Roman antiquity. So it proved an auspicious time for Brown, who was recognised for his land improvements, water-engineering and planting. As was his way, ever the resourceful, indefatigable polymath, he took advantage of every opportunity to promote his business, with a fourth, lucrative pillar to his practice: architecture. 'The celebrated Brown could not behold the scene without rapture, and urged the owner to build a house there.'[311]

Condition and style were important for the principal focus of any given country estate, the hard-edged country mansion in a soft, rural scene. He had noticed at Grimsthorpe how Vanbrugh had married his dramatic, innovative classical north front with the remaining old-world charm of the medieval castle. Brown tackled similar taxing problems of alteration, happy to turn his hand to plans and elevations to modernise the crumbling piles that clients inherited, and mastered a cohesive union of old and new in whatever mode owners desired.

OPPOSITE **January 2013, Burghley House, Cambridgeshire** The junction with Brown's new ha-ha.

ABOVE **Croome Court, Worcestershire (NT)** Motif on the hall cornice, English oak leaves and acorns intertwined.

155

Stowe October ye 22: 1750

Sir

I was from home when Mr Stevensons Letter came to Stowe which is the reason that it is not answer'd sooner. The Monument of the late Lord Cobham is one hundred and 10 feet high, the Statue of His Lordship is 10 Feet and three Inches of it; the Pillar with its Capitel and Bace are the Tuscan Proportion, but of difert members which I composed to make it more monumental, and to answer the octangular forme of ye Pillar. There is a winding Staircase that leeds up to the Captl which Staircase takes up 5 Feet and 10 Inches of the Diameter of the Pillar, the greatest Diameter of which is 10 Feet 6 In The Foundation of the Pillar is double Piled and double planked. If you have any intention of Building a Pillar of this kind if a draught of it or any other kind will be of use to you, you may command it from me. If you are determined in your Sort of Building, and has a Plan of it, if you will pleas to send me a rough Sketch of it, with ye Weight of a Cubrik Foot of the Stone I will put you in a way that you will be Sure to have your Building Stand. The Scaffolding of Building of this kind is ye greatest Arte in the whole, after ye Foundations. The Wind has a very great effect on Buildings that stand on so small a Base and should be well attended to in the Scaffold that it has not the least effect on the Building by laying Putlocks from the Standards to the Building as some unskilfully do. I again take ye liberty to and if I can be of least usefull to you I beg you command me, because I should have a double pleasure in your situation being my native Country. I am Sir Your most Obedient Servant,

Lancelot Brown.

Nine years at Stowe supervising Cobham's extraordinary projects had been an invaluable training in architecture. Since the octagon had become the symbol of enlightenment, Brown's octagonal prospect tower (see p.157) had caused particular comment, and prompted enquiries from further afield.

Hoping to expand his independent practice, Brown was aiming high in replying to George Bowes, a wealthy Whig MP with property at Gibside (County Durham) (see *left*).[312] Perhaps revealing himself as a little too keen to promote his abilities as an architect, on this occasion Brown did not land the commission, but it proved worth persevering.[313]

Although classical architecture remained popular with the ruling elite throughout his lifetime, there was a deliberate, experimental and theatrical trend towards Gothic revival. Batty Langley's reactionary book, *Ancient Architecture Restored* (1742),[314] found favour among Whig intellectuals who coupled national pride with a love of medieval history. Most architectural commissions in Brown's first five years of independent practice were probably thanks to an Oxford-educated gentleman architect from the Midlands, Sanderson Miller (1716–1780), hailed by William Pitt as 'the great master of Gothick', and responsible for mosaic decorations in the Gothic Temple interior at Stowe. In November 1749 he noted in his diary that he and Brown walked together for five hours in Stowe gardens, more than a simple tour of inspection. The previous month, Miller had been working on his design for a Gothic greenhouse at Enville, while Brown, after the death of Cobham, was contemplating future prospects. He must have welcomed Miller's flattering interest, and the chance perhaps to collaborate in his architectural projects for the Earl of Stamford at Enville (discussed on pp.92–94).

What is known, however, is that the next summer Brown accepted an invitation to visit Radway Grange, Miller's small Warwickshire estate overlooking Edge Hill, the famous Civil War battlefield. Both Miller's octagonal, castellated Gothic tower, inspired by the (twelve-sided) fourteenth-century Guy's Tower at **Warwick Castle**, and his lodges displayed refreshing profiles. Strong three-dimensional exteriors, as opposed to classical, flat façades with applied detail, were matched with interesting spatial interiors. His eclectic garden buildings were also well worth viewing, ideal for hospitality and meaningful, in keeping with the place's sense of history.

ABOVE **April 1991, Stowe, Buckinghamshire (NT)** The Cobham Memorial, based on the Gibbs design, but built and altered by Brown.

RIGHT **August 1991, Warwick Castle** Scots pines and shrubberies relieve the embattled austerity of Guy's Tower.

A definite rapport developed between the two men. They were the same age, both from unexceptional backgrounds, likeable and equally self-assured. If Brown were to bring Miller's designs to fruition, Brown's ambition for wider recognition might also be realised. Their mutual talents came to be accepted and admired by high-ranking, affluent leaders of society, many craving rural retreats to escape overcrowded, increasingly unsanitary and industrial cities.[315] Miller was remodelling the Old Shire Hall, a stone's throw from Warwick Castle, when Lord Francis Brooke commissioned Brown to upgrade the castle park, works which inspired the artists Canaletto and Paul Sandby.

Over a period of more than ten years, Brown earned £2,293 on this project (today about £332,000). Besides land and water improvements in the park, he modified the approach, courtyard and offices, rebuilt both porch and stairs to the Great Hall, and provided an ice-house. He also modernised Brooke's private accommodation by making walls thinner to gain more space.

Walpole was excited by the novelty and well-engineered scale of Brown's works, but remained unconvinced by his interior alterations:

One sees what this prevalence of taste does.... The view pleased me more than I can express; the river Avon tumbles down a cascade at the foot of it. It is well laid out by one Brown, who has set up, on a few ideas of Kent and Mr Southcote. Where he has attempted Gothick in the castle, he has failed woefully, a new apartment that is most paltry.[316]

So many cognoscenti flocked to Strawberry Hill in Twickenham to inspect Walpole's interpretation of Gothic architecture that opening times and numbers of visitors to his quixotic garden had to be strictly regulated. Brown must have numbered among those inspecting the charming, and surprising, irregular castle-like extensions to the Thames-side house. Six months after moving to Hammersmith, less than ten miles downriver, Brown submitted proposals for alterations to Francis Willoughby, 2nd Viscount Midleton's house at **Peper Harow** (Surrey): first, a two-and-a-half-storey, nine-bay stone-built elevation with castellated parapet, three-storey wings, half-size windows lighting the cellars, and a double staircase to the front door; second, an embattled elevation, with central bow, and windows with pediment ornamentation or plainly arched.

These somewhat hybrid classical/Gothic plans were rejected. A month later, May 1752, Brown returned, determined, ever the aspiring architect, and armed with fresh proposals.[317] These conformed to an accepted, classical pattern-book ideal: a simplified two-storey, dressed 'Elevation of South-West Front, with Bow window in center' with Venetian windows on end bays either side, and steps up to an unadorned door in the projecting central bay.

Since few of Brown's interior plans survive, those corresponding to the Palladian elevation are worth close inspection.[318] One idiosyncratic layout, in ink and grey wash, initialled 'LB' (see p.159), includes a stable court with coach-house, spaces for dung, 'and a space for breeding Pheasants Etc', a kitchen court, including three hog sties, wood- and peat-houses, a brew-house, a laundry court with a single privy and a double one outside. Brown intended both a grand stairway and back stairs for staff, and such calculated details as separate water closets for men and women and 'closets for servants to powder wiggs'. Compact, practical designs show originality in use of space: a basement for laundry, wash-house and dairy; a three-sided *piano nobile* (principal floor) for reception rooms, the drawing room extending into the central bay; bedchambers with dressing rooms; and an attic floor with staff bedrooms.

OPPOSITE **September 2003, Strawberry Hill, Twickenham, Middlesex** Horace Walpole's 'little Gothic castle': 'It was built to please my own taste, and in some degree to realise my own visions.'

RIGHT Brown's unsigned proposals for Gothic elevations, April 1752, to alter Lord Middleton's house at Peper Harow © Surrey History Centre

BELOW Brown's interior plan, initialled LB, to alter Peper Harow House © Surrey History Centre. Marrying the house to the setting with planting and sinuous paths, he thoughtfully suggested two discreet earth closets for gardeners, and one for maids in the Laundry Court (arrow).

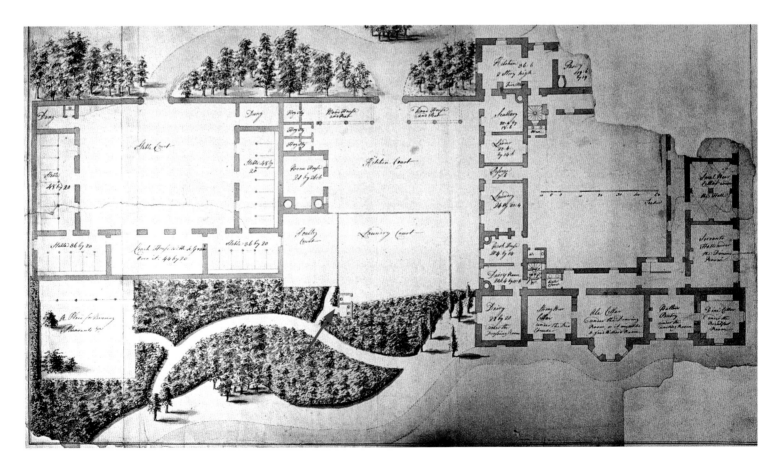

Despite Brown's best endeavours, a commission to upgrade the house was not forthcoming. The newly-wed Midletons could not make up their minds. It might have been a question of presentation. A naïve choice of scale for one plan, 'not quite 1" to 10ft', would not have engendered confidence in the accuracy of his building. As some consolation, he later (1757–58) worked to improve the setting. The old house was eventually pulled down and the Scottish architect and committed classicist William Chambers (1723–1796) built a smaller house (c.1765–68).

A complicated contract for Brown to remodel the Earl of Denbigh's house eventually went ahead at **Newnham Paddox** with the assistance of Miller's mason, Benjamin King, and carpenters from Stowe, Hobcraft and Smallbones. Progress was slow, intermittent and piecemeal, between 1754 and 1768, by which time Brown had in effect pulled down the old and fitted up a new Palladian house, at a total cost of £6220 5s 7d (today £902,000).[319] Walpole, on this occasion, gave his approval: 'a plain good brick front'.[320] Josiah Wedgwood, the resourceful pottery magnate, was impressed by the salon, specifically designed to display a fine collection of Van Dyck portraits: 'It is a very convenient house in the distribution of the rooms, & one, the Grand Drawing Room, is very magnificent.'[321]

Meanwhile, Sanderson Miller was spending time with a wealthy, 'grave young Lord of the remains of the Patriot Breed'. The 6th Earl of Coventry had just inherited a Jacobean house at **Croome** in Worcestershire, last remodelled in the seventeenth century. Seeing the grounds waterlogged by unprecedented summer rainfall, Miller did not hesitate to recommend Brown. Miller trusted the Northumbrian's ability to build a new house, having observed his capacity for both water-engineering and construction at Stowe and Warwick Castle. As soon as Brown secured the commission, he contacted a former collaborator, Benjamin Read, engineer and paviour, to act as foreman for his team. The first priority was to begin trenching the low-lying land, extending existing land drains and the artificial 'river' in order to create a mile-long lake with turns said to simulate those of the River Severn.

OPPOSITE July 1994, Croome Court, Worcestershire (before National Trust restoration) The nine-bay south front has low, square-angled eminences with pyramid roofs, Venetian windows on the *piano nobile*, and a portico, four unfluted columns flanked by cast stone sphinxes.

LEFT June 2009, Croome Court, Worcestershire (before National Trust restoration) Gilded door case.

BELOW Croome Court, Worcestershire (before National Trust restoration) Bronze door furniture.

RIGHT Croome Court, Worcestershire (before National Trust restoration) Entrance hall.

When satisfied that the environs were dry, Brown elected to build the new house on the substantial old foundations, incorporating existing chimneys and ensuring that the kitchen and other offices in the basement were connected to his extensive network of brick conduits underground. He was assisted by a range of reliable craftsmen including William Donn, a surveyor and builder (who later went on to establish his own practice); John Hobcraft, his trusted master carpenter at Stowe, Wotton and Newnham Paddox; the mason Robert Newman; and Francesco Vassalli, a decorative stuccoist.

The resulting house appears robust, and perhaps coarser than Brown's original proposal; it is a rather pedestrian amalgam of Vitruvian ideas from central figures in the development of English Palladianism: Burlington, Kent and Colen Campbell. Interestingly, there is also more than a passing resemblance to Miller's Hagley Hall (1754–60). On the short west side the central bay, derived from a half-octagon, shows an interesting early grasp of movement, possibly thanks to Miller's encouragement.[322] Brown

had been working at Syon (1763–68) alongside James Paine, a promising architect who is thought to have introduced the earliest three-sided bay window in a classical building.[323] Whatever the case, Brown kept up with modern trends.

The Croome interior is, at first impression, dignified, almost plain. A Doric screen with four fluted columns divides the entrance hall, and the carved and gilded doorcases are restrained. The main cantilevered staircase with iron 'bottle' balustrade is tucked away informally at the east end of the house. The house servants working in basement rooms lit by natural light through half-windows were also able to enjoy the park views. Coventry encouraged the talented Scot Robert Adam (1728–1792), who had studied in Italy, to decorate a tapestry room and the dining room. Joseph Rose Jr attended to the refined plasterwork in Adam's picture gallery in the west wing, overlooking Brown's 'new river'.[324]

Out in the park, Brown's island temple to the west and a rotunda summerhouse on the east vied for attention with Adam's smart Temple Greenhouse to the north and, later, his park seat to the south, the Owl's Nest.[325] Brown's and Adam's paths crossed elsewhere, but somehow they never seemed on close terms.[326] Adam was younger and may have been envious of Brown's popularity and relaxed familiarity with high-ranking clients. Or was he dismayed by his virtuosity? A quick assimilation of graceful Adam-inspired detail into Brown's own classical designs was soon all too apparent.

Coventry dedicated more time to his estate than to the country's politics. The wealthy Tory and recognised connoisseur lavished the finest materials on his classical, purpose-built country residence. The pivot of 'finely picturesque and powerful' panoramic vistas came to an astonishing overall cost: £400,000 (today £58 million). This included new three-sided stables and offices in red brick dressed with Bath stone, the obligatory ice-house and feature garden buildings, and an arboretum to rival Kew.[327] Within two years, Coventry wrote to Miller to express gratitude:

> Whatever merit Croomb may in future time boast, it will be ungrateful not to acknowledge you the primary Author… It was to your assurance that Nature had been more liberal to me than I apprehended… Mr Brown has done very well by me, and indeed I think has studied both my Place and my Pocket which are not always conjunctively the objects of prospectors. I am much obliged to you for the domestic comforts you wish me, and yet I think they may be too numerous…[328]

Flattery apart, Brown is the acknowledged architect of Croome.[329]

Following his wife's death, Coventry remarried in 1764, and swiftly charged Brown with another assignment, a more private residence for his bride. He built Springhill House with a thin, ashlar façade, set on a beautiful rise in a sixty-acre park not far from Croome. Well-appointed domestic offices included excellent beer and wine cellars.[330] It mattered not to Brown that he was sometimes paid two years in arrears. Coventry's lifelong friendship was ample reward.

Sanderson Miller enjoyed an income from his estate rentals, and so was able to offer designs free of charge to his friends. Brown, on the other hand, needed to earn a living. So Miller encouraged another acquaintance, Lord Dacre, to commission Brown to create a ten-acre pool on the boundary of the park at Belhus (Essex), and to improve the grounds with plantations and shrubberies. Later Dacre wrote to Miller with news of Brown who, by this time, was evidently expanding his business independently.

> He tells me he has the alteration of Burleigh and that; not only of ye park but of ye House which wherever it is Gothick he intends to preserve in that Stile: and whatever new ornaments he adds are to be so: For example in ye old Hall whose Sides he says is now quite naked: I advised him however not to Lace it too much: He says he wou'd give ye world you cou'd see his designs: having ye highest opinion of your Skill in this way;
>
> I asked him why he did not send them to you: that I knew of your good nature; but his answer was that ye Drawings were so large it was impossible. He wanted much to know if there was any chance of seeing you in this part of the world…[331]

In 1753 Brownlow-Cecil, 9th Earl of Exeter, was saddened when his wife, formerly Letitia Townshend, passed away leaving him childless. He had only just inherited **Burghley** (technically Cambridgeshire, though the postal address is Lincolnshire), but a generous £70,000 legacy (today about £10 million) proved a distraction. So when, in August 1755, an earthquake (discussed on p.72) affected the nearby town of Stamford and much further afield, Exeter certainly had the means to repair his damaged Elizabethan home. It was probably this that prompted him to call in Brown in the first place.

Records of the early programme for remodelling the grand house are sparse, and none of Brown's typically large plans survive. However, comparisons are revealing between William Cecil's original

architecture, depicted in a 1680s tapestry, and in drawings by Haynes (1755), with Brown's subsequent alterations, including shoring up the house because of the nearby fault line. At the same time, he ensured the environs of the house remained dry with the land draining away into his surrounding new ha-ha.

The original idea to build a great library by adding a 21-ft bay to the narrow west wing had to be abandoned, probably because structural damage was greater than first realised. After demolishing this wing to open a view of the north front, Brown went on to remove the old stables and all trace of other assorted buildings cluttering the area, before entirely grassing it over. This characteristic simplification set off the magnificent Elizabethan west front, making a dramatic, lasting impression on arriving visitors, its splendid gold doors reflecting afternoon sun. In opening up the north front as the main entrance Brown retained the ornamental ironwork gates and *clairvoie* railing by the seventeenth-century Huguenot iron-worker Jean Tijou, and addressed the problem of the palisade.

March 2007, Burghley House, Cambridgeshire Note an almost imperceptible level-change. Brown buried part of the original Barnack stone plinth to shore up the house and address the geological fault line (shown on John Haynes's survey, 1755) running just south of the house.

In place of the demolished wing, he had to copy and extend both the original low stone wall around the court and the iron grille. Later he decided to fill in and replace the court pond with a circular lawn. The essential slope of both drive and lawn, crucial for drainage, is barely apparent. The extensive ha-ha, probably constructed with stone from the demolition of the old stables and west wing, is at least 9 ft high in places. Yet it remains unseen from the approach road in the park (see p.239).

During long absences travelling in Italy, the earl found it expedient to offer Brown £1,000 per annum patronage (today £145,000), entrusting him to mastermind various sizeable projects with regular supervisory visits.[332] Brown paid his clerk of works, Aquila Cole, but Exeter also gave Cole additional money to distribute among workmen. The local architect William Legg's plan (1756) has Brown's

suggestions pencilled in: for instance, on the Chestnut Courtyard, 'LB For the Feeding and Fatting of Fowls'.[333] This detail is typical of his absorption in modernising administrative offices and the practicalities of everyday living. A real priority was to design a new brew-house in order to keep house staff, masons and ground force as fit and as content as possible. Brown also improved their working life with new kitchens, servants' quarters and domestic offices sandwiched between the kitchen court and his new stables.

Ever resourceful, Brown helped himself to ashlar stone from Exeter's nearby property, Wothorpe House, abandoned after an unhealthy water supply caused cholera. This was put to good use in his three-sided, nine-bay, two-storey stable range in restrained Gothic style. The battlements edge a hipped roof tiled in local Collyweston slate. His perfectionism, coupled with the renowned quality of local masons' workmanship, ensured that all his alterations respected and blended seamlessly with the original Elizabethan parts of Cecil's house. John Linnell (1729–1796), a woodcarver and cabinet-maker based in London's Berkeley Square, featured among skilled craftsmen who interpreted Brown's interior designs and clever use of space, doubtless also addressing water closets. His designs included ceiling decoration for the present library, north dining room, billiard room, chapel and ante-room. One

idea was to situate Coade stone virgin lamps[334] around the sides of the chapel in order to draw the focus away from the great fireplace towards the altar. Behind the altar was hung the earl's treasure, brought back from Venice, the magnificent Veronese altarpiece.

Exeter eventually remarried and by the late 1770s, his debts totalled £55,500 (about £8½ million). Consequently, he reduced Brown's annual payment to £750 (today about £107,000). When his bailiff, John Clarke, came to check the earl's personal account, he discovered that Brown had been overpaid. After promptly returning the amount owed, in April 1779, Brown finally closed the account. There was no apparent ill feeling as, two years later, he was invited back to submit plans for the Great Hall and stairs. However, in this case, Exeter preferred an earlier design by Robert Adam.

A footnote, here, in the context of Brown's interpretation of Gothic architecture, may explain 'an architectural mongrel' at **Tong** (Shropshire).[335] George Durant, an MP who had amassed a fortune in Havana, drove a hard bargain with the Duke of Kingston for an estate, a village and a house in poor repair. The rebuild, on the site of a medieval castle, cried out for a sympathetic interpretation. Brown submitted various plans and elevations, perhaps attempting to combine elements inspired by Walpole's Strawberry Hill Gothic

May 1998, Burghley House
Compare Brown's proposal for the south elevation (right: © The Burghley House Collection) with today's south front. In consideration of the fault line, he underpinned the house and rebuilt the south front with a façade. He raised the south garden level and removed steps to the door, allowing direct access to a spacious lawn. He heightened the central second-storey bays to screen high-ceilinged baroque staterooms and staircase and raised blank windows matching the height of the outer bay windows.

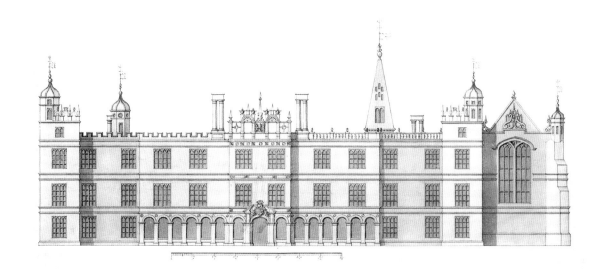

style and the ogee domes of Burghley's skyline. Durant chose to oversee the build himself and subsequently enjoyed all the credit for Tong Castle.

James Paine was one of the first architects to run a successful, independent private practice with clients as opposed to patrons. His interpretation of a restrained, less monumental Palladianism suited those with more modest means. Original elevations and plans show confident use of movement and his development of a convenient interior staircase, which must have influenced Brown's designs.[336] They worked in tandem, assigned the same specialist craftsmen

and admired each other's achievements. Paine masterminded the Earl of Scarborough's new country residence at Sandbeck, as Brown laid out the grounds; likewise for Baron Petre at Thorndon Hall (Essex). Paine, having also lost his father at an early age, was as compulsively driven as Brown. He too did not get on with Chambers.[337]

However, in the 1770s their relationship soured. Not only had Paine become resentful of Brown's royal patronage, but also, in competition, Paine lost a significant commission to Brown: the rebuilding of the Earl of Donegal's country house at **Fisherwick** (Staffordshire).

Brown had shrewdly offered to take on the extra responsibility for the carriage of the requisite fine materials, including quality stone from the ruins of Roche Abbey that he had negotiated with Lord Scarborough. This he used to fashion a superb hall floor inset with black Warwickshire marble.[338] Regrettably, Paine, when publishing his designs, chose to express sarcastic bitterness in print:

…what surprising genius's then must those be who are born architects? How much above every other order of men? But, as nothing is impossible with the great Author of Nature, so we have a genius of this kind, who, after having been from his youth confined against his nature, to the serpentine walks of horticulture, emerge, at once, a compleat architect, and produce such things, as none but those who were born with such amazing capability, could possibly have done…[339]

In due course, Humphry Repton came to Brown's defence:

In the dispute betwixt him and Pain the architect, the latter seemed to have the advantage because Brown left nothing in writing, but if we compare the houses built by each, we shall discover that Brown has left many good specimens of his skill while Pain never built a house that was comfortable without great alteration.[340]

A cemented relationship, so to speak, with one reliable gentleman builder, Henry Holland Sr of Fulham, secured a successful expansion of the architectural side of the practice.[341] One of Brown's closest friends, Holland supervised house alterations at Flambards in Harrow (Middlesex) while building a manageable residence for the Duke of Bridgewater adjacent to a medieval great hall and cloisters at

Ashridge (Hertfordshire). In 1769, inspired by travel in Italy, Rowland Holt III commissioned Brown to transform his red brick Tudor and Jacobean house at Redgrave (Suffolk) into an imposing, four-square Palladian mansion. Holland arranged for the delivery of timber and Portland stone for an Ionic portico and supervised the encasing of the house in white brick from nearby Woolpit.[342] Repton later recorded this refinement: 'Brown said "A red house puts a valley in a fever".'

The classical country house at **Claremont** in Surrey broke new ground: nine bays by seven, not in red but light yellow brick.[343] Robert Clive (1725– 1774), a colonial Major General, one of England's wealthiest peers, was better known as 'Clive of India' after his stint as Governor of Bengal. Having purchased Vanbrugh's Claremont estate from the Duke of Newcastle's widow, Clive 'never enjoy'd one hour's comfort' in the damp, old-fashioned house. However, he remained unconvinced by proposals for a neo-classical country house on higher ground submitted by Sir William Chambers, now sharing the position Architect of the King's Works with Robert Adam. To his astonishment, Brown won the prestigious commission, undoubtedly thanks to sensitive attention to Clive's requirements for a compact, neo-classical villa. Harking back to Peper Harow, the architectural tables had been turned.

Now the most sought-after architect in 'modern English taste', Brown recognised nascent talent, offering Henry Holland Jr (1745–1806), the able son of his friend and colleague, the opportunity to be

his Clerk of Works. Not long after, Holland Jr took on John Soane (1753–1837), the youngest son of a Reading bricklayer, just twenty years old, to work as clerk and draughtsman on £60 a year (today £8,700).

Lodging with the Holland family, and already showing signs of the flair and brilliance later recognised by the London establishment, Soane contributed several coloured elevation and ceiling plans for Claremont.[344] They include one idea for a dome, and perhaps the finest room: the rectangular hall, dressed with an oval ring of red *clairvoie* columns and oval relief plasterwork panels. Brown continued to explore every architectural possibility in compact interior layouts. He tried out embryonic ideas that influenced and inspired both Holland Jr and Soane, including cantilevered stairs, mock doors for symmetry, and skylights expanding feelings of contrast and space by allowing natural light to penetrate shadowy stairwells. His architectural forte was, without doubt, the disposition of offices. A light, spacious basement contained a vaulted room for Clive's large, sunken, indoor marble bath. This opened on to a discreet underground service tunnel, an efficient and original solution for bringing in food and fuel supplies.

Despite reusing red bricks from the old house for interior walls, costs rose to £15,584 (today about £1,834,000). Luxurious furnishings, including the finest gold-framed mirrors from Paris, amounted to almost £18,000 (about £2,260,000). Brown assured Clive that he considered every detail, including the 'Great Eating Room' and the library or 'Gold Room'.

Your Lordship may depend there has been no stone left unturned for the completion of Claremont. I flatter myself what is done will have the approbation of your Lordship and Friends.... Your Lordship will be pleased to remember that it is not a ceiling, a chimney Piece, fine Glasses or even Pictures that constitute Beauty. It is the harmonious disposition of the Whole which will ever please, and is far, very far above Fashion, whatever does not please I will alter...[345]

As it happened, Clive never moved in. He committed suicide in his London home following a bout of severe depression, perhaps brought on by public criticism and parliamentary suspicions about his vast wealth. It took six years before his executors paid Brown his final dues. In the interim, there were fresh horizons to explore and more challenges to face.

Charles Pelham, newly married, at **Brocklesby** in Lincolnshire, appreciated that his remote sixteenth-century manor house needed updating for his beautiful young bride Sophia.[346] However, he had spent a small fortune buying racehorses in order to breed thoroughbreds. The expansion of the stables was his priority, plus the provision of a gallop, because enclosures were curtailing popular race meetings on the outskirts of Lincoln.[347] Brown assessed the situation and promptly produced the requisite grand plan (1771) to develop the entire estate.[348] Besides being a halfway house on journeys north for ongoing projects at Burton Constable, the commission gave him the opportunity to spend time in his wife's county and to foster useful contacts for his sons' future careers. Two years later he returned for a further three

plumbing, a new house would then have been quite straightforward. In the event, the proposal was deemed too radical. Either young Pelham balked at the expense or he wished to remain living next door to his beloved horses. The original master plan shows what appears to be extra, partly erased, pencil marks, a mirror image of the house sketched around a court, an idea for an extension that was also dismissed. Brown penned in his account book a rare personal testimony to his labours, concerning 'A Plan for the Alterations of the House and Offices': 'A great deal of trouble was it to me.'[351]

Was Brown's 'trouble' the amount of time and effort he had invested? Or was it Pelham's late £300 payment (today £43,500), which arrived some three years after he had presented his first comprehensive proposal, bearing in mind that he still had to pay

days to concentrate on the alteration and glazing of the stables, and the construction of a brew-house, blacksmith's shop and wagon-house.

Meanwhile, Thomas White Sr (1736–1811),[349] a surveyor regularly employed by Brown, drew up two coloured plans for the park including a series of interlinked lakes: one, 'the ground round about the old Abbey'; the second, closely relating to Brown's contract (1776),[350] 'for the Improvement of Brocklesby Agreeable to the Building of a New House'. Considering Brown's keen instinct for business, and given that Holland Jr had married his daughter, had become a partner in the practice, and possessed measured plans for model houses with modern

his surveyor, contractors and labourers? The final compromise was to raise the ceiling of the East Hall to accommodate the Pelhams' fine collection of exceptionally large paintings. Afterwards, he arranged to stucco the northwest front of the red brick house with Knottingley lime, ensuring that both old house and new additions, now fully visible from his new approach road, were seamlessly united. Strangely, unlike most Brown commissions, the main park vistas today bear little relationship to the house. Why? His original, grand plan envisaged the park landscape to be centred on, and viewed from, a classical country house on a site overlooking his new waters, a house that was never built.[352]

CHAPTER SIXTEEN

FREEDOM TO ROAM

Art provided the impetus for changes to Paul Methuen's house at Corsham, Wiltshire. From 1762 to 1765, Brown effectively doubled the interior space in the east wing specifically to house a refined picture gallery, together with a new library, cabinet room, state bedroom and a novel octagon room.[353] The gallery is a 'three-cube saloon' with an elaborate plaster ceiling. Classical proportions, 72 ft long, 24 ft wide, were as fundamental as ensuring that the south-facing windows, parapet and stone vases of the new wing corresponded to the original part of the house.

Brown's garden buildings were rarely whimsical. Rather than being 'follies', they served a definite purpose, and attracted the family and their visitors to explore the wider landscape. To help clients visualise the carefully considered, intended destination, Brown, just as William Kent had done, set each feature – arbour seat, summerhouse, ice-house, column, lodge, boat-house or bathhouse – within the context of an attractive treescape, and often at an angle to the house. His small bathhouse at Beechwood (Hertfordshire, see p.177), for example, was intended 'to stand obliquely in order to show its side in perspective to ye windows of ye house'.[354] Thus his secluded bathhouse at Corsham merged into its vegetative surroundings with an air of medieval rusticity – a wonderfully sheltered, private way to commune with nature.

OPPOSITE **November 2009, Corsham Court, Wiltshire** A remnant detail of Brown's original design at the side of the bathhouse, an ogee-headed archway framing an old yew.

ABOVE **Corsham Court, Wiltshire** Brown's new picture gallery lit by large double-hung sash windows
© Corsham Court Collection

ABOVE LEFT **July 1994, Corsham Court, Wiltshire** Brown's bathhouse comprised a cold-plunge within an open loggia, plus a small changing room upstairs.

ABOVE RIGHT **November 2009, Corsham Court, Wiltshire** A door at the rear of the bathhouse allowed a discreet exit through a novel serpentine tunnel.

BELOW LEFT **July 2009, Wimpole Park, Cambridgeshire (NT)** Terminating the main view from the house, glimpses of the romantic Gothic tower, a sham-ruin built by Brown.

BELOW **August 2009, Wotton, Buckinghamshire** Wooden pillars of the restored rotunda frame views over the lake.

In the early 1770s, with the assistance of a local architect, James Essex, and his trusted foreman Biesley, Brown realised a long-envisaged sham Gothic ruin at **Wimpole**, Cambridgeshire. Rather than remaining true to Sanderson Miller's original design, he made the tower four storeys instead of three to match the scale of the park panorama, knowing that the eye would be disturbed if it appeared out of proportion. Equilibrium and safe building took priority over the fashion for medieval 'Englishness'. Jemima, Lady Grey, shared the news with her daughter Amabel:

The Tower is better for being raised, but the additions Mr Brown has quite changed from our plan, though he undertook to follow it and said that he liked it. That is, he has 'Unpicturesqued it' by making it a mere continuous solid object, instead of a Broken one. The wall – which is still going on – is continued entire *at the bottom from the whole Tower to the Broken one, and is to be fractured only at the upper part of the Gateway, which is I believe, to resemble our design. However as it makes altogether a greater object it wont do ill. And the upper part of the wall, if well done may yet be sufficiently varied.*[355]

Since his first encounter with Vanbrugh's classical rotunda at **Stowe**, Brown had remained partial to circular buildings at key vantage points, perfect for viewing the landscape in all directions.

The inspiration for his classical Palladian 'Round House' at Redgrave, Suffolk (actually octagonal), may have come from Tottenham, Wiltshire, where he had recently spruced up Burlington's 'Octagon' summerhouse (1743) with a new coat of stucco. At Redgrave the octagonal summerhouse with a domed roof terminates the lake, an arresting focal point, offering a destination for a walk and an opportunity for informal entertaining overlooking the waters. Complete with fireplace, it provided welcome comfort and shelter from the elements. It would be interesting to compare its measurements with Garrick's similar temple at Hampton, which could almost be Brown's (see p.45).

At Sherborne Castle in Dorset, Brown's neat contemporary dairy with Gothic façade made a feature in Lady Digby's flower garden, while screening the utilitarian offices in his organised service yard, connected by a service tunnel. Opposite, he tasked Henry Holland Jr with designing the classical glasshouse. Meanwhile, an exotic *clairvoie* in the middle took the eye away from the two differing architectural styles at either end of the garden.

BELOW LEFT **August 2008, Sherborne Castle, Dorset** Henry Holland Jr's classical glass-house and a *Gingko biloba* in the centre of the flower garden.

BELOW RIGHT **September 2003, Sherborne Castle, Dorset** A state-of-the-art interior for Brown's dairy with its Gothic façade.

The commission at Melton Constable (Norfolk) involved restoring an existing bathhouse that catches the eye in the park and is similar in profile to Spier's Lodge at Warwick Castle. The semi-hexagonal bay also calls to mind Brown's 'antique-embattled' remodelling of High Lodge at Blenheim, like a hunting-lodge within a medieval deer park. As well as building aviaries for breeding exotic pheasants, parrots and peacocks near the house, some country-house owners began to gather a motley collection of wild animals – sometimes for scientific observation, but mainly for amusement. It made sense to house their pet curiosities in secluded locations in the heart of the park.[356]

'Beastly buildings', utilitarian cowsheds, pigsties and kennels in model farm arrangements, such as those in the Middle Park at Burghley, were made prettier with turf roof or thatch, Gothic façades and quatrefoil windows. On a visit to Paris in August 1769, accompanied by his eldest son Lancelot, Brown may have seen the Royal Menagerie at the Palace of Versailles. Did this inspire his sandstone ashlar and brick menagerie at **Coombe Abbey**, Warwickshire? As usual, he thoughtfully provided accommodation for the keeper, stables for winter shelter for beasts from warmer climes, stores for food and bedding, and cart sheds. Upstairs, a decorative, hexagonal observation room allowed Lord Craven and his guests a fine view of the six-acre walled animal enclosure where the animals could drink from the edge of Brown's 'Great Pool'.

At **Castle Ashby**, Northamptonshire, Brown found himself in direct competition with Robert Adam. Adam proposed a modest, naturalistic layout, introducing a Chinese bridge over the lake. Brown, on the other hand, took great pains to pinprick through a tracing of a survey by Thomas Eyre III (1760) to create a much clearer and broader 'great General Plan'. This is approximately 6 ft by 5 ft on eight overlapped panels of heavy cartridge paper, for which he charged the Earl of Northampton £50 (today £7,250).[357] Typical of larger designs with a one-inch

border, it is accurate to a scale of 1 in. to 200 ft and drawn in iron-gall ink and wash. His recognisable 'dotting' indicates the removal of walls, hedges and even village buildings, and his intention to simplify the scene and open up panoramic views.

Subsequently, these innocent pinpricks have provided valuable ammunition to his critics as evidence of the fine gardens he swept away, so fuelling the anger of those who mourn the obliteration of earlier English gardens. According to his accurate historical outlines and dimensions, gardens at this time were mainly elaborate French- or Dutch-inspired. His dots also chart the significant, steady rise of the English landscape movement.

The clarity of Brown's plan, not to mention his engineering prowess, probably helped to land the commission. A combination of versatility, thrift and understated organisational skills in the use of space catered for every eclectic taste and aspiration in vistas new. Here Brown introduced a short walk

for the ladies to visit his Palladian dairy, where the garden front, in Ketton limestone, has echoes of Kent's Temple of Venus at Stowe. The courtyard elevation is relieved with an oval ox-eye window[358] in the parapet and an unusual wooden verandah made by his principal carpenter, John Hobcraft. The latter's considerable skills notwithstanding, Brown maintained full control over details of design: 'I cannot give direction about the alteration over the columns at the Dairy till I am on the spot.'[359]

On the other side of the house, at a distance, a longer circuit walk in the park leads to another classical Tuscan seat, also attributed to Brown. This was designed to terminate and furnish the principal view from the house beyond the lake, and is actually little more than a half-rotunda stage-set façade and screen, hiding a brick cottage for the keeper and an animal enclosure, safely tucked behind out of sight. Interestingly, on his plan of the same period for Weston Park (Staffordshire), rather than clutter a

OPPOSITE **November 2001, Castle Ashby, Northamptonshire** The Menagerie is attributed to Brown.

LEFT **Castle Ashby, Northamptonshire** Brown's Dairy has an unusual veranda with wooden lattice at the rear.

ABOVE **January 1998, Burghley Park, Cambridgeshire** The Gothic cowshed in Brown's model farm and dairy complex.

landscape with too many structures, Brown envisaged a multipurpose classical building with dairy and music room, overlooking a menagerie for bright exotic birds, later designed as the Temple of Diana by James Paine.

Nearby, nestling among evergreens on the perimeter walk, 'Knucklebone Arbour', a more countrified shelter, offered a pleasing view over a serpentine ha-ha and across the upper lake back to the house. The round wooden gazebo had a thatched roof and a patterned floor consisting of concentric circles of pebbles and sheep bones. Brown also agreed: 'The pulling down the old ice house & Building a new one in a very expensive manner & place £68. 0. 0. [today £9,850].'[360]

In the time before refrigeration, Brown was noted for his domestic ice-house. A small, egg-shaped brick structure, with a domed roof and tunnel entrance, it was invariably situated conveniently near lake, pond or river. The choice of wheat-straw thatch was deliberate, in order to provide extra insulation. Elsewhere, it was often more usual, and cheaper, to hide the ice-house under an insulating mass of earth, a 'hillock', concealed by planting.[361] Occasionally, as at Petworth and Compton Verney, a smart new ice-house made a

fashionable feature to show off on the approach drive on a sloping site near a lake or pond. This allowed draining water to filter through the sump at the bottom, thus maintaining a cool temperature. Ice was cut with saws, then stacked and compacted between layers of straw. With the entrance door facing as near north as possible and straw packed in the tunnel, the ice would keep for up to two years. The Croome ice-house has a sunken circular cavity about 10 ft across and 10 ft deep, almost certainly standard dimensions.[362]

Suggestions for a tea-house on the cliffs at Aldborough and a temple on Roe Hill, as an observatory tea-room, fell on stony ground at **Burton Constable** in Yorkshire.[363] Instead, avoiding the expense of an entire building, Brown proposed 'an archway or façade to terminate the menagerie avenue'.[364] In almost the same breath, he recommended castellated sham lodges, linked by an iron palisade, to screen domestic offices. He then suggested taking down the ash-house, moving the coal-house into the courtyard, hiding the wood yard behind the stables and altering the water-house into a square tower. That such mundane considerations as

improving drying yards and faggot yards, outhouses and 'stink piles' should exercise the energies of the royal gardener is hard to credit, yet it is key to understanding Brown, who appreciated how their look, and smells, affected the scene. Whether classical or rustic, grand or modest, a shelter and seat became an essential addition to the composition of the landscape for contemplation of the expansive vistas he had created or upgraded: 'cut down some trees to make an opening for a view of the house from Mrs C's [Constable] seat in the Park near the Bridge.... Icehouse to be placed near the Seat Clump in the park'.[365]

As people's lives were becoming far less confined, it is notable how many seats were proposed with ladies in mind so that they could savour the new views. They must have taken delight in the freedom to explore the wider park landscape in comfortable fashion. Attractive garden seats were doubtless welcomed, particularly in the chillier northern uplands, by those gentlemen commentators and weary garden tourists who would arrive, often unannounced, wanting to inspect the house and gardens, and paying the housekeeper for the privilege.

ABOVE LEFT Brown's undated, cross-section plan for the ice-house for Beechwood, Hertfordshire © The Beechwood School. Two elevations indicate what is to be built above and below ground.

ABOVE **August 2011, Compton Verney, Warwickshire** The restored ice-house gives an indication of how it looked when first built.

BELOW **July 1992, Harewood, Yorkshire** Perhaps a visual pun, a 'seat of wisdom', the Owl Seat interrupts the east wall of the kitchen gardens.

A straight road, militarily exact, as built by the Romans, offers no interesting diversion. Brown paid attention to finding just the right satisfying, curving drive up to the house. In the park the line of a drive may have appeared more meandering, but it had an important and gratifying role, enabling the arriving visitor to take in a series of changing vistas. Warwick Castle was the first distinctive landscape of scale where Brown's tree belts and judiciously placed clumps on high ground, closely modelled on Switzer's 'enfilade', successfully controlled a sequence of charming views, unfolding one by one on a leisurely perimeter drive.[366] In enlarging the lake at Petworth,

Brown removed the main approach through the valley, arranging for the coach road from Upperton to be built at a new, higher level, following the concave contour of the hill and offering panoramic, 'borrowed' views to the North Downs, beyond the park boundary. He brought together an extensive domain and, more than just negotiable, he made it attractively understandable.

New ridings, linked with the old, impressed visitors by their extent, and encouraged exploration on an indirect route, into the exciting unknown. In this way, Brown often doubled the distance from the main road to the house, adding to the anticipation of arrival. In

practical terms, his circuit drives through woodland enabled access to foresters for arboreal management, and facilitated the removal of cropped timber.

The journey towards **Appuldurcombe** (Isle of Wight) once led into the open park across acres of grassland, through scattered groves and individual trees placed seemingly randomly, but often asymmetrically, to engage and entertain the tourist. A sequence of views unfolded to left and right: a clump of trees on the horizon, a column, here a church spire, there a glimpse of the Channel. Finally came the grand revelation, the first dramatic glimpse of their final destination, the country house in its 'natural' setting.

ABOVE AND LEFT **November 1991, Temple Newsam, Yorkshire** A modest wooden Tuscan temple, an eye-catcher among stately beeches on the hill, makes a destination for a walk and an opportunity to see uplifting vistas across the wider park and back to the house.

Artificial undulations enlivened flattish terrain and were relatively easily made when digging ha-has and sunk fences, but mostly by disposing spoil from excavating the lake. A gentle rise along the way prompted the unsuspecting observer to look to one side or the other, perhaps towards a rotunda at left and, at the next hillock, an urn at right. The range of attractions was never intended to be seen all at once, unless from a boat bobbing on the waters. Each feature was concealed by planting, revealed suddenly and spectacularly in dappled glades of lawn edged with attractive shrubs, and then hidden again just as quickly in dense woodland, until the next enchanting surprise around the corner. Brown's circuitous approaches to Caversham (Berkshire) and to Wimbledon (Surrey, now Merton) found favour with Walpole.

A new Palladian house at Benham in Berkshire proved another versatile collaboration between Brown and Holland Jr. A pair of arched gates, with pediments, gate piers and a classical, rustic screen, still hides lodges on either side. The drive winds down a thickly planted hill in deep shade before visitors catch the first welcome glimpse of the water,

at a distance, across a swathe of pastureland. The gentle incline continues clockwise around the slope, whereupon, spectacularly, all at once, the visitor is confronted, as if by magic, with the classical Palladian house directly ahead.

Lodges and boundary walls added to feelings of security, and that in turn encouraged the family and their visitors to roam more widely within the park boundaries. The style of lodges mostly reflected that of the main residence, making a strong statement for travellers entering an estate from the public road. However, at Combe Abbey, Warwickshire, Baron Craven was wealthy enough to commission both an unconventional Gothic cottage, with central octagonal range and two wings, almost certainly designed by Brown, and a studied, neo-classical arch attached to a lodge by Holland Jr.[367] At **Clandon** (Surrey) Brown removed refined, crested, wrought-iron and gilt gates from the original forecourt to create space. He was content to reuse materials where possible, appropriate and prudent. So he rehung them to link his new pair of lodges, each with a pretty lunette window, probably also recycled from elsewhere.

OPPOSITE **October 2010, Appuldurcombe Park, Isle of Wight** Brown designed this old 'Green Drive' on the approach, traversing the high ground rather than the valley, so as to take in sea-views. The poet Gerard Manley Hopkins (1844–1889) once enjoyed walks in the park here.

RIGHT **Appuldurcombe House, Isle of Wight (EH)** Brown's drive formerly snaked in from the right. Notice the Scots pine, asymmetrically placed with cedars of Lebanon, on the opposite rear corner of the house, probably part of his design.

BELOW **September 2007, Clandon Park, Surrey (NT)** In 1776 Brown re-hung the ornate gates from the old house forecourt at the park entrance between his pair of single-storey, square classical lodges.

CHAPTER SEVENTEEN

KEEP ALL IN VIEW
VERY NEAT

Henry Hoare was naturally drawn into discussions concerning plans for his daughter's home at Tottenham House, in the heart of the ancient Savernake forest. He was especially engaged when his son-in-law, the 2nd Baron Bruce, invited Brown to remodel the gardens. The designer set about moving gate piers and demolishing the forecourt wall to install the requisite ha-ha. Unusually, he chose to retain the direct approach, whether out of respect for Burlington's original classical design or because the topography precluded an oblique, serpentine route.[368]

The banker made a rough sketch showing the house enclosed by a loosely snaking, oval belt with individual groves scattered around on one side of the straight road. On the other, he had sight-lines, or possible rides, drawn from the house towards Lord Hertford's prominent forest enclosure, a strong focal point. A caption on the reverse side of the paper reads: 'Brown's Idea for Improvement in the Levels so as to make one great *Whole*.'[369]

The country house was the hub. Every aspect framed by every reception room window and hall door mattered. This was how Brown developed a seamless, united landscape, with singleton trees or groves providing Claudian foreground interest, 'altering the old park wherever it is thought Necessary, in short to compleat the whole'.[370]

OPPOSITE **September 1989, Denwick Hills, near Alnwick** (see also p.131) Foreground remnants of a grove of beech, *Fagus sylvatica*, on the Great North Road (A1)

ABOVE **May 1992, Petworth, Sussex (NT)** A deer helps to create a neat, uniform under-canopy.

Hoare had clearly grasped the significance of the word 'whole' that appeared consistently in many of Brown's contracts and was part and parcel of his everyday terminology. Rather than random or piecemeal improvement, Brown put into practice Switzer's holistic philosophy.

Every site was different. Brown examined all land, timber and water assets in each client's portfolio, studying the entire workings and infrastructure of an estate, so as to offer the best advice and find solutions to problems, with a promising broad commitment: 'and giving the Whole a Natural easy and corresponding Level with the House, the Water and the Roads'.[371]

The simplicity of language typically understated the numbers of men and the intrinsic skills required to grade the landscape with corresponding levels, and underestimated the amount of time needed to achieve an agreeable, harmonious effect. In reality the task was unquestionably complex, as witnessed by the Earl of Breadalbane:

> *…dined yesterday at Ingestre; where there is a greater alteration of Mr Brown's direction than I thought possible. The garden is now bounded by a sunk fence, which brings in a most delightful prospect up to the Lodge in the Park, the grounds are all united by easy slopes running into each other & all the holes fill'd up, & the View is now very extensive along those lawns. A great deal of wood is cut down within the garden as well as without & a number of mighty fine old oaks appear which were hid, and a gravel walk is made round the whole thro' large oaks and flowering shrubs so far within the fence that the Eye goes over it & the great lawn appears part of the garden, the space between the walk & the fence being grass with old trees scattered in it, & likewise on the inside of the walk the wood is towards the garden cut for a considerable space in particular spots leaving only the great trees & grass under them.*[372]

All areas required appropriate investment and subsequent careful management. The key to organising and uniting variable components of the

ABOVE **March 2009** In Brown's day, it was common to stock the woods with colourful pheasants for sport, apparently easier to manage than native species.

OPPOSITE **June 1994, Milton Abbas, Dorset** Pevsner admired the exhilarating situation of this village, which Brown moved. The road (and the drains) snake down to his lake. His thatched cottages are little changed, cocooned with surrounding plantations.

domain, sprawling deer park, forest and farmland, was to provide extensive rides through perimeter oak and beech plantations. This brought significant sporting and financial returns, while the texture matured to give a great sense of place. Each gradation of landscape had to sit well with existing woodland ridings for fox-hunting, blending at the same time into adjacent working fields and outer 'rough parks' for hares, warrens and game.

It was not just the eye that was disturbed at **Milton Abbey** in Dorset. The village was far too close to Lord Milton's house for privacy, offending ears and, probably, noses. More importantly, it occupied the only suitable location for a lake, so, despite objections, it was demolished. Some materials were recycled, such as sound, heavy timber beams for use over fireplaces. The uprooted villagers, far from feeling abandoned, eventually settled into Brown's village, Milton Abbas, nestling in a narrow valley that he clad with trees. Each house was once shaded, according to old postcards, by a splendid horse-chestnut tree. Each pretty, uniformly thatched and rendered brick dwelling, large enough for two to four families, was set

back from the road, and far enough apart to prevent the flames spreading if the thatch caught fire.

Critics continue to accuse Brown of condoning, if not setting, a trend towards social upheaval and deprivation of the poorest. In the longer term, his drastic measures proved to be in the interest of most people, with landowners having acted responsibly in rehousing estate workers. Here, they left shabby hovels to move into viable, more attractive accommodation in upgraded surroundings.[373] Houses were situated on a sloping site to allow free drainage, with fresh-water pumps at regular intervals through the village. In reality, tenants enjoyed the perfect location, with better views than Lord Milton, of both the lake and St James's Church (later built by James Paine).

Wealth was no longer displayed in rococo gardens, fountains and fish canals; rather it was shown in the scale of lawns and 'natural' waters, in model farms and villages, and in the extent of plantations scattered across hills and vales. Brown caused many a wholesale transformation: '"Wilderness" with swamps, gorse and whin higher than a man on horseback, deep ridge and Furrow…. Now all is removed and at great Expense.'[374] No one could misconstrue his concise

directions: 'Three things must be attended to, Space, Cleanness & Shelter'[375] or 'Keep two men constantly employed in Mowing Thistles and Weeds'.[376]

Roadside gutters were to be cleaned out, clumps, gravel paths and drives weeded, molehills levelled. Often the same men and women in charge of husbandry on the farm worked on the gardens. Sometimes Brown thought it necessary to reorientate the focus away from a nearby town, as at Warwick and Petworth. Other designers' efforts paled in comparison. He maintained one over-arching principle, very probably repeated everywhere he worked: 'Keep all in view very neat.'[377]

Grass tolerates drought, grows quickly and well in England and suits its oceanic climate. For centuries, the traditional, perennial, pleasurable 'bird-haunted' English lawn has been widely admired. 'The antithesis of the French parterre' ironically stemmed from the Old French word *launde*: an open area for grazing deer. An early survey (1608)[378] for Wakefield Lodge has a broad acreage beside a large pond annotated as 'The Lawn'. Acres of green space, offering a civilising, calming effect, allowed space for outdoor entertainment long before Brown's time. By the

1730s, according to the Chelsea gardener Philip Miller (1691–1771), a great expanse of open grassland was popular with the upper echelons of society:

> Lawn is a great Plain in a Park or a spacious plain adjoining to a noble Seat. As to the Dimensions of it, it should be as large as the ground will permit, but never if possible less than fifty acres. As to the situation … it will be best on the Front of the House, and to lie open to the neighbouring Country and not pent up with Trees.[379]

Garrick milked the comedy of the ha-ha in his play, but Walpole recognised this dramatic departure from rectilinear garden geometry, the leading step in the change towards modern gardening and, by stretching boundaries, a consolidation of farmland.[380] Thanks to a discreet ha-ha, and sometimes an additional sunk fence in the middle distance, Brown's lawn became one delightful, seemingly continuous sweep across the view, often down to the edge of his lake. His spacious Salisbury Lawns at Chatsworth set off the famous Cascade (1703) descending the hillside.[381]

Contracts for drain works or road realignment promised the quickest route to re-establish order by sowing grass seed on a large scale, with a reassuring pledge: 'growing, levelling and sowing meadows and should any part of it fail, sow it over again till it does answer'.[382]

Evergreen, drought-tolerant clover with domed white flowers, Trifolium repens, competes well against most weeds. Its main bonus: its palatable leaves provide high-energy fodder for livestock. After clearing away great gardens in front of Petworth House, Brown laid sufficient quantity of 'good Mould' and obtained Dutch clover and grass seed to cover some 1,870 ft towards the road.[383] Again his (undated) Milton Abbey account details a huge quantity, enough for 140 acres of lawn, the seed bought from another of Brown's clients in the Thames valley: 'for 1,120 lbs of Dutch clover seed bought by S Freeman Esq of Fawley Ct & sent to Milton Abb. £32 13. 0. [£4,700]'.

Those clients spending only the summer months at their country estates welcomed the expediency and modernity of this open, gracefully contoured

'new look'. Whether surveyed from front steps or from reception room windows, a foreground expanse of grass aroused feelings of freedom. An effortless connection with the surrounding countryside invited easy exploration.

Each return visit generated further work, to 'correct every thing that was wrong', as long as the client could bear the cost.[384] The shrewd businessman made himself indispensable. Every consultation involved close study of local contours, leading clients to a deeper awareness of the qualitative value of land. The farming economy expanded. Livestock health improved as cattle, sheep and deer, no longer scratching around on common land, fattened on improved pastures. Eighteenth-century paintings reflect landowners' growing fascination with superior breeds of animals, taking their lead from George III. Sheep grazing close to the house became a common sight. Useful grazing grassland was extended by means of sunk fences and trenching 'to drain and divide the Meadows', while arable farming switched to the park periphery.

OPPOSITE **November 1991, Temple Newsam, Yorkshire** Opencast mining disrupted some areas of Brown's landscape, but an attempt was made to restore significant horizon plantations on view from the house, much as he had designed.

ABOVE **September 2009, Temple Newsam, Yorkshire** A view hardly changed since Brown's day. Acres of green grass calm and simplify the space for visitors and set off the Elizabethan architecture of the house.

BELOW **February 2007, Wimpole, Cambridgeshire (NT)** A serpentine sunk fence to drain and separate the pastures leads the eye to a series of evergreen holm oaks.

Mowing was best done when the grass was still damp from early morning dew. The mowers kept it neat by swinging their sharp, crescent-shaped scythes rhythmically back and forth before raking off the loose cuttings. Often the whole household assisted the gather. Mowing and haymaking, a social community event, with teamwork spread among villagers of all ages, was more important than ever to produce winter fodder for larger numbers of horses. Many clients indulged in a variety of field sports. Patrons of the Turf, including Lord Derby at Knowsley (Lancashire), were quick to appreciate the increased income from grazing as more 'pretty paddocks' were let out.

There was no need for trained gardeners, as harnessed oxen pulled rollers to level lawns. Greenswards proved ideal for organised summer games such as rounders (or baseball). Some sporting clubs attempted to play the ancient game of Real Tennis out of doors on smooth, levelled grass. 'Field Tennis' eventually became known as 'Lawn Tennis'.[385] Bowling greens were still common[386] but, after the rules of cricket were regularised, this competitive game with medieval origins began to supersede linear bowling, and exploited the wider availability of space.[387] One of the earliest recorded matches was played at Peper Harow (Surrey) in July 1727. The game was well established by the time Brown was employed by Viscount Midleton

to make improvements. Doubtless, as in many commissions, he left sufficient open space for the cricket ground.

The Earl of Sandwich, Brown's influential friend from Huntingdon, together with his clients Viscount Palmerston and Lord Temple, numbered among active patrons of cricket. At **Sherborne Castle**, where Alexander Pope had previously given advice, the grounds had declined despite Lord Digby's best efforts. Brown, doubtless inspired by following in Pope's footsteps, set about selective tree-felling. Eventually, acres of levelled lawn beyond Brown's new ha-ha made a perfect playing field. Here, in July 1782, the Duke of Dorset's team challenged an All England side. A vigorous man with an active mind, mixing with men of all ranks, Brown proved a great leveller in more ways than one. Enjoyable rural entertainment on gracious lawns contributed towards lowering barriers between gentlemen players and estate workers.[388]

Further north, at Burghley, his changes caused a workforce reduction from twenty-five gardeners to ten. 'The Environs to the House are now under Mr Brown's hands and are at present chaos, but seem to be coming into a handsome lawn, and the wood about it will be fine.'[389] Since, in 1773, a portable summerhouse and expensive new garden rollers

ABOVE **May 1998, Brocklesby, Lincolnshire** In contrast to Brown's open park punctuated with tree clumps and dotted trees, his sheltered riding is now appreciated by the local hunt.

BELOW **August 2008, Sherborne Castle, Dorset** Brown left ample space for a cricket field beyond his extensive new stone ha-ha on the left (or 'ah-ah' according to Mr Burnett, the agent). Note the contrast of open space with tree-punctuated parkland below Jerusalem Hill.

were purchased for £19 15s 0d (£2,863) and £35 5s 0d (£5,000) respectively, there seems a distinct likelihood that cricket was being played in the park by this stage.[390] Meanwhile, a new grandstand overlooking the racecourse west of Burghley's High Park proved popular with Stamford townsfolk.

Lincolnshire was renowned for its horses, and the Horncastle horse fair was the largest in the country. A strong tradition of fox-hunting in the region dates from about 1700, when a racehorse breeder, Charles Pelham, was joint master at **Brocklesby**. Owing to its remoteness, it was mainly tenant farmers and clergy who participated in four-day hunt meetings. The pack of hounds, fifty couples on average, secured its reputation when another Charles Pelham commissioned Brown to enlarge the stables and build new kennels away from the house.[391] The master plan (1771) for Brocklesby addressed many radical improvements. Brown persevered with consultations spread over more than ten years. This brought great changes to the house, the gardens, kitchen gardens and the surrounding park landscape: in effect, the whole fabric and management of the estate (see also pp.197 and 212–13). Taking account of his young client's sporting pursuits, he allowed ample room in the park for a gallop, or racecourse, and for a cricket field.[392]

In 1777, a 'New Inn' built nearby in Great Limber served the influx of visitors to the races. In spring 1780, despite his health problems, Brown faithfully reappeared, intent on overseeing coving and plaster embellishments in his new East Hall. The grounds did not escape inspection.[393] Two new 'iron rollers' were purchased from Hull for £5 (£725) each, one for the new lawn and the other, possibly, for the cricket square beyond the ha-ha. The estate carpenter made several long wooden benches for spectators, and painted a summerhouse, also costing £5, with four coats of olive green paint.[394] The Pelhams and their guests, meanwhile, occupied country chairs in a rustic temple summerhouse, specifically positioned in the garden to catch the afternoon sun, and offering an uninterrupted view of the cricket in the park.[395]

Viscount Torrington found Brown's 70-ft-wide rides through his newly created tree belts in their early stages of growth 'horribly staring, and disagreeable'.[396] Later, Arthur Young disagreed, recognising how Brown had assisted hunting: 'a beautiful place to plant a foxhunter'.[397] This commission differed from normal 'place-making'. A major, viable and secure sporting estate evolved in no small part thanks to Brown's methodical, conscientious advice and foresight: 'Brocklesby is not merely a domain: it is a kingdom.'[398]

Enclosures of common land and open fields, notwithstanding local politics and expenditure, also increased opportunities for employment in laying down plantations and securing boundaries.[399] Mrs Montagu described developments at Sandleford in Berkshire:

> The scene is extremely animated; 20 men at work in the wood and grove, and the fields around are full of haymakers. The persons employed on the work are poor weavers who by the decay of our manufacture at Newbury are void of employment, and not having been trained to the business of agriculture are not dextrous at the rake and pitchfork, but the plain digging and driving wheelbarrows they can perform and are very glad to get their daily subsistence.[400]

A long, high red-brick wall on the boundary of Syon Park is thought to date from Brown's modifications. Note also the miles of boundary wall at Petworth and Burghley. Brown strove for balance, proportion and quality of line in every detail, whether in park paling, iron rail fence or boundary walling, and appreciated how important it was to keep estate labourers and stonemasons in work through the winter months. Did he design the unusual deer fence consisting of tall spear-shaped wooden posts linked by wires and iron chain, encircling his Burghley gamekeeper's cottage? This thatched Round House, in the local rural 'mud and stud' tradition, doubled as a lodge for his new approach, now known as 'Brown's Cutting', leading from Ermine Street, the nearby Roman road.

A stone park wall stretching along Parkhill Road at Castle Ashby secured Brown's Menagerie. Here too he advised on a new fence and gates within the park:

1769 New Park Fence 12 pr acre common work with Two rails 7½ foot posts 18s [£130]

4 ½ foot pales 3 railed work with 10-foot post & pales from 6 to 9 foot

carpenters work £107 8s. [£15,600]

9 great gates @3gns [£442] a gate 6 little gates @ 2 gns. [£292]

a gate total carpenters work £254. 4.3 [£36,860]

Ditch round the New Park Fence 10d. a pole

Drains @ 8d. a drain 8s. 0d. [£58][401]

TOP March 2007, Burghley Park, Cambridgeshire Brown's Gothic gamekeeper's lodge reflects local traditional 'mud and stud' cottage buildings.

LEFT January 2013, Burghley Park, Cambridgeshire The annual upkeep and repair of frost damage to Brown's stone boundary wall, several miles long, is considerable.

ABOVE October 1995, Burghley Park, Cambridgeshire Note this unusual deer fence, surrounding the gamekeeper's lodge. Could this also be a Brown innovation?

Brown is thought to have designed a curious pair of wrought-iron Gothic gates at Tong Castle in Shropshire.[402] Keeping pace with change, neater, longer-lasting and discreet iron rail fences (also called 'wires'), made by local or estate blacksmiths, were paid for by pound weight:

Thomas Squire's Bill for the Rail Fence at Wimbledon Pk 42.3.9. [£6,090]

John Watridges Bill for painting the above fence 13.0.0. [£1,885]

Recd by the omission of the rough Rail Fence 21.0.0. [£3,045][403]

An ability to think in three dimensions, underpinned by engineering expertise, brought about a novel exploitation of space and topography. Rather than being secretly iconic, Brown's innovative subways were, in the main, down-to-earth service tunnels. They were constructed with a basic brick core, just as his conduits were, employing the cut and fill method, straightforward for a man who grew up in a mining area. A tunnel is thought to have existed at Stowe for bringing in stock to graze the Grecian valley, but has never been found. It may have been adapted from part of Brown's underground watercourse after his trial lake was abandoned. Perhaps, as a result, an idea began to germinate. His underground passages at Petworth and elsewhere allowed both the carting of ice and the safe

movement of animals to the menagerie with minimal disturbance to the family's garden walks. A large tunnel at Wimbledon, built high enough for a man on horseback, could take eight men abreast.[404] The Sherborne contract (1776) proposed a 'subterraneous passage' from the castle yard to ease the restocking of provisions, including pit coal, sea coal and coke. Brown's tunnels increased efficiency and a more peaceful equilibrium in the environs of the mansion.[405]

In the garden, disguised changes in level were skilfully designed to ease the flow of pleasure-ground walks. At Gatton (Surrey), the path from the house to the kitchen gardens negotiates a 'dry arch' built over the approach to the stables; it doubles as an agreeable eye-catcher. The side on view from the park is faced with tooled ashlar, as opposed to the rubblestone and brick on the stables side, a characteristic touch of thrift.

After Brown's death, Humphry Repton grasped every opportunity to study his work. In 1789, tackling only his second commission, he outlined a pleasure garden beside the lake at Holkham (Norfolk), with his lakeside walk passing through a tunnel.[406] Occasionally critical of Brown when it suited, Repton did graciously acknowledge specific strengths and new departures in his designs, in particular his assured serpentine contour on the plan, on the ground and even under the ground. He appreciated just how much Brown had integrated a variety of spaces into a surprising and harmonious whole:

The belts & rides which surround his parks, his breaking up of avenues by removing trees at irregular intervals, his predilection for serpentine lakes, inspired by Hogarth's line of beauty & his ingenious crossing of paths or drives, one above the other, by means of stone or rockwork bridges.… It often happens that a walk in a plantation or shrubbery is crossed by a road or drift way; this has been ingeniously obviated (I believe originally by Mr. Brown), by making one pass over the other, and where the situation requires such expense, a subterraneous passage may either be made under the carriage-road.…[407]

OPPOSITE TOP LEFT **October 2010, Appuldurcombe, Isle of Wight** An eighteenth-century wrought-iron gate.

OPPOSITE TOP RIGHT **November 2009, Corsham Court, Wiltshire** Brown's stone tunnel, just as at Nuneham Courtenay, for discreet and easy movement of cattle or sheep from the park, passes under the North Walk in the pleasure ground.

OPPOSITE BELOW **May 1994, Croome, Worcestershire (NT)** The lake circuit leads under the main road to Upton, with an affecting change of light, before the walk continues through flowering shrubberies towards St Mary Magdalene Church.

CHAPTER EIGHTEEN

MOVING HEAVEN

In 1717, the year after Brown was born, a powerful, classless and co-operative fraternity of landowners, architects, journeyman masons and independent craftsmen established the first Grand Lodge of Freemasons in London. The movement grew steadily. By the mid-eighteenth century hundreds of lodges were holding regular meetings, though not all were affiliated under the Grand Lodge system. Numbers of Brown's clients, and many associate masons and craftsmen, were involved in the fraternity.[408]

In Templar Freemasonry, the constitutional number required to open a 'Commandery' was eleven members, alluding to the true Disciples of Christ. This was represented by twin pillars on either side of a temple entrance, a symbolic gateway to enlightenment and wisdom. Was there some subtle significance, some hidden meaning, therefore, in Brown's eleven-window design for a greenhouse at Burghley? Or was it simply an extended orangery positioned strategically in the shadow of the Great Hall, so as to hide a complex of offices, laundry court and assorted fuel yards behind? Orange trees, rare plants and flowering shrubs, arranged outside in summer, were then protected from the prevailing west wind. Walpole remained unconvinced by this bastardised architecture somewhere between Gothic and Grecian: 'A noble pile! Brown is ornamenting the park and has built a Gothic greenhouse and stables, which are not bad, except that they do not accord with the House which is not Gothic.'[409]

OPPOSITE **May 1999, Croome, Worcestershire (NT)** Much of Brown's work endures, woven in with national identity.

ABOVE Brown's Plan (1771) for a sham bridge for Grimsthorpe, Lincolnshire (not executed). Courtesy © Lincolnshire Archives, with the permission of the Grimsthorpe and Drummond Castle Trust.

TOP **March 2007, Burghley House, Cambridgeshire** Brown's original Gothic greenhouse, with octagonal turrets to conform with the Jacobean skyline of the great house. The castellated parapet and perpendicular fluting over the arches recall decoration on Gibbs's Gothic Temple at Stowe.

ABOVE **September 2006, Wotton, Buckinghamshire** A masonic carving in the Orangery.

Philosophy and iconography in intellectual Masonic circles influenced many garden building designs, with inherent symbolism in chequered floors, obelisks and columns, pyramids and temples. Alexander Pope and William Kent numbered among those Freemasons who advocated garden grottoes to introduce a frisson of underworld mysticism into their communion with nature. Rocks represented 'Wisdom'. A grotto festooned in moss and ferns near a water-source suggested a mysterious retreat for the beguiling nymphs and fauns of the ancient world, guardians of life-giving water. Learned thoughts concerning the 'journey of life' and the theatre of the 'rocky path of virtue' were surely understood by Brown, and maybe even appreciated, but, a pragmatist at heart, he would use a grotto to disguise the artificial termination of a lake. This would probably help solve the problem of spoil disposal from building demolition or lake excavation.

Surviving contracts make no mention of grottoes, but where clients requested 'caves in fine taste', Brown ensured solid brick foundations before cladding their walls with shells, tufa, quartz and other sparkling minerals. He saw them as a spot to picnic, a shelter in a sudden rain shower that might serve as a judicious location for a cold bath or even to house a fishing-boat. Sabrina, goddess of the River Severn,

TOP **May 1999, Croome Park, Worcestershire (NT)** Brown's grotto, a feature on the circuit walk to take the eye off his dam, has been restored.

MIDDLE AND BELOW **May 1996, Brocklesby Park, Lincolnshire** The interior red brickwork of the curving grotto tunnel, and the side chamber, were once lined with wood, then covered with plaster, stones and fossils.

reclined inside a two-room crystal-encrusted grotto at Croome, Worcestershire. Here a passage from Virgil's *Aeneid*, engraved in Coade stone, might spark a visitor's imagination, transforming the sparkly caverns into a refuge for shipwrecked mariners.[410]

Fossils and petrified stones, supplied by Joseph Benerson of Eyam in Derbyshire, lined Brown's last grotto at **Brocklesby** (Lincolnshire), where a long, snaking brick tunnel created an intriguing diversion in the flat terrain, and where his young plantations were beginning to get established. The darkness of its side-chamber, or apse, was relieved by a single shaft of light from a slit window.[411]

Visitors emerged from the gloom, enticed by the light and the attractive ferns and trailing ivy foliage, to find lime-tree cuttings from Burghley framing a surprise rustic summerhouse tucked at the end of a hollow. An occasional resident hermit or holy man added, if not a spiritual dimension, certainly a memorable, theatrical experience.

More importantly, Brown altered the boring, flat Brocklesby terrain and screened the thoroughfare to his new kitchen gardens and kennels by 'throwing up road in Haburgh lane and a deep holloway'.[412] As a result, the fourteenth-century All Saints Church appears raised as if on a small hill. It became a focal

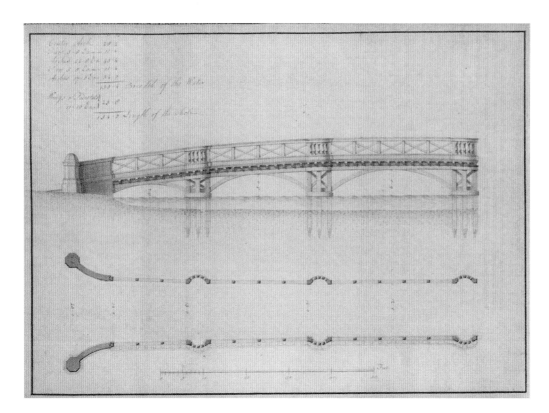

LEFT Brown's undated 'Plan of Intended Bridge to be placed over the New Water at Ashburnham', 12 x 20 ins., scale 1 in. to 6 ft © East Sussex Record Office. A more classical wooden bridge was chosen. Old oak piles are still discernible near George Dance's nineteenth-century stone replacement. The truss pattern of Brown's Crescent Bridge at Wotton (opposite, newly restored), though higher, shows how his bridge might have looked.

BELOW **November 2013, Compton Verney** Brown's workman-like stone bridge, carrying the main road and an approach to the house, has typical flatter, elliptical arches.

point, its environs neatened with new-laid paving, set against a backdrop of signature Scots pines and cedars.

A few classical freestanding greenhouses, showing more than a hint of Robert Adam's influence, survive from the latter part of Brown's career. His original drawing (1767) for **Ashburnham** (Sussex) has five bays. In the event, a seven-window greenhouse with cornice and parapet has each rounded window flanked by pilasters, and cost his client £600 (today £87,000).[413] Brown's substantial solid oak bridge with iron pins or screws at the joints, once on view from the house, has long since been replaced by George Dance's nineteenth-century stone bridge.[414]

Enthusiasm for *chinoiserie* persisted. Brown conceived a 'Crescent Bridge' at **Wotton**, Buckinghamshire, which, far from being Chinese, had a 100-ft single span and a 13-ft rise modelled on a truss-pattern principle by Palladio. As a picturesque eye-catcher, cleverly taking the eye off both the dam and the termination of the lake, the bridge succeeded admirably. He instructed gardeners to blend the structure into the setting. A surprise attraction, popular on the circuit ride, it was revealed without warning, its graceful arc recalling the charm of every willow-pattern plate before, almost as quickly, its silhouette was hidden by dense foliage. Later, visitors caught a partial glimpse, and then, further round the lake, an enchanting view spied at a distance across the water.[415] One of the last wooden bridges he built, according to Henry Holland's account after Brown's death (1783), was on Wimbledon Common, at this time owned by Earl Spencer.[416]

If not wooden, Brown's bridges were plain brick and functional, often concealing a weir: for instance at North Cray Place (Kent) and Luton (Bedfordshire) (see p.98). Greater numbers of masonry bridges were being built, in conjunction with better roads, following techniques developed and published by the French.

RIGHT **September 1997, Wotton, Buckinghamshire** Brown's Crescent Bridge has been rebuilt (1990s) to his original design and dimensions – based on Palladio's principles rather than the Chinese – but rather steep to negotiate easily.

ABOVE May 1997, MIDDLE September 2008, Burghley, Cambridgeshire The Lion Bridge is carefully positioned to make a principal vista from both the gardens and the house, crossing his 'new river' from 'Brown's Cutting', his new approach. The lions, originally Coade stone, were replaced in the nineteenth century by a local stonemason.

BELOW LEFT June 2014, Compton Verney, Warwickshire Restored lead Sphinx, attributed to John Cheere, previously painted to look like stone.

BOTTOM June 2011, Compton Verney, Warwickshire Sphinx Bridge, thought to be Robert Adam's design, built by Brown, bears more than a passing resemblance to Lion Bridge in Burghley Park.

Westminster Bridge, by the Swiss engineer Charles Labelye, took eleven years to build, opening in 1752. A fine stone bridge became an essential aspect of every professional improver's remit.[417]

Having replaced Brown's original wooden bridge at Chillington, Staffordshire, with a single-span stone bridge with balustrade and sphinxes, James Paine went on to design an even more impressive three-arch bridge across the River Derwent at Chatsworth. We will never know whether it was at Brown's suggestion, though it seems likely, that the bridge was set at an oblique angle to carry his new park road up to Chatsworth House.

As with most architectural proposals, Brown offered clients a choice when it came to upgrading approaches to cross over their 'new river'. The crossing was interpreted by some as if they were passing over the River Jordan to the Promised Land. In January 1773 Exeter commended his suggestions for Burghley, 'being both elegant.... I prefer that with three arches, shall not finally determine till we meet…'.[418]

Thomas Manton, a mason from nearby Stamford, soon began work and a year later was paid for the stone. As the bridge neared completion, a local contractor, Edward Thorpe and Co., earned £61 (today £8,845) and needed twenty-four wheelbarrows to dig out the mud for another eleven-acre stretch of water.

Since the 1730s, there had been commercial iron-ore smelting on an industrial scale in the Coalbrookdale region of Shropshire where Abraham Darby III (1750–1791) built the first metal bridge, the famous Iron Bridge over the River Severn (1777–80). This was fabricated with cast-iron elements fastened by keys, just as in a wooden structure. With several commissions in the area around this time, Brown kept abreast of developments in ironworks. In addition to his classical sham bridge at Scampston, Yorkshire (see p.99), his three-arch bridge, purposefully hiding a weir controlling the flow of the Swan Beck into the main lake, was admired for its cast-iron railings and for its economy. The upstream side was built in utilitarian red brick in English garden-wall bond with sandstone parapet and dressings; the side on view from the house was all smart sandstone.

William Constable, a northern client, was co-operative, forward-thinking and rigorous, ensuring that copious notes were recorded each time Brown put in an appearance at **Burton Constable**, near the Yorkshire coast. These 'Minutes of directions from Mr Brown' (1767–82) shed light on progressive drainage methods in the low-lying park:

> *To make the New part of the Lake abt 3 Feet deep, and the sides about 10 Inches higher than the Surface of the Water – make the sides sloping and keep the Edges a neat Turf. – Lay the Earth at the nearest advantage making the adjacent Grounds slope gradually to the edge of the Lake.*[419]

His men edged the lake with bricks buried under a coping of turf to prevent erosion, and removed medieval ridges and furrows in common fields beyond, so that the continuous grassy curves of the shoreline, kept high and dry, appeared completely natural. Then they tackled another reservoir.[420]

An ink and colour wash plan, 'A section through the intended bridge at Burton Constable… May 1778', is far removed from the early days of quick sketches on the reverse side of estimates. Here a more scientific cross-section for a sham bridge, hiding a dam of a double brick wall with gravel fill, is labelled with precise instructions regarding stone foundations and parapet. Brown was still experimenting, so the novel cast-iron balusters could well be his.

Four years later, he suggested further refinements to help labourers persevere through noxious snags and inclement weather to arrest leakages: 'Waste of Water in the Ponds. Mix Gravel & Earth to make a kind of batter or swurry and pour it in, to fill up the interstices.[421] Termination of the Menagerie Pond. – Mr B. will send a drawing.'[422]

An undated watercolour, probably by John Spyers, shows the bridge set diagonally, as at Chatsworth, so as to be seen from the house. Instructions on the reverse, in Constable's

August 1998, Burton Constable, Yorkshire On Brown's sham bridge, classical vase-shaped balusters are novel, made of sturdy and enduring moulded cast iron. Could they be another example of his advanced design or are they a later restoration?

handwriting, concern mixing paint to disguise the brick dam with a *trompe-l'oeil* painting of imitation rocks and cascades, using indigo, white lead and white sand.[423] Brown had an eye for the smallest details, aiming to achieve his version of the perfect way to 'heaven on earth'.

Orthodox English parish churches and chapels, also a rich, reassuring resource, sometimes adjoining the house, accommodated magnificent ancestral monuments that aroused feelings of family tradition and stability. This did not stop Brown. He dismantled St James's Church at **Croome** to make space to build his new stable complex, no mean task. He then rebuilt the church carcass in Bath stone in advanced, plain Gothic style, again with battlements and pinnacles reflecting Miller's influence. Robert Adam attended to interior plasterwork as Brown arranged the transfer of family memorials to the resurrected church. Nikolaus Pevsner[424] considered Brown's church at Croome 'one of the most serious of the Early Gothic Revival outside, one of the most elegant inside'.

The choice of location for his rebuild is noteworthy, the church acting as the park's principal eye-catcher, an uplifting sight on the brow of the hill above the house and intentionally visible from the windows. The church name was also changed to St Mary Magdalene. Had Brown been influenced by Madingley's church of the same name? It is of course appropriate, since, after his Resurrection, Christ first appeared to Mary Magdalene in a garden. What was more, on leaving the church, visitors' prayers were rewarded – as today – with the 'new river' snaking through park and pleasure grounds towards the Malvern Hills beyond, a stirring panorama and foretaste of heavenly Arcadia.

At Burghley, Brown cut *points de vue* through established lime avenues, intentionally aligning the views from the upper Pagoda Room on each of the spires belonging to St Mary's Church and All Saints' Church in the nearby town of Stamford. At Moccas (Herefordshire), he encouraged Sir George Cornewall to enclose the twelfth-century church, St Michael's, within the park. The octagonal spire of St Mary's Church, Hainton, is also thought to be a Brown modification, associated with *points de vue*, the eighth day, symbolising the new world order after Christ's Resurrection.

Another old chapel at **Compton Verney** (Warwickshire) was too close to be in keeping with the new classical house façade, as well as blocking the view to the lake. In 1772 all the Verney monuments and the sixteenth-century coloured glass windows were transferred across to Brown's restrained Italianate alternative, built in limestone ashlar. Its round-headed upper windows accord with those of the house's south front.[425] The Georgian chapel with 'a pretty Adamish interior' successfully hides the walled garden.[426]

St Bartholomew's Church, Binley (early 1770s), has been attributed to Brown. In the same period, the Earl of Scarborough commissioned a mausoleum chapel with classical bell-cote overlooking the Lincolnshire landscape. Since the setting of St Helen's Church, Saxby, is so memorable, could Brown be the architect, since he was undertaking commissions in Lincolnshire and Yorkshire?

RIGHT July 1998, Compton Verney, Warwickshire
Brown's Chapel (1772–76), one of few surviving
Georgian chapels, has a wooden triumphal arch
bell-cote.

BELOW St Bartholomew's, Binley, Warwickshire
(1773) Attributed to Brown, the grey sandstone
exterior is quite plain, but the neo-classical Adamish
interior is the opposite, 'in Venetian ballroom
taste' (Pevsner), with (*right*) the focal altar window,
Madonna and Child (1776), by William Peckitt
of York.

CHAPTER NINETEEN

THE 'KITCHING GARDEN'[427]

By the 1770s, in keeping with the perceived wisdom that more is less, designers had often reduced the number of eye-catchers to a refined summerhouse, a bridge and a church or nostalgic abbey ruin. Nature in all her finery, reflected in lively waters, filled in the gaps. Day-to-day living called for more down-to-earth priorities. Thanks to early experience on the Kirk Harle estate, and then given head gardener responsibilities at Stowe, Brown had become expert in every aspect of productive gardening: location, water management, hot walls, ordering stock and equipment, and pruning fruit trees.[428] He procured a variety of vegetable and fruit seeds, gooseberry and currant bushes, and raspberry canes for estates such as Wotton, Syon and Petworth from seedsmen and nurserymen including the Kensington-based John Williamson. According to clients' wishes, Brown was neither too busy nor too self-important to apply his mind to this essential aspect of people's lives. As with everything he turned his hand to, Brown became expert in methods for 'hastening forwards' salads and seeds.

OPPOSITE June 2009, Croome, Worcestershire (NT) Part of Brown's walled garden has been recently restored to productivity. Note the stone coping and also the buttress supporting the high red brick wall.

ABOVE June 2009, Croome, Worcestershire (NT) A section of cobbled road in the walled garden, with raised barrel for drainage.

LEFT **April 2008, Cole Green, Hertfordshire** Gates to smarten up the entrance to the walled garden were probably moved by Brown from another part of the formal gardens (see plan detail p.52).

TOP AND ABOVE **April 2008, Cole Green, Hertfordshire** An old lead label for a morello cherry tree and a buttress support to one of the inner corners of the walled garden.

Gardeners had been experimenting with protective mats to provide the requisite conditions to grow exotic fruits year-round: oranges, lemons, figs and vines, in glazed hothouse ranges. With coal readily available, more owners, especially those in the bleaker eastern and northern counties, commissioned kitchen gardens with double 'hot walls', where warm air from a furnace was circulated through a series of flues in the gap between the two layers of brickwork. His surviving account book mentions only new kitchen gardens at Knowsley, Lancashire (approximately four acres), and walled garden plans for Basildon (Berkshire), Charlton (Wiltshire) and Newton (Wales), the latter possibly an upgrade with hot walls and stoves. He failed to itemise many more walled gardens constructed as part of all-inclusive plans at other sites.

In 1755, Earl Cowper commissioned a small octagonal walled garden with hothouse at **Cole Green** (Hertfordshire.)[429] Typically, Brown caused ornate gates from elsewhere in the grounds to be dismantled and rehung to smarten the entrance 'gate-holes' of the new 'kitching' garden. The walls are 12 ft 9 ins high, in English bond, the ground sloping almost imperceptibly south to north. Sound advice concerning growing produce provided an extra incentive for clients to summon Brown to their rural estates.[430] The Tottenham agent relayed his suggestions to his employer:

> *Viewed the place for the new one very attentively – Said the shape of a Kitchen Garden was of little consequence, and that it must be adapted to the ground & the appearance it would have on the outside. Lord Shelburne's Gardens are 5 a. [acres] – he thinks one acre of this Ground will raise as much Garden Stuff as 2 of Lord Shelburne's. 4. a or 3 & ½ will be sufficient if no more can be conveniently taken in.*[431]

Local brickworks were inundated with orders, as Brown positioned new walled gardens, mostly on the east, away from the house, and where possible nearer to the high road for ease of transportation of produce to market. It made sense to isolate kitchen gardens. Widespread use of fresh, therefore noxious, stable-manure in untidy frame yards, together with rotting vegetables, and smoke fumes from hot wall furnaces carried on the prevailing westerly wind, all produced unpleasant odours.

Lord Warwick wrote to commend Brown to the Earl of Guildford:

> *and I never knew anyone more attentive and more understanding as well as more frugal in all those details, in and about a place as he is. As to the kitchen gardens, he can scarce want practice in them for in about ten years he has made upwards of 30 and sees them well stocked and not only that, but recommended proper gardeners to take care of them and also seen that they did so.*[432]

In addition, Brown tucked orchards behind protective walls, so that regimented rows of fruit trees would not detract from the different character and height of trees in the park. A broad swathe of beech screened the walled garden at Temple Newsam and provided an extra wind-break. He designed a 'Lady Walk' to hide the walls at Hainton, just as at Longleat, with 'shrubs, trees of curious sorts and Turf':[433]

> *this Shrubbery at the outside of the Piece of fine Natural wood which I thought had better been lett into the Park till I perceived … Embosomd in it. The Best Conceald and best situated fruitery and Kitchen garden I think I Ever saw…*[434]

Among many well-travelled clients, Admiral Lord Anson commissioned Brown, in addition to park improvements at Moor Park (Hertfordshire), to lay out extensive fruit and kitchen gardens. The celebrated 'Moor Park Apricot', brought back from the East, was cultivated here (the parent tree survived until 1840).

Following Brown's advice at Madingley (Cambridgeshire), a catalogue (1757), recording over a hundred assorted fruit trees, includes eleven varieties of grape growing on the south-facing end and middle walls, and in the field beside the walled

LEFT **June 2013, Fenstanton, Cambridgeshire** Might this pollarded veteran apple tree be one of Brown's original fruit trees in the Fenstanton Manor garden?

ABOVE Red peach, *Prunus persica*

garden.[435] A later order has recently come to light. In 1770 James Wood, a local nurseryman, supplied 'Lancelot Brown Esq. Lord at Fen Stanton' (formerly Huntingdonshire) with twenty-four fruit trees including apricot for his own garden:

3 Damsens	*2s. 3d. [£13.60]*
1 quince	*1s. 0d. [£6]*
4 Cheres	*3s. 0d. [£18]*
2 Plum	*0 1s. 6d. [£9]*
19 apels & pars	*0 14s. 0d. [£84]*
4 peches & Nectron	*0 4s. 0d. [£24]*
1 apricock	*0 1s. 0d. [£6]*[436]

Fruit-growing expertise helped to secure Brown's royal appointment for the close supervision of all royal kitchen gardens. His salary was fixed at £1,107 (today £160,500) per annum, with an extra £100 (£14,500) specifically for the challenging task of growing 'Pine Apples', and a further £100 for forced fruits. He oversaw the specialised business of growing pineapples, cucumbers and melons in a brick frame, methods learned from the Dutch by creating subterranean hot air from pits of tanning bark, dung and, later, underground water pipes from steam boilers. In addition to sourcing mats to cover melon and early fruit, clay pots, fruit trees and all manner of tools, Brown was held personally responsible for:

compost for the oranges etc, Fewel for the Hot houses and Stoves, Fruit and Sallad Baskets, … and an Engine to sprinkle Trees and Plants…. Carriages of the Kitchen Garden eatables and carriages of the King's Summer Fruit … from the several gardens daily by relays of men on foot to the Court….

The ground to be dunged and cropped with several varieties of eatables, and proper for his Majesties use, & the Trees pruned and nailed.[437]

Wilderness House at Hampton Court, Brown's home, probably influenced his designs for head gardeners' accommodation elsewhere, being conveniently adjacent to the productive, eight-acre complex of orchard, kitchen garden and two-acre melon ground, ideal for tours of inspection.[438] However, the pressure of having to supply fresh provisions daily for the royal household surfaced in disputes over salary. In 1765, he complained to the Treasury lords that he was still receiving the same remuneration as Lowe and Greening, his predecessors:

I was yesterday at the Treasury to get the Power which your Lordships have been so good as to grant for the Repairs for the Royal Garden at Hampton Court. But on looking it over, I found that the Bell Glasses, the Potts and orange Tubs were omitted which I daresay your Lordships have been misinformed about…. The King has desired strawberrys almost round the year which makes it Necessary to increase the Garden Potts and bell Glasses. I shall be extremely sorry if his majesty should want anything I can do for him which must be the case. If I have not those things granted, as it would be highly imprudent in me and to my family I lay out money in Purchasing New things which have always been found at the King's Expense, and the more so, as Prehaps [sic] I hold my Place more Precariously than any other Man as my own Health is so very bad, and even deserving does not always keep a man in Place. Suppose I was to Buy those things refused, and be turned out next week or Die, they all become the Kings as no man has a right to move a single Pott, Tub or Bell Glass or any other thing off the King's Ground and my family must loose it.[439]

His letter, with phrases underlined to convey the strength of his feelings, prompted the desired review. His pay almost doubled to £2,000 per annum (£290,000). A year later he requested additional payment, taking into consideration his responsibility for the wage bill for the entire royal gardens workforce:

Mr Brown presents his best respects to Mr Lounds and begs the favour to inform him in what manner he is to be paid for keeping the Treasury Garden and the Kitchen Garden at Windsor.

Mr Brown has constantly paid the People for those gardens has [sic] never received pay for them.[440]

Two years passed. Brown, still frustrated by the injustice, worried about his family's future, conscious that a severe asthma attack could suddenly end his life: 'I have constantly kept them & paid all the Expence [sic] out of my own pocket for near four years for which I have had no payment.'[441] Losing all patience when this too was ignored, Brown took his grievance directly to George III: 'Balanced this acct with His Majesty. See the state of it and the paper signed with the King's hand.'[442]

When criticisms were later voiced about the upkeep of the Hampton Court gardens, matters were settled in the same way. The king relied on Brown, his position was secure and the royal kitchen gardens took precedence. To save transporting substantial amounts of produce every day from Hampton Court, Brown hatched an integrated plan (1771) modestly titled 'Rough Sketch', to convert the royal grounds at Old Deer Park, Richmond, by removing hedges, and altering Bridgeman's raised terrace walk along the Thames 'into waving lawns that hang to the river in a most beautiful manner'.[443] The snag was that his chosen space for extensive walled gardens to supply all three royal residences, Royal Lodge, White House and Dutch House (Kew Palace today), was situated in those parts of the Wilderness open to the public. Brown preserved the rustic Hermitage as a romantic ruin, but caused an outcry after demolishing William Kent's iconic 'Merlin's Cave'. This subterranean timber structure with Gothic arched entrance had a thatched roof and plaster walls 'adorned with astronomical figures and characters' that must have been showing its age.[444] Mason could not resist publishing a satirical poem anonymously:

To Richmond come; for see untutor'd Brown
Destroys the wonders which once their own;
Lo! From melon-ground the peasant slave
Has rudely rush'd, and levell'd Merlin's Cave,
Knocked down the waxen wizard, seized his wand,
Transform'd to lawn what late was fairy-land,
And marr'd with impious hand each sweet design
Of Stephen Duck and good Queen Caroline.[445]

In the mid-1760s Brown returned home to Kirkharle, and gave an improvement plan for his birthplace. This included a kitchen garden, at a distance on a south-facing slope, with central 'stew' (fishpond) straddling the 'Vicarage Burn'. Meanwhile, at nearby **Wallington** (Northumberland), the estate Brown knew as a schoolboy, Sir Walter Calverley Blackett commissioned a plan for a lake at nearby Rothley. Here too, given his holistic *modus operandi* elsewhere, it seems highly likely that Brown advised improvements for the walled gardens, especially

re-routing a stream running through the middle in an underground culvert, and demolished part of the south wall so as to catch as much sun as possible, to negate problems in freezing temperatures. Typical of his practical-minded thoughtfulness, he then addressed the issue of security with the secluded, now open kitchen garden. He designed a small house into the north wall with a window above the glasshouses, to overlook the garden so that the head gardener could keep an eye on his produce. This also offered a fine view of Paine's bridge over the river. Brown brought up from Moor Park a hot wall and glasshouse specialist, William Ireland, to mastermind the building of this 'Owl House' range (named from the Calverley family crest).

Subsequently commending Ireland to Lord Bute as 'sober, industrious and honest', Brown called him back south to **Luton** (Bedfordshire) to supervise building and equipping his octagonal garden, with walls over 12 ft high, enclosing almost five acres, dissected by a diaphragm wall.[446] The supply of bricks was not a problem, as brickworks were plentiful in the region. By 1770, when Bute was away travelling in Europe,

Dr John Symonds, a Cambridge history professor, suitably impressed by the swift progress, reported: 'The kitchen garden actually looked as if it had been planted two years.'[447]

Gardening at Luton was of the highest calibre and pushed the known boundaries of horticulture. Later, in 1777, Bute wrote to thank the scientist-explorer Joseph Banks (1743–1820) for a valuable collection of seeds. Banks was by then the unofficial director at Kew. Bute let Banks know that he would be pleased to see him at the Luton garden together with his fellow collector, the leading botanist Daniel Solander, a gifted pupil of Linnaeus.[448] By 1783 between ten and twelve gardeners, overseen by a head gardener, were employed exclusively in the kitchen gardens and 'pinery'. A second head gardener managed a second team tending rare trees and floriferous shrub introductions in what must have been a fascinating and remarkable 'Flower Garden Wood'.

Meanwhile, back at **Burghley** once again, Brown relied upon Ireland to oversee all his model farm projects and, in particular, the building of a nine-acre walled garden, with an essential range of glasshouses, at quite a distance from the house, but close by the Great North Road. At the entrance, Brown suggested installing stone gate-piers that he had removed earlier from the garden environs of the great house. A deep, sloping ha-ha surrounding the walls and slips helped to drain the area's heavy clay, funnelling rainwater into several deep wells within the produce gardens. Lord Exeter seemed especially pleased: '10 Feb 1778 paid Wm Ireland his Lordship's present to him for executing Mr Brown's plans of the new works in Burghley Park. £350 [£50,750].'[449]

The effect on a client's private world was immense, with fewer encumbrances around the house. The family experienced liberating space and greater privacy, while the entire household reaped healthy benefits from reliable, sometimes exotic, ranges of fresh vegetables and soft fruit from the organised, well-stocked, almost hidden gardens. Brown's focus on down-to-earth realities of daily life, subsistence and self-sufficiency helped to improve both the quality and the economic infrastructure of remote rural estates.

OPPOSITE July 1988, Wallington, Northumberland (NT) The Owl House and glasshouse range.

BELOW A Plan of Burghley kitchen garden, unsigned and undated © The Burghley House Collection.

RIGHT Undated and unsigned plan for glasshouse range at Luton Park, Bedfordshire © The Bute Archive at Mount Stuart.

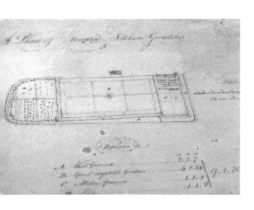

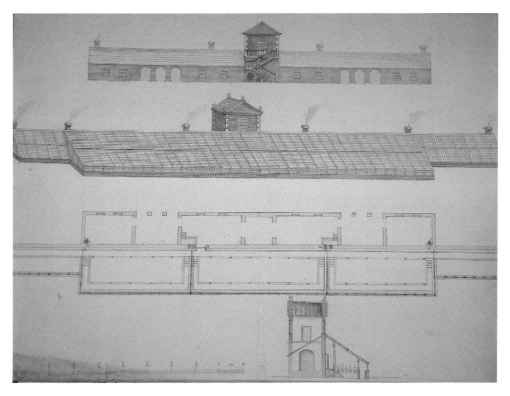

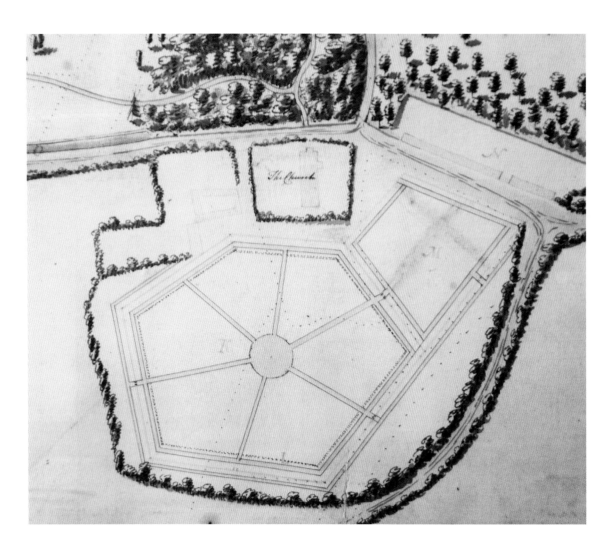

At **Brocklesby** he demolished unsuitable garden walls near the farmyard, and selected a better location beyond the church for an orchard and up-to-date productive gardens. His irregular hexagonal walled garden took three years to build and required thousands of 'Holland' bricks.[450] To avoid having to import bricks, it was probably Brown's suggestion to construct a brick kiln nearby in Great Limber village.[451] Coping stones came from nearby Killingholme Haven. Brinkscliff and Hawood quarries further afield in Yorkshire supplied stone for a stove and hothouse. A melon ground contained a glazed 'succession house' for tender fruit. In 1777 '40 fruiting Pine' (pineapples) cost £16 (£2,320). In 1780, a consignment of parcels of exotic trees arriving at Brocklesby perhaps included the *Gingko biloba*, still just surviving, and a fine, mature *Catalpa bignonioides* shading the head gardener's castellated house nearby.

With 560,000 bricks already in stock at **Charlton**, Wiltshire, William, Earl of Suffolk, was impatient for a plan for his kitchen garden so that he could calculate if he had the requisite quantity. Brown duly obliged.[452] The south wall was made deliberately low, as at Wallington, to avoid lingering frost pockets in winter. An imposing head gardener's house in the centre of the north wall includes a large half-moon window on the first floor overlooking the one-and-a-half-acre garden and parkland beyond.

In times of political unrest, Brown's integrated, productive settings made the future feel more secure. Little wonder clients were satisfied. With unrivalled and tenacious passion for progress, he encouraged gardeners to use the best, most advanced horticultural methods for growing fruit and vegetables and raising crops.

Always responsive to the conditions of each new site, Brown sought to improve air circulation for fruit

trees at **Wynnstay** in Clwyd, Wales. He obtained bricks from local brickworks for unusual horseshoe-shaped, south-west-facing kitchen garden walls.

In addition to a 10-ft plan, 'Alteration & continuance of the Water at **Heveningham Hall**', proposing a lake, planting and drives, Brown presented an ostensibly uncomplicated plan (1781) for the close environs of the neo-classical house in Suffolk designed by Sir Robert Taylor. This second plan was one of Brown's most sophisticated, and once more pushed the bounds of modernity. In an arrangement drawn from nature in curvaceous accord,

house, lawn, stables and conveniently adjacent walled garden to utilise the manure come together in one compact, cleverly arranged unit, enclosed in a foetal shape by the ha-ha. Even the elegant, easy line of his approach drive connecting to the wider world is reminiscent of an umbilical cord.[453] The novel, rounded double walling of the rebuilt kitchen garden, without corners, provided more available growing room for espaliers. The succinct appraisal by the French Rochefoucauld brothers, visiting after Brown's death, would surely have been music to his ears: 'The effect is one of neatness and harmony.'[454]

BELOW **October 2012, Heveningham, Suffolk** The curved kitchen garden south wall.

RIGHT 'Plan of Part of Heveningham . . . with the Intended Alterations by LB 1781' © Reproduced by permission of Historic England.

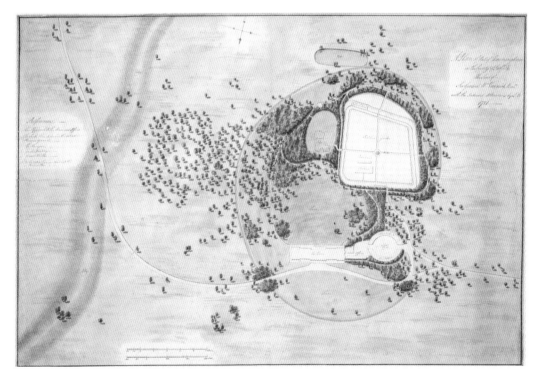

CHAPTER TWENTY

FULL-SCALE DRAMA

Of those countless millions of people who have visited **Blenheim**, in Oxfordshire, few would disagree that the park offers quite simply 'the finest view in England'.[455] It could be said that Brown had practised where Walpole preached: 'Prospect, animated prospect, is the theatre that will always be the most frequented.'[456] A stirring sight, comparable to the Tower of London or the Statue of Liberty, once seen Blenheim is never forgotten.

This was not quite the case when Brown first rode through the Triumphal Arch entrance from Woodstock town into Blenheim Park and paused to contemplate the palace and its setting. If this was the famous gift of gratitude from Queen Anne to her loyal general, the Duke of Marlborough, somehow Vanbrugh's imposing three-storey limestone bridge seemed the primary focus and was longer than the great Baroque palace itself. It was modelled on the Venice Rialto, with a 101-ft central span, and once contained more than thirty rooms for habitation and entertaining. Moreover, at the time of Brown's arrival, decades after it was begun, it remained unfinished. Presumably this was one of several reasons why the 4th Duke of Marlborough had called in Brown.

OPPOSITE **April 1991, Blenheim, Oxfordshire** An oak and an evergreen holm oak feature on a pleasure-ground walk (since grassed over) among daffodils.

ABOVE **August 2014, Blenheim, Oxfordshire** Brown's amphitheatre of space centred on Vanbrugh's great bridge, with Blenheim Palace out of sight, left. His great lake has made an impact on countless visitors since the eighteenth century.

What a disappointment it is to discover the bridge straddling the inconsequential River Glyme. Originally winding through the marshy valley below the palace, this narrow tributary of the Thames had been converted into a straight-sided, narrow canal, barely 3 ft wide, linking two negligible basins and totally out of proportion with the grand palace. The surrounding terrain was diverse, but rather barren and lacking sufficient planting interest. Both the approach and the look were plainly unsatisfactory. Brown was one of the few men with an imagination capable of comprehending just what Vanbrugh had visualised: a theatrical, well-watered setting grand enough to complement his great palace. Facing the biggest challenge of his career, he soon came up with a way to make it happen.

The solution was to dam the river to a height that would effectively flood one entire storey of Vanbrugh's bridge. This engineering was radical, exciting and courageous enough to convince the young duke. Brown introduced his right-hand man Benjamin Read as overseer, recommended 'above all others in this kingdom, next to himself'.[457]

First, they took pains to strengthen the bridge by encasing the walls of the lower rooms with stone from Woodstock Manor, the old palace ruins. Brown incorporated the old palace basin, 'Queen Pool', and nearby fish stews, to create one enormous lake as they raised the water level by damming the Glyme, intentionally flooding the reinforced ground-floor storey of the bridge. Surveys, calculations and trials were necessary to work out the correct level of the dam both to raise the water to the right level of the bridge and to flood the valley.

The duke understandably fretted about the staggering expense, over £21,000 (today £3,045,000). Six years passed before the lake could be considered safe and watertight, and then it took a further two years to fill all 150 acres. Brown's massive dam was more than 200 yards long, 30 ft high on solid limestone foundations and walls, infilled with Oxford clay sourced on high ground west of the dam, and mixed with gravel. Shaped like the neck of a bottle, it successfully held back the river in the southern valley at a bend where it turned eastward, and raised the level of water by nearly 17 ft. Brown disguised the dam with a 'Steep Walk' among shrubberies, with three plane trees strategically tucked well below it so that their roots were no threat. The original waterworks functioned unobtrusively, with only an occasional sluice gate repair in the underground spillway and additions to the clay core, until a recent major restoration (2009), undertaken to meet European and British flood management laws.[458]

Around the bend Brown organised an attractive, noisy distraction, his Grand Cascade, 60 ft wide at the crest, with great rocks held in place by barely noticeable ironwork. The lake waters disgorge into a widened, deepened, rechannelled and canalised Glyme. A wonderful destination for the duke's visitors exploring the pleasure grounds, the cascade proved a tremendous surprise and delight. To this day, most visitors never give a thought to Brown's massive dam around the corner.

In 1767 Brown encouraged the duke to enlarge the park by purchasing land to include his artificial canal, as if a 'natural' winding river, widening into a lake at the Lince, a wooded area. Here the river bank effectively forms another half-mile-long dam, spanned by Brown's typical workman-like sham bridge – brick, with eleven arches, again suggestive of enlightenment – and an elegant three-arch stone bridge, designed by Sir William Chambers, with lead sphinxes added later. A second cascade accommodates the changing level where the Glyme meets another tributary, the Evenlode, before feeding into the Thames.

Thomas Richardson's pen and green wash survey of Blenheim, 2 x 3 ft (1774), shows the great changes Brown achieved.[459] It clearly demonstrates the easy, flowing line, scale and natural style of Brown's walk through the pleasure grounds, across to the walled gardens, circumnavigating the great lawn that was 'frequently covered by sheep' and then back towards

LEFT **April 1991, Blenheim, Oxfordshire** Brown designed the seemingly natural Grand Cascade to take the eye off both his massive dam and the significant level-change between the lake and the river/ canal waters below. Concealed underground, an adjacent spillway and sluice gate allowed control of the flow. An engine house and pump were also installed nearby.

ABOVE **Blenheim, Oxfordshire** One of the many crown-like iron prongs across the top of the cascade (arrow). Could this have been Brown's solution to secure large rocks in position and at the same time to enliven the straight horizon line along the falls or a later restoration?

the palace.[460] Annotated in French, it successfully conveys a sense of the cohesive completeness of the grounds. The intention may have been to send a copy abroad, where *Le Jardin Anglais* (the English Garden) was becoming the height of fashion. Brown made designs for the Royal Palace at Laeken in Belgium, and his ideas later influenced parks in France, Germany, Sweden and Russia.

Walpole approved, describing the water as 'now amazingly beautiful it puts the bridge's nose out of joint'. The steep sides of the valley had become 'the bold shores of a noble river'.[461] Brown was exhilarated, finally satisfied that his scheme to corral the tributary waters of London's major artery delivered all that he had envisioned. Looking out across the greatest lake he had ever made, he was overheard exclaiming: 'Thames! Thames! Thou wilt never forgive me for this!'[462] Having served clients up- and downriver, Brown knew the Thames had played an inspirational role. Far from being pompous, he was overcome by the powerful effect of his new waters on his emotions and his feelings of patriotism.

Local legend has it that Henry II built a bower for his mistress, 'Fair Rosamund' Clifford, in the old Woodstock Park at Blenheim.[463] Long since an evocative ruin, it inspired Vanbrugh, Joseph Addison

and Thomas Clayton to compose a three-act opera, *Rosamund* (1707), which was altered with music by Arnold, and in 1767 performed at Covent Garden. Now it was Brown's turn to be affected by associated ideas of history and sentiment, but his proposal for a Gothic bathhouse fell on deaf ears. With a curving staircase either side leading to the upper storey, it would have charmed the eye reflected in the lake in the view across from the palace, while adding a strong subliminal link to both the park's medieval history and England's bygone royalty. Blenheim, more than most places, must have stimulated Brown's mind. Some believe that the formations of regiments and squadrons preparing for the Battle of Blenheim inspired the planting: 'in the vast space no void appears, its munificent execution a fittingly heroic tribute'.[464] Was it the Vanbrugh effect – a desire to add drama, with history playing its part? Brown kept thinking about Blenheim. Every return visit prompted plans for more improvements:

> I have supposed a Habitation for a Family on the corner next to the column some of the stone which has been pulled down in the sunk fence, may if your Grace pleases be made use of for the front; ... and I flatter myself that the Effect of the Building would be very proper for the situation.[465]

This and various other plans, including Palladian twin lodges suggested for Ditchley Gate, never went further than the drawing-board, even with the promise of a prudent reuse of stone. With the escalating expense of lake-making, the duke also rejected the idea of raising and crenellating the park wall near the Triumphal Arch in order to screen the houses overlooking the park, which would have effectively turned Woodstock into a fortress town. One wonders, since Brown labelled every single neighbouring house-owner on his large drawing, whether he had dined with them all. A sensible Gothic cart-house and stable near the kennels did go ahead, and the alteration and castellation of High Lodge (interestingly, originally advocated by Switzer),

as well as a two-storey building that included a menagerie and granary, 'for the easy turning of the Grain, and letting it fall for one floor to another which is the best way of keeping it sweet'.[466]

OPPOSITE **April 1999, Blenheim, Oxfordshire** The island does not feature on Brown's original plan. Presumably he decided to keep this section of the old causeway as a nesting haven, to save labour costs in removing it. Note three generations of beech to maintain his frame for the view.

BELOW **August 2014, Blenheim, Oxfordshire** Lombardy poplars add a vertical dimension to the edge of Brown's lake and lead the eye to the Column of Victory (1730), dedicated to the memory of the Duke of Marlborough by his wife Sarah.

August 2014, Blenheim, Oxfordshire A fine stand of cedars of Lebanon helps to screen the walled garden from the pleasure-ground walks.

Benjamin Read remained on Blenheim's books when Brown's contract finally ended. His know-how irreplaceable, Read worked there till he died in 1794. After Brown's death, the sovereign eventually came to see Blenheim. Amazed by the scale, as is everyone who contemplates the great waters for the first time, George III commented: 'We have nothing to equal this.' Evidently the king, with renewed enthusiasm, now turned his attention to his 'Virginia Water' on the edge of Windsor Great Park, which had been until then the largest man-made reservoir in the country.

An unparalleled sight, a calm sea of grass south of the palace, Brown's vast lawn at Blenheim, its scale on a par with his luxurious lake, stretched towards St Martin's church tower on the south horizon, and north towards St Mary Magdalene in Woodstock. An eye-witness account paints a picture of how Brown united and simplified the gardens:

> From the house, we visited the gardens; and here I am lost, not in confusion, but amidst scenes of grandeur, magnificence, and beauty. They are spacious and include a great variety of ground. The plain, or as artists term it, the lawn, before the palace, is kept in perfect order; not a single spire of grass rises above another. It is mowed and swept every other day, and is as smooth as the surface of a looking-glass. The gardener, who has lived twenty-five years upon the place, told us that he employed about sixty-three hands during the summer, in mowing, sweeping, pruning, lopping and in ornamenting the grounds.[467]

If internally the stratified structure of the mansion enforced status and segregation, out of doors society was effectively changing. In the open air, where they shared the same scenery, all ranks were gradually beginning to mix on more equal terms.[468] Just as Euston's jockeys enjoyed swimming in his lake, so here too farmers, gamekeepers, coachmen, gardeners, foresters and landowners all played sport, hunted and fished and worked together to manage what was slowly becoming a more democratic landscape, more convenient for all concerned: 'Blenheim may be seen every afternoon, from three till five o'Clock.... COMPANY who arrive in the morning may take the ride of the Park, or walk of the Gardens, before dinner, and after that visit the Palace.'[469]

Brown had contributed much towards putting Blenheim on the world stage. In March 1785 Thomas Jefferson, the future President of the United States of America, was appointed as Minister to France. The following spring he embarked on a tour of English parks, which later proved inspirational when he laid out his own grounds at Monticello. On reaching Blenheim, Jefferson noted in his journal that 200 people were employed in the park, with the turf mown every ten days. Brown's still immature trees were set among gnarled veteran oaks, but he admired the broad gravel walks and the Grand Cascade, set off by waving drifts of stag's-horn sumacs, *Rhus typhina*, on the right bank.[470]

> *The water here is very beautiful and very grand.... It is not laid out in fine lawns and woods, but the trees are scattered thinly over the ground, and every here and there small thickets of shrubs in oval raised beds, cultivated, and flowers among the shrubs.*[471]

One hundred years later, Sir Winston Churchill (1874–1965) was born and raised at Blenheim. He came to love the place deeply and appreciated just how much it had affected his life: 'The surroundings we shape for ourselves do more than we dream to shape us – especially when we are very young.'

September 2011, Blenheim, Oxfordshire The setting of Brown's great lake has now matured, with rather more trees than he originally envisaged.

CHAPTER TWENTY-ONE

ADVERSITY OF MAN & NATURE

I f Brown had come a long way from his rural roots, he remained down-to-earth and doubtless enjoyed rekindling memories of childhood haunts when the Duke and Duchess of Northumberland called on him to improve **Alnwick Castle's** setting. They thoughtfully included his first patrons among their dinner guests. Soon the Loraines invited Brown to return to **Kirkharle**, where he expressed his deep gratitude the best way he knew how, by addressing current capabilities for their estate.

A new laundry and offices followed and also the dismantling and rebuilding of better accommodation for estate workers a distance from the house. The kitchen garden straddling the burn was likely to have been cob-walled, as no trace remains today. A proposed circular approach, edged with iron railing, and a serpentine piece of water never materialised. Of course, his plan encouraged investment in tree-planting, including a narrow horizon-belt on the ridge beyond the Loraine house. As a result, given time, their 'woody theatre of stateliest view' rivalled nearby Wallington.[472] An eye-catching bell tower was added to St Wilfrid's Church, where the altar window still frames a veteran sycamore, one of several sheltering the little church of his christening.

OPPOSITE **June 1989, Alnwick, Northumberland** A lip cascade or weir on the River Aln solves the level-change, its unnatural straight line screened from the castle by a trinity of oak trees.

ABOVE **October 1989, Alnwick, Northumberland** A sycamore maple, *Acer pseudoplatanus*, the 'Tree of Liberty', and a mixed clump on the rise punctuate a sheep pasture, the central part of Brown's design from the Alnwick Castle ramparts.

Despite their very different upbringing, the Duke of Northumberland's patronage had developed into friendship. Both men were passionate improvers. During the late 1760s, having continued to embellish Syon, in Middlesex, Brown turned his attention to Alnwick Castle, the duke's principal seat. James Paine and Robert Adam had been remodelling the castle, once a Borders stronghold against raiding Scots, into a more comfortable if still imposing home. Just as at Chatsworth, Brown knew how to broaden and calm the River Aln below the ramparts, transforming it into an effective mirror.

A series of lip cascades, with modest drops, adjusted its levels and caused the river to tumble past Denwick Mill. Brown effectively re-aligned its course to flow in ever-widening oxbow bends eastwards towards the sea (see p.222).

The duke and duchess commissioned Brown to fill in the moat from the Bow Burn and to restore the old causeway from a new 'Garden Gate' (1776) to allow easy access to the gardens. Given the task of improving the surrounding sparse, craggy moorland, Brown established several ten-mile drives for the landscape-loving duchess. He ordered 1,200 trees to be planted annually on the upper slopes of surrounding hills for over twenty years, and to crown horizons on view from the castle. A few graceful, feminine beeches at irregular intervals still punctuate the Duchess Drive to the coast, while sturdy, masculine oaks pepper the Duke's Drive south towards Warkworth Castle.[473]

The Northumberlands and their guests spent convivial times on the castle's 'Pic-Nic Tower', witnessing a gradual transformation of the vistas. Beyond, in the distance, Robert Adam designed a 'pretend ruin' perched on Ratcheugh, a craggy ridge on the eastern skyline catching the warm glow of the setting sun. This Gothic summerhouse and

observatory was ideal to follow the Percy Hunt, and offered splendid views inland to the castle and to the Cheviot Hills or out towards the North Sea.

By 1770 most visitors considered Brown's pleasure walks at Alnwick the finest in England.[474] The duke had purchased a thirteenth-century Carmelite foundation, Hulne Priory, further west. Robert Adam and Brown collaborated in restoring the ruins, converting them into a Gothic summerhouse overlooking a menagerie. Here the views of the Cheviot Hills were so inspiring that Brown, emboldened by his Blenheim work, suggested throwing a dam across the valley to create a sensational lake. However, that November, tumultuous storms and floods swept away both the new cascades on the River Aln and the castle causeway.

Yet again, nature's unpredictable whims had defeated the visionary. His scheme had to be abandoned, owing to the magnitude of the flood damage and the resulting expense of making good. Besides, the land was deemed to give too valuable an agricultural yield to be sacrificed for a great reservoir even bigger than that at Blenheim, which, more importantly, might have insured against further serious flooding as a result of extreme adverse weather. The next summer, James Brindley came from Staffordshire to oversee the rebuilding of the cascades – as it happened, one of his last undertakings.[475] Afterwards Thomas Biesley, who had been employed by Brown since 1756 supervising pleasure grounds and park planting at Syon, came north to be foreman, overseeing seventy-five workers. He, together with Thomas Call, the Duke's own gardener, continued to implement Brown's ambitious planting programme in Hulne Park and on ten miles of drives around Alnwick.

His collaborators may have served him long and loyally, but Brown's extraordinary success rattled the architects Sir Robert Taylor and Sir William

LEFT **April 1990, Hulne Park, Alnwick, Northumberland** Brown once dreamed of creating a 200-acre lake here, an ambitious plan that was never realised in the view to the Cheviot Hills. Note a sprinkling of mature park trees below Brislee Hill, remnants of Brown's planting in the valley below Hulne Priory.

BELOW **July 1991, Hulne Priory, Alnwick, Northumberland** An eye-catching sycamore maple, *Acer pseudoplatanus,* a 'Tree of Liberty', welcomes the visitor to the romantic ruin, on a rise above the River Aln.

Chambers. They both considered him little more than an upstart who had invaded their territory.[476] Having been knighted abroad, and sharing the post of King's Architect with Robert Adam, Chambers mourned traditional gardening arts. He had introduced extravagant Moorish, Ottoman and Chinese features to Princess Augusta's gardens at Kew, as a grandiose interpretation of imperial trade and influence made possible by victory against the French. Any works by the 'friend of nature', in other words Brown, seemed to him tediously uninspiring in comparison, little more than common pastureland:

> *in this island it is abandoned to kitchen gardeners, well skilled in the culture of salads, but little acquainted with the principles of Ornamental Gardening. It cannot be expected that men uneducated, and doomed by their condition to waste the vigor of life in hard labour should ever go as far in so refined, so difficult a pursuit.*[477]

The label 'kitchen gardener' has adhered to Brown's name ever since. It has been repeated by critics and sneering rivals, and has resulted in lasting misconceptions. Wisely, Brown chose to ignore all this. As it happened, a road known as 'Love Lane' divided Old Deer Park, improved by Brown, from Kew where the grounds were improved by Chambers – an irony not lost on gossips at court:

> *Brown, who Chambers may excel*
> *But n'er could 'capabilitate' so well.*[478]

When William Robinson, Clerk Itinerant to the Board of Works, began questioning Brown's *modus operandi*, and making accusations about his neglect of the king's gardens at Hampton Court, Brown chose to put pen to paper to defend his position with vigour:[479]

> *Hampton Court Nov 3rd 1770*
>
> *Sir,*
>
> *I received your Letter and must acknowledge to you that I have lived long enough not to wonder at anything therefore it did not surprise me.*

> *I believe I am the first Kings Gardiner that the board of works ever interfered with and they have taken time which seems odd, the first was when I received a very extraordinary Letter from a gentleman of the board of works under the colour of Friendship, at a time when I found it necessary to discharge three men.*
>
> *I seldom use ephithets otherwise I would translate that letter as it deserves because I know both the owners meaning and his conduct on that subject.*
>
> *I believe if any Person had a right to have censured my conduct, it was the surveyor of the Gardens, which would have been very agreeable to me, because I know the gardens are in exceeding good order and I can assure you that I lay out a hundred pounds a year upon them more than my predecessor did. My wish and intention is to see them in better order than ever I saw them in and I have stopped at no expense in procuring Trees and Plants nor grudged any number of hands that were necessary, I this day went through the Garden and my Foreman told me, they have more hands than they know how to employ, but you Sir have only done your duty. You will be so good as to inform the Gentlemen of the Board of Works that* Picque *I pity, that the insolence of office I* Despise, *that* Ideal *Power I laugh at and that* real *Power I will ever disarm by doing my Duty.*

> *I am sir your most obedient Sevt.*   *L. Brown.*

> *PS The gravel at Hampton Court is totally worn out. I have been obliged in the course of this year to break it up three times, otherwise it would have been as green as grass.*

Again underlining select words to convey his anger, Brown felt sure of his ground. He patently loathed vestiges of malicious pomposity and petty officialdom. His letter provoked indignation, as shown in a letter from the Whitehall Office of His Majesty's Works to the Lords of the Treasury. One of the signatories was none other than Sir William Chambers. Losing Lord Clive's commission for the Claremont house to his adversary, and his release from further consultation at Milton Abbey, where Lord Milton continued to employ Brown, had dealt another blow to Chambers's pride and stoked his resentment.[480] The pique that Brown had pitied most was that of his arch-rival.

Since it was impossible to undermine Brown's influence at court, Chambers sought to regain the moral high ground in matters of gardening taste. His publication *Dissertation* (1772) contained sound, informative opinions but, regrettably, in advocating a strange assortment of oriental ideas, the highly respected professional misread the mood of the times and the state of English gardening. An opportunity to articulate his animosity in print proved irresistible:

> *Whole woods have been swept away to make room for a little grass and a few American weeds. Our virtuosi have scarcely left an acre of shade, nor three trees growing in a line, from land's End to the Tweed, and if their humour for devastation continues to rage much longer there will not be a forest-tree left standing in the whole Kingdom.*

Walpole, appalled, wrote to William Mason:

> *I have read Chambers' book. It is more extravagant than the worst Chinese paper, and is written in wild revenge against Brown; the only surprising consequence is that it is laughed at, and it is not likely to be adopted, as I expected, for nothing is so tempting to fools as advice to deprave taste.*[481]

It was not Brown's style to publish a rebuttal. He was content to let his work speak for itself, and never wavered from a personal vision honed through years of experience. Sadly, the legacy of the printed word will outlive his more transitory landscaping creativity.

With his eldest son, Lancelot, studying law at St John's College, **Cambridge**, Brown became friendly with the Master, Dr Powell, and with Professor Mainwaring, a well-known theologian. They both shared his fervour for 'modern' gardening. After a flood in 1770 and inadequate repairs, in 1772 they called him in to direct the rebuilding of the river bank and welcomed suggestions to improve the Fellows' Garden walks. Powell generously arranged to donate

March 1998, St John's College, Cambridge The Bridge of Sighs over the River Cam (1831) seems appropriate to Brown's unfulfilled proposal to create a lake to prevent flooding, and to improve and unify the setting along the Backs while reflecting the magnificent college architecture.

the first £500 (today £72,500) of the estimated £800 (£116,000) for the project, with the rest raised by subscription. Afterwards, with a local gardener, John Fortin, appointed to carry out Brown's suggested planting improvements, they agreed: 'the remainder of the old yew hedge by the side of the garden wall be taken away, and that the wall be covered with Phylyrea [sic] and other plants proper for a wall'.[482]

Dr Powell and St John's College Fellows arranged the presentation of a silver cup costing £52 (£7,540) to Mr Brown for his services in improving their walks. The following year, whether commissioned by Powell or stimulated by the unique ambience and history of the town, Brown created a bold plan (58 x 30 ins). He proposed enclosing surrounding fields with curving belts of trees and shrubs as a boundary screen, 'varied and against the road', and a ribbon walk winding through shrubberies and small copses, with willows and pines accompanying and softening the bridges.[483] His imaginative scheme would widen the River Cam into a mirror lake effectively centred on King's College and would reflect the medieval architecture of its fine chapel in his new waters.

Full of good intentions, Brown had, rather naively, underestimated college politics. His radical idea caused great disquiet. The competitive dons of the other five august colleges were simply not prepared to spend huge amounts of money, or subordinate their various lands, to allow King's College to dominate. On this rare occasion, Brown's normally persuasive charm and magnetism proved powerless. To save embarrassment, the University Senate presented a tasteful silver tray, delicately engraved with unusual, serpentine seed-like beads, formalised flowers and leaves, in recompense for his trouble. His plan later influenced, and probably continues to inspire, college authorities to maintain sufficient quality 'thinking' space. An understated legacy, The Backs remain effectively unified.[484]

Elsewhere, nature was equally determined not to be accommodating. Lakes silted up, deteriorating into stagnant, swampy marshland or abandoned puddles. Coventry wrote to Brown to request:

a man of Practice & sound Distinction for that Important work. Could Mr Read be spared as he first made the head, he would be the fittest person to restore it. I believe the roots of the Trees have been a chief cause of the Fissures in the bank....[485]

Troublesome topographical and geological conditions tested Brown's perseverance at Milton Abbas, Dorset, and Gawthorpe (now Harewood, Yorkshire). In periods of heavy rainfall and subsequent flooding, he mastered the over-abundance of water to lasting benefit. He adapted his designs accordingly,

drawing the water, almost a blue 'necklace', across large plans, creating a chain of two or three interconnected lakes, and sometimes including a separate silt-pond. Brown's series of five reservoirs changed the entire character of the Woodchester valley above Stroud (Gloucestershire). Such pragmatic manipulation of water made the best use of local resources, eased conservation and, crucially, limited risk of further flooding. Impressive, gratifying, affecting prospects, whether awe-inspiring acres of open water introducing space, new light and life, or becalmed, secluded, dappled river tracts for both contemplation and sport, the illusion of one continuous 'river' across clients' land attracted attention like a magnet, lifted spirits and enhanced feelings of security. In the long term, as we have already seen, better drainage improved the landowners' finances by making more land available for arable and livestock farming, securing higher rents on leasing and increasing the potential for long-term investment in timber. Increased numbers of game and wildfowl provided good sport. Angling grew in popularity. Healthier fish lurking in healthier waters under alders and willows made for better coarse fishing. Thanks to his designs, the social life of affluent families expanded, with boating, sailing and skating.

At the other end of the spectrum, in terms of scale, one of Brown's last and least-known lakes, created to reflect the old ruins of Newsham Abbey near **Brocklesby**, Lincolnshire, made an idyllic, secluded spot for picnics and boating. In the 1780s, despite ill health, he made an effort to travel there, intent on improving Pelham's water supply. Changes included the removal of an island, the installation of an expensive double-force pump, more elm pipes laid, covered with gorse, and new water closets installed in the house.[486] After his death, Brown's estate received payment for work on a boathouse, and a plan and elevation for an intended stone bridge.[487] Meanwhile, Pelham, a keen sailor, took possession of a luxurious English oak pleasure barge, festooned with curtains and cushions, to cruise his romantic 'Abbey Water'.[488]

CHAPTER TWENTY-TWO

TRANSITION

Brown and the Hollands, father and son, proved an effective building team. In 1773, the bond between families was strengthened when Henry Holland Jr married Bridget, Brown's elder daughter. Her dowry was considerable.[489] It followed that his son-in-law, just as capable, and by this stage methodically running the building and disbursement side of the practice, should become a partner. Brown went on to back Holland's London property developments: Hertford Street, Park Street, four houses in Hereford Street and the Hans Town scheme.

Their collaboration at **Broadlands**, Hampshire, brought about the conversion of a seventeenth-century house by squaring its E-shape into a classical, Italianate villa.[490] They then faced the entire house in white brick, rendered in part to give the appearance of stone, and added new sash windows, Portland stone dressings and porticoes on east and west fronts. For the interior Brown designed a fine Palladian oak staircase, brought in Joseph Rose the Elder for expert plasterwork, and invited the neo-classical artist Angelika Kauffmann (1741–1807) to paint ovals on his elaborate salon ceiling. After over six years of alteration, the house now pleased Viscount Palmerston more than any other, with elegant reception rooms embellished by magnificent paintings and furniture brought back from his Grand Tour. Brown was satisfied, but remained self-effacing: 'I am now at Lord Palmerston's which I think is turning into a respectfull [sic] Place.'[491]

OPPOSITE July 1998, Benham Park, Berkshire A Brown/Holland Jr collaboration, 1772-75, ashlar and stucco. Here the nine-bay north front has a triangular pediment, carved roundel and swags.

ABOVE July 1993, Cardiff Castle, Wales The inner precinct where the keep was once encircled by a Brown walk.

With as much drive as his father-in-law, Holland Jr in an ambitious, entrepreneurial move soon took over a key role as Clerk of Works at the Mews, Charing Cross (1775–83). He designed Brooks's Club, St James's (1776–78), and worked on both the Theatre Royal and Covent Garden Theatre (now the Royal Opera House). When visiting the capital, Brown liked to stay with the young Hollands in their house in Hertford Street. Another joint commission, an extensive modernisation of Lord Bute's London house, again with John Soane assisting, was conveniently round the corner in South Audley Street. They also worked together at **Cardiff Castle**, where Brown cleared the inner precinct of buildings, laid it to lawn and filled in part of the moat, while interior modifications of the west range were overseen by Holland Jr. His romantic idea to turn the keep into a ballroom proved too much for the studious Bute, and was flatly rejected.

A reliable partnership, the royal gardener and his young partner, acting as an alternative to Robert Adam, were also in popular demand for building country retreats. They dovetailed their talents to offer clients the whole package: a neo-classical house with self-contained ancillary buildings, within a viable and attractive setting. In addition to alterations to his banker Robert Drummond's great house at Cadland, on the Hampshire coast, a compact thatched, fishing *cottage ornée*[492] went ahead, based on a double octagon.

At **Benham** (Berkshire), Brown's three-storey freestone and stucco Palladian house was fronted by a dignified Ionic portico with plain, unfluted columns.[493] A significant departure in eighteenth-century house development, a small, circular, double-height vestibule with alcoves and second-floor gallery, a 'tribune' later adopted by Soane, featured a domed skylight to throw light on to the floral mosaic floor below.

Lady Craven grumbled about the expense, but the entrance hall, a long saloon with fine ornamental plasterwork, was the height of sophistication, where generous windows created a light, airy atmosphere with outstanding views of the park. Meanwhile

Trentham was 'wonderfully altered from the grand to the modern'.[494] The Holland/Brown partnership added pediments, Corinthian pilasters, a balustrade parapet to the south front, and a new east wing extension. Their sophisticated solution to unify old and new was to render the entire building with white Egyptian cement.

The iron balustrades of Holland's Triumphal Arch and lodge at **Berrington** (Herefordshire) were made from Spanish cannons captured during the American War of Independence. Attractive colonnaded screens hid his stable court, dairy, laundry and other offices. His neo-classical house, with a striking red sandstone façade, stands graciously, encircled by a deep apron ha-ha like a stage set, in easy communion with Brown's splendidly conceived 'scenery'.[495] Most visitors pause on the steps to take in the wide, pastoral panorama, their eyes attracted by shimmering water in the distance. Here are uplifting views against the backdrop of the Welsh hills, and, incidentally, in late summer, splendid 'Ladies' Tresses' orchids in the grass. A sturdy, mature oak dominates the middle ground on a perfectly rounded knoll, Brown's *tour de force*.

Far from slowing down, despite his advancing years Brown took on another joint commission with Holland to remodel the house at **Nuneham Courtenay**, Oxfordshire. They added a third storey to each of the two original wings of the villa, reached by a new top-lit staircase. An extension on the south side made for a complete reorganisation of offices and staff accommodation. This allowed rooms on the west to be converted into reception rooms that offered the best views over the Thames valley, where, much to the delight of Earl and Countess Harcourt, Brown provided direct access into the gardens.

George III and Queen Charlotte frequently stayed with their friends the Harcourts at Nuneham, and sought their advice in the development of Windsor Park. Of all the estates improved by his master gardener, Nuneham was the king's favourite, 'the most enjoyable place I know'. Walpole eulogised All Saints Church, which the earl had converted into a classical temple: 'the principal feature in one of the most beautiful

ABOVE **January 2003, Sandleford Priory (now St Gabriel's School), Berkshire** Brown installed the window to light Mrs Montagu's dining-room.

LEFT **July 1998, Berrington Hall, Herefordshire (NT)** Brown's easy, uncluttered approach.

landscapes in the world'.[496] An added bonus, Revd William Mason designed a romantic flower garden, though the width of the grass paths on his plan seems to have concerned him more than the shape or contents of the beds.[497] He sang Brown's praises in verse:

> *Great Nature!*
> *Him the Muse shall hail in notes, the living*
> *Leader of Thy Powers*
> *Which antedate the praise true Genius claims*
> *From just Posterity:*
> *Bards yet unborn shall pay to Brown that tribute*
> *fitliest paid*
> *In strains, the Beauty of his Scenes inspire.*[498]

Mrs Elizabeth Montagu, the blue-stocking intellectual, commissioned the architect James Wyatt (1746–1813) to rebuild and Gothicise **Sandleford Priory**, Berkshire, once the home of Augustinian canons. She was grateful that her celebrated friend tailored landscape improvements according to her limited finances. The widow mentioned his name many times in animated correspondence:

> *Mr Brown by removing a good deal of ground*
> *and throwing it down below to raise what was too*
> *low, while he sunk what was too high, has much*

improved the view to the south and having at my request made a fan light over the East window so that the arch formed by the trees is now visible. These rooms are the most beautiful imaginable.[499]

His many celebrated achievements in landscaping and lake-making have overshadowed Brown's architectural works, which some consider pedestrian in comparison with Vanbrugh's Baroque flamboyance, or the later imaginative designs of the Wyatt dynasty or of Soane. Small fan windows were already lightening dark townhouse hallways. Here Brown's tripartite window, an exterior ogee arch and three sashes surmounted by a delicate, segmental top, covered almost the entire east wall of the converted chapel, to confirm his architectural invention and resourcefulness better than any written theory paper. His sensitive response to a dear friend's wish to enhance the elegance of her dining room let in more than copious amounts of light, more than a romantic, uninterrupted view, an arched roof of 'twilight groves'[500] by his new waters. This original window underscores Brown's advanced philosophy in realising a significant transition, a delightfully contemporary and unifying relationship between house and landscape.

CHAPTER TWENTY-THREE

THE MYSTERY
OF THE GARDEN

In 1758 the banker Charles Raymond planted a vine at his home, Valentine's, in Ilford (Essex). Ten years later a slip was taken and the cutting heeled against the wall of William III's 'exotics' greenhouse in a secluded corner of the Privy Garden at **Hampton Court**. As it grew, gardeners trained its branches into a protective glasshouse, its roots reaching down into the palace sewers, perhaps accounting for its remarkable survival.

The productive royal vine, *Vitis vinifera* 'Schiava Grossa', or 'Black Hamburg', is now a living legend, probably the oldest vine in the world, and certainly the largest, extending the entire length of a 72-ft glasshouse (built later). For two weeks each August, gardeners harvest bunches of sweet dessert grapes, the yield sometimes as much as 700 lb (320 kg) in weight. Since 1935, grapes have been sold annually to the public rather than supplying the sovereign's table.[501] A pleasant rosé wine may be made to toast the man responsible, 'the Genius of the Place'.

Unfortunately, Brown was far too busy to write down his ideas about 'place-making'. However, having crossed the Channel to Paris on at least one occasion, he felt sufficiently qualified to make comparisons between the French style of gardening and the current, quite different fashion at home.[502] Science was of such consequence to Brown that he repeated his words in the postscript when corresponding with Revd Thomas Dyer of Marylebone about a plan for a client in France (see *overleaf*).[503]

OPPOSITE **May 1991, Harrow School Lake (formerly Flambards), Middlesex** A temple seat was once here.

ABOVE Ripening grape vine, *Vitis vinifera* 'Schiava Grossa' or 'Black Hamburg'.

In France they do not exactly comprehend our Ideas on Gardening & Placemaking which when rightly understood will supply all the wants, all the Elegance & all the Comforts which mankind wants in the country, & (I will add) if right be exactly fit for the owner, the Poet & the painter. To Produce these effects there wants a good Plan, good execution, a Perfect Knowledge of the Country & the objects in it, whether natural or artificial & infinite Delicacy in the Planting etc, so much Beauty depending on the Size of the Trees and the Colour of their Leaves to Produce the effect of light and shade so very essential to the perfecting of a Good Plan as also the hideing what is disagreeable and shewing what is Beautifull, getting shade from the large Trees & sweets from the smaller sorts of Shrubbs etc. I hope they will in time find out in France that Fashion has little to do with a good English Garden or House, a word which in my opinion disgraces Science wherever it is used. I daresay you will think I have said enough & therefore will only add that I am with sincere respect your oblig & obed Sert

Lancelot Brown

They will in Time find out in France that Place-making, & a good English garden depend entirely upon principles & has very little to do with Fashion, for it is a word that in my opinion disgraces Science wherever it is used.

There was no escaping the annoying, worn-out, frivolous cliché overused by every commentator and aspiring social climber. Trends in gardening, lake-making, forestry, exemplary walled gardens, model tenant farms and menageries involved several sciences: engineering, arboriculture, horticulture and husbandry. The word 'fashion' obviously exercised an expert who, whether he liked it or not, led the way in matters of style.[504] These few lines, where Brown expressed his clear thinking so passionately, now formulate an ideal brief for every aspiring landscape designer.

One other letter adds a surprising footnote to Brown's approach to improvement. On this occasion Amabel, Marchioness de Grey's daughter, wrote to her cousin, knowing that her mother was with her and always appreciated hearing any news of Brown.[505]

… Now I must request you to inform Mama that a great Man has paid us a visit, which Visit (as happens sometimes with great men) has ended in very little. You will guess that I mean the illustrious Mr Brown, who walk'd unexpectedly into the Garden on Tuesday Morning, & din'd with us in his way to Hawnes. He did not pay much Attention, or open any Scheme relative to the middle of the Garden. He saw that the water might appear to come from one Wood & flow into the other, but he did not know that a winding Water through a strait Avenue might not look inconsistent, & if the Avenue was destroy'd, & part of the Wood clear'd away it might unravel part of the Mystery of the Garden. In short he did not think that any material Alteration could be made anywhere, unless the whole Stile of the Place was chang'd, except cutting down a few Trees. – Neither could I persuade him to make any Sketch for the Grove, (a Pen and Paper he thought would do more Harm than Good, the Trees should be mark'd upon the Spot) nor did he seem to enter into a compleat Alteration but propos'd, if we thought it too thick "or would remove that Nightmare" to cut down three diagonal Rows from the near End of the Gravel Walk.

Although not convinced, and – vexed by Brown's sudden, unannounced arrival at **Wrest**, she could not resist a touch of scepticism – Amabel faithfully reported and underlined Brown's thoughts. Like many improvers with neither university education nor training in architecture, he had developed a crossover range of skills by subscribing to pattern books, often employing the same craftsmen as other high-ranking competitors. In his case, know-how was polished by an extra, less common ingredient: imagination. In his informal approach and authoritative thinking, he was highly sensitive to a garden's atmosphere. It was important to keep that extra frisson of mystery, that touch of history or that surprise discovery, that pleasurable, sometimes exciting unknown, pursued by all explorers, great and small, young or old.

When David Garrick was thwarted in his ambition to build a classical temple beside the Thames to give due homage to William Shakespeare, it was Brown's imagination that solved the actor's dilemma (see p.45). A busy public thoroughfare from Staines to Kingston ran in front of his villa at Hampton, barely a mile upriver from Hampton Court. Brown had recommended building a tunnel underneath to link the house to the garden, a suggestion acclaimed by Dr Johnson: 'Davy! Davy! What can't be overdone, may be underdone.'[506] Little wonder Garrick loved an idea that would add a touch of drama to his Elysian river garden. He would be able to enjoy a mysterious grotto, just like Pope's.

Visitors emerged from the shadowy, underground passage, as if from a cave on Prospero's isle, to discover a sublime Thames-side garden basking in sunlight. Their mysterious rocky journey ended in a wonderful surprise. A graceful, weeping willow, wafting in the breeze, framed the octagonal Grecian temple housing a fine sculpture of the immortal bard.[507] Brown went on to plant shrubs and trees to screen the road. Walpole brought over a suitable gift for Garrick, a fellow Freemason, some cypress trees (*Cupressus sempervirens*), as potent emblems of the sanctity of life and immortality.[508]

Just as Brown's star had risen in the area of landscape improvement, Garrick played an equally

ABOVE AND BELOW **September 2003, Hampton, Middlesex** Garrick's Thames-side garden is now a public park with restored grotto tunnel. Here, centre stage, a visitor is studying a map to get her bearings and comprehend the garden's layout including a classical temple to honour the Bard, William Shakespeare. Robert Adam played golf through Brown's tunnel, and Garrick kept one of the golf balls as a memento.

energetic and inspirational role in the rise of theatre. In 1769, five years after Shakespeare's bicentenary, he wrote the script and organised the music for a special Shakespeare Jubilee Pageant by the river at Stratford upon Avon. He built a large rotunda based on one in Ranelagh Gardens, to hold 1,000 spectators. Unfortunately, heavy rain caused this special occasion to be cancelled. However, they later performed the pageant ninety times in the popular Theatre Royal, Drury Lane, London.

At this time, public entry to this theatre was, surprisingly, far from grand. Every visitor had to negotiate a dark, probably dank, narrow passageway from a courtyard. This succeeded in heightening their expectations. What a contrast they experienced upon entering into the atmospheric, candlelit, richly embossed auditorium. In similar vein, Brown designed enjoyable carriage drives as if sublime scenery for his friend's stage set: tree tunnels of shade relieved by random dappled clearings, an occasional organised view of a temple seat or a 'pretend river', before venturing out into the bright expanse of open park on the way to the house.

Undoubtedly, having experienced lively outdoor entertainment with music, spectacle and fireworks, Brown delighted in expanding open-air theatrical tradition to make each arrival and departure an unforgettable experience. The ha-ha made the house appear as if on a raised stage, framed by wings of pleasure-ground scenery. He balanced light and shade in a variety of views, whether boats bobbing on his waters, deer chasing across park pastures, or men and women hay-making, sheep grazing, swallows and swifts winging.

No one disputes that Brown built on the foundations, and in some cases, amphitheatres, laid by an exceptionally gifted predecessor. As an author and director of a number of plays, Vanbrugh's exaggerated view of life, his theatricality, filtered through to architectural designs, nowhere better exemplified than at Blenheim. All the same, in 1760, Walpole had dismissed the Blenheim landscape as tired. Years later, he changed his mind: 'I used to think it one of the ugliest places in England; a giant's castle who had laid waste of all the country round him. Everybody now allows the merit of Brown's achievements there!'[509]

The articulate commentator and Brown, the diligent, high-flying improver, recognised and sparked off each other's ideas in their attempts to conserve and interpret English history. They both prepared the ground for an emerging profession. Neither the first nor the only improver to create mirrored lakes, Brown outclassed other designers in scale, in variety and artistry. Onlookers wondered at his skilful levelling, which, coupled with considered planting, stabilised the land and embedded his lakes seductively into the landscape as if from time immemorial. Centre stage, reflecting lawn and vibrant arboreal palette, his majestic waters sparkled like crown jewels, man and nature in perfect harmony.

Since a Stamford mason carved the date 1577 on the ceiling of **Burghley's** western entrance, there have been countless visitors. One, Lady Grantham, observed: 'On way [to Newby] stopped at Burleigh. Mr Brown has smoothed & laid out the grounds, having levelled & pared away the House till he has given it appearance of higher situation.'[510]

Revd William Sawrey Gilpin, on returning, was also struck by the major changes made by Brown.[511] In simplifying the scene, clearing away stables, barns and garden ornament clutter, he set off the magnificent Elizabethan architecture to great effect. He improved everyday management and use of the grounds, enabling sporting events to flourish, while moulding and artfully dressing the landscape to add impact. Visitors turning off the Great North Road took a new, more direct approach to the house, 'Brown's Cutting'. After passing through his young beech and oak shelter belt, they were confronted with a sleek, neo-classical entrance archway and then glanced at his 'Round House', a thatched country lodge[512] for the gamekeeper complete with kennels (see p.191). Moments later they admired his modern model farm, a *ferme ornée* with pretty Gothic cattle shed and dairy (see p.175).

Continuing the journey, as their carriage eased down a shaded, tree-lined incline, they noticed a mysterious change of terrain. The hill had been specifically hollowed out to add to their anticipation by hiding the view, before, at the bottom of the slope, they arrived suddenly into bright daylight, welcomed by four great lions

ABOVE **June 2008, Burghley, Cambridgeshire** Brown left one original Cecil tree as a gate guardian, a veteran lime tree, now known as Queen Elizabeth's tree. Nearby he planted a spreading oriental plane and a cedar of Lebanon (left) to make a significant trinity.

BEOW **April 2008, Burghley, Cambridgeshire** The Elizabeth Gate, north-east, counterbalancing the similar gateway south-west, 'Brown's Cutting', exemplifies holistic place-making.

reclining either end on the ramparts of Brown's fine stone bridge. As they crossed his 'river' to 'a world apart', the rise of the bridge automatically causing them to turn their eyes, they were confronted with the exceptional Elizabethan house, and Tijou's dazzling, gilded gateway.[513]

Later, sharing his thoughts about Burghley with Lord Harcourt, Brown, the thrusting pioneer of modern comforts, was acutely aware of the significance of the Cecil heritage: 'This is a great place, where I have had 25 years pleasure restoring the monument of a great minister to a great Queen.'[514]

He conceived a new gateway, the 'Elizabeth Gate'. More than a straightforward restoration, more than adding to the impact of arrival, and even more than an understated, matchless contribution to the running of the Burghley estate, Brown's art had become, in effect, four-dimensional in evoking the power and emotional awe of the history he cherished.[515]

October 2011, Syon Park, Middlesex Some trees, including Scots pine and swamp cypress (centre left), date from Brown's planting, where two poplars (centre) are probably later replacements in this pleasure-ground setting.

OPPOSITE September 1992, St James's Park, London Many Londoners and overseas visitors enjoy the park daily, but it is still possible to find a peaceful corner under stately plane trees.

Some believe Brown underscored divisions in local society by introducing a visual endorsement of a landowner's power and influence, in defining newly enclosed lands to create greater privacy for clients by screening ordinary settlements and public roads with great plantations of oak and beech. Brown's 'mind's eye' spurred him on. No doubt he envisaged casual spectators, estate staff included, pausing, as he frequently did, to admire and appreciate these belts as guardians with a reassuring presence, emphasising a stimulating progression of seasonal beauty within a great space. Perhaps, in modern terms, he could be called the world's first 'minimalist'— his rather Spartan, formulaic approach and recognisable 'Brownian' style displayed a rewarding rhythm and a selective palette of trees, shrubs and flowers that could appeal to the imagination.

A German aristocrat, Prince Pückler-Muskau (1785–1871), on a carriage tour of English parks singled out these boundaries as perhaps the most successful and rewarding component of a strong 'sense of place':

Very many parks in England – especially those from the old days by Brown (the Shakespeare of horticulture, so to speak), who combined noble poetry with a good deal that was clumsy, square and rugged; or those that are the work of his students, who were only able to imitate his faults without achieving his beauties – are surrounded along the perimeter wall with a narrow, almost regular, belt of mixed planting, in which, parallel to the wall itself, is laid a boundary drive, where the wall is mostly seen glinting between the trunks.[516]

Taking in the Syon landscape when Brown's trees were in their prime, he was again discerning: 'Syon House has another park laid out by Brown, the Shakespeare of English garden arts, and in his grandiose style, but particularly strange in its magnificent mature specimens of foreign trees, which we only grow in greenhouses.'[517]

The prince repeated this literary analogy at Blenheim, another sensational and moving *coup de théâtre*. One January visit prompted a fresh metaphor: 'My eye feasts on the ever-changing pictures like those in a magic-lantern.... One cannot but admire Brown's great genius when wandering through this park. It is the Shakespeare-Garden of England.'[518]

Returning home enthused, Pückler-Muskau determined to pursue similar improvements and to allow public access to his Muskau estate. He recognised that Brown's parks were for both the convenience and the profit of those who lived there, but were also freely available for the delight of a wider society.

As regards public access, the royal St James's Park had been opened to Londoners and had been highly popular for entertainment since Charles II's day, when its Grand Canal was considered to be the French designer Mollet's masterpiece. Brown, newly appointed by George III as Gardener at St James's, drew up a plan. Many historians believe that, apart from closing one end to create Horse Guards Parade, nothing much was done to alter the formal layout, until John Nash's naturalising improvements in the Regency period.[519] However, a brief news-sheet clipping suggests otherwise, that in 1770 work had already started to naturalise Charles II's canal:

> Mr. Brown, the Engineer, commonly called Capability Brown, is to have the new modelling St. James's Park; but till the Arches of the Drains are settled, the Ground cannot be covered in. The principal Point intended is to give a full View of Whitehall to the Queen's Palace, and also of Westminster Abbey, to effect which almost all the Trees on that Side will be taken away.[520]

Typical of Brown here, with drainage and conduit work always the first priority, a survey (1770) shows the canal endorsed with pencil marks, to indicate 'Rosamund's Pond' near 'James' gat' with the street filled in, indicating his intention to unite both water features.[521] One can imagine him instructing his men about his 'principal Point' for the park, just as at Cadland: 'NB. None of the Views must be interrupted by Planting.'

Conscious of the history in the heart of the capital, Brown planned to unite, emphasise and preserve the commanding triumvirate relationship between the Queen's Palace (today Buckingham Palace), Whitehall, the seat of political power, and the venerable medieval Westminster Abbey where all the kings and queens of England had been crowned. A more fascinating example of the emotional power of English designed landscape would be hard to find.

CHAPTER TWENTY-FOUR

LOVE OF COUNTRY

Prime Minister Chatham trusted Brown, the 'honest man of sentiments much above his birth', and counselled a cousin's wife: 'You cannot take any other advice so intelligent or more honest.'[522] Since their first acquaintance at Stowe, besides achieving uncommon upward social mobility, it seems that Brown had closely followed William Pitt's career as he rose to be Paymaster General. Pitt's marriage to Cobham's niece, Hester Grenville, had followed a romantic proposal at Wotton: 'in all the beauty of its deep shades of oak, softening lawns and tranquil waters, like a lively smile lighting up a thoughtful countenance'.[523]

Pitt, who once famously acknowledged that 'the parks are the lungs of London', involved himself in landscape improvements at Wotton and at his home in Chevening, Kent, doubtless a welcome distraction from political tensions, besides being an antidote to the swarming squalor of the capital's streets. In 1766, as Britain was making territorial gains in America and the Caribbean, and to the east in India, Pitt became Prime Minister and was created Earl Chatham. He campaigned for the cause of liberty and the rights of the individual with an empathy for ordinary people that earned him the nickname 'The Great Commoner'. Knowing that William Pitt had been educated at Eton and played cricket there in his young 'Patriot' days, Brown elected to send his eldest son Lancelot there. The school had an excellent reputation and was not socially exclusive. Brown's allegiance to Pitt verged on hero-worship: 'I knew, after forty years' experience, that no man loved his country more.'[524]

OPPOSITE **November 2015, Burghley, Cambridgeshire** The summerhouse.

ABOVE **August 2009, Wotton, Buckinghamshire** A tranquil, pastoral view of the Warrells.

Another admirer of the Prime Minister, though a complete stranger, Sir William Pynsent welcomed Chatham's opposition to a 10s (ten shillings, now £72) tax on a hogshead of cider, critical to his local Somerset economy. Consequently, having no offspring, he chose to bequeath his country estate, **Burton Pynsent**, to Chatham, who turned to the royal gardener for advice. Brown, much taken by a nearby prominent spur of land high above Sedgemoor Plain, could envisage a 150-ft high Tuscan column in memory of the generous landowner, as both prospect tower and eye-catcher, close to the edge of the high escarpment. What was more, every time the Somerset Levels below were purposely flooded and refreshed, the man-made farming territory became an awe-inspiring seascape. Brown reported directly to the Prime Minister:

> *I called at your Builder's in Bath but found he was set out for your house the same day I arrived at that place. I shall have some opportunity of talking to and giving him the best advice in my power concerning the construction of Pillars, the scaffolding and etc. Agreeable to my promise, I have sent you by your Steward a design for the Pillar which I hope will merit your approbation; if there are any parts you disapprove of, we can very easily correct them when I shall have the honour of seeing you. The figure I have put on the pedestal is that of Gratitude, conveying to Posterity the name of Pinsant; which indeed he himself has distinguished and without flattery done in the most effectual manner by making you His Heir. On this topic I could say more, but my silence convey my respect. And that your King and Country may be long, very long, very long blessed with your unparalleled abilities will be the constant wish of Sir, your most obliged and most obedient, humble servant.*[525]

August 2001, Burton Pynsent, Somerset Brown's commanding 150 foot high Tuscan column on Troy Hill overlooks the Somerset Levels. An internal spiral staircase leads to the cupola. In WWII, iron railings around the base were dismantled. An urn replaces the figure, 'Gratitude', that must have weathered.

As soon as the landmark was finished and cased in Portland stone, Brown thought it best to approach Lady Hester, by then a close friend and confidante: 'Pardon my Zeal! Pardon my Vanity, but I wish above all things to know [how] my Lord does, and how the Pillar pleases his Lordship.'[526]

History does not relate her husband's reaction, but one story bears repeating. One evening Chatham and Brown, both improvers in their different ways, met by chance and dined together at Staines. As he took his leave, doubtless exaggerated with a benevolent flourish, the Prime Minister offered a parting shot: 'Now, Sir, go and adorn your country!' Brown's quick response, with wit hinting at the characteristic unease of a middle-aged man about the government, was: 'Go you, my Lord, and save it.'[527]

Subsequently Chatham began to suffer debilitating bouts of gout and mental illness, causing Brown grave concern, judging by supportive letters to Lady Hester:

I need not tell your Ladyship my feeling is everything where Lord Chatham's Interest, or his Happiness is concerned; pleasant Truth is a comfort, even bad news when we know the worst of it is better than being in suspense; if of an incurable sort we must make use of Philosophy, and submit to the dispensating of Providence.[528]

God knows best what can be done for such distracted Times, but Lord Chatham's Life will ever have a great influence on the Peace & Happiness of this Country.[529]

Having wisely avoided most involvement in politics, Brown now took every opportunity to speak out on Chatham's behalf, going so far as to act as intermediary when the earl fell out of favour with George III over the handling of the American war. Walpole assured Lady Ossory: 'Mr Browne was not the king's playfellow'.[530]

Meanwhile, deeply worried, Brown wrote to console Lady Hester:

Madam, I am just returned from a long Northern expedition on which I have spent many anxious hours, on account of Lord Chatham's health, where however I had the comfort to find one universal Prayer one wish that his Lordships life may be preserved to save this Devoted sinking Country, but alas, I am doubtful it is too far gone, even for his Lordship to redeem us.[531]

A profound love of country comes as no surprise. Gardeners are, on the whole, patient optimists who welcome each changing season, the next new growth and harvest. Marriage to Bridget and devotion to his family underpinned Brown's work, and was the motivation to secure their future. The considerable accomplishments of his self-assured offspring reflect not only Brown's strengths but those of their mother. Bridget cared for the family over long periods when he was absent from home. Success brought its own problems. Brown feared too much self-importance, both for himself and his children.

Where foremen recognised Brown's vision and strove to live up to his high ideals, his three sons declined to follow in his demanding footsteps and chose careers typical of period gentry. After Eton, Lancelot Jr studied law at Oxford, Cambridge and Lincoln's Inn before becoming a barrister. In 1779 he was elected to parliament with the encouragement of the Earl of Sandwich, a good friend of the family, serving as MP for Totnes for four years. Later becoming a Gentleman of the Privy Chamber (1795), Lancelot Jr maintained connections with Kirkharle, acting as sponsor at the christening of the 9th baronet. John, the second son, worked for his father for a short period, and was probably expected to join the practice. However, again thanks to Sandwich, in 1772 John accepted a commission in His Majesty's Navy. He served on board *Nautilus* in the American War, and was involved in several skirmishes in New York, causing his parents great anxiety. Not the first-born, 'poor Jack', as he was called in family letters, may have been Brown's favourite, though one missive expressed characteristic parental irritation, when John dared to brag about a fast journey to Southampton in a time

Brown considered impossible: 'I will give up the sea to him but the land he had best leave to me.'[532]

An adventurous, free spirit, probably as dynamic and patriotic as his father, John was promoted to Captain in Brown's lifetime, later advancing to Admiral of the Blues. Thomas, the youngest son, entered the church and married Susannah, daughter of Revd Samuel Dickens. They lived quietly, not far from Fenstanton, in Conington, Cambridgeshire. In 1774, the elder daughter, Bridget, gave birth to a baby girl, their first grandchild, further cementing the bond of friendship between the Brown and Holland families. A meeting with a woman who had tragically lost four of her five sons moved Brown to counsel his younger daughter Margaret, 'Peggy', who was often in his thoughts:

I have sometimes thought that there are more people made happy by Labouring under considerable difficulties than those of Easy affluent Circumstances, who have not tasted the bitter draft of affliction.… my constant wish & Prayer is for all your happiness you may be sure.

A second letter has Brown still pondering:

I should have added that she was not without strong feelings at the end of each of her melancholy misfortunes as there always came a Shower of Tears, but you see there were none of her misfortunes could be prevented by Human prudence, there was nothing that was wicked, nothing profligate and there Christian hope & fortitude of mind was her only resource.

Later, he empathised with Peggy, who was fretting and unable to make up her mind about a proposal of marriage: 'I pitty the feeling & distress of your mind, I wish to God, it was in my power to alleviate your distress & give comfort to you.'

Brown tried his best not to put pressure on his daughter, simply offering 'blessing & advice but *no commands*'. Yet, in a postscript, like all fathers with daughters he simply had to make his wishes known:

'Hope you will find that the best thing you can do is marry Mr Gee.'[533]

One Richard Cosway pencil sketch has Brown sharing a decanter of wine with Lord Craven and an old Northumbrian friend, Robert Shafto. Here was a man who enjoyed life. Forward-looking and friendly, and far from arrogant, Brown also gave free advice. Josiah Wedgwood valued his taste and opinion, not to mention his society connections, and eagerly showed Brown the new jasperware tablets he had perfected to set into chimneypieces. Unsurprisingly, the landscaper preferred natural colours.

He expressed his strongest approbation and even admiration of what he had seen. He preferred them greatly to sculpture in marble, and would make use of them himself as an architect when he had an opportunity.… This gentleman, if there is any confidence to be placed in the greatest apparent sincerity and earnestness, means really to serve us, and he gives for his reason – because we deserve it.[534]

Extended travel gave time to reflect not only on the needs of his fellow men but also to observe cyclical renewal, nature's way of offering celebration and comfort, hope and inspiration. Severe asthma attacks undoubtedly forced him to confront his mortality, but he persevered with that resource of 'Christian hope & fortitude of mind'.

Growing older, and easily able to afford retirement, a weary Brown simply would not let go. In 1781, after two visits to Stanstead (Sussex), he supplied Richard Barwell 'with very fair descriptive drawings', as usual, understating exhaustive plans for house, offices, farms, stable, greenhouse and chapel. He also immersed himself in complex plans for major modifications to **Belvoir Castle**:

1779 3928 acres by Spyers @ 1/- [today £7.25] an acre my journey to Belvoir Castle included Christmas 1782 £300 [£43,500] Plans of different stories & elevations of the fronts taken by Spyers £20 [£2,900] General Plan for alterations of whole place with various offices Plan for

putting offices in new attic storey to castle all with these drawings in a book £300.[535]

In February 1782 William Hervey's journal notes a Brown visit with plans for a house at Ickworth (Suffolk), which, though not adopted, proved influential, as a later postscript suggests: 'Lancelot Brown may have helped to choose the exact site and may have planned the gardens. I have heard my father say that he designed the serpentine road which formerly led to Ickworth Lodge that is now a grass track.'[536]

On 1 January 1783, John Haverfield became by warrant 'Chief Gardiner of our Royal Gardens', almost certainly on Brown's recommendation. He knew him well. The Princess of Wales's gardener at Kew had supplied trees for both Luton and significant improvements at Richmond for which Brown had been paid an extra £2,500 (£362,500).[537]

His health rapidly deteriorating, and conscious of his frailty, Brown's thoughts concerned those he loved. In February 1783 he called in the attorney John Edison, 'of Coopers Hall, London Gent.', a friend and associate for the best part of his professional life. Brown was anxious to be fair to his offspring, adding a codicil to a will made four years earlier regarding land in Lincolnshire to be inherited by his second son, John.[538]

The end came suddenly, the very next day, Thursday 6 February, at about nine in the evening. Returning from dinner in Piccadilly with Lord Coventry, one of his closest friends, Brown dropped dead on the pavement outside his daughter's house in Hertford Street. He was sixty-seven years old. An obituary writer assumed that 'a violent blow he received when falling in a fit in the street' caused his death.[539] It is more likely, as Walpole believed, that his asthma caused a seizure in the freezing night air. The family laid Brown to rest at St Peter and St Paul Church in **Fenstanton**, his manor in Huntingdonshire (now Cambridgeshire). Perhaps it was his wish, or theirs, that he should lie on the north side of the church, facing his native county, in an unmarked grave. Later they placed an unusual crenellated monument in Gothic Coade stone on the north inside wall of the church. Mason's epitaph, for once without a trace of satire, is testimony to the admiration and respect of his contemporaries.

Ye sons of elegance who truly taste
The simple charms that genius art supplies,
Come from the sylvan scene his genius grac'd
And offer here your tributary sighs
But know that more than genius slumbers here.
Virtues were his, which arts best powers transcend.
Come ye superior train, who these revere,
And weep the Christian, Husband, Father, Friend.

November 2013, St Peter and St Paul Church, Fenstanton,
Cambridgeshire (formerly Huntingdonshire)

An anonymous obituary summed up the thoughts
of contemporary admirers:

His great and fine genius stood unrivalled, and it
was a peculiar felicity of it that it was allowed by
all ranks and degrees of society in this country, and
by noble and great personages in other countries.
Those who knew him best, or practised near him,
were not able to determine whether the quickness
of the eye, or its correctness, were to be most
admired. It was comprehensive and elegant, and
perhaps it may be said never to have failed him.
Such, however was the effect of his genius that
when he was the happiest man, he will be least
remembered, so closely did he copy nature that his
works will be mistaken. His truth, his integrity and
his good humour were very effectual and will hold
a place in the memory of his friends, more likely to
continue, though not less to be esteemed...[540]

The country boy had amassed a fortune; by today's
standards he was a millionaire. The first article
of his eleven-page will underscores his principal
dedication to his profession. He bequeathed 100
guineas (£15,225), over and above his wages, to
Samuel Lapidge, his right-hand man, charging him to
complete all unfinished contracts, to employ William
Ireland as his foreman and to collect any outstanding
bills.[541] Each house servant received a year's salary
over and above their wages. His eldest son, Lancelot
Jr, inherited his surveying instruments, treasured
tools of his achievements. He expressed love for his
daughter Bridget 'with an unchangeable affection',
and bequeathed a further £1,000 (£145,000) to add to
her considerable marriage dowry. Bridget, his widow,
was naturally well looked after. Besides all household
goods, furniture, paintings, personal belongings,
coach and horses, she inherited, along with Edison
and Henry Holland Sr, estates and premises in the
counties of Lincoln, Huntingdon and Cambridge.

George III had come to rely on Michael Milliken, a
talented Scot and 'safe pair of hands' brought down by
Brown from Chatsworth to supervise the royal gardens
at Richmond. Soon after the news of Brown's death

had reached the royal ear, he went over to Richmond gardens and in a tone of great satisfaction said to the under-gardener: 'Brown is dead! Now Mellicant you and I can do here what we please.'[542]

If the King saw Brown as a benevolent dictator, Walpole was plainly upset by his death. He shared his thoughts with William Mason, asking if he too was concerned. Having previously claimed he did not care about everyday whims and petty politics, 'who is grubbed up or transplanted', on this occasion, Walpole recognised the importance of defining Brown's place in history, 'Lady Nature's second husband' after Kent. In actual fact he took the view that 'the second monarch of landscape' had improved on his predecessor's 'puny clumps'. Unusually, he struggled to find the right words and suggested that Mason could perhaps improve on his 'bad epitaph':

With one lost Paradise the name
Of our first ancestor is stained;
Brown shall enjoy unsullied fame
For many a Paradise regained.[543]

People were still talking about Brown the following July when Lady Maynard pronounced:

A great genius ... does not shut a door like an
ordinary man. Apply this to the little ground of
Lord Godolphin, in St. James's Park: it was laid
out by Capability Brown, and though an object
of the smallest kind, is able to exemplify his very
transcendent ability.[544]

In Suffolk Brown's ideas to restore the church destroyed in a fire at Fornham St Genevieve were abandoned, and the remaining tower left a picturesque ruin in the park.

Elizabeth Montagu missed her friend greatly:

I found Sandleford improved by the attention
of the great Mr Brown, my pleasure in these
improvements was mixed with regret for his
death.... Brown was certainly a man of great
genius.... Happily for me he made a plan for all
that is to be done here.[545]

A year later he was still in her thoughts, and helping to motivate improvements:

What I left a rivulet assumes the air of a river
charming walks on its banks and through the
wood make me think with gratitude of the late
Mr Brown by whose plans all these things were
accomplished and we are still following the same
directions happily he had given us a design for
everything that intended to be done here and we
are now embellishing the grounds to the south and
making an approach to the house which will be
far preferable to the present.[546]

The Earl of Exeter built a 'shrine', a secluded summer pavilion among the shrubberies and cedars overlooking the Burghley waters, to house Brown's portrait, a copy of the one by Nathaniel Dance.[547] Meanwhile, Lord Coventry, perhaps more than most, mourned the loss of his friend:

I write from a house which he built for me
which without any pretension to architecture, is,
perhaps, a model for every internal and domestic
convenience. I may be partial to my place at
Croome, which was entirely his creation, and, I
believe, as hopeless a spot as any on the island.[548]

He commissioned a Coade stone casket to place by the lake, with the inscription:

To the Memory of Lancelot Brown
who by the powers of
his inimitable and creative genius
formed this garden scene
out of a morass.

Later, reminiscing in a letter to Repton, Coventry confirmed that he held Brown in especially high esteem as an artist.[549] On the earl's death, in 1809, his great-grandson planted an acorn beside the Brown memorial.

CHAPTER TWENTY-FIVE

EPILOGUE

STILL CAPABLE

Each pleasing Art lends softness to the mind
and with our studies are our lives refined.[550]

As trees planted after the Restoration were reaching their glorious prime, deep thinkers, Whately, Jefferson, Burke and Mason among others, were preoccupied in searching for meaning in the language of grass, flowers and trees, and consequence in the purity and exclusivity of landscape. Elizabeth Montagu, too, expressed this common thread: 'Art was better employed in beautifying the rural scene than any other work of taste.'[551]

Despite a fondness for amusing play on words, Brown was a compulsive man of action rather than a wordsmith, and had no urge to 'book' his place in history; he was far too busy to commit to paper his thoughts regarding the art of landscape. Besides, others were saving him the trouble, particularly Walpole, who was determined to record the significance of 'natural' English gardening at its zenith:

> *Extraordinary that having so long ago stumbled on the principles*
> *of landscape gardening we should have persisted in retaining its*
> *reverse, symmetrical and unnatural planting.... It was fortunate*
> *for the country and Mr. Kent, that he was succeeded by a very able*
> *master; and did living artists come within my plan, I should be glad*
> *to do justice to Mr. Brown; but he may be a gainer, by being reserved*
> *for some abler pen.... An open country is but a canvass on which*
> *a landscape might be designed.... If we lose sight of the propriety*
> *of landscape in our gardens, we shall wander into the fantastic*
> *sharawadgis of the Chinese....*[552]

OPPOSITE **April 1999, Harewood, Yorkshire** A fine example of what Richard Bisgrove calls 'memorable landscapes that appeal directly to the soul rather than the intellect'.

A mostly reliable, well-read eye-witness, though sometimes carried away, Walpole heightened society's patriotic fervour by celebrating 'new masterstrokes' to modern gardening. Whereas William Kent had merely 'chastened or polished' the 'living landscape', Brown had then 'transformed' rural views. Perhaps the reality of modern, radically unconventional landscapes, combined with Adam Smith's hypothetical publication *The Theory of Moral Sentiments* (1759), had stimulated Walpole's 'Eureka' moment:

July 2009, Wimpole, Cambridgeshire (NT) Repton reintroduced a *clairvoie* screen, urns and terrace gardens.

We have discovered the point of perfection. We have given the true model of gardening to the world; let other countries mimic or corrupt our taste; but let it reign here on its verdant throne, original by its elegant simplicity, and proud of no other art than softening nature's harshnesses and copying her graceful touch.[553]

'Propriety' and 'perfection' defined the heady heights that Brown had reached in his holistic consideration of a memorable, pleasingly contoured and practical working landscape that resonated with elements of English history. His works were

developing their own legible story line, rather like the pages of an open book, with clients initiated into the punctuation of his planting. 'Such a school of landscape cannot be found on the face of the world.'[554]

Unusually for him, Walpole struggled to find the correct term to describe this new contemporary art, first of designing landscape gardens, then, over time, refining and superintending them: 'I have a mind, should you approve of it, to call designers of gardens, gardenists, to distinguish them from gardeners; or landscapists. I wish you would coin a term for the art itself.'[555]

Neither definition entered common parlance, unlike his delightful word 'serendipity'. The term 'landscape architecture' for this emerging profession was coined only later and only later still was Brown acknowledged by most as its father.

Equally, his notable achievements in crossing social barriers are defined in a letter from Henry Holland Jr to Humphry Repton. As partner and son-in-law, Holland was best placed to assess an exceptional career:

No man I ever met with understood so well what was necessary for the habitation of all ranks and degrees of society: no one disposed of his offices so well, set his buildings on such good levels, designed such good rooms, or so well provided for the approach, for the drainage, and for the comfort and conveniences of every part of a place he was concerned in. This he did without ever having had one single difference or dispute with any of his employers. He left them pleased, and they remained so as long as he lived.[556]

Since Henry Holland Jr opted to concentrate on architecture, his brother-in-law, Lancelot Brown Jr, presented all his father's designs to Repton. It is therefore conceivable that Brown's leather-bound folio albums containing surveys, plans and Spyers's watercolour illustrations provided both impetus and inspiration for Repton's famous, highly prized 'Red Books'. Discovering the mere mention of the celebrated name 'Mr Brown' advantageous to business, Repton began his proposals by tactfully expressing his appreciation before proposing certain changes: 'Everything at Ashridge is on a great scale of substantial and permanent grandeur.'[557]

Appreciating that laying out a 'natural' landscape was the most complicated of all gardening commissions, he was particularly complimentary in his Red Book for Gayhurst (Buckinghamshire): 'The water in the park, though it consists of several pieces of different levels, has the effect of being in one single sheet when seen from the house; this was very ingeniously executed by Mr Brown.'

The more Repton surveyed Brown's works, the more he realised how fundamental it was for a good landscape gardener to have knowledge of building:

Mr Brown's fame as an architect seems to have been eclipsed by his celebrity as a landscape gardener, he being the only professor of the one art, while he had many jealous competitors in the other. But when I consider the number of excellent works in architecture designed and executed by him, it becomes an act of injustice to his memory to record that, if he was superior to all in what related to his own particular profession, he was inferior to none in what related to the comfort, convenience, taste and propriety of design in the several mansions and other buildings which he planned.[558]

Lacking the support of a wide network of contractors and foremen, Repton failed to convince landowners that they should invest in grandiose schemes for new houses. Nevertheless his picturesque 'before and after' watercolour proposals, with copious amounts of written advice, proved highly popular. By raising flaps of paper, as if by magic, Repton revealed attractive and imaginative solutions to what he considered design faults. Consequently, some Red Books offer an unparalleled, lasting legacy, the 'before', giving a painterly record of Brown's park and garden views, maturing to sensational effect.

Repton's first publication, *Sketches and Hints on Landscape Gardening*, included, so as to distance himself from Brown in clients' eyes, occasional, selective criticisms of his predecessor's style, which should perhaps be taken with a pinch of salt. His Red Book for Thoresby, for instance, argued that his predecessor had a liking for sluggish water. The more likely scenario is that landowners neglected regular maintenance and de-silting of reservoirs and spillways. Repton did reposition some kitchen gardens but preferred conservatories, balustraded terraces and floral rosaries to utilitarian aspects of everyday life.

Abroad, *Le Jardin anglais* was gaining popularity in mainland Europe. Catherine the Great of Russia was among the first to appreciate the new simplicity of the English landscape. The empress enthusiastically copied down a couple of hundred pages of the French edition of *Whately's Observations on Modern Gardening*[559] and corresponded with Voltaire: 'I passionately love gardens in the English style, the curved lines, the gentle slopes, the ponds pretending to be lakes, the archipelagos on solid ground, and I deeply disdain straight lines…. I should say my anglomania gets the better of planimetry.'[560]

Catherine purchased John Spyers's album containing original watercolours of Hampton Court gardens when Brown was in charge. She was so inspired that she began to seek English designers and gardeners for her own lands and commissioned the famous 'Frog' Wedgwood dinner service illustrating settings of great estates.[561] Later the botanist, designer and garden writer John Claudius Loudon (1783–1843) declared 'White Birch Park', the backdrop for Pavlovsk Palace, the most beautiful example of the English landscape garden in the Russian Empire.[562]

Travelling artists arrived to capture the extraordinary cleanness of Brown's works. They supplied a growing number of clients with paintings for their reception rooms, while drawings of improved views kept engravers and print shops busy. Somehow, wherever they worked, their pictures were idealised, all too similar: the house above the lake, framed by trees. Certain younger, up-and-coming, equally ambitious designers began to find Brown's domesticated parkland boring and predictable, with only one sterile mood, 'somnolent tranquillity'. They ridiculed Brown's imposing plantations as military invasions and evidence of Whig power and affluence. To be fair, Sir Uvedale Price (1747–1829) respected Brown's line. He also recognised that great strides had been made in the arrangement and management of trees and grudgingly praised his pleasure grounds, before going on to land a final blow:

> *In the garden scene at Blenheim the gravel walk appears in great perfection; the sweeps are large easy & well taken; & though in wild & romantic parts such as artificial bands destroy the character of the scenery, yet in gardens, where there must be regular borders to walks, an attention to the different curves is indispensable & the skill that is shown in conducting them, though not to be rated too high is by no means without its merit. That was Mr Brown's fort & there he was a real improver, for before him, the horror of straight lines made the first improvers on the new system, conceive that they could make too many turns. His misfortune (& still more that of his employers) was, that knowing his fort, he resorted to it upon all occasions, & carried the gravel walk, its sweeps, & its lines, to rivers, to plantations & universally to all improvements; not contented with making gardens, many parts of which he well understood, he chose to make landscapes, of which he was worse than ignorant; for of them he had the falsest conceptions.*[563]

Among those who favoured a romantic air of abandonment, the poet Richard Payne Knight (1750–1824) famously portrayed Brown as 'Thin meagre genius of the bare and the bald'.[564] Walpole was enraged: 'The abuse of Brown is as coarse and illiberal as it is cruel and unjust.'[565]

Some thought Brown's landscapes too 'smooth' and deemed a wilder, rugged look more picturesque, going so far as to advocate unkempt landscapes. Where the royal designer was more than aware of the aesthetic value of ruins, he never recommended neglect of the setting – rather the reverse. His was a hard act to follow. Perhaps such perfectionist standards and 'too high-keeping' management style had proved not only challenging but too expensive to maintain. W.S. Gilpin believed Brown's 'floating' lake and planting at Roche Abbey had contrived a beautiful valley scene, 'too magnificent and too artificial an appendage to be in unison with the ruins of an abbey'.

Even so, Gilpin acknowledged one great achievement: real pleasure in being subtly made to take a 'pause'. Brown's words to Hannah More (p.129), 'Now there ... there ... at another part ... now ... and then another subject', suggest energy, excitement, movement. The observation of landscape on the move, sitting in a comfortable carriage, offered immense fun, and satisfaction in experiencing the powerful effect of scale and ever-changing variety of surprise vistas. Brown's style was the very opposite of 'static', which the word 'picturesque' implies.

A major influence on aesthetic taste was sweeping Europe. The Welsh romantic painter Richard Wilson (c.1713–82), patronised by both the Earl of Coventry and Henry Hoare, and the royal artist Paul Sandby (*c.*1730–1809) numbered among a new breed of native artists who were making landscape fashionable. Sandby's classical studies, influenced by Claude Lorraine, were imbued with a light reminiscent of Italy and an almost tangible, harmonious feeling of social stability. Wilson's works include a few patrician parks improved by Brown: several versions of the memorable vista between two landscapes, from the royal Richmond Gardens towards Syon, three versions of Moor Park, as well as Ashburnham, Croome, Chatsworth and the River Dee near Eaton Hall (Cheshire). A series of six different Wilton views depicts young cedars on both sides of the river, their trunks neatly shredded (trimmed), a fastidious detail perhaps indicative of a Brown consultation. Paul Sandby painted thoroughbreds grazing on the Wakefield Lodge lawn, and several views of Cardiff Castle, Luton Hoo and Nuneham Courtenay, whereupon William Mason avowed: 'in a short time (Sandby) will be that Claude Lorraine, that Browne assured him he was'. George Stubbs (1724–1806) set his thoroughbred horses and wildlife paintings against the backdrops of Euston,

Eaton, Patshull and Peper Harow. Peter de Wint (1784–1849) painted deer in Lowther Park, Cumbria.

The artistic legacy of Brown's transformations to the look and feel of parkland cannot be overstated. At the tender age of twelve, the giant among artists J.M.W. Turner (1775–1851) undertook a watercolour study of Nuneham Courtenay. He went on to explore natural space and light in many Brown parks, radical, 'natural' settings, now accepted as pleasingly traditional: Ashburnham, Harewood, Lowther Castle and Syon. One dreamy painting of Petworth, a favourite haunt, given his recognisable, atmospheric soft-focus treatment, is now considered among his finest works and has immortalised Brown's foreground stand of quintessential English oaks. Recently, David Hockney included paintings of Sledmere (East Yorkshire) in his landmark 'Bigger Picture' exhibition. Artists and photographers will continue to capture changing aspects and moods from dawn to sunset: pleasing hummocks, depressions and ridges, emphasised by low winter sun or frost. His works can still excite, surprise or soothe; or they are just breathtaking.

LEFT Joseph Mallord William Turner (1775-1851), *View of Nuneham Courtenay from the Thames* (1787). Gouache, graphite and watercolour on paper © Tate, London 2016

OPPOSITE **November 1989, Alnwick, Northumberland** A beech grove by the River Aln at Denwick Bridge. Brown's beech belts and groves, majestic visual assets for over two hundred years, deserve restoration.

We must balance the weight of many complimentary, emotional and sometimes lyrical opinions, on the one hand, against some surprising vitriol on the other. Mrs Delaney was astonished to see no sign of George London's gardens at Longleat which, before the turn of the eighteenth century, had cost the first Viscount Thynne a reputed £30,000 (today £4,350,000). Brown had not set out to destroy these decorous gardens on a whim. A prolonged drought had hastened reorganisation of the territory in direct response to the essential need for water. Should a calamitous fire break out, it was vital to be able to pump up water to the house, using the prototype fire engine. Notably, to prove Brown's respect for the past, several works survived his alterations unscathed: Switzer's bastion garden at Grimsthorpe, Bridgeman's amphitheatre at Claremont, and the walled garden or *hortus conclusus* at Chatsworth, known as 'Queen Mary's Bower'.[566] Visiting Alnwick, more than a century after Brown, Sir Walter Scott also saw fit to censure him:

Oct 7th Drove out with the Duke in a phaeton, and saw part of park, which is a fine one, lying along the Alne. But it has been ill-planted. It was laid out by the celebrated Brown, who substituted clumps of birch and Scottish firs for the beautiful oaks and copse which grows nowhere so freely in Northumberland. To complete this, the late Duke did not thin, so the wood is in a poor state.... We came by the remains of the old Carmelite Monastery of Hulne, which is a very fine object in the park. It was finished by De Vesci. The gateway of Alnwick Abbey, also a fine specimen, is standing about a mile distant. The trees are much finer on the left side of the Alne, where they have been let alone by the capability-villain.[567]

The unforeseen low cost of coal had affected the duke's income. His estate suffered as a result, with countless birch and Scots pines intended as nursery trees left uncropped. Wherever landowners neglected the upkeep of grounds, or if subsequent designers made mistakes, the famous Brown took the blame. The Poet Laureate William Whitehead (1715–1785) foresaw such negative judgments and imagined a conversation between Dame Nature, half angry and half flattered, and her peerless imitator at Nuneham:

I may have my revenge on this fellow at last
For a lucky conjecture comes into my head,
That, whate'er he has done, and whate'er he has said,
The world's little malice will balk his design:
Each fault they call his, and each excellence mine.[568]

None mourned the passing of formal English gardens more than Sir Reginald Blomfield, Thomas Mawson, and even Laurence Whistler: 'He had few ideas and the chief of them was negative: to destroy formality wherever found… [and re Claremont] just as at Stowe, Kent enriched, then Brown ruined the scheme.'[569] The twentieth-century designer David Hicks concurred: 'I find almost tragic the work of Capability Brown, who destroyed so many fine avenues and marvellous English gardens.'[570]

On the other hand, garden historian Hugh Prince argued persuasively: 'It was manifestly absurd to try to impose straight lines upon the invincible undulations of the English countryside.'

Perhaps Brown's greatest legacy is his name, a name still capable of provoking lively debate, his image on occasion as battered as Flora's statue at Madingley. In 1992 Tom Stoppard crystallised the Age of Enlightenment in his amusing play *Arcadia*, addressing the dichotomy, the unending battle of taste between formal and natural design, and argued for the comparative significance of literature, painting and landscape as opposed to the science and mathematics of the natural world. Following in Garrick's footsteps, one character, Lady Croom, loves 'natural' gardening and ridicules her useless gardener as 'Culpability' Brown:

Lady Croom: But Sidley Park is already a picture and a most amiable picture too. The slopes are green and gentle. The trees are companionably grouped at intervals that show them to advantage. The rill is a serpentine ribbon unwound from the lake, peaceably contained by meadows on which the right amount of sheep are tastefully arranged. In short, it is nature as God intended, and I can say with the painter, 'Et in Arcadia Ego' – Here I am in Arcadia', Thomasina....

The author and researcher Hannah Jarvis combats the argument by deploring a decline from 'thinking' to 'feeling':

Hannah: There's an engraving of Sidley Park in 1730 that makes you want to weep. Paradise in the age of Reason. By 1760 everything had gone – the topiary, pools and terraces, fountains, an avenue of limes – the whole sublime geometry was ploughed under Capability Brown. The grass went from the doorstep to the horizon and the best box hedge in Derbyshire was dug up for the ha-ha so that fools could pretend they were living in God's countryside.

May 2006, Madingley, Cambridgeshire A statue of Flora ornaments Brown's still extant circuit walk.

In short, Brown's grounds required less upkeep than old-style, formal gardens, suiting those aristocrats who moved to their country estate for only a few weeks or months of the year. Skilled gardeners disappeared behind his new garden walls, screened by vegetation, a distance from the house where they could experiment in growing fruit, vegetables and flowers in a productive, sheltered 'vegetable manufactury'. A sweet-smelling, rural idyll, Arcadia, a pleasant change from chaotic, stinking streets around their London townhouses, with a minimum of noise and distraction around the house, replaced business with leisure, and gave welcome recuperation from hectic social lives or burdensome responsibilities of power. Secure and, above all, manageable landscapes were sophisticated, agreeable to the eye, comfortable

to negotiate, perfect for entertainment, contemplation and romance.[571] Despite all this, some continue to judge his works boring, facile and sterile, facetiously diminishing the value of a lake, a framed view, broken by clumps or single trees. Each new generation, just as their forebears, must make up their own minds.

The improver would not have been familiar with the word 'sustainability', but this could be the clue to the survival of so much of his handiwork. He successfully found the pulse of our relationship with nature: wonderful but best kept under control? A very English response![572]

A new appreciation of Brown landscapes has twenty-first-century landscape architects and land managers recognising the ongoing validity of his ideas in terms of ecology and management. Challenges face the present generation of landowners, witnessing mostly over-mature, disjointed fragments of original design: how and, at what point, to intervene to recover a landscape of quality.[573] Decisions to revive ageing parks, replanting lost trees and decaying belts, or to re-engineer dams and clear silted lakes are complex, ongoing and costly, a daunting, perhaps impossible process when a site is in fragmented ownership.

Outdoor work is sometimes constrained by planning. Both earlier and subsequent layers of significant design have to be evaluated, particularly where public funding is involved. Effective restoration and new work are rooted in, enabled, and occasionally provoked by thorough historical research.[574] Must conservation stifle creativity? Some naturalists, preferring forests of mixed native trees, seem loath to recommend replanting those Brownian belts that have deteriorated, and consider dominating beech plantations contrived. Consequently, single-species ribbon plantations, enjoyed by passers-by for centuries, crowning park horizons and bringing the landscape together, are now in grave danger of disappearing altogether. Enchanting and uplifting in spring, with their delicate fresh green, later their rusty bronze foliage warms autumn views, often well into

winter. Exact re-creation is, of course, impossible, but if the context and layers of history that make a site worthwhile are fully understood and appreciated, today's landscape architects will arrive at enlightened solutions for sympathetic regeneration, in order to banish the air of abandonment that can so easily pervade a garden and park. Conservation will always require intervention, new work, new funding and, surprisingly, new thinking.

Close scrutiny of an historic estate, a serpentine ha-ha or approach drive here, a sheet of water there, might suggest Brown's style but not necessarily his involvement. Many eighteenth-century designers and surveyors introduced similar features. His contemporaries, and those who later emulated his ideas, never quite achieved his extravagant, even heroic scale of lake-making and planting. 'Bird's-eye' engravings, paintings and drawings cannot be taken too literally. Who knows if artistic licence was taken to alter the position of trees, and even the topography, to suit their composition? Similarly, surviving plans were not necessarily fully implemented. If he returned several times, were his refinements ever recorded? Old surveys, first edition Ordnance Surveys and early photographs help to identify his work. Perhaps the remnant legacy of his signature planting is better seen in early aerial photographs.

Undoubtedly the best method of survey remains to walk the ground, in order to identify pockets of tree species available to an eighteenth-century designer, and to assess their positional strength and whether they provide living proof of Brown's vision. Rigorous research and aesthetic vigilance are not confined to archives. Park managers and head gardeners walk the ground together, much as Brown would have done, to observe critical components, to absorb atmosphere, to avoid the monotonous predictability of symmetry and, above all, to maintain standards. Best practice, in keeping with the spirit of the place, calls for a perfectionist eye for detail in line and in nurture. The bone structure has to be beautiful. Notice how a limited number of varieties and asymmetric

positioning as punctuation trees form significant 'bones', controlling and framing vistas.

'Place-making' at Trentham (Staffordshire) began with a monastic settlement, later, thanks to Brown's radical alterations, becoming a landscape of great scale. In turn, his lake became a backdrop to magnificent Italianate terrace gardens by the Victorian architect Sir Charles Barry. Sadly, industrial expansion in the Staffordshire potteries nearby polluted the river so badly, in 1911, that the house was abandoned. As it disintegrated into a ruin, the local council took over the gardens as a municipal park.

Recently, developers embarked on a major restoration, realising that Trentham is situated within an hour and a half's drive of 21 million people. They commissioned two extraordinarily different designers to upgrade the lakeside setting. Tom Stuart-Smith addressed the cultural and textural context, and, inspired by Barry's lines, took his contemporary 'river' planting template 'for an epic tapestry of control'. The Dutchman Piet Oudolf envisaged great meanders where visitors can lose themselves, wandering through tall, waving prairie grass amid massed colour and tone-coordinated herbaceous planting. Hailed as one

of the most advanced modern designers, he considers himself a free-thinker unencumbered by history. Yet his work has real echoes of Brownian informality in the use of the serpentine, as much as his 'action-man' drive and prodigious determination. His larger-than-life personality, his close supervision of process, line and naturalistic planting, if with a much wider and possibly more colourful plant palette, is followed months, or a year or two later, by suggestions for refinement.

In addition, the modern equivalent of the menagerie, a monkey zoo, sounds through Brown's beech woods. Too dense through decades of neglect, the woods are now in the process of being thinned and managed. His waters, teeming with carp, bream, roach, perch and pike, are a great recreational haven for boating and anglers, and sparkle with light and life, to rival any natural lake.[575]

Modern society is hugely more complex. Giant caterpillar trucks and mechanical diggers are spectacularly altering contours of the land, to construct a tangled web of motorways, new towns and shopping centres. Such schemes are no longer one person's vision, despite the influence of Brenda Colvin and Sylvia Crowe in softening motorway landscapes by tree belts and wild

July 2011, Trentham Gardens, Staffordshire Brown's great lake is the backdrop to Charles Barry's Victorian terrace gardens, recently recreated by Tom Stuart Smith.

flower verges, with high banks to conceal traffic streams and deaden noise. There seems little likelihood that one individual will ever again determine wide-reaching changes to match Brown's personal achievements.

> *The Landscape Gardeners*
> *Brutal shuddering machines, yellow, bite into*
> *given earth.*
> *Only rich Whigs, commanding labour,*
> *Once had earth shifted, making lakes, and said*
> *– And it was true – 'We are improving Nature'.*[576]

It took Brown many years to achieve his desired effect. He encountered not only adverse climate conditions, but problems with manual labour, communication, transport, experimentation and supply of materials. The task is even more multi-faceted and onerous today, with additional delays caused by stagnating bureaucracy and often a frustrating, convoluted planning process. In an age of increasingly grim 'urban reality' a tolerant, long-term view is essential. Historians, biologists, ecologists, engineers and planners in dialogue need doses of Brownian good judgement, integrity, resilience and perseverance in partnership.

The best traditions of English parkland continue to have worldwide appeal, especially in America, Australia and Canada. Questions concerning improvement remain constant. Brown's surviving plans will continue to inform and inspire future generations: the expert choice of line, and the remarkable variety of uses for free space and ways of making the most of resources, are just as relevant in engendering optimism for tomorrow's horizons. A positive, perfectionist philosophy will prevent undergrowth eating into any significant line, particularly edges of lakes. Today, highly trained professionals and artists, rather than serving a sprinkling of wealthy lords and ladies, disseminate universal principles in the cultural language of 'natural' landscape, to the benefit of millions.

At the turn of the millennium, the landscape architect Kim Wilkie explained a commission for Heveningham (Suffolk) as: 'History with a future – putting in a design two hundred years late.' Wilkie praises Brown's understanding of terrain, and confirms his accuracy in the assured line and the fluid curves in graceful harmony, on perhaps his most spontaneous colour-washed plan (1781). A few tantalising details differ from other well-tried plans. Brown was still adapting his designs: hedges on the approach, and a pavement encircling the new-built walls of the house. Perhaps he had come to realise that a little regularity in the close environs of the house assisted its integration into its surroundings, an idea that Repton went on to develop in a more eclectic manner. Brown may have purposely intended planting many oaks to restore a sense of the medieval deer park, an association with the past in keeping with the local story of the 'Elizabeth Oak'.[577]

Veteran Scots pines terminate the lake. Brown's foreground frame for the Palladian house, a trinity of sturdy oaks, recently pollarded to prolong their life, offers a sense of continuity. Faced with English nature specialists wishing to protect a special nature reserve, particularly an area of alders by the lake, Wilkie focused on interpreting 'brownifications',[578] original proposals that were never fully implemented because of the designer's death. A compromise was reached

October 2012, Heveningham, Suffolk Kim Wilkie's curvaceous amphitheatre, encircled by clipped holm oaks, is punctuated in Brownian fashion with asymmetrically-placed cedars of Lebanon.

in creating a temporary island, while later the alders were gradually replanted downstream.[579] The spring-fed, meandering lakes have now been cleared of silt, extended and crossed by a new bridge, with vistas reopened to Huntingfield Hall and the church spire in Walpole village.[580] A phased implementation of planting, at the rate of thirty acres a year, is establishing enclosure and accentuating undulating folds of land. Every year, a team of arboriculture specialists sweeps in to keep woods pristinely manicured in Brownian fashion, if with modern equipment.

Much of the outer park landscape may be viewed from a public road through the park, not from a slow, swaying horse-drawn carriage, but fleetingly from the smooth comfort of a car: an open and tailored 'whole' stirs hearts and minds just as Brown envisaged.[581] The water seems never-ending. The entire valley flows and luxuriates with clean, harmonious lines. After all, Brown's account does refer to 'Heaveningham'!

On the south side of the house, Wilkie has broken away from traditional restoration with an innovative scheme to contour the land instead of gloomy, overgrown Victorian terraces. Here a smooth grass spiral unfolds asymmetrically like the shell of a giant snail, evocative of Bridgeman's turf amphitheatre at Claremont, encircled above by a walk, sheltered by clipped evergreen holm oaks at regular intervals. A rectangular reflection pool on the house terrace below this spacious, contemporary foreground sits comfortably with and leads the eye to the Brownian park panorama beyond.

A pleasurable and cerebral pursuit, the act of viewing a landscape garden may be learned, and read like the pages of a book. Even if some pages are missing as we move through a landscape, we understand more about the space surrounding us. Spectators see not merely the world in front of their eyes, but a composition of that world, a way of appreciating their surroundings. Where some Brown works have been built over or degraded, many manicured settings have survived the passage of time and the increasing pressures of population: 'Gardens are tellers of tales. The skills of the designer allow the tale to be heard.'[582]

The emotive story of land carries on. Complacency is not an option. Like Shakespeare's plays, Brown's landscapes will always demand re-evaluation and reinterpretation, with still more to be discovered above and below ground or buried in archives. The outlines of some important scripts survive, the range and depth of some proving cinematically advantageous for film and television. A good design story will always be worth retelling: new designers will be encouraged to provide new scenery, whether with public funding or private initiative, to ensure the survival of fundamental, balanced, asymmetric Brownian concepts, his original, theatrical tour of discovery and liberating sense of space. Long after the last tree of Brown's 'woody theatres' has shrivelled and fallen, his art will live on in the desire to manipulate a gloriously atmospheric, integrated yet practical environment. The stage will always need setting.

Since before the Druids erected Avebury's stone circles, the surroundings Britons created have reflected their beliefs. At the dawn of the eighteenth century, Joseph Addison appreciated that there was more to a 'landskip'[583] than a composed, naturalistic 'view' with pictorial effect. Though manners were more formal then in polite society, men and women experienced the same feelings and aspirations as we do now. The sight and strength of what we consider beautiful affects the part of the brain governing emotional response, arousing melancholy or nostalgia, perhaps even religious fervour. Water possesses a seductive power to touch our innermost selves, 'as much use in the landscape as Blood in a Body'.[584] Landscape has the power to ease solitude, blow away cares and make one feel happy to be alive. Landscape is where some choose to celebrate commitment, or remember a loved one.

The incisive, unimpeded line of Brown's lake edges may have been swamped by reeds and vegetation, but his restful waters still attract like magnets. The interplay of shimmering light within the surrounding rigid landmass creates a softer, soothing, ever-changing space. Sanctuaries teeming with wildlife are married to the land as though they had always been there.

Gentle exploration of a landscape park, away from aggressive commotion and pollution in town or city, alleviates stress, gives comfort and enriches mind and spirit. Today at Sandbeck (Yorkshire) infinite acres of uninterrupted meadowland seem to converge on the walls of the house. Oblivious to the semicircular arc of the ha-ha, visitors explore the wide expanse of parkland with their eyes until, drawing near, they are surprised to find a deep, wide trench, in spring filled with lemon-yellow cowslips and sky-blue forget-me-nots.

Mavor believed Brown 'viewed nature with the enthusiasm of a lover', stripping her back to her most calming and beguiling simplicity.[585] My view is that, rather than a love affair, his was a business-like contract with nature 'to correct and mend and inlarge'.[586] There is no easy path to design. Rivals and cynics did not shake Brown's confidence. Interestingly, where Catholics still took no part in public life, Brown was the improver of choice for Protestant and Catholic landowners alike. They trusted in his ability and his vision. A missionary resolve, stemming from his Christian faith, has to be judged in the context of his times, when men openly expressed their beliefs. A long dedication by Thomas Bruce, Earl of Ailesbury, on his column at Tottenham, for instance, concludes 'but above all of Piety TO GOD, FIRST, HIGHEST, BEST, whose blessing consecrateth every gift, And fixeth its true Value'.

'A beautiful prospect delights the soul.'[587] Elevated vistas prompted equally elevated thoughts, with some clients naming distinct landscape features Jerusalem Hill, Paradise Hill or Heaven's Gate. Placing eternity on the horizon was conducive to contemplation. New, uncluttered views, 'free from the detail of allegory',[588] were far removed from the fashion for classical myths of 'Vice and Virtue', or occasional extreme sexual innuendo, as displayed in odd baroque and rococo gardens. For visitors arriving at Stowe's Bell Gate, the first gratifying, and possibly most memorable sight, the Gothic Temple of Liberty surrounded by Brown's companion planting, lifted eyes and imaginations heavenward.

An undeniable 'rightness' in Brown's planting made man's handprint appear negligible, far from reality.

This controlling, diligent forester abandoned pencil and paper to refine by eye, instinct and experience rather than by the rule, preferring to be on hand to advise, to ensure that saplings were weeded, every withered branch, thistle or bramble banished, and to mark every tree that needed felling with an axe. Woods were not tamed wilderness, rather a valuable crop to be nurtured with as much rigour as the kitchen garden. The irony is that his characteristic, asymmetric settings and 'unsquared' groves came to be seen as models of freedom of expression, living manifestations of the ideal of liberty. Most remain unaware of the imported trees Brown chose to plant, and accept them as typically English, rolling countryside and deer park. They can be felled for timber, or succumb to age, disease or tempest, and be replaced in easy stages, as and when necessary, without adverse effect.

Brown's most powerful influence was so subtle that it has been either taken for granted or overlooked. More than thirty trees figure throughout the Bible, as metaphors and in parables, from Eden's tree to the rod of Jesse, to the acacias growing outside Jerusalem, from the staple olive tree to the vine, from the poplars of Syon to the tree of Calvary. Swathes of planting, advocated by Brown and his fellow improvers, gave landowners hope by invigorating tired landscapes, and laid the foundations of grand 'tree cathedrals' later valued by the Victorians.

This precious 'added value' to the English landscape, in drawing the eye towards and preserving the centuries-old iconography of parish churches and romantic abbey ruins, with evergreens to suggest eternity, endorsed the many stabilising traditions of his Christian forefathers. Time and again Brown's skilful planting emphasised their evocative history and spiritual significance and fused the medieval aesthetic with the rightness and single-minded reverence of religion. No other building offered such meaningful support and emotional reassurance. What was more, the moral goodness of a 'Christian landscape', an engaging and uplifting setting, resonated with and was enjoyed by all ranks.[589]

William Fordyce Mavor (1758–1837), witnessing Brown's work at Blenheim in its early maturity, appreciated that this 'mighty master of picturesque

*Nunquam minus solus
quam cum solus*
NEVER LESS ALONE
THAN WHEN ALONE

(Motto on Brown's bookplate)

embellishment' had brought considerable benefit to the welfare and education not only of those who worked there, but large numbers of the visiting public. Blenheim and Luton Hoo had been packaged and made available as an edifying terrestrial paradise, exemplifying ideal science: 'Brown possessed an originality of conception, a poet's eye, and an instinctive taste for rural embellishment … to the picturesque landscape which pleases the sight, [Blenheim] adds the moral landscape that delights the mind.'[590]

A just and honest man, his northern charm and sense of humour undoubtedly helped Brown's popularity as he grasped every opportunity to advance in social circles. Occasionally brooding in 'philosophick strain', Brown suffered his share of anxiety, disappointment and ill health, doubtless missing his family when away from home. He persevered. He furthered friendships with educated churchmen and lived by both the holy book and sincere Whig values: certainty and liberty, charity and thankfulness.

The bell-tower crowning his native church at Kirkharle reflected his serious side, as much a sign of Christian faith as his formally confessed last will and testament. His contemporaries chose a memorial to salute this conviction, his familial love and loyal friendship. Here was a man who led by example, both peace-maker and place-maker, moving heaven and earth to defend and 'pass on' uncompromising ideals to his children, and to the foremen, foresters and nurserymen his business relied on.

Look again. Value the coherence and simplicity of focus and, rather than the direct line, the appealing and intriguing, oblique approach. Cherish the rhythm, wonder at the scale. In his considerate response to people, place and history, Brown showed how to read land in a natural way, to spot capability, develop every potential known to science and, lastly, to contrive a pause for a view to be appreciated. He rode hills and dales, surveyed the measure of fertile, green pastures and lingered to soak in the serenity of gentle waters. Out on the land, he must have felt closest to his Creator – whose vision he sought to emulate. His choice of motto, 'Never less alone than when alone', hints at a significant, reassuring presence accompanying him on his life journey.

As Monet is to waterlilies and Van Gogh to sunflowers, so 'Capability' Brown has become synonymous with almost every open, man-made and contoured landscape that engages and inspires. Much more than a quirky nickname lives on. Brown bequeathed an enduring generosity of design to the improving world, the gift of landscape.

APPENDIX

THE PICTURE TODAY

While Brown is considered one of the founding professionals in the art, the term 'landscape architecture' was first used in Regency times by the Scotsman Gilbert Laing Meason.[591] Over time, a notable addition to the vocabulary of landscape has been the adjective 'Brownian', an evocative hallmark for any romantically serpentine setting.

According to Rocque (1746), compared with a later map (1776), it seems the population of Wimbledon village doubled, from approximately 500 to approximately 1,000 people, and of those twenty gardeners are named, and thirty lords or gentlemen. It was obviously a very desirable location to live, and so it has remained. In 1780 Hannah More penned:

> *The Bishop of St Asaph and his family invites us to Wimbledon Park, Lord Spencer's charming villa which he always lends to the Bishop at this time of year. I did not think there would have been so beautiful a place within seven miles of London. The park has such a variety of ground and is as un-Londonish as if it were one hundred miles out.*[592]

Forty years later Wimbledon Park was the venue for a celebratory garden party and Grand Fête attended by Queen Victoria soon after her accession. Elsewhere occasional aquatic night fêtes with large numbers of sailing ships saw musicians playing from rowing boats, as fireworks, and lanterns hanging in surrounding trees, created extraordinary reflections on the water. Brown contributed, and continues to contribute, an immeasurable boost to culture and heritage as, down the decades, special and popular events have been held in the unthreatening, open space of his parks. We have the opportunity to walk the same paths as our ancestors and significant figures of history, such as Charles Darwin who, in a letter to his sister, described how a therapeutic stroll in Moor Park, where he used to study ants, would make him relax and enjoy the odd nap: 'as pleasant a rural scene as ever I saw, and I did not care one penny how any of the beasts or birds had been formed'.[593]

During the course of the nineteenth century some writers mocked park improvers, but the art of gardening was widely disseminated, with horticultural magazines more accessible. A growing class of Victorian entrepreneurs and industrialists found every aesthetic, economic and sporting reason to commission smaller, private parks laid out along straightforward Brownian principles.[594] Several designers and surveyors, basing their reputation by association as 'pupil of the celebrated Capability Brown', or offering designs 'in the manner of Mr Brown', lacked his imagination and 'force of genius'.

Designed in 1841, Victoria Park in east London is thought to be the capital's oldest public park, funded by selling off a royal property, St James's House. In the north, authorised by Act of Parliament (1843), Birkenhead Park attracted considerable public funds, over £103,000 (almost £15 million) for a successfully picturesque scheme designed by Joseph Paxton (1803–1865) along recognisably Brownian principles, and became the inspiration for New York's Central Park. Another Act (1846) 'to amend the Act to facilitate the Enclosure and Improvement of Commons' specifically encouraged the establishment of philanthropic town parks for public health and enjoyment.

By 1886 there were over 4,000 landscape parks in the country. Brown's all-consuming ambition and impossible dream 'to finish England' was closer to being realised.

> *The stately Homes of England, How beautiful they stand, Amidst their tall ancestral trees, O'er all the pleasant land!*[595]

While his trees were silently reaching marvellous maturity, disapproving opinions, with little real substance, continued to be handed down from generation to generation. The professional designer John Claudius Loudon (1783–1843) exchanged the spade for the pen and joined the ranks of Brown's critics:

> *What first brought him into reputation was a large sheet of water which he made at* Stowe, *in which, as in all his other works, he displayed the most wretched and Chinese-like taste. Wherever his*

levelling hand has appeared, adieu to every natural beauty! See every thing give way to one uniform system of smoothing, levelling and clumping of the most tiresome monotony, joined to the most disgusting formality.[596]

At the same time, he praised the fact that Tottenham Park, thanks to the benevolence of its owner, was always open to local inhabitants, 'who drive, ride or make gypsy-parties at their leisure'. Later, possibly in reaction against dreary, over-polluted industrial townscapes, those who preferred intricate, floral displays and colourful 'outdoor carpets' remembered Brown as the 'great intermeddler'.[597] Bedding was cheaper because labour was still cheap, and plants were grown under glass and heat. As the century drew to a close, the architect Sir Reginald Blomfield (1856–1942) launched into garden design, and then into print with another broadside attack:

While Mr Brown was removing old pieces of formality he was establishing new ones of a more extensive and mischievous consequence.… Kent was followed by 'Capability' Brown, who began as a kitchen gardener, but he took the judicious line that knowledge hampered originality. He accordingly dispensed with any training of any kind and rapidly rose to eminence.[598]

Likewise, Thomas Mawson (1861–1933), a prominent landscape architect, deploring the creation of acres of 'undistinguished' parkland, laid the destruction of so many English historic formal gardens firmly at Brown's door.

THE HERITAGE LANDSCAPE

Conservation and environmental regeneration are not just twenty-first-century concerns. Change occurs through cycles of growth and decline, formality and wilderness, nurture and neglect. Most landowners down the ages wish to keep up appearances within their means and understanding, and are committed to the duties of inheritance. Gardens are often most vulnerable when new owners take over. However, in recent times, both the value of green space and the realisation of its imminent loss have increasingly concentrated minds. At Chillington, Peter Giffard fought against the Department of Transport's decision to route the M54 motorway through the Brown landscape. In 1971 Staffordshire

County Council supported his efforts by designating the park as the county's first historic parkland Conservation Area, though this was not enough to stop the motorway from clipping a corner of it.

Landscape is in constant flux. The 1976 drought, causing trees much stress, contributed to both beech bark disease and a devastating outbreak of Dutch elm disease, *Ophiostoma novo-ulmi*, a fungus carried by the elm bark beetle. The death of about ten million trees, including Brown's elms, completely changed the experience of the English landscape. Other diseases – 'bleeding canker', *Pseudomonas syringae pv. Aesculi*, affecting horse chestnut trees, and *Chalara fraxinea*, 'ash dieback' – are causing great concern nationwide. *Phytophthora ramorum*, or 'sudden oak death', initially identified in 2007 in the south-west, is still spreading, threatening both oaks and beech.

Since few new landscapes of scale are being created, the protection and regeneration of eighteenth-century models, such as the 'naval seascape' at Thoresby for the Pierrepont family, becomes even more imperative. Following World War I, changing agricultural practice and urban development have destroyed almost half the country's historic parkland.[599] Relatively few private designed parks remain.

With Heritage Lottery funding, the National Forest project is creating a variety of accessible landscapes for the future in the midland heart of the country, landscapes to celebrate and interpret the multi-layered 'land shapes' and culture of the past. The Woodland Trust works towards regeneration and sustainability, encouraging everyone to value and map veteran trees, and is involved, for instance, in replanting at Moccas (Herefordshire), where Brown incorporated sacred old oaks and yews of character into his schemes. Now his trees, diligently planted for future generations, are themselves veterans. Decay is not necessarily a bad thing. Ancient hollow trees, playing their part in the countryside's ecology, add quality to the landscape while hosting a bio-diversity of insects, including rare beetles associated with dying timber.

A re-evaluation in the management of parks has led to regeneration methods sympathetic to the natural cycle, leaving some fallen timber for ecological reasons and planting young among the old. Although the Forestry Commission has an agenda of mass planting of woodland on acquired lands, the significant value of natural and historic environments has at last earned wider recognition. Natural England are providing more funding and publicity for designed landscape appraisal and training in conservation, restoration and forestry programmes.

Countrywide schemes to protect and replace important trees will help to maintain and regenerate the local character and distinctiveness of a valued landscape. Numbers of landowners embarking on Countryside Stewardship schemes are anxious to keep the emotional connection of Brown's footprint on the land. Where his master-plans survive, together with those surveys commissioned soon after his improvements, they will undoubtedly be a source of inspiration.

If the 1987 hurricane was a wake-up call, bringing home with brutal force the realisation that surviving aspects of Brown's designs are fragmentary, fragile and fast diminishing, the millennium helped to focus minds on time and consequence, and on the value of making, and leaving, a mark. In 2000 the Lowther Estate in Cumbria, jointly with English Heritage, commissioned research into the background, history and detailed design concepts of the castle site and grounds. A team of landscape and garden historians, architects and engineers spent almost a year on the Lowther Castle and Garden Conservation Plan, both the basis and the catalyst for a significant, ongoing regeneration project.

English Heritage landscape architect advisers, in close collaboration with the Garden History Society, the Association of Gardens Trusts and County Gardens Trusts researchers, compiled a Register of Parks and Gardens to highlight their importance, to afford some protection to the historic environment and to encourage wider accessibility. Brown's works have been recognised and recorded, most recently on the online web resource Parks and Gardens UK, an educational heritage project that maps the past to understand and serve the present, and to help plan future landscapes. Environmental organisations have greater understanding of the built fabric of our heritage, and of the cultural and aesthetic importance of the settings. Meanwhile, with considerable restoration experience, particularly in the last thirty years, and in the light of drought and flooding, the National Trust is advocating more space for water in its upland territories, more planting to prevent topsoil being washed away by flood, and better management of rivers, catchments and existing drains so that land retains its natural sponge-like qualities.

The Brown 'brand' helps to promote tourism. Sales of estates have exploited Capability Brown's name as a major selling point, even where the links are tenuous. A surprising number of his parks survive in good or fairly reasonable condition because they are valued. Many that were once private are today open to the public. Huntsmen and women (now confined by law) continue to chase foxhound packs across his territory following a laid scent; shooting syndicates target game in habitats created specifically for the purpose. Cricket is played on many a spacious levelled lawn before the house. Farmers and gamekeepers tend livestock; schoolchildren attend to botany or, if lucky, picnic and catch minnows. Some lakes have fisheries where fishermen still patiently await their catch; sea scouts and cadets, among many others, go canoeing and boating.

Established country estates remain valuable open amenities, attracting huge numbers of visitors for horse trials, racing, carriage-driving, sheep-dog trials, angling competitions and game fairs, horticultural and country shows. Some parks host paint-ball games, others stage classical, jazz or pop concerts, often with a dazzling climax of fireworks.

Many parks such as Chatsworth enrich lives by featuring in art, literature, television documentaries and films, and enhance the quality of life, driving or cycling through, walking the dog or enjoying picnics. Parks are often the first play area or wilderness that small children explore outside their home, a first view of the wider world, magical places for exercise, solace, therapy and romance.

Some landscapes, it must be said, have lost their special space and perspectives, where the only clues to a Capability Brown park are perhaps street names in residential developments, such as Cedar Rise or Lancelot Close.[600] Late 1950s tower blocks built incongruously in the middle of pleasant grounds at Mount Clare, Roehampton (Surrey), dwarf the Georgian villa. Nearby a featureless concrete and glass Sixties college is an inappropriate distraction. Quite a few Brown sites are similarly built over or badly degraded, whether dissected by motorways or with massive, overbearing power cables, telecommunication masts or power stations dominating the views.

Bureaucratic problems regarding listed landscapes may hamper, or at least delay, moves towards upkeep and regeneration. Planning permission is required, for instance, to reinstate Brown's footpaths within the ice-house coppice and west lawn at Compton Verney House, an English Heritage Grade II* landscape.[601] A recent wind farm in the view from Castle Ashby detracts from the ambience. In this all too crowded island, open spaces remain under threat from piecemeal urban expansion. The modern, pressured world needs to hold on to the best of its green space. Where some county councils have acquired and opened country parks with large recreational areas, they have tended to emphasise wildlife and the natural environment, with little interest, or perhaps funds, to reinstate worthwhile aspects of Brown's original plan. Dialogue between improvers, designers and naturalists will stimulate lateral, sustainable and sensitive solutions to designs for life.

Designed landscapes are wildlife havens. Gatton Park (Surrey) hosts the largest island heronry in the country, thanks to Brown's mid-1760s intervention. The Engine Pond feeds like a natural stream with cascades into the main lake. Various Brown parks and lakes contain annotated Sites of Special Scientific Interest (SSSI), including sections of Syon Park bordering the Thames. Here, from the early 1750s to the late 1770s, Brown planted up the vistas specifically to unite both sides of the river. The park still 'holds hands' across the river with the royal landscape of Richmond Old Deer Park, now in part assimilated into Kew Gardens, a World Heritage site. The Thames Landscape Strategy, a welcome recent initiative, is highlighting, restoring and protecting these Arcadian views along the reaches of the capital's river. Such is the respect for Brown's infinity views that planners are now taking his ideas into consideration.

Television has contributed to a massive rise in the popularity of golf, a sport that seems tailor-made for parkland settings (to the horror of some purist garden historians), with some unexpected advantages. First, over twenty golf courses laid out in Brown parks provide consistency and continuity for a high-quality, textured grassland that is resilient and stable. Secondly, thousands of golf-club members, with the privilege and active well-being of regular visits, are grasping the feel of eighteenth-century landscape. They appreciate well-manicured, 'natural' surroundings and vistas as much as any wealthy landowner and his circle two hundred or more years ago. New tree planting to delineate different holes on a golf course could conform to Brown's ideas and retain the 'feel' of his design.

PARADISE REGAINED[602]

In September 1917 an auction catalogue for the sale of mature ash and poplar at Stowe hailed Brown as 'a famous forester'. Since the National Trust agreement (1989) with Stowe School, a comprehensive renovation programme has been unfolding to preserve the prestigious historic landscape gardens.[603] It began by draining and cleaning out the lakes before gradually restoring garden buildings: Cobham's Pillar, the Grecian Temple, Grotto, Conduit House and so on. Extensive tree planting continues to recreate eighteenth-century pleasure-ground walks alongside experimental planting of flowers and flowering shrubs, including roses. Visitors to the Grecian Valley, the epitome of Brown's contribution to Stowe, find it difficult to conceive of the contours of the serpentine sweep as man-made. Scots pine and cedars of Lebanon tower above rolling slopes of grass that, in late spring, are threaded with cowslips.

Great clearances have been made at Prior Park College, originally built by the entrepreneur Ralph Allen. Pupils and staff enjoy superb vistas towards Bath. The National Trust has restored the circuit walk and shrubberies, excavated Alexander Pope's upper pool and cascade, overlooked by a statue of Moses striking the rock, and reinstated the link with Brown's extended waters below. Claremont, Radley (Oxfordshire), Langley Park (Norfolk) and Newton (Somerset) number among other educational establishments in Brownian settings.

Sadly, the advent of the car has changed beyond recognition Brown's imaginative theatre of approach in some sites, the situation aggravated by poor positioning of car and coach parks or insensitive visitor facilities. Brown's approach drive from Newbury to Sandleford Priory, a girls' private school, has long gone. Traffic cuts through the western view on the A34, maintaining an ever-present hum. In the early 1990s a few lost cedars of Lebanon were replaced. A tall oak still stands in a strong position by the house on the south lawn, planted in 1743 by Elizabeth Montagu to mark the birth of her only child, a son, nicknamed Punch, who died as a baby. Having lost infant children himself, Brown would have empathised.

In 1996 the opportunity to 'recreate the story' of Brown's first major integrated commission was at last addressed. When the Croome estate came up for sale, the National Trust acquired 270 hectares (670 acres) of the park with the help of a £4.9 million grant from the Heritage Lottery Fund and a generous donation from Royal & Sun Alliance. More recently, the Croome Heritage Trust purchased the Grade I house, the hub of the landscape, and agreed to lease it into the care of the National Trust. Where great plane trees still frame the views from the lake, towering elms along the river's edge have gone, as also a great English oak central to the north vista, marking the heart of the park; 45,000 replacement trees and shrubs have been planted in the Trust's largest ever restoration project. Rather than rod, rule and compass, the workforce has employed global positioning satellite technology and comparison with Brown's plans to ensure historical accuracy.

Croome is considered one of the country's twelve most exceptional parkland sites, its mile-long river-lake, deemed one of Europe's most important artificial lakes, a significant wetland Site of Special Scientific Interest, and 'the fountainhead of the English landscape style'.[604] Managing a regeneration programme is complex here. The National Trust is rightly committed to the conservation of flora and fauna and wildlife habitats. Lateral thinking among many agencies concerned has resulted in multi-disciplinary compromises.[605] Where Brown's lake has been reopened and cleaned, the Trust has compensated by providing new lagoons, marshland and reed beds to re-establish wildlife, close to the M5 motorway that slices through the western park, and along the north end edge, in order to filter the water before it reaches Brown's lake. 50,000 cubic metres of silt and vegetation have been spread over neighbouring fields, improving the soil. Where large portions of the park were used for arable farming, similar concessions are enabling reversion to more appropriate hay meadows. Over and above sound-bite 'sustainability', a discerning eye and Brownian attention to detail are needed in managing the territory with a balanced, integrated approach to ecological and aesthetic change. There has been a tendency to overcrowd new planting, particularly shrubs. It is far better to follow the maxim 'more is less', taking care not to overcrowd or obstruct the views and to avoid the feeling of being hemmed in. Space allows enjoyment of the best features.

Visitors making forays into the park will then appreciate Brown's vision: 'the controlled views, long walks, tiered trees and eye-catching golden garden buildings placed in the landscape.[606] If the public could be given the chance to explore the landscape by horse-drawn carriage, recreating that pleasurable eighteenth-century experience, a moving, ever-changing, living panorama would better any wide-screen vision.

North America boasts every conceivable category of natural landscape, some awesome. In 1858 Frederick Law Olmsted (1822–1903), inspired by European tours, and the landscape architect Calvert Vaux (1824–1895) together designed the first common green accessible space, Central Park, in New York, based on Brownian principles. Later, the world-famous twentieth-century landscape architect Sir Geoffrey Jellicoe dreamed of an elaborate theme park: Moody Historical Gardens, at Galveston in Texas, dedicated to the changing fashions of landscape and garden design through the ages:

Ponder on the past not as the past but as a pointer to the future.… The world is moving into a phase when landscape design may well be recognised as the most comprehensive of the arts. Man creates around him an environment that is a projection into nature of his abstract ideas.…
We are promoting a landscape art on a scale never conceived of in history.

For Jellicoe, the English country estate was the pinnacle, the greatest contribution we have made to the history of art. It was not merely an essay in the organisation of space; it would symbolise a way of life, maintaining a balance between the intellectual and the biological. Jellicoe planned all sections of the Galveston theme park to illustrate garden styles rather than the work of individual garden designers. He made one exception, intending two entire sections devoted to 'Capability' Brown in recognition of his pioneering contribution to the complex art of landscape. Sadly, this original, forward-looking project to demonstrate man's shaping of his environment never went further than the drawing-board.

Perhaps the oldest tree in England, the 'Bowthorpe Oak' stands less than a mile from where Brown rented Witham Manor house when working at Grimsthorpe Castle. It features on Captain Armstrong's Survey of Lincolnshire (1778), with a measured girth of 36 ft (today more than 39 ft). Inside, among other carving, are the initials 'LB'. Whether they are Brown's is arguable. What cannot be disputed is that 'Capability' Brown left a considerable and enduring mark on our landscapes.

BIBLIOGRAPHY

Amherst, Amelia, *A History of Gardening* (Bernard Quaritch, London, 1896)

Bapasola, Jeri, *The Finest View in England - the Landscape and Gardens at Blenheim Palace* (Blenheim Palace, 2009)

Batey, Mavis, and David Lambert, *The English Garden Tour* (John Murray, 1990)

Batey, Mavis, and Kim Wilkie, *Arcadian Thames* (Barn Elms, 1994)

Berrall, Julia S., *The Garden - An Illustrated History* (Penguin, 1978)

Betts, Edwin Morris, *Thomas Jefferson's Garden Book* (American Philosophy Society, 1944)

Bisgrove, Richard, *Paradise Gained: History, Art and Politics in the English Garden* (2005)

Bond, James, and Kate Tiller, ed., *Blenheim - Landscape for a Palace* (Alan Sutton & Oxford Uni. Dept for External Studies, Gloucester, 1987)

Brown, Jane, *The Art and Architecture of English Gardens* (Weidenfeld & Nicolson, 1989)

Brown, Jane, *The Omnipotent Magician* (Chatto & Windus, 2011)

Bruyn Andrews, C., ed., *The Torrington Diaries 1781-1794* (Eyre & Spottiswoode, 1938)

Burnett, David, *Longleat* (Dovecote Press, 1988)

Cambridge Gardens Trust, *The Gardens of Cambridgeshire* (2000)

Campbell, Susan, *Charleston Kedding - A History of Kitchen Gardening* (Ebury, 1996)

Campbell-Culver, Maggie, *A Passion for Trees - The Legacy of John Evelyn* (Transworld, 2006)

Cantor, Leonard, and Anthony Squires, *The Historic Parks and Gardens of Leicestershire and Rutland* (1997)

Clarke, G.B., ed., *Descriptions of Lord Cobham's Gardens at Stowe 1700-1750* (Buckingham Record Office, 1990)

Clifford, Joan, *'Capability' Brown* (Shire Publications, 1974)

Colvin, H.M., *A Biographical Dictionary of British Architects* (John Murray, 1954; rev. edn Yale University Press, 1995)

Cook, Olive, ed., *The English Country House* (Thames & Hudson, 1984)

Daniels, Stephen, *Humphry Repton* (Yale University Press, 1999)

Dixon Hunt, John, and Peter Willis, eds, *The Genius of the Place* (Paul Elek, 1976)

Drake, John, *Wood and Ingram - A Huntingdonshire Nursery 1742-1950* (published privately, 2008)

Eliot, Simon, and Beverley Stern, eds, *The Age of Enlightenment*, Vol.2 (Open University Press, 1979)

Fedden, Robin, and Rosemary Joekes, eds, *National Trust Guide* (Cape, rev. edn 1977)

Fleming, Laurence, and Alan Gore, *The English Garden* (Michael Joseph; rev. edn Spring Books 1988)

Girling, Richard, ed., *The Making of the English Garden* (Macmillan, 1988)

Gordon, Catherine, *The Coventrys of Croome* (Phillimore & National Trust, 2000)

Gowing, C.N., and G.B. Clarke, *Views of Stowe* (Buckinghamshire County Museum & Stowe School, 1983)

Gray, Todd, *The Garden History of Devon* (University of Exeter Press, 1995)

Hadfield, Miles, *A History of British Gardening* (Spring Books, 1969)

Hadfield, Miles, and Robert Harling, *British Gardeners - A Biographical Dictionary* (Condé Nast, 1980)

Hall, Ivan and Elizabeth, *Burton Constable Hall* (Hull Museum & Art Galleries/Hutton Press, 1991)

Harding, Stewart, and David Lambert, *Parks and Gardens of Avon* (Bath Press, 1994)

Harris, Eileen, *British Architectural Books and Writers 1556-1785* (Cambridge University Press, 1990)

Harris, John, *No Voice from the Hall* (John Murray, 1998)

Harvey, John, *Early Gardening Catalogues* (Phillimore, 1972)

Harvey, John, *Early Nurserymen* (Phillimore, 1974)

Hertfordshire Gardens Trust and Richard Bisgrove, *Hertfordshire Gardens of Ermine Street* (1996)

Hickman, Clare, *Therapeutic Landscapes* (Manchester University Press, 2013)

Hinde, Thomas, *'Capability' Brown - The Story of a Master Gardener* (Hutchinson, 1986)

History of the County of Oxford, A, Vol.12: *Blenheim: Park from 1705* (Oxford, 1990)

Hodgson, Revd, *A History of Northumberland* (1827)

Horwood, Catherine, *Gardening Women* (Virago, 2010)

Hoskins, W.G., *The Making of the English Landscape* (Guild Publishing, rev. edn 1988)

Howman, Luke, *British Landscape Painting of the 18th Century* (Faber, 1973)

Hussey, Christopher, *English Gardens & Landscapes 1700-1750* (Country Life, 1967)

Hyams, Edward, *'Capability' Brown and Humphry Repton* (Dent, 1971)

Jackson-Stops, Gervase, *An English Arcadia 1600-1990* (The National Trust, 1992)

Jacques, David, *Georgian Gardens* (Batsford, 1983)

Jellicoe, Geoffrey and Susan, *The Landscape of Man* (Thames & Hudson, 1975, rev. edn 1995)

Jones, Barbara, *Follies and Grottoes* (Constable, 2nd edn 1974)

Kelly, Alison, *Mrs Coade's Stone* (Self-Publishing Association, 1990)

Lacey, Stephen, *Gardens of the National Trust* (National Trust Enterprises, 1996)

Laird, Mark, *The Flowering of the Landscape Garden* (Penn, 1999)

Leach, Peter, *James Paine* (Zwemmer, London, 1988)

Leach, Terence R., *Lincolnshire Country Houses and Their Families*, Pt 2 (Laece Books)

Lewis, W.S., and Ralph S. Brown, eds, *Correspondence of Horace Walpole*, 1935

Lockett, Richard, *A Survey of Historic Parks and Gardens in Worcestershire* (Hereford & Worcester Gardens Trust, 1997)

Loudon, John Claudius, *In Search of English Gardens* (National Trust Classics, Century 1990)

Mawrey, Gillian, and Linden Groves, *The Gardens of English Heritage* (Frances Lincoln, 2010)

Meir, Jennifer, *Sanderson Miller and his Landscapes* (Phillimore, 2006)

Milward, Richard, *Wimbledon Two Hundred Years Ago* (Milward Press, 1996)

Mitchell, Alan, and John Wilkinson, *Trees of Britain and Northern Europe* (Collins Pocket Guide, 1982)

Morris, Richard, *Churches in the Landscape* (Dent, 1989)

Mowl, Timothy, *Historic Gardens of Dorset* (Tempus Publishing, 2003)

Mowl, Timothy, and Brian Earnshaw, *Trumpet at a Distant Gate* (Waterstone, 1985)

Mowl, Timothy, and Diane James, *Historic Gardens of Warwickshire* (Redcliffe Press, 2011)

National Trust Volunteers, *Stowe Tree Guide* (2011)

Parry, James, ed., *Rooted in History: Studies in Garden Conservation* (National Trust, 2001)

Payne Gallwey, Sir Ralph, *The Book of Duck Decoys* (London, 1886)

Pevsner, Nikolaus, *The Buildings of England*, County Series (Penguin/Yale University Press)

Phillips, Charlotte, and Nora Shane, eds, *John Stuart, 3rd Earl of Bute (1713-1792)* (Luton Hoo Estate, 2014)

Picard, Liza, *Dr Johnson's London 1740-1770* (Weidenfeld & Nicolson, 2000)

Plumptre, George, *Garden Ornament* (Thames & Hudson, 1989)

Porter, Roy, *English Society in the 18th Century* (Penguin, 1982, rev. edn 1991)

Price, Uvedale, *Essays on the Picturesque* (London, 1810)

Prince, Hugh, *Parks in England* (Pinhorns, 1967)

Pugsley, Steven, ed., *Devon Gardens - An Historical Survey* (Alan Sutton, 1940)

Reed, Michael, *The Georgian Triumph 1700-1830* (Routledge & Kegan Paul, 1983)

Roberts, Jane, *Royal Landscape* (Yale University Press, 1997)

Robinson, J.M., *Temples of Delight - Stowe Landscape Gardens* (Pitkin Pictorial & National Trust, 1994)

Rose, Graham, *The Traditional Garden Book* (Dorling Kindersley, 1989)

Ruffinière du Prey, Pierre de la, *John Soane, The Making of an Architect* (Chicago & London, 1985)

Sanecki, Kay N., *Ashridge – A Living History* (Phillimore, 1996)

Sanecki, Kay, *Old Garden Tools* (Shire Publications, 1979, rev. edn 2004)

Scarfe, Norman, *Innocent Espionage – The La Rochefoucauld Brothers' Tour of England in 1785* (Boydell Press, 1995)

Sproule, Anna, and Michael Pollard, *The Country House Guide* (Century Hutchinson, 1988)

Stroud, Dorothy, *Humphry Repton* (Country Life, 1962)

Stroud, Dorothy, *Henry Holland* (Country Life, 1966)

Stroud, Dorothy, *'Capability' Brown* (Faber, 1975, rev. edn 1984)

Stuart Thomas, Graham, *Gardens of the National Trust* (Weidenfeld & Nicolson, 1979)

Stuart, David C., *Georgian Gardens* (Robert Hale, 1979)

Switzer, Stephen, *An Introduction to a General System of Hydrostaticks & Hydraulics, Philosophical & Practical* (London: Printed for T. Astley, S. Austin and L. Gilliver, 1729)

Symes, Michael, *Mr Hamilton's Elysium* (Frances Lincoln, 2010)

Symes, Michael, and Sandra Haynes, *Three Eighteenth-Century Gardens: Enville, Hagley & the Leasowes* (Redcliffe Press, 2010)

Taylor, Kristina, and Robert Peel, *Passion, Plants and Patronage, 300 Years of the Bute Family Landscapes* (Artifice, 2012)

Thacker, Christopher, *The Genius of Gardening* (Weidenfeld & Nicolson, 1994)

Turner, Roger, *'Capability' Brown and the Eighteenth-Century Landscape* (Phillimore, rev. edn 1999)

Tyne & Wear Museums, *'Capability' Brown and the Northern Landscape* (Exhibition Catalogue, 1983)

Underdown, David, *Start of Play* (Allen Lane, Penguin, 2000)

Victoria County Histories, The (Institute of Historical Research, University of London)

Walford, Edward, *Old and New London*, Vol.6 (Cassell Petter & Galpin, 1880)

Wilkinson, Gerald, *A History of Britain's Trees* (Hutchinson, 1981)

Williamson, Tom, and Liz Bellamy, *Property and Landscape* (George Philip, 1987)

Williamson, Tom, *Polite Landscapes: Gardens and Society in Eighteenth-Century England* (Sutton, 1995)

Willis, Peter, *Capability Brown in Northumberland* (Northumberland & Newcastle Society, 1981)

Woodhouse, Adrian, *Capability Brown of Kirkharle* (limited edn, Kirkharle Courtyard, 2000)

Woods, May, *Glass Houses* (Aurum Press, 1988)

Wright, Neil R., *John Grundy of Spalding, Engineer 1719–1783* (Dept. of Recreational Studies, Lincoln County Council, 1983)

Wulf, Andrea, and Emma Gieben-Gamal, *This Other Eden* (Little Brown, 2005)

JOURNAL PAPERS/ARTICLES

GH: *Garden History* Journal

Adshead, David, 'The Design and Building of the Gothic Folly at Wimpole, Cambridgeshire', *The Burlington Magazine* (London), Vol.CXL No.1139, February 1998

Bate, Sally, 'Lancelot "Capability" Brown didn't build any kitchen gardens in Norfolk, or did he?' (*Norfolk Gardens Trust Journal*, Autumn 2015, pp.4–7)

Brighton, Trevor, 'Chatsworth's Sixteenth-Century Parks and Gardens', GH 23:1, Summer 1995

Brown, David, 'Lancelot Brown and his Associates', GH 29:1, Summer 2001

Cowell, Fiona, 'Richard Woods; A Preliminary Account part II', GH15:1, Spring 1987

Hall, Elizabeth, 'Mr Brown's Directions: Capability Brown's landscaping at Burton Constable 1767–1782', GH 23:2, Winter 1995

Hay, C.S., 'The History of Sandleford Priory' (Newbury District Field Club, 1981)

Hingston, Elizabeth, 'Ashburnham Place, East Sussex', GH 29:1, Summer 2001

Jacques, David, 'Lancelot Brown: The Professional Man', *Landscape Design* 1978, Vol.121

Jacques, David, 'The Chief Ornament of Gray's Inn: The Walks from Bacon to Brown', GH 17:1, Spring 1989

Jacques, David, 'Warwick Castle Grounds & Park 1743–1760', GH 29:1, Summer 2001

Laird, Mark, 'The Culture of Horticulture: Class, Consumption, and Gender in the English Landscape Garden', in *Bourgeois & Aristocratic Cultural Encounters in Garden Art, 1550–1850*, Vol.23, ed. Michel Conan, in the series *Dumbarton Oaks Colloquium on the History of Landscape Architecture* (Dumbarton Oaks, USA, 2002)

Lennon, Ben, 'Burlington, Brown and Bill', GH 39:1, Summer 2011

Mayer, Laura, 'Landscape as Legacy: the Gothick Garden Buildings of Alnwick, Northumberland', GH 39:1, Summer 2011

Meir, Jennifer M., 'Development of a Natural Style in Designed Landscapes between 1730 and 1760: The English Midlands & the work of Sanderson Miller and Lancelot Brown', GH 30:1, Spring 2002

Mowl, Timothy, 'Rococo and Later Landscaping at Longleat', GH 23:1, Summer 1995

Phibbs, John, 'Point Blank', GH 35:1, Summer 2007

Phibbs, John, 'The Persistence of Older Traditions in Eighteenth-Century Gardening', GH 37:2, Winter 2009

Phibbs, John, 'Mingle, Mass & Muddle: The Use of Plants in Eighteenth-Century Gardens', GH 38:1, Summer 2010

Phibbs, John, 'The Structure of the Eighteenth-Century Garden', GH 38:1, Summer 2010

Roberts, Judith, '"Well Temper'd Clay": Constructing Water Features in the Landscape Park', GH 29:1, Summer 2001

Shields, Steffie, '"Mr Brown Engineer": Lancelot Brown's early work at Grimsthorpe Castle & Stowe', GH 35:2, Winter 2006

Shields, Steffie, '"A Profusion of Water", The Grenville Landscape of Wotton House', *New Arcadian Journal* 65/66, December 2009

Symes, Michael, 'Flintwork, Freedom & Fantasy: The Landscape at West Wycombe Park, Buckinghamshire', GH 33:1, Summer 2005

Symes, Michael, 'Charles Hamilton at Bowood', GH 35:2, Winter 2006

Thompson, John, 'Remarks on the Effect of the Lombardy Poplar in Park Scenery', *Gardener's Magazine* Vol.1, 1826, pp.16–20

Till, Eric, 'The Development of the Park and Gardens at Burghley', GH 19:2, Autumn 1991

Wade, Sybil, 'The Historic Landscape of St Gabriel's School Grounds' (April 1997)

Willis, Peter, 'Capability Brown's Account with Drummond's Bank 1753–1783', *Architectural History* 27, 1984

For gazetteer of attributed Brown Sites/Works please see online database: www.parksandgardens.org

NOTES

ABBREVIATIONS

AO Archive Office
BL British Library
CL Central Library
BOD Bodleian Library, University of Oxford
EH English Heritage
GHS Garden History Society
HE Historic England
HL Huntington Library, California

ICE Institute of Civil Engineering, London
PRO Public Record Office
MET Metropolitan Museum New York
NPG National Portrait Gallery
NT National Trust
PGUK Parks and Gardens UK Online resource
RHS LL Royal Horticultural Society,
    Lindley Library, London

RIBA Royal Institute of British Architects, London
RO Record Office
RS Royal Society, London
SM Soane Museum, London
UL University Library
VCH Victoria County Histories

1   www.measuringworth.com. See also Jim O'Donoghue, *Consumer Price Inflation since 1750, Economic Trends*, No. 604, pp.38–46.
2   Edward Connery Lathem, ed. *The Poetry of Robert Frost* (1969): 'The Road Not Taken'.
3   The Great Storm, October 1987, caused immense, irretrievable damage in the south, particularly to vulnerable, shallow-rooted beech trees, still in full canopy. At Cadland, almost all Brown's coastal Scots pines fell like 'pick-up sticks'. Eighty per cent of the mature trees at Uppark (Sussex) were lost. Fallen mature trees at Petworth, in the care of the National Trust since 1947, totalled over 750, interrupting Brown's seamless boundary belt and creating unsightly gaps on the horizon, and so destroying the reassuring sense of permanent calm. It took over twenty years for replacement trees to recreate harmonious enclosure. Head Gardener Trevor Seddon seized the opportunity to complete part of Brown's over-ambitious plan for the park that had never been fully realised, planting 34,000 trees including swamp cypress and white willow, with nurse silver birch, 'to sculpture' the south-west end of Brown's lake.
4   Lord Exeter acquired a copy to put in Brown's summerhouse as a memorial by the lake at Burghley. It now hangs in the Pagoda Room close to a window overlooking the gardens and his lake.
5   Stroud p.202. An anonymous obituary.
6   W.S. Lewis, ed. *A Notebook of Horace Walpole* (New York, 1927), pp.29–30.
7   Horace Walpole, *Essay on Modern Gardening*, 1771.
8   Emily J. Climenson, ed. *Passages from the Diaries of Mrs Philip Lybbe Powys 1756 to 1808*, p.195.
9   Enclosures by private Act of Parliament began about 1730 and became common from 1750. Twenty-one per cent of England was enclosed in this way. There were over 5,000 Acts dealing with almost 7 million acres of land, about two thirds of which had been arable and one third common or waste.
10 Batty Langley publications include *A Sure Method of Improving Estates* (1728) and *New Principles of Gardening* (1728).
11 Dorothy Stroud, *Capability Brown* (Faber & Faber, London, 1975; rev. edn 1984), p.30.
12 Kevin Nichols, *Begotten in Silence* (Mayhew McCrimmon Ltd, 1978).
13 Brown's name was originally spelt with an e. Coincidentally, Lancelot Browne (d. 1605), the physician to Queen Elizabeth I and James I, wrote a commendatory letter prefixed to Gerarde's *Herbal* (1st edition 1597). A career in gardening seems somehow to have been predestined.
14 Kirk Harle, named from 'the church by the stream', is now a hamlet known as Kirkharle. Harle in early English also meant 'from the hare's land' or 'from the *battle land*'.
15 Reverend John Hodgson, *History of Northumberland* (1827), part II, vol. 1. Hodgson was vicar of nearby Kirkwhelpington.
16 Sir Lambton Loraine, 11th Baronet, *Pedigree & Memoirs of the Family of Loraine of Kirkharle* (1902). Loraine's uncle had married the Earl of Carlisle's daughter at Castle Howard (Yorkshire), celebrated for great architecture and thought-provoking, grand vistas, almost as if the recreation of a Roman province.
17 In 1698 Thomas Savary (1650–1716) reported to the King, and to the Royal Society, obtaining a patent for his steam pump design. In 1712 Thomas Newcomen (1664–1729) built a successful, working steam engine at Dudley Castle mine.
18 A Turnpike Trust was a group of people empowered by a private Act of Parliament to take over a section of road, erect gates upon it and charge tolls to the road users in order to keep the roads in good repair.
19 In 1710 there were 167 peers; by 1790, 220 peers.

20 By 1808, c.200,000 acres of fen in Lincolnshire had come under cultivation by drainage.
21 Wealthy landowners involved in the drainage and exploitation of fenland, with drainage expert John Grundy Sr (c.1696–1748) acting as agent.
22 Perhaps Loraine, whose mother was Elizabeth Vyner, introduced Brown to his Lincolnshire cousin, Sir Robert Vyner, with estates at Gautby and Tupholme, a fellow MP of Banks II. Brown may have accepted land in Lincolnshire in lieu of cash payment for his advice. His will (Huntingdon CRO.1692) bequeathed land there to his second son, John, possibly including Fishtoft, Osbournby and Donnington.
23 Lincoln Record Society, Vol.45, *Letters & Papers of Banks*, p.180, no.247, & p.183.
24 Sir Gilbert Scott, *Personal and Professional Recollections* (1879), p.2.
25 Stroud, p.205.
26 Stephen Switzer, *Ichnographia Rustica; or, The Nobleman, Gentleman, and Gardener's Recreations containing directions for the general distribution of a country seat into rural and extensive gardens, parks, paddocks, &c., and a general system of agriculture*; illus. from the author's drawings. (D. Browne, London, 1718, 1742, republished Garland Publishing Inc. 1982, Preface, pp. xvii & xix). *Ichnographia* comes from the Greek word meaning 'ground plan'.
27 BOD. MS. Eng. Misc.c.114. f.201. Letter dated 1724, Stephen Switzer to Dr William Stukeley.
28 Grimsthorpe Castle's north front was completed after Vanbrugh's death (1726), probably by Nicholas Hawksmoor (c.1661–1736).
29 Lincolnshire AO. 5Anc8/21/5, p.252. The work on the causeway bridge was completed by a Mr Bannister, because by then Brown was working permanently at Stowe.
30 Lincolnshire AO. 3Anc 4/35A. Grundy Survey Book of Grimsthorpe (1753). The engine house was eventually demolished and rebuilt as the head gardener's cottage beyond 'The Groves'.
31 BOD. Royal Gardener Charles Bridgeman (1690–1738) was a key figure in the transition to naturalistic gardening.
32 HL. STTF Box 69 bundles 2 & 3. 'Indevoring to mend the Head of the River in ye wood' [4 men] 11–18 January 1741; also 'wheeling to make ye new Hedg (Heud) cross ye Pond' [6 men 24 days] 26 January 1741.
33 The idea was inspired by an allegorical essay by Joseph Addison in *The Tatler* (1709), describing the Elysian Fields.
34 Half of the busts are carved by Peter Scheemakers (1691–1781), the other eight by John Michael Rysbrack (1694–1770).
35 Soane Museum, Stroud papers.
36 HL. Stowe Vols 168. Pt 1 (of 2).
37 Steffie Shields, *A Profusion of Water, The Grenville Landscape of Wotton House*, New Arcadian Journal 65/66, December 2009, pp.59–71. Richard Grenville's 'Bargain Book' concerning agreements and labour payments records two significant areas of early activity with reference to water, coinciding with enclosures (1741–43). The nature of this improvement, similar to 'New Works' he was undertaking at Stowe, fitted the Brown profile. Grenville's first recorded 'gratuity' or 'expenses' payment, one guinea to the 'Stowe Gardiner', appears in the 1742 Wotton Day Book.
38 Clarke, *Descriptions*, p.83.
39 *Ibid.* p.79.
40 *Ibid.* p.124. Changes continued, so the guidebook was amended and extended every year. Seeley's later collection of engraved views of Stowe (1750) illustrates columns, temples and garden buildings, including the Keeper's Lodge.

41   *Ibid.* pp.81–82. Gibbs's Boycott buildings were originally finished with pyramidal tops (1728), the east as a belvedere with an octagon room, the west as a 'Dwelling-house for a Gentleman'.

42   HL. STTF Box 69, Bundle 10. James Scott bill for garden seed, 1744/45. Scott's Nursery, c.1740–60, covered eight acres at Turnham Green in West London.

43   According to Seeley's 1744 guide it was built above the ice house.

44   Thomas Whateley, *Observations on Modern Gardening* (1770).

45   After the Seven Years War, the temple, originally with windows, was adapted by Richard Grenville, Earl Temple, and named the Temple of Concorde and Victory (1763).

46   Both Grimsthorpe and Stowe accounts refer to Mr Barnes or 'Barn ironmonger'.

47   Soane Museum, Stroud papers. Brown's letter to Cobham, dated 24 February 1746, found by Mr David Easton, London.

48   Sir Charles Browne at Kiddington (Oxfordshire), the Duke of Grafton at Wakefield Lodge (Northamptonshire), the Duke of Marlborough at Langley (Buckinghamshire), Lord Brooke at Warwick Castle and Earl Denbigh at Newnham Paddox (Warwickshire). In 1748 Lord Guernsey approached Brown about the alteration of the Great Pool at Packington in the Forest of Arden (Warwickshire). See Chapter 4.

49   The column was moved (1756) to its present position near the church.

50   In 1957 the figure of Cobham was destroyed by lightning. A replica was installed by the National Trust (2000).

51   Gowing & G.B. Clarke, *Views of Stowe* (Buckinghamshire County Museum & Stowe School, 1983), Plate 21, Cat. no.59, *Grecian Valley from the New Grotto*, by J.C. Nattes.

52   Edward Walford, *Old and New London* (1878), Vol. 6, Ch. XXXIX, p.542.

53   Castle Ashby Archive, Brown's letter dated 6 May 1771.

54   Also known as Dame Barbara Mostyn.

55   Rector of Woodstock. *Guide to Blenheim* (11th edition, 1820) quotes Lady Mostyn, daughter of Sir Charles Browne, of Kiddington. I am grateful to Sarah Furze for this information.

56   At Bowood, an entry in Lady Shelburne's journal reads: '5 August 1765 Mr Brown the gardener came to dinner and spent the evening giving directions to his men.'

57   Janet Waymark, *Sherborne, Dorset* (GH 29:1, Summer 2001, p.70). On another occasion, Captain Digby wrote in his diary: 'Captain R. went with regret to Minterne before breakfast sorry to lose any of Mr Brown's company.'

58   H. Walpole, *Correspondence 32*, p.148. 1 October 1773.

59   Stroud, p.82.

60   The architect for Shakespeare's temple, said to be modelled on Burlington's Chiswick House, has never been identified. A payment of £720 from Clutterbuck, in three instalments, in Brown's Drummond's account might suggest James Clutterbuck, a 'mercer' who was Garrick's adviser and acted as his banker. Brown lived only half a mile from Chiswick House, and this temple, minus the Palladian portico and columns, bears a striking resemblance to Brown's rotunda summerhouse at Redgrave in Suffolk. Brown paid the Fulham builder Henry Holland Sr in 1756 and 1757, exactly the period when Garrick was building the temple. Holland later oversaw building works at Redgrave. See p.173.

61   I am grateful to Suzannah Fleming for information about David Garrick's garden.

62   Lincolnshire AO. Stubton VII/E/1 Vol.1. Letter dated 1 August 1777 from Thomas Heron to his brother, Sir Richard Heron, principal secretary to the Lord Lieutenant at Dublin Castle.

63   Ibid.

64   BL. Add.69795, f.105. Letter dated 1 September 1778.

65   In 1766, James Fitzgerald, Viscount, of Taplow (MP 1747), was created 1st Duke of Leinster, Ireland's premier peer. His Dublin home (Kildare House, later Leinster House), was first built in 1745–48 on the unfashionable, south side of the city. A model for the White House in Washington, it is now the seat of the Irish Parliament.

66   BL. Add.69795. Letter from Lord Hardwicke, 10 December 1767.

67   *Ibid.* Letter to his daughter Margaret.

68   E.W. Harcourt, *The Harcourt Papers*, Vol.VIII. Letter to Lord Harcourt.

69   Wiltshire & Swindon RO. CR/A2932, Brown's letter, September 1761.

70   *Ibid.* Brown's letter, March 1764.

71   *Ibid.* 9/35/52, Brown's letter to Lord Bruce, March 1765.

72   Stroud, p.138. Letter to Peggy (Margaret).

73   SM. Stroud papers. Letter from York to Mrs Elizabeth Montagu (1720–1800), an intellectual friend of Dr Johnson and Horace Walpole, known as 'Queen of the Blue-Stockings' for her entertaining salons.

74   RHS Lindley Library. Brown's Account Book dates from 1764, but there are references to some payments and contracts from 1759 onwards.

75   *Ibid.*

76   Named after mathematician Edmund Gunter (1581–1626).

77   In 1737, to reduce the margin for error, instead of the traditional open sights, the celebrated mathematical instrument-maker Jonathon Sisson improved the theodolite by adding a telescope.

78   Thomas Greening the Younger (1710–57).

79   North Yorkshire RO. ZNK X 1/9/119, MIC 930, 15 December 1769. I am indebted to Mrs Val Hepworth for this information.

80   RHS LL. Brown's Account Book, p.114.

81   I am grateful to Kevin Rogers for sharing his research. The 'Kentian' cascade at Stowe may have been a collaboration of Brown and Sanderson Miller.

82   This plan is comparable to both the early 1750s Syon plan and the later 1760s Aynho plan.

83   Herts RO, Youngsbury Plan c.1769 [DE/A/2845]. Hills Plan West Sussex RO, Add. Mss 48,149.

84   West Sussex RO. Petworth House Archive. Egremont's wife and George Grenville's wife at Wotton, where Brown had worked in the 1740s, were sisters.

85   The former Egremont House in Piccadilly, built by Matthew Brettingham 1756–61, now called Cambridge House, became part of a new development in 2013 likely to become the most expensive property in England.

86   I am grateful to my cousin Corinne Bible, a graphologist, for this analysis of Brown's handwriting.

87   West Sussex RO. PHA 6623. Letter to Lord Thomond, October 1764.

88   David Jacques, 'Lancelot Brown: The Professional Man', *Landscape Design* (1978), Vol.121, p.27.

89   BL. Add.61672, f.119. Letter to the Duke of Marlborough, 26 August 1765. Paviour Benjamin Read was Brown's chief engineering foreman after Stowe.

90   I am indebted to David Brown for charting payments in Brown's Drummond's Bank account.

91   RHS LL, Brown Account Book, p.11. Concerning Branches (Suffolk), W. Brown was probably Brown's cousin, William Brown. See also A.W. Skempton, A Biographical Dictionary of Civil Engineers in Great Britain and Ireland, p.498.

92   BL. Add.69795. Letter from Lord Craven.

93   Wiltshire RO. CR/A2932. Reference to Christian Sanderson, an associate 1761–66, and again 1771–83.

94   Leeds AO. T.N. Estate Accounts: Brown's 1769 letter to Lord Irwin from Ashburnham.

95   'Anthony Gerrit' is recorded as the agent after 1776 supervising the 'new work'. There are large payments to 'Anthony Garret' from 1772 to 1779 in Brown's Drummond's Bank account. The sizeable amounts paid perhaps indicate that, besides implementing the improver's plans at Brocklesby, Garrett also worked for Brown elsewhere over the same period.

96   Burghley Archive Day Book, 24 June 1777.

97   Wiltshire & Swindon RO. 9/35/52. January 1765.

98   *Ibid.*

99   Wiltshire RO. 1300/1920. October 1768.

100   Wiltshire RO. 9/35/52.

101   Wiltshire RO. 1300/1911.

102   Wiltshire RO. 1300/1934. Brown letter dated September 1765.

103   H. Walpole, *Correspondence 9*, p.285. Letter to Lord Montagu, 4 July 1760.

104   Stephen Switzer, *The Nobleman, Gentleman and Gardener's Recreation* (1715) re-published as *Ichnographica Rustica* (1718, 1742).

105   Lincolnshire AO. Yarb5/2/17/1. A road from Brocklesby to Brigg accounted for with echoes of Brown's meticulous instruction: 'Nov 14 1778 pd George Houlton for covering the New Road. 18ft wide 18 inches thick at the centre decreasing gradually to 6" stuck at the edge with chalkstone 15" thick & with gravel 3" according to the agreement made with him to be 8/6 per rod £177 13s. 8d.'

106   BL. Add.69795. Henry Fox's letter dated August (1755?).

107   Thomas Whately, *Observations on Modern Gardening* (1770).

108   Leeds AO. TN Corr. Brown's letter to Viscount Irwin, 5 March 1771.

109   Bowood Muniments. Contract, Article 6, 10 August 1762.

110   Timothy Mowl & Brian Earnshaw, *Trumpet at a Distant Gate*, p.187.

111   In 1790 these walks took 12 men a week to mow.

112   Elizabeth Hall, *Capability Brown at Burton Constable*, GH 23:2, p.161.

113   Hall, GH 23:2, p.158, No.3.

114   *Ibid.*, p.161, no.19. 1782.

115   Ashridge Repton Red Book. 'The deep walled ha-ha invented by Brown was seldom used by him but to give a View thro some glade, or to give some security to a terrace walk, from whence as my late friend Mr Windham used to say "it is delightful to see two bulls fighting without the possibility of danger".'

116   John James (c.1672–1746), architect/surveyor/carpenter, wrote an English translation of a book by A.J. Dezallier d'Argenville, *La Theorie et la Pratique du Jardinage* (Paris: J. Mariette, 1709): *The theory and practice of gardening* (London: Maurice Atkins, 1712), which includes the making of parterres, mazes, garden buildings, and many other ornaments.

117 West Sussex RO. PHA 7428, Shortgrove contract, 24 July 1753, Article 3. 'To build a Wall along the said Fosse of five feet high sufficient to keep up the Earth and to lay a proper coping of Clay with earth along the same etc.'

118 Madingley Hall, Cambridgeshire. Contract with Sir John Hynde Cotton, dated 16 November 1756.

119 *Ibid*.

120 Essex RO, D/Dby A365/1, 22 April 1763, Audley End contract.

121 Cambridge UL.

122 Adelaide Drummond, *Retrospect & Memoir* (Exeter, 1915). 'Our host [Paget?] ... then brought out a book in which was a plan by Mr Brown for the improvement & development of that steep hill (a high & rather steep hill pretty well covered with shrubs) as a pleasure ground'. This book probably resembled the leather-bound folio of watercolour plans recently brought to light at Belvoir Castle. Proposals were said to have been only partially implemented.

123 David Jacques, *Capability Brown at Hampton Court*, Hermitage Magazine (April 2003), pp.52–55. The albums (c.1778) are in the Hermitage Museum, St Petersburg.

124 David Jacques, *Warwick Castle Grounds & Park 1743–1760*, GH 29:1, Summer 2001, p.55, a comment by Lord Brooke.

125 Warwickshire RO. CR2017/A5 (Microfilm MI416), Newnham Paddox Building Book (1743–81).

126 British Geographical Society. August 1755, Lincoln. The Lincoln Mercury 394 (1755) reported damage at four villages on the south side of the Humber: 'the walls of some [houses] fell down', suggesting an intensity of at least VI on the Mercalli Scale. I am grateful to Rod Conlon for drawing to my attention an article by David L. Bates, 'When Earth Her Entrails Shook' (*Northamptonshire Past & Present*, Vol.V, No.4 (1976), pp.55–68).

127 Boston Library, Lincs. Transcription of Minutes of the Corporation of Boston, Vol.V, p.669. Minute 565A, 22 August 1755. I am grateful to Sandra Sardeson for drawing these Minutes to my attention.

128 Huntingdon RO. Acc.1692. In Brown's will, dated 26 March 1779, he left Bridget's brother John Wayet £10 for a mourning ring. In January 1753 'Mr Brown' accompanied Sir Francis Dashwood to a meeting in Lincoln to discuss the River Witham Navigation. Dashwood, of West Wycombe and Hell Fire Club fame, with estates in Lincolnshire, Nocton and Well, is known to have consulted Brown, while John Wayet, his brother-in-law, was later elected as one of Boston's four commissioners responsible for this major scheme.

129 Huntingdon RO. Acc.1692. Brown's will, dated 26 March 1779, records his ownership of land in Lincolnshire including at Donnington, where Browntoft Lane still exists today.

130 Shirley Jeffrey, *Croome Park: tracing the vision of Capability Brown* (Dr Martin, J.C. Lowry). Warwick MA 2002.

131 BL. Add.69795, 6 June 6 1775. Letter to Revd Dyer.

132 Horace Walpole, *Correspondence 9*, p.223. Letter to George Montagu Esq., 20 August 1758.

133 *Ibid.*, 31, p.355. Letter to Lady Ossory, 31 August 1782.

134 Janet Waymark, *Sherborne, Dorset* (GH 29:1, Summer 2001, p.67). The lake cost the comparatively small sum of £322 9s 0d, today over £47,000.

135 Switzer, S, *An Introduction to a General System of Hydrostaticks & Hydraulicks, Philosophical & Practical* (1729, 2 vols).

136 I am grateful to Kate Harwood for sharing her research at Southill.

137 Northamptonshire RO, Map 4210, survey dated 1608.

138 Northants RO. I am grateful to Rod Conlon, Northants Gardens Trust, for sharing his research into Wakefield accounts.

139 I am grateful to Richard Howlings for drawing to my attention his paper 'Wakefield Lodge and other Houses of the Duke of Grafton', *Georgian Journal* Vol.III (1993), pp.43–61.

140 West Sussex RO. Petworth House Archive. Contract dated June 1755.

141 *Ibid*. Letter to Lord Egremont, August 1755.

142 *Ibid*. Contract, 4 May 1756, 4th Article.

143 In 1782 a new beam pump was constructed at Coultershaw Mill, powered by a water wheel, to improve the water supply. It seems likely, given his engineering work elsewhere, that years earlier Brown had worked to the same end.

144 British Museum. Heal, 74, 2. My thanks to Karen Lynch for sharing this information, after having recently found a signed Brown account for Lord Middleton for a survey and plan for Shillingley, Sussex.

145 Sir Ralph Payne Gallwey, *The Book of Duck Decoys* (1886). 'Truly this county was the home of Decoys, for I am able to give a list of no less than 38 of these contrivances as formerly existing in Lincoln.... The Decoys of Lincoln chiefly flourished in its eastern and southern portions, notably between Sleaford and Crowland, and from Wainfleet to Boston.' There is a description of a Victorian decoy, unchanged from eighteenth-century methods. 'At the Hoo, near Welwyn, 8 miles WNW. of Hertford, is a small trap Decoy (constructed 1870) belonging to Lord Dacre, and used only to supply household wants. The one cage that is

attached to the pool is 30 ft long, 12 ft wide and 9 ft high, and is covered with wire netting. When the fowl swim up the ditch under the cage they are entrapped by means of a falling door, worked by a wire from a distance.'

146 G.B. Clarke, *Seeley's Description* (1744), p.136.

147 The earliest true description of a Decoy occurs in the *Universal Magazine*, April 1752. In 1795, Williams of Wrangle constructed a four-pipe decoy at Packington.

148 Sherborne Castle Archive. Accounts record the purchase of both wild duck and fish to stock the new lake. Several other accounts include payments for netting at a time when Brown was involved in lake-making. Duck were sold for 4d each in 1776, equivalent to £2.40 today.

149 Payne-Gallwey. At Chillington the 100-acre lake had two pipes. At Holkham, on the marshes, there were traces of an old decoy and its pipes half a mile north of the church. The lake here attracts immense numbers of wildfowl every winter, many of which remain to breed. At Lowther Castle, in the park, an oval-shaped pool, of about three acres, is known as 'the Decoy'.

150 An abbreviation of the Dutch 'ende-kooy' or 'Duck Cage', a trap pronounced d'coy, to distinguish it from the decoys, the live tame duck that attracted wildfowl by their calls.

151 Stroud, p.147, quotes from James Paine, *Plans of Noblemen's and Gentlemen's Houses* (1767).

152 Estate workers carried out improvements without Brown's master eye. When offered 2,000 nursery cedars of Lebanon from Wilton, Herbert replied gratefully, requesting 4,000! This planting has been compounded by succeeding generations who continued to plant cedars in memory of relatives, so that now the park scenery seems somewhat dense.

153 Richard Milward, *Wimbledon Two Hundred Years Ago* (1996), p.40.

154 *Ibid*.

155 HL. Letter, 4 July 1758, William Pitt to Lady Hester Pitt.

156 *Wynne Diaries III*, p.126. In July 1804, the diarist Elizabeth Wynne explored Wotton's grounds. 'Wotton, 22nd July. Sunday. I took the entire round of the gardens, three miles and was much delighted with the walks, which are much more natural than those at Stowe. Lady Buckingham seems to be very partial to this place, where she spent the first years of her marriage. We were invited by Lord Bm. into the Boat who was rowed about the lake by his two sons, and were some time upon the water.'

157 Brown gave similar advice at Packington, Petworth, Chatsworth and Bowood.

158 Thomas Whately, *Observations on Modern Gardening* (1770), pp.84–88. In the mid-1990s Michael Harrison came to repair the ha-ha, a two-week job. He never left. An exemplary restoration is still being undertaken by owner David Gladstone and his untiring landscape manager. Tracing the history from the ground up, Harrison has, single-handedly for the most part, cleared lakesides, undergrowth and multitudes of self-seeded trees, uncovered original gravel drives and walks, and repaired numerous architectural features: temples, bridges, seats. Then, following up an in-depth historical survey, and consultation with both the Countryside and the Forestry Commissions, a five-year restoration planting plan for the pleasure grounds was drawn up. Stumps of Scots pine which were logged after World War II have been faithfully replaced in the same locations. With studious attention to detail, close observation and thoughtful discussion, the Brown way, Gladstone and Harrison have now carefully replanted the major vistas, so that Wotton continues to intrigue the imagination and charm every visitor: 'while the setting sun shoots its last gleams on a Tuscan portico, which is close to the upper basin, but which from a seat near this river is seen at a distance, through all the obscurity of the wood, glowing on the banks and reflected on the surface of the water' (Whately).

159 Thomas Whately, *ibid*.

160 Edwin Morris Betts, *Thomas Jefferson's Garden Book* (1944), p.112.

161 Thomas Hinde, 'Capability Brown – the Story of a Master Gardener', p.62, from J. & N. Eddowes, *A History of Burghley House* (1797), p.189.

162 *Ibid*. Before WWI, and in the 1950s and 1984, these wooden plugs have rotted, causing floods that damaged the dam.

163 In the nineteenth century these eleven acres were expanded to 26.

164 Later replaced by a Victorian stone bridge.

165 Edward Stevens, c.1770, possibly reworked in the style of Inigo Jones from an earlier monument (Tillemans, c.1729). The column has now been moved to the Duchess Walk in the east gardens.

166 Sherborne Castle Archive. 1756.

167 See p.51 re Packington. Also at Burghley as mentioned, and at Wotton, a survey (c.1649) has a drawing of a great lake superimposed that was first planned by Brown in the 1740s; later, too, at Ashburnham and Burghley, surveys are overdrawn with suggested changes to the water.

168 A similar apron ha-ha is found at Lacock Abbey, where Brown worked in 1755.

169 Brown was also involved in alterations at Stamford's wife's estate at this time, Dunholme Massey, including a new green drive to the church.

170 At Croome, a land drain supplied water from a reservoir in the neighbouring 'New Field' north, originally fed through lead pipes into Brown's grotto and thence, as at Enville, to top up the lake.

171 M. Symes & S. Haynes, *Three Eighteenth Century Gardens: Enville, Hagley and the Leasowes* (2010), p.128. The cascades, requiring further repair in the next decade, are seen in a mid-1760s painting by Anthony Devis.

172 In the 1820s head gardener James Brown was working in this Lamport area and is believed to be responsible for the features. Head gardeners are not generally landscapers! The likelihood is that the gardens would have needed considerable restoration, de-silting and cutting back, as in every generation.

173 David Burnett, *Longleat*, p.110. Contract, October 1757.

174 There is a similar sophisticated connection between house drains and sluices at Dunham Massey. Also Thoresby lake waters were used to flush through the drains of the old house.

175 Walpole, 16, p.28.

176 Daniel Defoe, *A Tour through the Island of Great Britain*, 8th edn (London, 1778), Vol.III, p.52. Improvements included a Palladian arch on the approach and, as the Enville proposal, a neat Tuscan pillar on the hill in memory of Herne's aunt, Frances Napier, as depicted in a Paul Sandby engraving. The column was later transferred to Mount Stuart on the Isle of Bute.

177 A nineteenth-century pinetum and Edwardian Italianate rose gardens have changed the character of many picturesque views from the house, currently under development as a hotel and adjoining golf course.

178 The lines of the river are now much altered by water-flow and silting, which has also caused the island to rejoin the mainland.

179 Arthur Young, *Northern Tour*, 1771, Vol.1, p.24.

180 BL Add.69795. Letter, 1773.

181 The tufa has now been moved to a rockery. Many cascades have been altered during subsequent lake restorations. Unattractive concrete structures now divide certain lakes.

182 Sussex RO. Petworth House Archive 7428.

183 Well House, Arthur Road, Wimbledon, the only Spencer building to survive in Wimbledon, is the probable site of Brown's engine house. The deep well silted up and was 34 years later dug out to 563 ft, a domed brick building was put over it, and it was still in operation by 1815. In 1875 it was converted into a dwelling.

184 Staffordshire RO.

185 PRO/30/29/2/68-69. Contract (1759).

186 Beds & Luton RO. L 30/14/315/2. Letter dated 15 March 1773 from Dr Beilby Porteus to Thomas Robinson, 2nd Baron Grantham (1738-86). I am grateful to Kate Harwood for drawing this to my attention.

187 RHS LL. Brown account book, p.13. 1765.

188 Byng, *Torrington Diaries*, Vol.3, p.128, June 1792.

189 ICE. Brindley notebook (1761-62). 7 January 1762.

190 West Yorkshire Archive Service, Leeds. Temple Newsam Estate Accounts 12/10.

191 RS. *Philosophical Transactions* (1673-1775), Vol.47. Letter LXIX, April 1752, pp. 415-28, with diagrams; also various folios of designs. Also a Catalogue of the Civil and Mechanical Engineering Designs 1741-92 of John Smeaton, FRS. It seems likely that Brown collaborated with Smeaton at Thoresby, the Duke of Kingston's estate in Nottinghamshire, in designing and installing a water-house, wheel and pumping machinery for the engine.

192 Wilts RO. 1300/1912, December 1765.

193 *Ibid.*, October 1768.

194 Stroud, p.114.

195 Bowood Archive, Lancelot Brown Plan (1763).

196 Entire villages moved on Brown's advice, besides that at Bowood, included Swynnerton (Staffordshire) and Milton Abbas (Dorset).

197 BL Add.57822, f.155, Brown's letter to George Grenville dated 22 June 1764.

198 Fiona Cowell, *Richard Woods: A Preliminary Account part II*, GH 15:1, 1987. I am indebted to Fiona Cowell for her help.

199 Beds AO. 30/9a/9/124, Lucas papers, 19 September 1769. Probably a reference to John Bunyan, *Pilgrim's Progress* (published 1678), begun while imprisoned in Bedford jail. 'The Enchanted Ground' is an area through which the King's Highway passes, with air that makes pilgrims want to stop to sleep. If one goes to sleep here, one never wakes up.

200 Ed J.J. Cartwright, *Travels through England* (Camden Society, 1889). Richard Pococke visited Stourhead in July 1754. 'Two large pieces of water are to be made into one and much enlarged for which the head is making at great expense'. The lake was completed and filled by 1757.

201 Messrs Hoare & Co., Archive, London. There is no record of payment to Brown in Hoare's personal account. Hoare made regular imbursements, from May 1752, to a Mr Sanderson. The name is quite common. Is it coincidence that, two years later, a Mr James Sanderson was employed as Brown's foreman at

Warwick Castle? Then again, this might refer to Christian Sanderson, another key collaborator from 1761.

202 Messrs Hoare & Co., Archive. Letter dated 1763. Hoare's choice of words was inspired by Alexander Pope's poem: *Epistle IV, To Richard Boyle* (Lord Burlington; 1731) about Stowe gardens: 'Consult the Genius of the Place in all; (Nature) ... Paints as you plant, and as you work, designs.'

203 David Brown, *Nathaniel Richmond Gentleman Improver* (University of East Anglia Thesis), September 2000, p.182. Revd Joseph Spence's letter (1751) to Revd Wheeler.

204 Walpole mentions coming across Brown in Paris.

205 Jane Brown, *The Omnipotent Magician* (2011), p.143. In 1760 Brown was proposed for membership of the Society for the Encouragement of the Arts, Manufactures and Commerce, undoubtedly useful for making contacts and being introduced to clients.

206 I am grateful to John Phibbs for showing me a watercolour labelled on the reverse 'Chichester Cathedral - Mr Browne' (not in Brown's handwriting).

207 Cipriani had decorated the magnificent Red Drawing room ceiling at Syon.

208 RHS Brown Account Book, p.121. 'Wm Constable 1774 in July or August paid for & sent 2 Clerisseau paintings £32 8' (£4,640).

209 *Antony and Cleopatra*, Act 2, Scene 2.

210 Grimsthorpe Castle Archive: F. Wood Survey (1830). Switzer's Bastion Garden survived into the nineteenth century.

211 WSRO CR/A2932. Corsham Archive. The identity of the lady 'Blagrave' remains a mystery.

212 Revd William Mason, *The English Garden* (1772).

213 In the 1930s this soil and turf, raised by 6 or 7 ft in some areas, was removed to reveal the ground plan of the Abbey. Now under the care of English Heritage. The ruin is surrounded by chain link fencing, which detracts from the beauty of the setting.

214 Austen chose to satirise people's love of gloomy thrills in *Northanger Abbey*, writing about Henry VIII: 'Nothing can be said in his vindication, but that his abolishing Religious Houses and leaving them to ruinous depredations of time has been of infinite use to the landscape of England.'

215 John Drake, *Wood & Ingram - a Huntingdonshire Nursery* (2008) pp.28, 29 and 48.

216 The best-known of many elm varieties, *Ulmus x hollandica* or *Ulmus major*, first raised in 1760 in Huntingdon, may have been included in this order.

217 J. Whitaker, *A Descriptive List of the Deer Parks and Paddocks of England* (Ballatyne & Hanson, London, 1892).

218 John Heywood, *A dialogue Conteynyng the Number in Effect of all the Prouerbes in the Englishe Tongue* (1546): 'Plentie is no deinte, ye see not your owne ease. I see, ye can not see the wood for trees.'

219 Stephen Switzer, *Ichnographia Rustica* (1718), p.86.

220 Hall, GH 23:2, *Minutes*, Tuesd Oct.15th 1782, p.160, No.13.

221 A 20th-century auction catalogue: 'Auction at Stowe - September the 19th 1917 - JACKSON STOPPS AND CO. NO BUYER OF ASH AND POPLAR SHOULD MISS THIS SALE. Having measured and valued timber in every part of the country we can still confidently assert that there is no place where one can see such length girth and soundness in the park of Stowe chiefly planted under the direction of the famous forester "Capability Brown".'

222 Lincolnshire AO. Stubton VII/E Letters, Vol.1. Thomas Heron to his brother Richard at Dublin Castle, Ireland.

223 Michael Symes, 'Charles Hamilton at Bowood', GH35:2, Winter 2006, p.206. Bowood House Archive, contract with Earl of Shelburne dated 10 August 1762. At Bowood many cedars were planted in the 1770s, after Brown's time, possibly at the suggestion of Charles Hamilton.

224 Brown's Drummond's account has additional payments to Richard Bagley and William Burchell, nurserymen in Fulham; Richard Butts, Kew Green; Samuel Bailey, seedsman, Bishopsgate(?); Oliver Cromwell & Co., Kensington; John Franklin, Lambeth Marsh; William North, then James Shiells, Lambeth nursery; Hewitt & Co. nursery, Brompton Pk; Cross & Co., seedsmen, Fleet St; Davis & Co., seedsmen, Snow Hill; and Richard Lewis, Balls Pond Rd nursery. I am indebted to David Brown for this information.

225 Laird, p.284. In 1773 at Burton Constable, Brown, Jardinier du Roi, imported trees from Centre de l'Arbres for £49 10s (£71,800) for spring planting, including 300 8-ft elms, 14 7-ft limes and 30 planes.

226 At Newnham Paddox (Warwickshire), 150 trees planted behind the stables, individually fenced with post and rails, mark the beginnings of a nursery.

227 Lincolnshire AO. Yarb. 9/4. Later created Baron Yarborough (1794), Charles Pelham went on to plant more than thirty million trees.

228 Nottingham UL. PWF 2256/1-2. G. Byng's letter to 3rd Duke of Portland.

229 Laird, pp. 276-77 (Wilts RO.1300/1913), Tottenham Park, *Minutes of Mr Brown's Proceedings*, October 1768.

230 *Ibid.*

231 Stroud, p.30.

232 David Jacques, *Warwick Castle Grounds & Park 1743–1760*, GH 29:1, Summer, p.61.

233 Note that, according to PGUK, in 1924 a Forestry Commission census recorded that one of the few remaining plantations of pure beech was found at Beechwood Park, Hertfordshire.

234 Arthur Young, *A General View of the Agriculture of the County of Lincoln* (1799). 'The Duke of Ancaster has woods to the extent of 4 or 500 acres. Cuts at 18 years growth, the whole underwood cut and the larger growth taken down in succession.... Takes out the sticks that will not pay for standing. The cold wet land gives the best wood. It is bought for the purpose of fencing new and old enclosures. The 18 years would not do for this. That of two to three growths of 54 years does for these purposes.'

235 Uvedale Price, *Essay on the Picturesque* (London, 1794). Price refers to an oak avenue conserved by a Cheshire landowner despite Brown having condemned it.

236 Walpole to George Montagu, 4 July 1760.

237 Thomas Whately, *Observations on Modern Gardening* (1770).

238 Laird, p.277. December 1765.

239 Essex RO. T/M298/1 and D/DU205/19. Percy Wyndham O'Brien, later Earl of Thomond, coloured the 1727 survey, marking 'the land in hand' green. In July 1754 Brown agreed a £610 (£88,870) contract, followed 17 months later by another £490 (£71,000) contract.

240 Egremont House, one of the few great London town houses still standing, is also known as '94 Piccadilly', with an entrance façade in St James's Square. Matthew Brettingham (sometimes called the Elder) rose from bricklaying to supervise the construction of Holkham Hall, eventually becoming one of the country's better-known architects.

241 West Sussex RO, Petworth House Archive.

242 PRO. 30/29/2. Trentham Contract (1759).

243 Hall, GH 23:2, *Minutes*, p.155, 8th Sept 1772, no.18.

244 *Ibid.*, p.157, 21 Sept 1775, no 8. Clumps on the East Lawn at Burton Constable were to be trenched to 2 ft, at 2s 6d per square rood. (Today, where trees have deteriorated or been felled, trenches may still mark the location and extent of a clump.)

245 *Ibid.*, p.158, Mr Brown's Directions, Aug 3 1776, no 1.

246 *Ibid.*, p.160, Minutes of Directions & Observations by Mr Browne, Tuesd Oct 15th, no.7.

247 *Ibid.*, p.156, 4th Sept 1773, Hints from Mr Brown, no.15.

248 David Jacques, *Warwick Castle Grounds & Park 1743–1760*, GH 29:1, Summer, p.56, Fig.5. See fenced in clumps in Mrs Delaney's sketch (1753) of Warwick Castle mount and environs. Also p.59, Fig.7, a plan for the 'Family Clump'.

249 Castle Ashby Archive.

250 Hannah More had come up to London from Gloucestershire. She quickly became a member of Dr Johnson's 'blue-stocking' circle, a respected educationalist and philanthropist, and one of the most influential women of her day.

251 Stroud, p.201.

252 I am grateful to Glynis Shaw for this information. In June 2012 the Clwyd Branch of the Welsh Historic Gardens Trust planted a Diamond Jubilee oak tree at Wynnstay as a replacement 'Queen Tree'.

253 West Sussex RO.PHA 7428. Shortgrove contract (24 July 1753).

254 J. & N. Eddowes, *A History of Burghley House* (1797), pp.8–9.

255 John Phibbs has recorded about 400 mounds in the park at Langley, Bucks. Many gardeners, believing that even young trees would fare better on a mound of earth, followed this practice well into the nineteenth century.

256 Hall, GH 23:2, *Minutes*, p.154. Hints from Mr Brown, 8 Sept 1772, No.6.

257 *Aesculus carnea* or red chestnut may also have been introduced by Brown. Pope's poem *Epistle IV, To Richard Boyle* (Lord Burlington; 1731) inspired by Stowe gardens mentions 'scarlet chestnut'.

258 I am grateful to Gary Webb, Grounds Manager, Compton Verney, for this information on lime trees.

259 Not popular among some naturalists, for its colonising, but sycamore timber is now more highly prized than oak.

260 Michael Symes, *Mr Hamilton's Elysium* (2010), p.109.

261 I am grateful to Camilla Hair, whose research has led to the suggestion that both these trees may indicate the owner's involvement with Freemasonry.

262 Wilts RO.1300/21.

263 John Thompson, 'Remarks on the Effect of the Lombardy Poplar in Park Scenery', *Gardener's Magazine* (1826), Vol.1, pp.16–20.

264 Charlecote, Coombe Abbey, Madingley, Blenheim and at Southill.

265 H. Walpole, 28, Letter to Mason, 6 September 1775, p.220, about Marquis de Girardin's garden at Ermenonville, the first example in France of an English garden.

266 Pollarded following Royal Mid-Surrey golf club fire (2001).

267 Maria Johnston's watercolour of Coombe Abbey, *View from the South-west* (1797), illustrates three trees breaking the corner dividing the old house from William Winde's classical west wing.

268 In 1970 Elvaston Castle was the first public Country Park to be opened in England.

269 Until recent engineering works (2011), three great planes helped to screen the downside of Brown's great dam at Blenheim.

270 The Madingley cedar near the house has since been replaced with a blue cedar, *Cedrus atlanticus*.

271 Mulgrave House, built by Sir Philip Stephens, has gone, but the large plane tree survives by the lake in the grounds of the Hurlingham Club. Similarly at Flambards, now part of Harrow School golf-course, a plane tree marks a focal position on the hill above the lake, as at Castle Ashby (see p.127).

272 The Lucombe Oak on the Alton Estate, Roehampton, in the grounds of Mount Clare, has been designated a Great Tree of London.

273 Knowsley Park Archive. I am grateful to Dr Stephen Lloyd for this information

274 Besides 10,000 Scots pine seedlings, Audley End records also include 1,300 larches, limes, silver firs (*Abies* species), Portugal laurels, Carolina poplars and birches, and 3,000 alders.

275 David Jacques, 'Warwick Castle Grounds & Park 1743–1760', GH 29:1, Summer, p.51, from J.C. Loudon, *A Treatise on Country Residences* (London, 1806), p.486.

276 John Phibbs, 'Point Blank', GH35:1 (2007). The 0 degree in geometry, or 'point blank' in the view from the house, is one example of Phibbs's theories on Brown's use of geometry.

277 The same idea may be seen on the hill between Weston Park (Staffordshire) and Tong Castle (Shropshire).

278 Kate Harwood has suggested that a triple Scots pine set may have also been a hallmark of the gentleman architect Sanderson Miller, one of Brown's mentors at the start of his career.

279 Lady Luxborough was one of the first to develop an ornamental farm, or *ferme ornée*, at Barrells in Warwickshire. According to Stephen Switzer, The *Appendix* to *Ichnographia Rustica* (c.1729, published 1742), this rural gardening is said to have 'been the practice of some of the best genius's of France, under the title La Ferme Ornée'.

280 BL. Add. 69795 2 June 1775. Also Stroud, p.157.

281 At Audley End today, the former laundry court, brew-house, wood- and coal-houses remain hidden behind great banks of box.

282 Wilts RO. 1300/1920, 1 October 1768, Tottenham. *Memorandums for Mr Winckles*.

283 Hall, GH 23:2, *Minutes*, p.156.

284 West Sussex RO. PHA 6623. Contract, May 1753.

285 Madingley College Archive.

286 John Phibbs, *Ibid*.

287 John Phibbs, 'Mingle, Mass & Muddle, the Use of Plants in Eighteenth Century Gardens', GH38:1, Summer 2010, p.40.

288 John Phibbs, 'The Persistence of Older Traditions in Eighteenth-Century Gardening', GH37:2, Winter 2009, p.183.

289 Ornamental thorns such as *Crataegus crus-galli* or Cockspur thorn and *Crataegus phaenopyrum* or Washington thorn had been introduced by this time.

290 Cambridge UL. A leather-bound folio.

291 Cadland Estate.

292 Royal Society, London. *Philosophical Transactions* (1673–1775), Vol.52. Letter I. Revd David Wark recommended the use of furze in fencing the banks of rivers and intermixed with gravel in dams, at one-tenth the expense of using faggots.

293 Laird, 1774. Twenty years previously Williamson supplied Syon, Petworth and Belhus.

294 Catherine Horwood, *Gardening Women* (Virago, 2010), p.97. I am grateful to Gwen Grantham for drawing this to my attention.

295 Wilts RO. 1300/1920, 1 October 1768. *Memorandums for Mr Winckles*.

296 *Ibid.* Nursery Book 1785, Tottenham Park.

297 British Museum Collection, 1897,0505.557, Mary Delany collage album.

298 Charlotte Phillips and Nora Shane, eds, *John Stuart, 3rd Earl of Bute (1713–1792)* (Luton Hoo Estate, 2014), p.39. I am grateful to Pat Livesey and Nora Shane of Luton Hoo Walled Garden Research Group.

299 Alnwick Castle Archive. I am grateful to Susan Darling for this information.

300 Metropolitan Museum, New York. MM48974. c.1764.

301 Could this possibly be the tree-seat featured in Zoffany's painting *Three daughters of the Earl of Bute*?

302 Laird, p.389, reference George Mason, *An Essay on Design in Gardening* (London, 1768), pp.47-48.

303 Brocklesby Estate Office. I am grateful to Bill Spink, landscape architect, who informed me of the scale of the flower garden.

304 Lincolnshire AO. Yarb. 9/4. 1776 contract, 2nd article.

305 BL, Add. 69795. Undated letter. Frederick Nicolay (1728-1809), previously assistant dancing master to the Prince of Wales, rose to become Page to Queen Charlotte and Keeper of the Queen's Music Library.

306 Anonymous, *The Rise and Progress of the Present Taste in Planting Parks, Pleasure Grounds, Gardens, &c, from Henry the Eighth to King George the Third; in a poetic Epistle to the Right Honorable Charles, Lord Viscount Irwin* (1767).

307 At Ampthill, Ring Hill at Audley End, the Mausoleum at Bowood, Queen Mary's Bower at Chatsworth, Warren Hill at Peper Harow, Temple Copse at Wilton, Round Hill at Wycombe Abbey, and at Dynfwr.

308 Laird, p.281, Brown's Lowther plan (1771). Careful restoration of Lowther Castle gardens has recently begun.

309 John Phibbs, 'The Persistence of Older Traditions in Eighteenth-Century Gardening', GH37:2, Winter 2009, p.183, quoting William Mavor's description of planting at Blenheim.

310 Taylor & Francis (1959): Sir Joshua Reynolds, *Discourses on Art*, p.202.

311 Sir Thomas Hugh & Arthur Clifford, *A Topographical & Historical Description of the Parish of Tixall* (1817).

312 Durham RO. D/59/C1/3/11.

313 In 1757 architect James Paine completed a column at Gibside, dedicated to Liberty, approximately 135 ft high, rising above an avenue of oaks.

314 Re-issued as *Gothic Architecture, improved by Rules and Proportions* (1747).

315 The population of England doubled to ten million over the course of the eighteenth century.

316 Walpole 9, p.121, 22 July 1751. Letter to Lord Montagu.

317 *Ibid*. G145/92/43. Peper Harow plan, May 1752.

318 Surrey History Centre. 1567/3, G145/91/8, G145/91/9. Peper Harow plans dated April 1752.

319 The house was demolished in 1952; Brown's stable range, with Gothic entrance, survives. ('Gothic' is sometimes 'Gothick' when referring to the eighteenth-century revival.)

320 Walpole, *Journal of Visits to Country Seats* (1772), XVI, p.63.

321 Soane Museum, Stroud papers. Letter to Bentley, his partner.

322 Michael McCarthy, *The Origins of the Gothic Revival* (1987). Bay windows were something of a signature in Miller's house alterations, Gothic in his case, first at his own Radway (Warwickshire, c.1746), then Adlestrop (Gloucestershire, c.1750), Arbury Hall (Warwickshire, 1751) and possibly also Ecton Hall (Northamptonshire, c.1756). I am grateful to Jonathan Williams who drew this to my attention.

323 Also at Glentworth, Scarborough's estate outside Lincoln, at Benwell Tower (Northumberland) for Brown's friend Shafto, at Chatsworth (Derbyshire) and at Whitley Beaumont (Yorkshire), where Paine married Richard Beaumont's sister. Later, at Weston (Staffordshire), Brown's contract (1765-67) included creating a lake and planting, where Paine added a bridge over the lake and a temple greenhouse.

324 Metropolitan Museum, New York, Robert Adam plans. This fine room was originally intended as the library.

325 Catherine Gordon, *The Coventrys of Croome* (Phillimore & Co. Ltd, 2000), p.117.

326 Brown remodelled Hulne Priory (Northumberland) to include a menagerie and a Gothic summerhouse adjoining a fifteenth-century tower, with Adam providing interior designs.

327 Broadway Tower, later built by James Wyatt for Coventry (completed 1798), is said to have been inspired by Brown.

328 Worcestershire RO. CR 125B/153. Letter dated November 1752. I am grateful to Mike Cousins for drawing this to my attention.

329 Society of Antiquaries, London: *Plan of the principal Floor of Crome Court*.

330 Three miles south-east of Broadway, now Spring Grove House and largely remodelled in the nineteenth century.

331 Essex CRO. 125B/473. Letter to Sanderson Miller dated May 1756. I am grateful to Mike Cousins for drawing my attention to the Dacre correspondence.

332 Burghley Archive, Day Books.

333 Eric Till, 'Capability Brown at Burghley' (*Country Life*, 16 October 1975), pp.982-85.

334 In 1771 Mrs Coade established a very successful stoneware 'Manufactury' in Lambeth. Coade Stone, a stoneware between earthenware and porcelain, resisted all the elements through a careful selection of ingredients and a long firing.

335 Built in 1765, damaged by fire in 1911, Tong Castle was demolished in 1954. A hexagonal Gothic 'Convent Lodge' survives as an isolated feature on view from the M54 motorway (1977) cutting through the landscape. Gates, gate piers and

flanking walls thought to be designed by Brown were moved from their original position in Tong to the entrance to Villiers Ltd, Marston Road.

336 James Paine, *Plans, Elevations and Sections of the Noblemen and Gentlemen's Houses* (1767).

337 In London, Paine employed John Devall, Master Mason to the City of London (1760-84). Brown employed Devall at several sites, including Broadlands (Hampshire). Samuel Watson, the carpenter for Stowe's 'Grecian capitels', continued to work for Brown through the 1760s and collaborated with Paine at Chatsworth. The Yorkshire-born Joseph Rose the Elder (1723-1780), gifted at ornamental plasterwork, and considered 'the first man in the Kingdom as a plasterer', worked for Adam at Syon (Middlesex) before working for Brown at Broadlands (Hampshire); he was also employed by Paine at Glentworth (Lincolnshire), Sandbeck, and possibly at Temple Newsam, sites in Yorkshire where Brown was also involved.

Similarly Brown, Paine and Robert Adam relied on the well-known Birmingham locksmith Thomas Blockley for ornate brass, gilt and cast door furniture. Brown's bank account records annual payments to Blockley (1773-80).

338 The Fisherwick stables remain (now converted into dwellings) but the Palladian house is gone. The only evidence pointing to the excellence of Brown's design is a detailed schedule of work amounting to £9,406 (today about £1,364,000).

339 Paine, *Plans, Elevations and Sections of Noblemen's Houses* (2nd ed., 1783), I, pp.ii-iii.

340 Stroud, p.167.

341 Holland worked at Bowood in 1754 and may have recommended his Fulham neighbour for improving the grounds. Brown took over as paymaster at Bowood when Adam was also working there. Among other work, Holland assisted Paine in the alteration of Earl Scarborough's London residence, Lumley House, in South Audley Street (1756-82).

342 The house at Redgrave burnt down in 1945, and was finally demolished in 1960.

343 RIBA Library Drawings Collection. Coloured elevation and ceiling plans. Now known as Claremont Fan Court School. The German architect Friedrich Wilhelm Erdmannsdorff's Palladian design for Schloss Wörlitz was partly modelled on Brown's preliminary studies for Claremont House.

344 Soane was involved in Brown's practice until his 1778 departure for Italy, assisting Holland at Claremont, 1772-74, Benham, 1773-75, Cadland, 1775-78, Brook's Clubhouse, 1776-78, the Dairy for Hill Park, Kent, major alterations to 73 South Audley Street for Lord Bute, and in house speculation in Knightsbridge.

345 BL.MSS Eur G37/67/3 ff.9-10. Letter to Clive dated 3 October 1773.

346 The house had been remodelled in 1603, and again in the 1730s by William Etty.

347 Lincolnshire AO. Yarb. 9/4. £2,286 (£331,500). In 1772 Pelham spent £154 7s 0d (£22,370) on brood mares. Also Yarb. 5/2/1/5 Acct Bk p.51, 'mares covering'. Also Francis Hill, *Georgian Lincoln* (Cambridge University Press, 1966), p.66. Races on flat and steeplechase courses both north and south of Lincoln city lasted up to five days. However, c.1770, the enclosure of open spaces, such as Waddington Heath, caused these events, popular since the seventeenth century, to be cut back.

348 Brocklesby Estate Office: November 1771 survey mapped 1,947 acres of land, an area of undulating Lincolnshire chalk wolds at Brocklesby, Little Limber and Newsham, surrounded by heath and rabbit warrens, with relatively few trees, which cost 3d (today £1.80) per acre. Grand 'Plan for the Intended Alteration' on twelve joined folio sheets, measuring 93 x 72 ins.

Bill Spink, landscape architect, comparing modern mapping with overlays of the Brocklesby plan, has verified Brown's accuracy.

349 Deborah Turnbull, 'Thomas White in Yorkshire', Yorkshire Gardens Trust Newsletter 3 (Winter 1997/98). White worked for Brown at Chillington, Sandbeck and Temple Newsam, and was living not far away at West Retford. He was also involved at Burton Constable, and went on to make a career in arboriculture and as a landscape designer, especially in Scotland, where his naturalistic designs reflect much Brownian influence. Both Brown's and White's plans are in Brocklesby Estate Office. One plan, no. 59b, illustrated in Stroud, 1984 edn, incorrectly labelled as Brown's, is in fact White's.

350 Lincolnshire AO. Yarb. 9/4.

351 RHS Lindley Library. Brown's Acct Bk, p.86. He made a similar comment at Highclere and in the account, recently discovered thanks to Karen Lynch, for a survey at Shillingley, Sussex.

352 Following Brown to Brocklesby some years later, Repton must have studied his plans. To the Duke of Portland he subsequently suggested building a classical house overlooking the lake at Welbeck Abbey, a proposal that was also refused.

353 This room has since been altered.

354 Beechwood House Archive.

355 David Adshead, 'The Design and Building of the Gothic Folly at Wimpole, Cambridgeshire', *The Burlington Magazine* (London, February 1998), Vol.CXL, No.1139, pp.76–84. Letter dated 1772. I am grateful to Kate Bryce for drawing this article to my attention.

356 Knowsley and Longleat Safari Parks, both Brown settings, continue the tradition of the menagerie, with enclosures for wild animals.

357 Castle Ashby Archive. Brown's plan, now very faded, is backed with coarse hessian, and nailed top and bottom to two wooden hangers, an inch in diameter.

358 Also seen in Brown's remodelled offices at Burghley.

359 Castle Ashby Archive. The Dairy and Dairy walk were constructed 1765–66.

360 RHS Lindley Library, Brown Account Book, p.28.

361 At Wotton the small island grotto, a square brick chamber originally faced with stone, partly covered under a mound, is possibly a converted ice-house.

362 F.B. Yorke, *Icehouses*, Ancient Monuments Society's Transactions (1956), Vol.4, pp.126–32. 'The main timbers of the roof are supported at their base by a circular stone wall ... reminiscent of the construction of a New Stone Age hut.' I am grateful to Rod Conlon for drawing this article to my attention.

363 Hall, GH23:2, p.155.

364 Hall, p.167.

365 Hall, p.161.

366 David Jacques, 'Warwick Castle Grounds & Park 1743–1760', GH 29:1, Summer, p.61. 'Brown's design at Warwick was a practical expression of Switzer's written word.'

367 The brick boathouse on the lake here, marked on a 1778 map, is also almost certainly Brown's.

368 Tottenham House, built in 1742, was demolished and rebuilt in 1820.

369 Wiltshire RO, 1900/1933.

370 Janet Waymark, 'Sherborne, Dorset', GH 29:1, p.79, Contract, Article 4 (February 1776).

371 Essex RO, D/Dby A365/1, 22 April 1763, Audley End Contract, Article 4.

372 Staffs RO, L30/9/17/9, 1756, Breadalbane's letter to his daughter.

373 John Soane later mentioned Brown's name in advising John Stuart about building a new village at Allenbank.

374 Ivan & Elizabeth Hall, *Burton Constable Hall*, Hull Museum & Art Galleries & Hutton Press (1991).

375 Hall, GH23:2 (1995), p.155, 8 September 1772, no.17.

376 *Ibid.*, p.159, 9 September 1780, No.5.

377 *Ibid.*, p.156, 4 September 1773, No.21.

378 Northampton RO. Map 4210. I am grateful to Rod Conlon for drawing this survey to my attention.

379 Philip Miller, *Gardener's Dictionary* (1731).

380 John Phibbs believes Brown's talent was most original in fusing what was seen as the restoration of the ancient countryside of England with productive agriculture and forestry.

381 Chatsworth Cascade was designed by the French hydraulics engineer M. Grillet.

382 Longleat (Wiltshire) contract dated October 1757.

383 West Sussex RO, Petworth House Archive, 3rd Contract, Article 4, June 1755.

384 Warwickshire RO L6/1326. Letter from Brown to George Lucy, dated 17 April 1762, 'concerning the ordering of trees'.

385 The Lord Aberdare, *The Royal and Ancient Game of Tennis* (Wimbledon Lawn Tennis Museum), p.18. In 1767 William Hickey reported: 'In the summer we had another Club which met at the Red House in Battersea Fields, nearly opposite Ranelagh, a retired pretty spot.... This club consisted of some very respectable persons.... The game we played was an invention of our own and called Field Tennis, which afforded noble exercise.... Our regular meetings were Tuesdays in each week.... The Field which was kept in high order and as smooth as a bowling green.... Besides our regular days some of the members met every evening during the summer months to have a little Field Tennis.' By 1793 Field Tennis became so popular that the *Sporting Magazine* commented: 'Field Tennis threatens ere long to bowl out cricket.'

386 A bowling green is shown on Brown's plan for Hainton.

387 David Underdown, *Start of Play* (2000), p.67.

388 John Byng, *The Torrington Diaries*, Vol. II (Eyre and Spottiswoode, London, 1935), p.329. Torrington describes 'a grand match England v Hampshire' for 1,000 guineas won by England in June 1791, as 'rural entertainment' attended by local society. In September 1791 a cricket match between Marylebone and Nottingham, with another grand prize of 1,000 guineas, at Upper Meadow, Nottingham, was attended by 10,000 spectators.

389 Lincolnshire AO. 3Anc 9/1/12. Marchioness de Grey's letter to her sister-in-law, Lady Heathcote, dated 17 August (1760?).

390 Burghley Archive, Day Book, 1773.

391 *Country Life* (10 February 1934), pp.144ff. Brown's kennels were replaced in 1795 by a grander design further south by James Wyatt.

392 Judging from surveys, the ground west of the ha-ha appears never to have been planted with trees, and has always been a cricket field.

393 Lincolnshire AO. Yarb. 5/2/17/1. Robert Kebblewhite was paid for plasterers' work in the 'Great Room' and staircase.

394 *Ibid.*

395 *Ibid.* I believe this to be the temple west of the Greenhouse. Curiously, it does not feature in Pevsner. Despite the recent ban on fox-hunting, both Brocklesby and Hainton huntsmen continue a tradition of friendly rivalry, and in addition, they play annual cricket matches in the two Brown parks.

396 Byng, Vol. II, p.391.

397 A. Young, *Journal* (1799).

398 Henry Thorold, *Lincolnshire Houses* (Norwich, Michael Russell Ltd, 1999).

399 Private enclosures dating from the sixteenth century had been mainly concerned with drainage and enclosure of marshes.

400 Wade, p.21.

401 Castle Ashby Archive, 1768–9.

402 I am grateful to Advolly Richmond for drawing these gates to my attention. These Grade II listed gates are thought to date from c.1765 and are now in a factory in Wolverhampton.

403 RHS LL, Brown Acct Bk, p.37, c.1780, eventually settled after his death.

404 Now closed, the tunnel still exists under Arthur Rd, Wimbledon, opposite the junction with Home Park Rd.

405 Tunnels were also built at Benham, Brocklesby, Claremont, Corsham, Radley, Moor Park, Southill and Warnford.

406 H. Repton, Holkham Red Book. 'This sort of surprise, though easily practised in hilly country, will appear a perfect wonder in Norfolk'.

407 H. Repton, *Theory & Practice of Landscape Gardening* (1803) & *Observations on the Theory and Practice of Landscape Gardening* (1805), p.201.

408 I am grateful to Camilla Hair for her (unpublished) research into eighteenth-century Freemasonry.

409 H. Walpole, July 1763.

410 Croome Estate Office. A bill from Mrs Coade dated 3 July 1778 was paid by Brown. In 1999 investigations by the archaeologist Rob Cleary revealed that white calcite, purple amethyst, Blue John (feldspar), fossils, shell and coral had been used.

411 Lincolnshire AO. Yarb. 5/2/17/1. The fossils etc. have disappeared. Pevsner describes the grotto as 'like a dank London tube', dating it c.1810. However, Brocklesby accounts detail construction in 1782–84.

412 *Ibid.* The Brocklesby plan (1771) corresponds to this account by showing extra markings and dashes by the church, to indicate his intention to lower the level of the lane.

413 East Sussex RO, ASH4357, Ashburnham family archive. 1777. Later, c.1845, refaced with Ashburnham red brick and grey headers; the central door was moved to the end to accommodate camellias, now the oldest in Britain. Brown's similar orangery at Redgrave (demolished in the 1960s) had a façade with decorative stone rosettes, surmounted on the parapet by urns and statues dedicated to the four seasons.

414 *Ibid.* Several plans survive for the intended bridge.

415 The wooden bridge has been restored to great effect.

416 Althorp, Spencer Archive.

417 RIBA 37092. Brown's plan for a single-span stone bridge at the Hoo (Hertfordshire) displays two differing treatments at either end. However, William Chambers won the commission. It is worth noting that in 1771 Earl Spencer commissioned Brown's collaborators the Hollands, father and son, to build Battersea Bridge across the Thames to make a convenient route to Wimbledon Park.

418 BL. Add. 69795. Letter dated 4 January 1773.

419 Hall, GH23:2, p.157. 21 September 1774. No.14.

420 *Ibid.*, p.158. 30 September 1775. No.18. 'Continuation of the Lake into Muddy Stanks [fish ponds]. Make a Clay Wall against the East side over Sievy Close & also Stanks Close if necessary; by making a trench 1½ foot wide & so deep till you come to the Clay & fill this trench with strong Clay – Then make a Dam across the drain & pen up all the water you can get this winter.'

421 *Ibid.*, p.160. 15 October 1782, No.10.

422 *Ibid.*, p.160. 15 October 1782, No.8.

423 This might explain traces of white paint still seen under Brown's middle bridge at Luton.

424 N. Pevsner, *The Buildings of England - Worcestershire*.

425 After the Compton Verney Arts Centre was opened, graffiti added disturbing, inappropriate notes to otherwise calming vistas. A big swastika and 'Shakespeare was here', daubed in white paint on the walls of Brown's Georgian church, were allowed to remain as 'artistic statements'.

426 N. Pevsner, *The Buildings of England - Warwickshire*. In 1931 the sixteenth-century coloured glass in the windows was removed and sold. An obelisk marks the spot by the lake where the chapel once stood.

427 BL. MSS Eur. G37/61/2 f.42. Letter to Clive 20 March 1771. Brown refers to the 'Kitching Garden' in a postscript.

428 Switzer, *Practical Fruit Gardener* (1724). Switzer recommended orientating kitchen garden walls 20 degrees to the east, rather than the usual north-south layout, to make the best use of sun to warm the walls. I am grateful to Neil Porteous for this information.

429 Hertfordshire Archives, DE/P/A8, 1755-64.

430 Basildon Park, Knowsley and Newton Castle, for instance. In 1780, more than a decade after his first contract, Brown was paid £10 (today £1,450) for a set of hothouse plans for Corsham.

431 WSRO 1300/1913. By 1767 the replacement kitchen garden was laid out.

432 Letter to Earl of Guildford, 1758, 16 March. Bodleian Library, North MSS d7 f.111. I am grateful to Christine Hodgetts for drawing this letter to my attention.

433 Longleat Archive, 1759, 3rd contract.

434 John Phibbs, 'The Structure of the Eighteenth Century Garden', GH38:1, Summer 2010, pp.20-34, from *Journal of a Tour thro' England and Wales* (1769) (London School of Economics Coll. Misc.38), Vol.II, ff.76-77. At Trentham, plantations to screen the kitchen garden, which had already been built, were included in Brown's contract. At Holkham, the kitchen gardens were built from 1781 to 1786, and though they cost about £1,115,000, were screened with planting in the first year. See also Tom Williamson, *The Archaeology of the Landscape Park Garden design in Norfolk, England, c.1680-1840*, BAR British Series 268 (Oxford, Archaeopress, 1998), p.102.

435 Cambridgeshire RO, 588/E27.

436 I am grateful to the late John Drake for sharing this information from James Woods's accounts in private ownership.

437 Royal Archives, Windsor. Geo/16835.

438 Hermitage, Russia. In a John Spyers album bought by Catherine the Great, one watercolour depicts the Melon Ground with frames and fruit trees, as seen from the cherry house in the north-west corner. Thanks to David Jacques for this information.

439 PRO. T1/451/420-421, 16 November 1765.

440 PRO. T1/455/412-413, letter to Charles Lounds.

441 PRO. T/468/328-329, letter to Thomas Bradshaw, 16 May 1768.

442 RHS LL. Brown Acct Bk.

443 Arthur Young.

444 *Gentlemen's Magazine* (June 1735).

445 William Mason (1725-97), *Heroic Epistle*.

446 Brown's original plan was for a kitchen garden south, near the lower lake and borehole. This would have been on view from the approach and from the lake. The existing open site higher up was chosen beyond the stables, so convenient for manure!

447 Luton Hoo Walled Garden Project.

448 H. Carter, *The Sheep and Wool Correspondence of Sir Joseph Banks* (1978).

449 Burghley House Archive. 1778 Day Book, p.90.

450 Pitt's son-in-law, Charles Stanhope, remodelled the gardens and built a hexagonal kitchen garden at Chevening, Kent, perhaps with advice from Pitt and/or Brown.

451 Lincolnshire AO. Yarb. 5/2/1/5 1774, Acct Bk, 'Bricks making in the yard at Great Limber £142 15s 3d [today £20,700] ... 290,000 common bricks, 31,985 pantiles, 13,750 dressed bricks, 1050 rigg tiles, 13,000 clinkers, 360 large gutter bricks.'

452 RHS LL. Brown Acct Bk, p.140. 'To plans for the kitchen garden & Stove, for a General Plan for the House & kitchen offices & also some stables for water to be made near the house £80' (Today £11,600).

453 A central well, peach-house, melon ground, hothouses and grape-house figure in the four-quartered kitchen garden situated beyond a horseshoe-shaped stable court. In the event, rather than straight walls the client opted to build self-supporting crinkle-crankle walls, typical of Suffolk.

454 Norman Scarfe, *Innocent Espionage - The La Rochefoucauld Brothers' Tour of England in 1785* (Boydell Press).

455 Jeri Bapasola, 'The Finest View in England - the Landscape and Gardens at Blenheim Palace', p.17, from *Vitruvius Britannicus*, 1725, Vol. III, plate 71.

456 Walpole, *Essay on Modern Gardening* (1785 edition).

457 BL. Oxford Journal, 26 July 1794.

458 With possible loss of life downstream in Bladon were the great dam to fail, safety, rightly, has to come first in any engineering decisions. A major restoration, 2009, was instigated in line with the 1975 Reservoir Act, recent European legislation and the 2010 Flood & Water Management Act. The clay core was corrected by digging a 1m-wide trench to remove eroded and breached sections and back-filling with bentonite (a form of clay) slurry. Rather than discreetly underground

as Brown designed, a new 80m-long serpentine spillway was created on the downstream face of the dam for sufficient overflow capacity, a bed of Armorloc concrete blocks laid, topsoil replaced and reseeded. The Grand Cascade was regrouted and the sides reinforced with concrete and limestone boulders that are all too uniform. Repairs were carried out to the 'penstock' or underground sluice gates. A walkway was created around the dam and a fully accessible viewing stand overlooking the cascade. One hopes new planting will eventually transform the present, unfortunate municipal effect.

459 BL. Add. 71602. 'A Reduced Plan of Blenheim Park Gardens and Plantations adjoining in Oxfordshire belonging to His Grace the Duke of Marlborough. Made in June 1774 by Thomas Richardson surveyor, Queen Ann St, Cavendish Square, London'.

460 Mavor, p.45.

461 Walpole, 10, p.309.

462 Walpole, 32 p.152, n.8. Also *Public Advertiser* (London), Wednesday, 9 September 1772; Issue 11097, 'Mr. Capability Brown, the great Arbiter of British Taste, a few Days ago, standing in Blenheim Park, and surveying with infinite Delight the very magnificent Piece of Water which had been suggested by his Fancy, and finished under his Direction, was overheard to say, Thames! Thames! Thou wilt never forgive me for this!'

463 Bod. Ms. Top.Gen.d.14f.14v), William Stukeley drawing (1724), *A View of Blenheim Castle from Rosamund's bower*. Rosamund was buried not far away at Godstow Abbey, by the River Thames.

464 Thomas Whateley, quoted by Osvald Siren, *China & the Gardens of Europe of the 18th Century* (1950), p.54. I am grateful to Sheila Love for drawing this to my attention.

465 BL. Add. 61672 f.119, Brown letter to Marlborough dated 26 August 1765.

466 Jeri Bapasola, *ibid.*, pp.82, 83.

467 *Letters of Mrs. Adams, the Wife of John Adams*, Vol. II, 1840. London, 3 October 1787.

468 James Bond & Kate Tiller, eds, *Blenheim - Landscape for a Palace* (1987). The leading landscape architect Hal Moggridge writes: 'The late eighteenth century was an age of egalitarian thought, arising from the ideas of the Enlightenment. Many of Brown's clients would have sympathised with the sentiments expressed by Jefferson in drafting the American Declaration of Independence that: "all men are created equal and independent". Brown himself, coming from a modest background, must have agreed and indeed his designs often appear to espouse the idea that all appreciate the landscape in the same way, regardless of their class status.... The passage of time, the additions and subtractions of succeeding generations have not diminished the emotional impact of this great landscape.'

469 *A New Description of Blenheim* (1797) guide, foreword. Now awarded World Heritage status, Blenheim attracts over 350,000 visitors annually.

470 William Fordyce Mavor, *New Description of Blenheim* (1789).

471 Edwin Morris Betts, *Thomas Jefferson's Garden Book* (American Philosophy Society, 1944), April 1786, three years after Brown's death.

472 Hodgson, *History of Northumberland* (1827) Part II, Vol.1, p.243. Today little remains of this planting. In the mid-1990s, in view of the significance of this landscape on his formative years, a long overdue restoration scheme was initiated, and the small lake he suggested creating by widening the burn has been made recently. An inappropriate, poorly placed Christmas tree plantation near the church ought perhaps to be felled.

473 Alnwick 'North Demesne', or 'The Pastures', is unquestionably one of Brown's best surviving works and a good place to read his landscaping, an entire 180 degrees of unspoilt panorama from the battlements. A twentieth-century programme of restoration, initiated by the 10th Duke of Northumberland, remained faithful to Brown's plan and followed the same methods, planting Scots pine and larch to provide protection for young beech belts on exposed hills and boundaries. The back and front zones of plantations were alternately felled and replanted so as to maintain uninterrupted enclosure on the skyline. Once the beeches were established the nurse trees were harvested, leaving the canopies of the single species belt to unite in a glorious ornamental crown. Successive tree belts are silhouetted against the sky as far as the eye can see, with clumps and punctuation trees scattered across the pastures.

In 2002 Jane, Duchess of Northumberland, initiated a monumental garden project, the Alnwick Garden, in the castle's 12-acre walled garden. She commissioned a master plan from the Belgian landscape architect Jacques Wirz to deliver 'one of the finest contemporary gardens in the world' that would also provide great benefit for the local economy. Thousands of tourists now flock to see the illuminated waterworks, grand cascade and the planet's largest tree-house. The surrounding horizons and sweeps of parkland are of comparable, if not arguably more, significance.

474 Thomas Pennant, *Tour in Scotland, 1769* (Birlinn, Edinburgh, 2000), p.22, originally published by John Monk (Chester, 1771), pp.31-32. the disappointed commentator Pennant thought the Alnwick gardens inconsistent with the

grandeur of the castle, 'trim to the highest degree, and more adapted to a villa near London than the ancient seat of a great baron'. I am grateful to Jonathan Williams for drawing this to my attention.

475 The mill here has been demolished. Robert Mylne's single-span stone bridge (1768) survives.

476 One wonders if Robert Adam drew criticism when, having failed to win the contract for improving Castle Ashby park, he went on to design both house and setting at Kedleston (Derbyshire).

477 William Chambers, *Designs of Chinese Buildings* (1757).

478 William Woty, *History of Hertfordshire* (1778), p.104. I am grateful to Dr Elizabeth Cripps for drawing this to my attention.

479 PRO. T1/479/86-87. Brown's letter to Mr Robinson at the Board of Works.

480 John Calcraft commissioned Brown to improve Ingress Abbey (Kent), including installing a kitchen garden, a site which Chambers had altered considerably for a previous owner.

481 Walpole 28.34, Letter to Mason, Strawberry Hill, 25 May 1772.

482 Thomas Baker, *History of the College of St John The Evangelist, Cambridge* Part II (1869, edited by John Mayor), p.1085.

483 Cambridge UCL.

484 'The Backs' were indeed enclosed, a valued asset for the townsfolk as much as for students and tourists. Other than Brown's expansive lawns setting off St John's College, the area is broken up by tree-lined paths. From 1979 to 1994, following the loss of elms to Dutch elm disease, a Backs committee planned replanting and management. More recently the landscape architect Robert Myers drew up a sensible, responsive Landscape Strategy for the Backs (December 2007), 'to improve the legibility, coherence and visual quality of the landscape as a whole'.

485 BL. Add. 69795.

486 Lincolnshire AO, Yarb. 5/2/17/2.

487 *Ibid.*, Yarb. 5/2/17/3. In c.1833–40 Adam Smith built a stone Gothic bridge with ornamental figures which I believe is Brown's design, especially since the end arch doubles as a tunnel to allow a walk under the bridge.

488 *Ibid.* The barge cost £120 15s 0d (today £17,500).

489 London Metropolitan AO, 1773 Hampton Q/EV/051. Indenture of five parts. February 1773 (Hanover Square, St George's Parish, with Anne Compton widow of Earl of Northampton, Castle Ashby) signed by Brown, Lancelot Jr, Mary Holland, Henry Holland Sr and Henry Holland Jr, John Edison, his lawyer, and Rob Burton.

490 Holland Jr made further improvements in 1788.

491 WSRO, 9/35/52. Letter to Lord Bruce, 16 October 1772.

492 Destroyed by fire in 1916. Cadland House was built on the same site in 1934, encapsulating the remains of the original cottage.

493 Designs for houses at Doddington (Cheshire) and Brentford (Middlesex) were not executed.

494 Byng, *Torrington Diaries* 3, p.128.

495 The word 'scenery' was first used in the 1770s as 'decoration of a theatre stage'. The earlier word 'scenary' came from the Italian 'scenario'. 'Scene' + 'ery' meaning 'a landscape or view, a pictorial scene' was used from 1777.

496 Walpole, p.176.

497 Bodleian Library. MS Eng.d.3842 Fol.87, letter dated to Earl Harcourt 26 September 1772.

498 William Mason, *The English Garden* (3 volumes, 1772–82).

499 Sybil Wade, *Sandleford Priory, the Historic Landscape of St Gabriel's School Grounds* (1997). Letter dated 9 July 1782.

500 Hinde, p.202.

501 Grapes were sent to hospitals treating injured soldiers in WWI.

502 Walpole, 'Correspondence' 7, p.325.

503 BL. Add. MS 69795. Letter dated 6 June 1775 to Revd Dyer. Also Stroud, p.157.

504 John Phibbs, 'The Structure of the Eighteenth Century Garden', GH38:1, Summer 2010, p.31. 'Mr Brown seems to have set the fashion and one invariable plan of embellishment prevails; namely, that of stripping the near ground, entirely naked, or almost so, and surrounding it with a border of shrubs, and a gravel walk, leaving the area whether large or small, one naked sheet of greensward.' Taken from William Marshall, *On Planting and Rural Ornament*, 2 vols [1785] (G. & W. Nichol, London, 1803), 1, p.281.

505 Beds AO. L30/13/12/52. Amabel Grey's letter to her cousin Mary Robinson, Lady Grantham.

506 Stroud, p.81.

507 Timothy Mowl & Diane James, *Historic Gardens of Warwickshire* (Redcliffe, 2011). Garrick had Hogarth design a serpentine chair, reputedly made from the wood of the mulberry tree in the garden of the house where Shakespeare died, and is sitting on it in Zoffany's painting *The Garden at Hampton House, with Mr and Mrs David Garrick Taking Tea* (1762).

508 This riverside section of Garrick's garden is now a public park recently restored as part of the Thames Landscape Strategy. Cypresses have again been planted near the grotto.

509 Walpole, 39 p.435. Letter to Lord Conway, 6 October 1785.

510 Beds RO L30/11/240/22. Mary Robinson, Lady Grantham's letter, 5 July 1782.

511 Bodleian MS Eng. Misc. e.489, William Gilpin, *Highland Tour* (1776): 'Every thing however yᵗ was disgusting he has removed. He has [choked] yᵉ avenues; he has given some form to yᵉ slopes; and has led yᵉ approach through a winding valley; in yᵉ very path wʰ nature herself wᵈ have chosen as yᵉ [satiat⁹] the magic of yᵉ is so great yᵗ it has given yᵉ house a new situation: from a bottom he has raised it upon a hill.' I am grateful to John Phibbs for drawing this quote to my attention.

512 Typical of Lincolnshire's mud and stud dwellings.

513 Today's car or coach visitors, entering the park from the north as in Elizabethan times, experience little of Brown's visually heightened 'theatre' of arrival. They have to walk far out into the middle of the park to witness Burghley's finest prospect. However, the house, lake and Lion Bridge make an undeniably dramatic backdrop to the popular Burghley Horse trials, which attract over 150,000 visitors annually.

The balance between preserving the past and planning for the future is always challenging. Change cannot and should not be prevented. New design, if thoroughly informed, should be actively encouraged to uplift a historic setting. Careful research and consultation are undertaken before pre-application planning and proposals are agreed. A 12-acre area below the head of Brown's lake at Burghley, cleared and planted with specimen trees, now serves as a relaxed and informal contemporary sculpture garden. This, and a new, educational yet fun-filled one-acre garden designed by George Carter (2007) and dedicated to William Cecil, the founder of Burghley, constitute the 'Gardens of Surprise', to mark the retirement of Lady Victoria Leatham, a direct descendant and for many years Burghley's remarkable custodian. These new gardens, using twenty-first-century technology to power its water features and lighting effects, 'are like nothing a visitor has seen before'.

514 Stroud, p.79, from E.W. Harcourt, *The Harcourt Papers*, Vol. VIII (1778), p.266.

515 Elizabeth I never stayed at Burghley House because of an outbreak of smallpox.

516 *Andeutungen über Landschaftsgärtnerei* (Wiesbaden: Marix, 2010, p.31; first publ. 1834). I am grateful to James Bowman for this and the next two references.

517 *Erinnerungsbilder*, Pückler's unpublished travel album (scrapbook), 1826.

518 *Briefe eines Verstorbenen* (Insel Ausgabe, Vol. 1, p.260; Letter 10 (7 January 1827), first publ. 1830/31). Also *Prince Pückler-Muskau*, Vol. III, p.253.

519 PRO Works 6/13,233, Brown's undated plan for the garden (copy in Spencer House). In the 1820s John Nash was commissioned to restore and extend the lake. His and others' subsequent tree-planting and building now mostly block the intended principal vistas of Brown's original scheme.

520 *Public Advertiser* (London), 6 September 1770, Issue 11126. I am grateful to Joy Uings for drawing this newspaper cutting to my attention.

521 PRO Works 32/71.

522 Kristina Taylor, 'Through the Keyhole: Foreign Affairs in the Country', *Historic Gardens Review*, Autumn 2001/Winter 2002, No.9, p.26.

523 Wotton Guide Book, September 1754.

524 PRO Chatham MSS. Also Stroud, p.187. Pakenham Correspondence.

525 PRO Chatham MSS 8/24/163, 10 September 1765.

526 PRO Chatham MSS 8/24/171, 10 September 1767. The column, dating from as early as the 1770s, now scarred by graffiti, was once crowned by an arcaded lantern, surmounted by the statue. Valdré later altered the base. In the late nineteenth century the figure was replaced by a drum and urn.

527 Stroud, p.185.

528 PRO 8/24/175, 12 October 1772.

529 PRO 8/24/179, 15 July 1775, letter not in Brown's hand. The next day Brown wrote to his son Jack in America; not received till 10 November.

530 Walpole, 32, p.152, 7 October 1773.

531 PRO Chatham MSS.

532 BL Add. MS 69795 Brown correspondence, as also following three quotes.

533 *Ibid.* Eventually Peggy chose to marry James Rust of Huntingdon after her father's death.

534 Stroud, p.150. Wedgwood's letter to his partner Bentley, dated 20 June 1776.

535 RHS Lindley Library, Brown Acct Bk. Later Brown's executors were paid £495 (£71,775). Belvoir Archive, the Brown folio album of plans and Spyers' illustrations. James Wyatt was later commissioned to alter the castle, and there seems little doubt that Brown's grand plan was a major influence on later landscaping improvements.

536 Journals of William Hervey (1755–1814), 1 February 1782.

537 James Brudenell, Keeper of the Privy Purse (Baron Brudenell, 1780). Drummond's Bank Account covering 1775–78.

538 Huntingdon RO. Acc1692. Brown's will dated 26 March 1779.

539 *Morning Chronicle and London Advertiser* (London), 8 February 1783, Issue 4284: 'Thursday morning, Feb. 6, 1783, about nine o'clock, died Lancelot Brown, Esq. of Hampton-Court, aged 67. His death was probably occasioned by a violent blow he received falling in a fit in the street, as he was returning from a visit at Lord Coventry's house in Piccadilly to the house of his son in law in Hertford-street. For above thirty years he had laboured under a very troublesome asthma, and though he bore it with an uncommon degree of fortitude and good spirits, yet at times, it reduced his life to alarming situations, and had lately prevailed so as to make him consider himself as drawing near that period, which he believed (with great strength of mind and resignation) as the price of a future state of perfect happiness.'

540 Stroud, p.202.

541 Later Lapidge apparently took to drinking heavily and quarrelled with Holland Jr. He went on to work for Repton at Bulstrode and Chalfont House.

542 Walpole, Correspondence to Mason, II, p.304.

543 Walpole 29, pp.285-86.

544 *Morning Post and Daily Advertiser* (London), 30 July 1783, Issue 3266. I am grateful to Joy Uings for drawing this to my attention.

545 Lapidge carried on Brown's commitments here and elsewhere, leaving a foreman in charge.

546 Wade, p.23.

547 Burghley Archive. The summerhouse is thought to have been Brown's design with carved neo-Jacobean tympana. Masons were sent to view the banqueting house at Chipping Camden (Gloucestershire).

548 Stroud, p.203.

549 BL Add. 69795. Brown Correspondence.

550 William Constable, Brown's Catholic client.

551 Wade.

552 Walpole, *Anecdotes of Painting in England*, Vol. IV (1771), including his essay *On Modern Gardening*. Sir William Temple (1628-95) used the term 'sharawadgi' to denote beautiful, irregular Chinese designs of fantasy in his essay *Upon The Gardens of Epicurus; or of Gardening in the year 1685* (Chatto & Windus, 1908).

553 Walpole, *Essay on Modern Gardening* (1770).

554 *Ibid.*

555 Walpole, *Correspondence with Rev. William Mason*, II, letter dated 10 February 1783.

556 H. Repton, *Theory and Practice of Landscape Gardening* (1803).

557 Ashridge Red Book.

558 Stroud, p.66, from Repton, *Theory & Practice of Landscape Gardening* (1803), p.266.

559 I am grateful to Professor Boris Sokolov for drawing this to my attention. He writes: 'Russia developed a calm and pure Brownian style, whose presence could still be felt as late as the 1820s (for example, in the White Birch Park in Pavlovsk). Even during the later 19th century, these Brownian landscapes continued to be seen as iconic images of the refined Russian culture.'

560 1772.

561 The Hermitage Museum, St Petersburg. About 180 watercolours and sketches in an album by Brown's surveyor, John Spyers.

562 J.C. Loudon, *The Encyclopedia of Gardening*, 1827, p.26.

563 Uvedale Price, *Essays on the Picturesque* (London, 1810), pp.149-50.

564 Williamson & Bellamy, *Property & Landscape*, p.154.

565 Walpole, *Correspondence* with Mason II, p.366.

566 Mary, Queen of Scots.

567 Sir Walter Scott, *The Journal of Sir Walter Scott* (1890, republished 1939-1946), p.299.

568 Stroud, p.192. William Whitehead, *The Late Improvements at Nuneham Courtenay*.

569 Laurence Whistler, *Sir John Vanbrugh* (Colsden Sanderson, London, 1938).

570 David Hicks, *My Kind of Garden* (Antique Collectors' Club, 2000).

571 After a recent change in the law, it is now possible to arrange weddings in a Brown park.

572 Dr Judith Rossiter, unpublished essay, *Whither the Wilderness*, Madingley ICE, University of Cambridge.

573 At Burghley, 6,000 new trees are being planted each winter. Each tree costs £50 to plant and protect.

574 In 2015 the Garden History Society merged with the Association of Gardens Trusts to form one national charity, The Gardens Trust, to support independent County Gardens Trust charities to research and comment on planning proposals affecting registered and locally listed landscape parks and gardens so as to inform and highlight concerns.

575 The course of the river was moved in the 1870s. In the twentieth century when Trentham was in the ownership of the Coal Board there was much subsidence damage to the lake.

576 Geoffrey Grigson, 1974.

577 An Elizabeth Oak, an ancient pollard, survives to this day. Legend has it that the queen shot a deer from this oak.

578 Jane Brown, *op. cit.*, p.193. The word is used in Lady Irwin's journal.

579 Robert Adam Architects have designed (2000) new features: eye-catcher temple, boat-house, new classical bridge, small orangery and belvedere in the walled garden, and extensions to the lodge houses.

580 Repton's advice was to straighten the 'river'.

581 Wilkie has used Brown's tested technique by raising a mound to screen the road from the house.

582 Gilly Drummond.

583 'Landskip' is a term first found in seventeenth-century poetry.

584 William Gilpin, *A Dialogue upon the Gardens at Stowe* (1748). In discussing the Serpentine River: 'Water is of as much Use in a Landskip, as Blood is in a Body; without these two Essentials, it is impossible there should be Life in either one or the other. Yet methinks it is a prodigious Pity that this stagnate Pool should not by some Magic be metamorphosed into a crystal Stream, rolling over a Bed of Pebbles. Such a quick Circulation would give an infinite Spirit to the View. I could wish his Lordship had such a Stream at his Command; he would shew it, I dare say, to the best Advantage, in its Passage thro' the Gardens. But we cannot make Nature, the utmost we can do is to mend her.'

585 W.F. Mavor, *New Description of Blenheim* (1789).

586 Erddig Family Book. Letter from John Lawry to Philip Yorke, 10 November 1767, reference to Sir Samuel Fludyer's estate, Lee, near London.

587 Joseph Addison, *Spectator* No. 411, 21 June 1712.

588 Thomas Whately.

589 Tim Richardson, *Daily Telegraph*, 25 August 2007, on his book *The Arcadian Friends: Inventing the Landscape Garden* (Bantam, 2007). Richardson deplored how the rich iconography of early-eighteenth-century prospects was replaced: 'Brown's landscapes are nothing more than the monotonous re-creation of the comfortably familiar.... Brown drained the landscape of meaning and dissent.'

590 W.F. Mavor, *New Description of Blenheim* (1789, 4th edn 1797). 'In this singularly picturesque landscape, the beautiful and the sublime are most intimately combined: all that can please, elevate, or astonish, display themselves at once....'

591 Gilbert Laing Meason, *The Landscape Architecture of the Great Painters of Italy* (London, 1828).

592 VCH. Vol.1V(1912).

593 *The Correspondence of Charles Darwin* (F. Burkhardt et al., eds, Cambridge University Press 1985).

594 Williamson & Bellamy, *Property & Landscape*.

595 *Blackwood's Magazine* (1827). The term 'stately home' first appeared in this poem by Felicia Hemans (1793-1835), a literary contemporary of Wordsworth. Later, Noël Coward parodied the poem in song.

596 J.C. Loudon, *Observations on Landscape Gardening* (1802).

597 Astronomer W.H. Smyth (1788-1865) of Hartwell was the first to use this term against Brown in *Aedes Hartwellianae* (1851). I am grateful to Kate Bryce for drawing this to my attention.

598 Sir Reginald Blomfield, *The Formal Garden in England* (1892, 1901), pp.14, 85.

599 English Heritage, *Valuing our Heritage*, January 2007.

600 Barnet, London.

601 See note 425.

602 Stroud, p, 202. Walpole's letter to Mason after Brown's death.

603 The National Trust, *Rooted in History: Studies in Garden Conservation* (2001).

604 *Ibid.*, p.144.

605 Similarly, the National Trust in a recent restoration at Wimpole left the upper lake purposely untouched because there are many rare 'ancient wetland' invertebrates, water-voles and an occasional otter.

606 Sue Herdman, *National Trust Magazine* (Summer 2008), p.38.

INDEX